47.95

Springer Series on Social Work

Albert R. Roberts, DSW, Series Editor
Graduate School of Social Work, Rutgers, The State University of New Jersey

Advisory Board: Gloria Bonilla-Santiago, PhD, Sheldon R. Gelman, PhD, Gilbert J. Greene, PhD, Jesse Harris, DSW, Michael J. Smith, DSW, and Barbara Berkman, PhD

 **Elaine P. Congress, MSW, DSW,** is Director of the Doctoral Program and Associate Professor at Fordham University Graduate School of Social Service. Dr. Congress has published extensively in the area of cultural diversity and ethical issues in social work practice, family treatment, school social work, and social work education. Very active in the National Association of Social Workers, Dr. Congress currently serves on the Board of Directors and chairs the Ethics and Professional Standards Committee. She is Assistant Editor for the journal *Crisis Intervention and Time Limited Treatment* and has chaired several major conferences on cultural diversity and families.

MULTICULTURAL PERSPECTIVES IN WORKING WITH FAMILIES

Elaine P. Congress, DSW
Editor

Springer Publishing Company

Copyright © 1997 by Springer Publishing Company, Inc.

Springer Publishing Company, Inc.
536 Broadway
New York, NY 10012-3955

Cover design by Margaret Dunin
Production Editor: Susan Gamer

Second Printing

98 99 00 01 / 5 4 3 2

Library of Congress Cataloging-in-Publication Data

Multicultural perspectives in working with families / Elaine P. Congress, editor.
    p.   cm.—(Springer series on social work)
    Includes bibliographical references and index.
    ISBN 0-8261-9560-1
    1. Family social work—United States.   2. Minorities—Services for—United States.   3. Ethnicity—United States.   4. Multiculturalism—United States.
    I. Congress, Elaine Piller.   II. Series.
    HV699. M85   1997
    362.82—dc21   96-40363
                                                CIP

Printed in the United States of America

Dedication

I would like to thank Dean Mary Ann Quaranta for her continual support and encouragement throughout my years at Fordham.

I would like to dedicate this book to professional social workers and social work students who daily work with culturally diverse clients and their families.

Contents

Contributors

Patricia Brownell, DSW, is Assistant Professor at Fordham University Graduate School of Social Service. Before joining Fordham's faculty, she spent 27 years in public sector social work, where she worked as a planner, researcher, and administrator for domestic violence programs. Dr. Brownell has previously published in the area of domestic violence and elder abuse.

Jeanette Burgos-Servidio, ACSW, is the director of the family-based treatment program at the Coalition for Hispanic Family Services. This is a program designed to work with emotionally disturbed children and their families.

Robert Chazin, DSW, is Professor at Fordham University Graduate School of Social Service. He has studied extensively the psychosocial aftermath of the Chernobyl disaster, as well as immigration issues for Soviet Jews. He has served as a mental health consultant to various social service agencies and has trained clinicians working with Soviet Jewish immigrants. He maintains a clinical private practice, working with individuals, couples, families, and groups.

Roslyn H. Chernesky, DSW, is Professor and Chair of the Administration Area at Fordham University Graduate School of Social Service. She is the author of many journal articles and book chapters on women in management and feminist approaches to administration.

Carol Cohen, DSW, is Director of the BA in Social Work Program at Fordham University. She is the coordinator of the Fordham University Program for the Development of Social Work Practice with Groups and has published on various issues in social group work.

Marlene Cooper, PhD, is Assistant Professor at Fordham University Graduate School of Social Service in New York City. Dr. Cooper has written a number of journal articles and book chapters in the clinical area, especially on family issues, obsessive-compulsive disorder, and single-subject research design.

Susan Bair Egan, MSW, is the Assistant Dean at Fordham University Graduate School of Social Service. She has previously presented material on the topic of multiple roles of women students.

Irene A. Gutheil, DSW, is Associate Professor and Co-Chair of the Practice Area at Fordham University Graduate School of Social Service. She has published extensively in the area of gerontology and practice, has written *Working with Older People: Challenges and Opportunities*, and heads the Ravissson Research Center on Aging.

Howard J. Hess, DSW, is Associate Dean at Fordham University Graduate School of Social Service. The author of multiple publications in the area of HIV/AIDS and practice issues, Dean Hess was the former Director of the Doctoral Program.

Carol P. Kaplan, PhD, is an Associate Professor and Co-Chair of the Clinical Area at Fordham University Graduate School of Social Service. She has written extensively on clinical issues with children and adolescents.

Judith A. B. Lee, DSW, is Professor at the University of Connecticut. The author of a book on empowerment, she has published extensively in the area of homeless women, empowerment, group work, and substance abuse. She is a past president of the Advancement for Social Work with Groups.

Maxine Lynn, MSW, is Director of Field Education at Fordham University Graduate School of Social Service. The former Vice President of the American Association of

Social Group Work, she has had much experience in group work and has published previously on group work and cultural diversity.

Yolando Mayo, DSW, is an Assistant Professor at Hunter College School of Social Work. A former first Vice-President of the New York City Chapter of the National Association of Social Workers and present member of CSWE Commission on racial, cultural, and ethnic diversity, she has previously done research on machismo and gender issues among the Hispanic population.

Steven McFadden, ACSW, is the executive director of London Terrace Psychotherapy Services, a mental health center serving gay and lesbian clients. Mr. McFadden is also an Adjunct Instructor at Fordham University Graduate School of Social Service.

Manuel Muñoz, CSW, was formerly the clinical coordinator of the Roberto Clemente Family Guidance Center. He is presently with the Center for Family-School Collaboration of the Ackerman Institute for Family Therapy.

Danielle Nisivoccia, DSW, is an adjunct Associate Professor and supervisor in the Stay in School Project at Fordham University Graduate School of Social Service. She has published previously in the area of field instruction and practice with families and children. Dr. Nisivoccia is currently chair of the children and families services committee of the New York City chapter of NASW.

Carmen Ortiz Hendricks, DSW, is Director of Field Education at Hunter College School of Social Work. She is currently the president of the New York City chapter of NASW. On the editorial board of the *Journal of Multicultural Social Work,* she has written and lectured on the topic of cultural competency.

Ana Paulino, EdD, is Associate Professor at Hunter College School of Social Work. She has published in the area of immigration and Dominicans.

Mary Ann Quaranta, DSW, is the Dean of Fordham University Graduate School of Social Service. She is a past president of National NASW and has served as Chair of the Reaccreditation Commission for the Council of Social Work Education.

Kathleen Romano, PhD, is Senior Psychologist at Montefiore Medical Group in the South Bronx and Assistant Professor of Family Medicine, Department of Family Medicine, Albert Einstein College of Medicine. Dr. Romano also has a private practice in Manhattan.

Virginia Strand, DSW, is Associate Professor and Director of the Family Violence Center at Fordham University Graduate School of Social Service. She has previously published in the area of sexual abuse of children and has conducted research on women with histories of sexual abuse.

Lynn. M. Tepper, PhD, is Director of the Institute of Gerontology at Mercy College, Principal Investigator of "Project: Age Well," and Associate Clinical Professor at Columbia University. Her clinical practice at Columbia Presbyterian Medical Center is primarily with an ethnically and culturally diverse elderly population with psychosocial issues that affect their health and well-being.

Sandra Turner, PhD, is Associate Professor at Fordham University Graduate School of Social Service and Co-Chair of the Practice sequence. She has published in the area of alcohol abuse, prevention of adolescent substance abuse, and women.

Luis Zayas, MSW, PhD, is Associate Professor at Fordham University Graduate School of Social Service in New York City. He has written extensively in the area of Hispanic children and adolescents.

Foreword

Mary Ann Quaranta

Cultural diversity is one of the greatest riches of the United States of America as well as one of its greatest challenges as we move from the metaphor of a melting pot to that of a beautiful mosaic. In the next century, we hope there will be a search for a basic national identity of our values as a democratic society as we, at the same time, continue to embrace differences along with the tremendous treasures of the multicultural nature of our society.

The idea for this book emerged from the conference held at Fordham University in fall 1993 under the able leadership of Dr. Elaine Congress, the editor of this volume. The impetus for the conference developed from the faculty's belief that there was an educational need for social workers and practitioners to engage in continuing dialogue about how we can increase knowledge and skills in working with families with diverse backgrounds in different settings. The conference was keynoted by such prominent persons in the field as Dr. Monica McGoldrick, Dr. Nancy Boyd Franklin, and Harry Aponte. The presentations were followed by workshops on a range of different subjects, some of which provided the starting points for the chapters in this excellent book. The fact that the conference was oversubscribed speaks of the need for educating social work students and practitioners about ways to work more effectively with families from diverse backgrounds.

Social work has always valued tolerance of difference in persons from different groups and has championed any efforts to protect persons and populations from discrimination and oppression. Although some of the issues, challenges, problems, and dilemmas faced by the social work profession today are the same, in some ways, as they were for previous generations of social workers, there are many new elements that should be included in our ongoing work.

Not the least of these new elements is the growing globalization of the earth, and the growing awareness of the need for all peoples to gain in understanding of other cultures. There is also expanding knowledge from a range of disciplines and professions on the complexities of cultures and of the fact that there can be considerable difference and conflict within, as well as between, cultures.

The social work profession and all of its members have a fundamental responsibility to expand their knowledge of the cultures of the various client populations they serve. This includes a realization that many of the theories of social work, and of the allied disciplines and professions from which it draws knowledge, are based on Western thought and ideology. Many of the assumptions made about human behavior are based on what has been the dominant orientation in our society.

With the growing diversity of persons entering our country, it is not possible for a practitioner or educator to have an in-depth appreciation of the nuances of such a broad range of cultures. Many perspectives constitute the way a culture is defined—language, mores, philosophy of life, religious orientation, views on family, and so many other variables.

Given the need to be understanding and sensitive to cultural differences, certain basic social work principles must guide us in our practice. We certainly must let the client lead us in relevant ways to an understanding of the nuances of the cultural differences pertinent to the area of concern. We can, as we have always done, learn a great deal about differences from studying the client's situation from a range of perspectives.

We must, at all costs, avoid the danger, the damage, and the disaster that can come from stereotyping, so pervasive in our society and so tempting a trap. Our commitment as social workers is to individualization. Yes, we should be guided by some general understanding of areas, in which there may be cultural differences, as in child-rearing customs, male and female role patterns, and attitudes towards intergenerational communication. But by all means, we must avoid characterizing people on the basis of generalizations and beliefs about how people from certain cultures behave.

Astute assessment skills are required to distinguish between cultural patterns and dysfunctional behavior. Similarly, our interventions must be governed by cultural appropriateness and culturally acceptable approaches.

This book will provide excellent guidance to students and practitioners in many areas of interest.

Preface

Elaine P. Congress

Although Sigmund Freud has been credited with being the original family therapist—when he treated little Hans's father for the child's fear of horses—family therapy emerged as a significant treatment model after World War II with the return of many servicemen to families they barely knew. Some of the main forces contributing to the development of family therapy have been psychoanalysis, general systems theory, studies of schizophrenia, marital counseling and child guidance, and group therapy (Goldenberg & Goldenberg, 1991). As the father of psychoanalysis, Freud recognized the importance of family relationships in the development of individual symptoms; and an early family therapist, Nathan Ackerman, first applied psychoanalytic principles to the study of the family. Most family theorists begin with the premise that a family is a system and that if any part of the system changes, the whole system (family) changes. Early studies of the etiology of schizophrenia saw certain types of families as conducive to the development of schizophrenia. In contrast to individual treatment, child guidance and marital and group therapy all stressed working with more than one individual at a time.

A major figure in the development of family therapy, Murray Bowen, once commented that even when he worked with only one person in a family, in reality he saw all family members (Bowen, 1978). Whether a therapist sees clients individually or collectively, maintaining a family perspective has been considered essential for effective clinical practice (Hartman & Laird, 1983).

Taking a family-oriented perspective, this book is written not only for the family therapist who usually sees families in their entirety but for all clinicians who work individually or collectively with families.

Although all families have culturally diverse backgrounds, this book will focus primarily on issues of policy and practice relevant to clinical work with the increasing number of families from backgrounds other than Western European. It is well known that the United States is culturally diverse. In many cities today one of every two families is from a background other than Western European, and by the middle of the next century the majority of American families may be from backgrounds other than Western European (U.S. Census, 1988). This diversity is increasingly evident in our social, health, and educational institutions. Despite much current discussion about cultural sensitivity and competence, there is concern that most of these institutions have an American, white, middle-class perspective (Ho, 1987).

Most of the past literature on family therapy—with some notable exceptions (Boyd-Franklin, 1984; Ho, 1987; McGoldrick, Pearce, & Giordano, 1996)—has focused primarily on treatment issues with white middle-class families. In contrast, this book primarily explores families from cultures other than Western European, and the word *culture* is used as a generic term that includes ethnicity, race, national origin, and religion (Lum, 1992).

Although religion and race are subsumed under culture, class is not. It is essential for the clinician to consider the socioeconomic class of the family to avoid inaccurate cultural generalizations (Devore & Schlesinger, 1995). Often families who have recently emigrated to the United States or who have been the victims of generations of discrimination are poor. Many of the families described in this book are from a low socioeconomic class, but certainly not all culturally diverse families are. In working with culturally diverse families the therapist must always be cognizant of what economic resources are available to the family, as this often affects its functioning.

The chapters are not meant to be all-inclusive. Instead, I have chosen to include those issues that appear to be in the foreground of multicultural practice with families.

Section One focuses on both "micro" and "macro" issues in the assessment of families. Assessment of families, in contrast to more traditional assessment models for individuals, occurs concurrently with the beginning of treatment. A good assessment should include an understanding of family boundaries, rules, roles, and structure. Scales for measuring successful, borderline, and dysfunctional families have been developed (Beavers, 1982; Olson, 1986). The ecomap describes the family in relation to the presence or absence of outside resources (Hartman & Laird, 1978). By the use of genograms the clinician is able to learn more about family relationships both currently and in the past (Bowen, 1978; McGoldrick & Kerson, 1985).

When I first began to teach students about assessing families, I became increasingly aware that there was not a family assessment tool designed specifically for culturally diverse families. Yet more and more families whom professionals see in their practice are from different cultural backgrounds. Of concern also was the fact that many clinicians often make sweeping generalizations about culturally diverse people. For example, a Puerto Rican family that has lived in New York City for several generations and an undocumented Mexican family that recently arrived in the United States are often both described as Hispanic. The culturagram was developed to assist clinicians in assessing more accurately families from diverse cultural backgrounds.

Chapter 1 discusses how clinicians can use a culturagram in their work with culturally diverse families. The culturagram is valuable not only for assessment but also for planning treatment and empowering culturally diverse families. An earlier version of this chapter appeared in the November 1994 issue of *Families in Society* (Congress, 1994).

Most people seek professional help because of family problems (Gurin, Veroff, & Feld, 1960) and are seen in family and mental health agencies. No matter how knowledgeable and skilled a practitioner is about the treatment of culturally diverse families, the agency context can influence successful treatment of these families. Chapter 2 can help clinicians assess their agency in terms of promoting cultural competency. Dr. Chernesky, who previously has written on women's issues in administration, now focuses on cultural diversity and agency practice. She suggests that an agency must be in the foreground in promoting culturally competent practice and must continually practice self-assessment of cultural competence in its board of directors, chief executive officer, planning committees, staff, and policies and programs.

Section Two focuses on family issues at various stages in the life cycle. In recent years much of previous theory on expectable life-cycle tasks and transitions have been challenged, if not completely rejected (Carter & McGoldrick, 1988). Trends such as adolescent parenthood, more unmarried partnerships, greater employment of women with young children, and "College at 60" programs all suggest other than traditional ways of looking at family development. Because a crisis can occur at any point in the new family cycle (Congress, 1996), this section explores issues in working with culturally diverse families in crisis across the life cycle.

The opening chapter of Section Two (chapter 3) focuses on the multicultural triangle of child, family, and school. Dr. Ortiz Hendricks stresses the need to understand these differing cultures in order to empower culturally diverse children of school age and their families. The clinician who works within the school is described as a cultural mediator who must act as an ''interpreter'' between the culture of the family and the culture of the school. The chapter concludes with several self-assessment inventories for clinicians to use in promoting culturally competent practice.

Adolescence has long been regarded as a traumatic period for families and as a crucial developmental task for adolescents because it usually involves separating and becoming more independent of parents. This time is especially challenging for culturally diverse families. Often parents from different cultural backgrounds are still very influenced by their original culture, whereas their adolescent children wish to follow mainstream American peer culture. When poverty is also a factor, family conflict may escalate and threaten to destroy the family. In chapter 4, Dr. Carol Kaplan and Miguel Muñoz present an ecosystemic model for clinicians based on reframing multiple versions of reality, using a strengths perspective, and focusing on solutions to help culturally diverse adolescents and their families negotiate the life-cycle challenges of adolescence in poor communities.

Adult women at the end of the 20th century often function in multiple roles. Not only are many women wives and mothers; they are also employees and students. More than half of all women with children under 6 years are employed outside the home (Carter & McGoldrick, 1989). Assuming multiple roles often leads to stress and conflict. This may be especially acute for women of color, who are more likely to be single heads of households (Hicks & Anderson, 1989). Not only have women with young children increasingly entered the job market, but they also have returned to college and graduate schools. Chapter 5 reports on an important study, conducted by Assistant Dean Susan Egan, a university administrator at a graduate school of social work, on the stresses and social supports of women with multiple roles. This chapter is useful for clinicians working with culturally diverse women who assume multiple roles.

Most clinicians are cognizant of the aging of our society. Whereas 11% of the total population was elderly in 1980, 22% will be over 65 by 2030 (NASW, 1993). The culturally diverse elderly are increasing in number much more rapidly than the White elderly. As the life expectancy of people increases, more and more older people will spend their later years living within extended families. Chapter 6 explores the aging family from a cultural perspective. Theories on aging, including disengagement theory, activity theory, and the new substitution theory, are discussed in terms of their applicability to culturally diverse older people and their families. Guidelines and successful examples of family therapy with culturally diverse older persons and their families are presented.

Section Three focuses on special populations. This section is not meant to be all-inclusive but instead features chapters on families whom therapists increasingly see in their practice.

One of the most devastating crisis events for families is the death or serious illness of a parent (Webb, 1994). The AIDS epidemic has had a serious impact on families, which has become increasingly acute in recent years as more and more women of color have become HIV-positive or developed full-blown AIDS. As most of these women are parents, the number of AIDS orphans has increased dramatically. Chapter 7, written by Dr. Kathleen Romano and Dr. Luis Zayas, addresses the ways in which children and families cope with HIV/AIDS and death and suggests interventions that have been useful in work with these families. Case examples are used to illustrate effective treatment for orphaned children and adolescents.

The next chapter in this section (chapter 8) explores issues in working with immigrant families in transition. Whereas early immigrants were primarily of Western European background, recent immigrants are more likely to come from the Caribbean, Central and South America, or Asia (Foner, 1987). Dominican families, one of the fastest-growing Hispanic immigrant groups, are the primary focus of this chapter, which traces the three stages of immigrants' experience—(1) premigration and departure, (2) transit, and (3) resettlement—and notes the immigrant's family response at each stage. To help clinicians in their work with immigrant families, important assessment and treatment issues are presented.

Within the past decade there has been a rapid increase in the number of Russians entering the United States. Although this immigrant group comes from a country with a very different language, political system, and culture, it has received much less attention in professional literature than other immigrant groups have. Often there is a tendency to make generalizations about Russian immigrants. In chapter 9, Dr. Robert Chazin focuses on the diversity of Russian immigrants who have come from different sections of Russia. Issues of transit and resettlement, especially in terms of individual and family expectations, conflicts of dependence versus independence, and the effects of lowered social economic status, are addressed. The chapter concludes with examples of therapist interventions with Russian multigenerational families.

In chapter 10, Steven McFadden proposes that gay and lesbian families represent diverse cultures. Often gay and lesbian families must cope with societal bias against them. Unlike racially and ethnically diverse families, gay and lesbian families must explain their culture to their families of origin. Culturally diverse gay and lesbian families may have a double stigma in terms of their relationship with the outside world. This chapter explores various developmental life-cycle issues for the gay and lesbian families, such as coming out to family and friends and having and raising children. Suggestions are made to enhance clinicians' practice with gay and lesbian families.

Although most literature focuses on issues of Hispanic women, especially in terms of their roles as wives and/or parents, chapter 11 of this volume concentrates on an often neglected topic: machismo and manhood in Latino families. Dr. Yolanda Mayo explores the effects of immigration on Latino men and challenges the commonly accepted professional belief that machismo is negative and counterproductive to family functioning. The importance of therapists' understanding Latino men in their cultural context is stressed to ensure a positive outcome for therapy with Latino families.

Section Four features specific problem areas that family therapists who work with culturally diverse families encounter. The focus is on the most timely topics as well as the least explored. In chapter 12, Dr. Virginia Strand describes therapeutic work with culturally diverse mothers of incest families. Traditionally, clinicians have blamed the mothers of incest families by stressing either their complicity, ineffectiveness, or dependence on male perpetrators. Instead of blaming the victims the author takes the position that culturally diverse women of incest families are often doubly stigmatized. Clinicians frequently do not understand the cultural context in which the abuse occurs nor do they understand women's behavior in relation to their cultural backgrounds. Examples of incest in families from different cultural backgrounds are presented and suggestions are made to clinicians about working with mothers and culturally diverse incest families in general.

In chapter 13, Dr. Brownell explores domestic violence in different cultural groups. Policies and programs related to domestic violence that try to separate victims from their families are often ineffective with culturally diverse families. It is suggested that interventions with victims of domestic violence would be more effective if clinicians understood more about the cultural context of clients and their families.

Substance abuse is recognized as a major social problem that has a negative impact not only on external social structures but also on internal family functioning. In chapter 14, Dr. Sandra Turner and Dr. Marlene Cooper explore how the incidence of substance abuse, as well as help-seeking and treatment choices for substance abuse problems, may differ among cultures. The discrimination that many culturally diverse families experience is seen as contributing to substance abuse problems. Specific treatment issues, including engagement, assessment, and choice of intervention, are discussed in terms of culturally diverse families; and specific examples illustrating successful work with culturally diverse families with a substance-abusing member are presented.

In chapter 15, Dr Howard Hess focuses on practice issues with gay and ethnically diverse families that have been affected by the HIV/AIDS epidemic. Although most of the early HIV/AIDS victims were gay white men, this disease has recently increased dramatically among African Americans and Hispanics, especially in large cities. A treatment model that stresses a multisystem approach and empowerment of the family is developed to help clinicians in their work with families with victims of the epidemic.

Section Five is titled "Beyond Family Therapy" to suggest that there are multiple treatment models to use in therapeutic work with culturally diverse families. The opening chapter of this section (chapter 16), written by this author from the perspective of a family therapist and by Maxine Lynn from the perspective of social group work, discusses the use of family therapy and social group work with a Lebanese boy and his family. Significant issues in family therapy and social group work are explored, with suggestions for interventions with culturally diverse families.

The next chapter in this section (chapter 17) explores the use of an empowerment group model with homeless women and their families. Dr. Judith Lee and Dr. Danielle Nisivoccia propose that homeless women with substance abuse problems have had to endure multiple oppressions. Empowerment groups combine a focus on substance abuse and recovery with developing a critical awareness of the connection between clients' personal history of addiction and oppression. Specific principles for practice are developed, to help clinicians work with homeless women of color.

A recent phenomenon, especially with the increase of AIDS orphans, has been that of grandmothers raising children. For many years informal extended-family support systems have helped families when parents, because of illness or death, were not able to raise children; but in recent years grandmothers are raising children in a more formalized relationship, through kinship foster care arrangements. The last chapter in this section explores the development of groups of culturally diverse grandmothers who provide mutual support in their renewed role as parents. Case examples of a group of Hispanic grandmothers and African American grandmothers are presented. Dr. Cohen discusses cultures other than ethnicity—such as the culture of family crisis, agency, and group culture—and their impact on the treatment of culturally diverse grandmothers and their families.

The book concludes with a discussion of ethical concerns as well as the future direction of therapeutic work with culturally diverse families. Promoting social work principles of self-determination, confidentiality, and informed consent often presents ethical dilemmas in practice with culturally diverse families. How will the newest trends of managed care affect therapy with multicultural families? Contrary to popular opinion, this author believes that the focus on short-term, goal-directed treatment will be very effective in work with these families.

REFERENCES

Beavers, W. R. (1982). Healthy, midrange, and severely dysfunctional families. In F. Walsh (Ed.), *Normal family processes* (pp. 45–66). New York: Guilford.

Bowen, M. (1978). *Family therapy in clinical practice*. New York: Jason Aronson.

Boyd-Franklin, N. (1989). *Black families in therapy: A multisystems approach*. New York: Guilford.

Carter, B., & McGoldrick, M. (1989). *The changing family life cycle: A framework for family therapy* (2nd ed.). New York: Allyn and Bacon.

Congress, E. (1994). The use of culturagrams to assess and empower culturally diverse families. *Families in Society, 39*, 531–540.

Congress, E. (1996). Family crisis: Life cycle and bolts from the blue. In A. Roberts, Ed., *Crisis management and brief treatment: Theory, technique, and applications* (pp. 142–159). Chicago: Nelson-Hall.

Devore, W., & Schlesinger, E. (1995). *Ethnic-sensitive social work practice* (4th ed.). New York: Macmillan.

Foner, N. (1987). Introduction: New immigrants and changing patterns in New York City. In N. Foner (Ed.), *New immigrants in New York* (pp. 1–33). New York: Columbia University Press.

Goldenberg, I., & Goldenberg, H. (1991). *Family therapy: An overview*. Belmont, CA: Brooks/Cole.

Gurin, G., Veroff, J., & Feld, S. (1960). *Americans view their mental health*. New York: Basic.

Hartman, A., & Laird, J. (1983). *Family-centered social work practice*. New York: Free Press.

Hicks, S., & Anderson, C. (1989). Women on their own. In M. McGoldrick, C. Anderson, & F. Walsh (Eds.), *Women in families: A framework for family therapy* (pp. 308–334). New York: Norton.

Ho, M. (1987). *Family therapy with ethnic minorities*. Newbury Park, CA: Sage.

Lum, D. (1992). *Social work practice and people of color: A process-stage approach* (2nd ed.). Pacific Grove, CA: Brooks/Cole.

McGoldrick, M., Anderson, C., & Walsh, F. (1989). *Women in families: A framework for family therapy*. New York: Norton.

McGoldrick, M., & Kerson, R. (1985). *Genograms in family assessment*. New York: Norton.

McGoldrick, M., Pearce, J., & Giordano, J. (Eds.). (1996). *Ethnicity and family therapy* (2nd ed.). New York: Guilford.

National Association of Social Workers. (1993). *Social work with older persons: Understanding diversity*. Washington, DC: NASW Press.

Olson, D. H. (1986). Circumplex Model VII: Validation studies and FACES III. *Family Process, 26*, 337–351.

U.S. Bureau of the Census. (1988). Projection of the population of the United States by age, sex, and race: 1988 to 2080. In *Current population reports* (Series P-25, No. 1018). Washington, DC: U.S. Government Printing Office.

Webb, N. (1994). *Bereavement in children*. New York: Guilford.

Assessment— Micro and Macro Approaches

Using the Culturagram to Assess and Empower Culturally Diverse Families

Elaine P. Congress

During the past 25 years there has been a dramatic increase in the number of immigrants who annually enter the United States. Previously, immigrants were predominately from European countries, but recent immigrants are more likely to be of Asian, West Indian, or Latin American backgrounds (Foner, 1987). Although there were many more immigrant men than women at the beginning of this century, current immigrants have included more women. Because new immigration policies favor the reunification of separated families, the number of immigrant families has increased (Foner, 1987). These changing immigration trends increase the likelihood that a family therapist will work with a culturally diverse family, often from a background other than European.

There has been increased recognition of the need to promote culturally competent practice throughout the institutions of our society. The need for a cross-cultural perspective has been seen as essential for those who

Note: An earlier version of this chapter appeared in the November 1994 issue of *Families in Society: The Journal of Contemporary Human Services*. Copyright © 1994 Families International, Inc.

work in a school setting (Allen-Meares, 1992). The importance of cultural sensitivity for those in the health field who work with patients with differing concepts of health, illness, and treatment has been stressed (Congress & Lyons, 1992). Despite increasing recognition of the growing diversity in our society, many family therapists continue to assess and treat culturally diverse families from a White, American, middle-class perspective (Ho, 1987).

Although cultural competency in practice with diverse families is of considerable importance, the number of books on cultural diversity and family therapy is limited (Boyd-Franklin, 1989; Ho, 1987; Logan, Freeman, & McRoy, 1990; McGoldrick, Pearce, & Giordano, 1996). Although the Ethnic-Sensitive Inventory helps therapists increase their sensitivity to the effect of their values on culturally diverse clients (Ho, 1991), no comparable self-assessment instrument exists for the family therapist.

CULTURAGRAM IN FAMILY ASSESSMENT

The culturagram, an assessment tool that focuses specifically on different aspects of culture, was developed to help practitioners better understand and empower culturally diverse families (Congress, 1994). This tool supplements two existing family assessment tools—the ecomap (Hartman & Laird, 1983), which delineates the relationship of the family to the outside environment, and the genogram (Bowen, 1978; McGoldrick & Gerson, 1985), which studies intergenerational relationships among family members. Neither the ecomap nor the genogram focuses specifically on cultural issues. Although generalizations about different ethnic groups have been helpful to family therapists in practice with culturally diverse clients (McGoldrick, 1996), current practice with culturally diverse families has stressed the importance of individualizing families from different cultural backgrounds (Green, 1995).

Overgeneralization in terms of racial or ethnic group characteristics may lead to incorrect stereotypes about families with whom the therapist is not familiar. To describe one family as Hispanic and another as Black does not promote sensitivity to cultural difference. A Puerto Rican family who has lived in New York City for 30 years may be very different from a Mexican family without legal documentation living in rural Texas. An African American family that relocated from a small southern town to a northern city will be unlike a Haitian family that entered Florida last year. Use of the culturagram helps the family therapist clarify differences among individuals and families from similar racial and ethnic backgrounds.

Culture should be viewed not as a singular concept but rather as incorporating "institutions, language, values, religious ideals, habits of thinking, artistic expressions, and patterns of social and interpersonal relationships" (Lum, 1992, p. 62). The culturagram enables practitioners to understand different aspects of culture in terms of a specific family.

COMPONENTS OF A CULTURAGRAM

The following topics are included in a culturagram:

- Reasons for immigration
- Length of time in the community
- Legal or undocumented status
- Age at time of immigration
- Language spoken at home and in the community
- Contact with cultural institutions
- Health beliefs
- Holidays and special events
- Impact of crisis events
- Values concerning family, education, and work

A culturagram model that social workers can use in work with culturally diverse families is presented in Figure 1.1.

Although all 10 areas should be included in assessing the impact of culture on the family, the areas may vary in significance. For example, family, education, and work values affect daily functioning, whereas holidays and special events may have an impact only at certain times of the year.

Reasons for Immigration

A family's reasons for emigration to a new community are of great importance. Many emigrants leave their country of origin to follow other relatives or friends to the new country; others leave to escape extreme

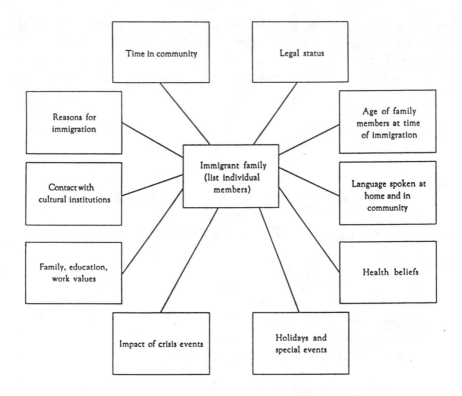

Figure 1.1 Culturagram.
From Congress, E. (1994). The use of culturagrams to assess and empower culturally diverse families. *Families in Society: The Journal of Contemporary Human Services, 75*, 532. (Copyright © 1994 Families International, Inc.)

financial deprivation, political oppression, or religious discrimination in their homelands. Some families migrate within the United States, from a rural to an urban environment, especially because rural communities have suffered extreme economic depression during recent years. Some immigrants expect that they will ultimately return to their home communities; others know they cannot ever return. Family therapists who see immigrant families must be cognizant of these factors, as the following example illustrates:

In a first interview a family therapist in a neighborhood counseling center noted that a 10-year-old Guatemalan child seemed very depressed. In completing the culturagram of the family, the practitioner explored why the family had come to the United States and learned that this family, which belonged to a dissident political group, had narrowly escaped death before arriving in California. A recurrent theme for this child and her family was that they could never go home again. Cut off from the country with which they were familiar, this child and other members of the family were experiencing difficulties in adjusting to a strange, alien country and had no hope of returning to their homeland.

Length of Time in Community

The longer a family lives in the United States, the more likely its members are to become acculturated. A family that immigrated recently may be more likely to adhere to its original cultural beliefs than a family that arrived many years ago (Longres, 1991). This is true both for families that have emigrated from other countries and for those that have moved from a rural to a more urban environment.

Given the task of following up on missed medical appointments, a clinic family worker learned that an immigrant family from rural Honduras had not brought their child for a return appointment. This 8-year-old boy had previously been brought to the emergency room by ambulance after he was hit by a car but was not admitted to the hospital. In completing the culturagram, the worker discovered that the family had been in the United States for only 1 month and did not know how to use public transportation to return for follow-up care.

Often family members arrive in this country at different times. For example, women from South American countries may enter the United States first as servants and then send for children, who may have been entrusted to the care of other relatives. In these families, mothers may be more acculturated than are their children. Family therapists need to be sensitive to these differences when they work with culturally diverse families.

Legal or Undocumented Status

Learning about the legal status of individual members of the immigrant family is an important aspect of the culturagram. Puerto Ricans are free to enter the United States as American citizens. Many immigrants enter legally under newly expanded immigration policies. A third group of newcomers, including students and household workers, acquire visas to stay for a specified period. Finally, some new arrivals may enter the country in secret or choose not to return to their country of origin after their visas expire. Without proper documentation many of the last group fear deportation. To live in the United States in constant fear of discovery and deportation has a detrimental effect on the functioning of immigrant families. Current antiimmigration legislation such as Proposition 187 in California has increased many immigrant families' fear of disclosure. Families fearful about deportation may become withdrawn and isolated (Foner, 1987). Often families with undocumented status avoid formal social and health services, as the following example suggests.

> A 2-year-old Mexican child was admitted to the hospital with a very high fever and tentative diagnosis of pneumonia. The mother had not previously sought medical care for the child, and a neglect charge was considered. After talking to the mother in Spanish, the social worker learned that the mother feared deportation as she was undocumented.

Sometimes clinicians who work with culturally diverse families find it difficult to learn the legal status of immigrant families. Family members may view professional clinicians as representatives of the Immigration and Naturalization Service. Before completing this part of the culturagram, it is essential that the family therapist develop a trusting relationship with the family. Clients and their families must be reassured about confidentiality and at times advised about community resources that support and advocate for undocumented people.

Age at Time of Immigration

Children acculturate more quickly than their parents. While attending school and participating in peer relationships, children quickly learn English and often serve as family interpreters, which may create problematic role reversals (Chilman, 1993). These differing rates of acculturation often lead to family conflict between Americanized adolescents and traditional parents, as this case example indicates:

> A mother and her 16-year-old daughter were seen on an emergency basis in a mental health clinic. The previous night their arguing had been so severe that the police had been summoned by a concerned neighbor. The conflict arose when the daughter wanted to date a boy "just for fun," which is typical social behavior for American adolescents. The mother, on the other hand, wanted her daughter to choose one boy for marriage so that people would not think that her daughter was a tramp.

Although elderly people may have less contact with American educational, social, and work institutions, it should not be assumed that all older people identify strongly with the culture of their country of origin. Although older people who have recently entered the United States may be more involved with their original culture, those who have lived in this country for many years may be very influenced by the culture of their new community (Gelfand & Barresi, 1987).

In completing this part of the culturagram, the family therapist becomes more aware of the ways in which age affects individual acculturation as well as family conflict caused by differing rates of acculturation.

Spoken Language

Speaking one's native language is a significant factor in maintaining one's cultural background (Devore & Schlesinger, 1991). Many social and educational institutions in which large immigrant populations are seen provide bilingual services. Often, children of immigrant families learn English quickly, although their parents continue to speak their native language only. Frequently, only the native language is spoken at home, with English spoken in the larger community. In completing the culturagram, the family therapist must learn what language individual family members speak, as this may be crucial to family functioning.

A Dominican family was referred for family counseling; poor communication was identified as the presenting problem. In completing the culturagram, the family therapist learned that the parents spoke and understood only Spanish, whereas the adolescent children understood Spanish but spoke only in English.

Contact with Cultural Institutions

Many culturally diverse families may be members of churches, ethnic schools, and social clubs to which people from similar cultural backgrounds belong. Contact with cultural institutions is one way in which immigrant families maintain their cultural identity (Gelfand & Fandetti, 1986). Family therapists must become aware of the cultural institutions that affect the lives of their clients. Religious rituals affect the daily lives of many immigrant families (Devore & Schlesinger, 1991). The therapist must learn whether (1) the family regularly attends an ethnic place of worship, (2) the children are enrolled in an ethnic school for religious instruction and/or general education, and (3) the children attend bilingual classes within the public education system.

Health Beliefs

Many immigrants have beliefs about health that are quite different from American medical practice (Congress & Lyons, 1992). These differences alter the way immigrants describe their state of health as well as their illnesses. Furthermore, the access and utilization of health care facilities for diagnostic and treatment procedures may vary among immigrant groups. For example, many Puerto Ricans consult a spiritualist before going to a medical doctor for a health problem. Asians seldom view symptoms as psychological and thus do not seek treatment from mental health clinics. Some West Indians seek medical treatment only when they are ill. Thus, preventive care under managed care programs may be avoided. Family therapists, however, must not depend on cultural generalizations about families they see but rather should study these families' unique beliefs about health, illness, and treatment.

Holidays and Special Events

Particular cultural groups often follow different religious rituals. For example, Puerto Ricans often celebrate the Feast of the Three Magi with gifts and parties. Sometimes special events are linked to transitional events such as births, marriages, and deaths. For Greeks, marriage is highly celebrated, and for the Irish, funerals are extremely important (McGolddrick, 1996). Such information should be included in the culturagram.

Impact of Crises Events

Although families from all cultures are affected by crises, certain stressors may have a particular impact on members of a cultural group. For example, losing a job may be particularly traumatic for a member of an ethnic group in which employment is essential to self-esteem. Also, the death of a grandparent may take on greater importance for a family whose culture stresses the veneration of older family members. Traumatic stressors such as rape may have an especially negative impact on women and their families if female virginity before marriage is an important value (Congress, 1990). Relocating to a different country or moving from a rural to an urban community can precipitate a crisis for a family: former coping skills may no longer work, and family members must learn new ways to adapt to a strange environment (Drachman & Ryan, 1991).

Family, Education, and Work Values

The values of individual members as well as of the family as a whole are influenced by their cultural background. Their values may differ on key issues such as family, education, and work. For example, many Hispanic and Asian families perceive the needs of the collective group (family) as being more significant than those of the individual (Devore & Schlesinger, 1991). In one instance, knowing the cultural values of a Dominican family helped an American-born family therapist understand an adolescent boy's decision to forgo educational opportunities in favor of supporting his family.

Immigrant parents usually want their children to succeed in this country and view education as an important step toward achieving this goal. It is important to assess the family's values concerning education and the educational process. For example, many Asian families stress the importance of high scholastic achievement (Shon & Ja, 1982). The Hispanic family may be influenced by the value of respect in their contact with school officials (Congress, 1990), which may inhibit Hispanic parents from questioning school authorities about their children. Each family's values concerning education must be explored.

Cultural values with regard to work provide important material for the culturagram. Some immigrants held high-status positions in medicine or higher education in their countries of origin and may have been forced to take low-status jobs, such as factory worker or taxi driver, in the United States. This may be embarrassing for the immigrant family. Also, during the recent recession many immigrants had to struggle to find any work at all. Immigrant families that view work as essential to self-esteem find it extremely difficult to cope with unemployment.

Sometimes women are able to secure domestic or factory work more readily than men, and this may create conflict in families in which men traditionally assume the role of provider. Many immigrant families come from a background in which all family members work. For example, some immigrant families run small groceries and restaurants in which children work alongside their parents. Many family therapists may be concerned that this arrangement will jeopardize the school attendance or peer relationships of immigrant children.

DIVERSITY AMONG FAMILY MEMBERS

In completing the culturagram, the family therapist may become aware of important differences among family members that affect acculturation and family functioning. For example, family members enter the new country at different ages. In addition, some family members may have been in the United States longer than others and thus may be more acculturated. These differences can create stress and conflict in immigrant families. Such issues are especially prevalent in families whose children become socialized to American culture through the educational system (Tseng & Hsu, 1991). Families may experience conflict when a child no longer wants to attend a cultural institution promoted by the family or wants to associate with peers at the expense of family-related activities. Family therapists should note these differences but avoid allying themselves with a particular family member. In the following example, a beginning family therapist does not follow this principle:

> A woman from the Dominican Republic and her 14-year-old daughter were seen in a family counseling center because the daughter wanted to see her friends in the afternoon after school rather than help care for her three younger siblings. The family therapist told the mother that in America children see their friends after school rather than care for younger siblings. Because the therapist sided with the daughter and did not attempt to reconcile conflicts within the family, the family never returned for another session.

The culturagram helps family therapists understand the diversity of cultural beliefs among family members. Such knowledge can be used to understand and reconcile differences. Family members may not even be aware that other family members have differing values and beliefs.

> In completing the culturagram of a Puerto Rican family that had immigrated 5 years earlier, the family therapist began to explore the differing values of

family members with regard to education. The youngest daughter had won a scholarship to a prestigious college in a distant state. Encouraged by school personnel, the daughter wanted to take advantage of this opportunity. The mother, however, was adamant that the daughter should not leave home but rather should attend a local community college. The mother, who suffered from diabetes and hypertension, believed that the daughter should stay at home and care for her. The daughter, on the other hand, was influenced by American values of individual educational achievement and wanted to pursue her education away from home. Exploring the value differences between the daughter and her mother helped the family understand its members' differing needs. The daughter stated, "I just thought my mother was jealous of me having this opportunity. I never knew how important keeping the family together was for her." Her mother commented, "I always wanted the very best for my daughter. I really can see how this college would provide the best education for her."

USES OF THE CULTURAGRAM

Assessment

Although assessment begins in the first interview, the process continues throughout contact with the family (Hepworth & Larsen, 1993). Information about the first five areas of the culturagram can usually be obtained in the first interview with the family, whereas the last five areas often are not explored until much later. Some information may be learned by direct questioning; other material can be obtained indirectly. For example, a family therapist first learned of the significant crisis caused by a grandparent's death when the family's children were taken out of school for 2 weeks during exams to return to Puerto Rico for the funeral. Information about a family's values often comes out indirectly in work with the family, not through direct questioning.

Some information, however, can be ascertained through direct questioning and exploration. The following questions can be used in completing the culturagram.

1. What brought you to the United States? Why did you decide to leave (county of origin)?
2. How long have you lived in the United States? In this community?

3. Do you have a green card? There are agencies that can help people secure a green card.
4. How old were you when you came to the United States?
5. What language do you speak at home? In the community?
6. What clubs/groups do you belong to?
7. When you are sick what do you do? Where and to whom do you turn to for help?
8. What kinds of family parties do you have? What holidays do you celebrate? How do you celebrate?
9. What particular events have been stressful for your family?
10. Do you believe everyone should have a high school/college education?
11. Do you believe that the man should be the family breadwinner?

Empowering Families

Families can be involved in the development of their own culturagram. Their involvement may empower family members by helping them see themselves and their cultural background as important. In completing the culturagram, however, the family therapist must strive to be open and encouraging. Being judgmental or critical defeats the goal of the culturagram to strengthen and empower families. Completing the culturagram with an immigrant family helps each member to see his or her own story of transition and relocation as unique and worthwhile.

IMPLICATIONS FOR FAMILY THERAPISTS

The culturagram is a powerful tool for helping family therapists assess and intervene appropriately with culturally diverse families. It is rooted in a model of cultural pluralism that stresses the intrinsic value of culturally diverse families pursuing their own styles, customs, values, and language while recognizing that differing degrees of acculturation do occur (Lum, 1992). The culturagram allows family therapists to do the following:

- Understand the complexities of culture as it affects families.
- Individualize families beyond cultural generalizations.

- Become sensitive to the daily experience of culturally diverse families.
- Develop differential assessments of family members.
- Involve the family in understanding its cultural background.
- Discover specific areas for intervention.

As more and more immigrants enter the United States each year, family therapists can make use of the culturagram as an assessment tool to understand and work effectively with culturally diverse families. The culturagram is useful with families from many different cultural backgrounds. Although this assessment tool is most helpful with families that have recently immigrated, it has also been used effectively with families who have been in the United States for many years.

REFERENCES

Allen-Meares, P. (1992). Prevention and cross-cultural perspective: Preparing school social workers for the 21st century. *Social Work in Education, 14,* 3–5.

Bowen, M. (1978). *Family therapy in clinical practice.* New York: Jason Aronson.

Boyd-Franklin, N. (1989). *Black families in therapy: A multi-systems approach.* New York: Guilford.

Chilman, C. (1993). Hispanic families in the United States: Research perspectives. In H. P. McAdoo (Ed.), *Family ethnicity: Strength in diversity* (pp. 141–163). Newbury Park, CA: Sage Publications.

Congress, E. (1990). Crisis intervention with Hispanic client in an urban mental health clinic. In A. Roberts (Ed.), *Crisis intervention handbook: Assessment, treatment, and research* (pp. 221–236). Belmont, CA: Wadsworth.

Congress, E. (1994). The use of culturagrams to assess and empower culturally diverse families. *Families in Society, 75,* 531–540.

Congress, E., & Lynn, M. (1994). Group work programs in public schools: Ethical dilemmas and cultural diversity. *Social Work in Education, 16*(2), 107–114.

Congress, E., & Lyons, B. (1992). Ethnic differences in health beliefs: Implications for social workers in health care settings. *Social Work in Health Care, 17*(3), 81–96.

Devore, W., & Schlesinger, E. (1991). *Ethnic-sensitive social work practice* (3rd ed.). New York: Macmillan.

Drachman, D., & Ryan, A. (1991). Immigrants and refugees. In A. Gitterman, *Handbook of social work practice with vulnerable populations* (pp. 618–646). New York: Columbia University Press.

Foner, N. (1987). Introduction: New immigrants and changing patterns in New York City. In N. Foner (Ed.), *New immigrants in New York* (pp. 1–33). New York: Columbia University Press.

Gelfand, D., & Barresi, C. M. (Eds.). (1987). *Ethnic dimensions of aging.* New York: Springer Publishing Co.

Gelfand, D., & Fandetti, D. (1986). The emergent nature of ethnicity: Dilemmas in assessment. *Social Casework, 67,* 542–550.

Green, J. (1995). *Cultural awareness in the human services.* Englewood Cliffs, NJ: Prentice-Hall.

Hartman, A., & Laird, J. (1983). *Family-centered social work practice.* New York: Free Press.

Hepworth, D., & Larsen, J. A. (1993). *Direct social work practice: Theory and skills* (3rd ed.). Chicago: Dorsey Press.

Ho, M. K. (1987). *Family therapy with ethnic minorities.* Newbury Park, CA: Sage Publications.

Ho, M. K. (1991). Use of Ethnic-Sensitive Inventory (ESI) to enhance practitioner skills with minorities. *Journal of Multicultural Social Work, 1,* 57–67.

Logan, S., Freeman, E., & McRoy, R. (Eds.). (1990). *Social work practice with black families.* New York: Longman.

Longres, J. (1991). Toward a status model of ethnic sensitive practice. *Journal of Multicultural Social Work, 1,* 41–56.

Lum, D. (1992). *Social work practice and people of color: A process-stage approach* (2nd ed.). Pacific Grove, CA: Brooks/Cole.

McGoldrick, M., & Giordano, J. (1996). Ethnicity and family therapy: An overview. In M. McGoldrick, J. Pearce, & J. Giordano (Eds.), *Ethnicity and family therapy* (2nd ed., pp. 1–27). New York: Guilford.

McGoldrick, M., & Gerson, R. (1985). *Genograms in family assessment.* New York: W. W. Norton.

McGoldrick, M., Pearce, J., & Giordano, J. (1996). *Ethnicity and family therapy* (2nd ed.). New York: Guilford.

Shon, S., & Ja, D. (1982). Asian families. In M. McGoldrick, J. Pearce, & J. Giordano (Eds.), *Ethnicity and family therapy* (pp. 208–228). New York: Guilford.

Tseng, W., & Hsu, J. (1991). *Culture and family: Problems and therapy.* New York: Haworth.

CHAPTER 2

Managing Agencies for Multicultural Services

Roslyn H. Chernesky

Along with the increasing emphasis on ethnically sensitive and culturally competent social work practice that emerged in the 1970s (Tully & Greene, 1994), there has been a more recent yet growing recognition that social agencies must also attend to broader ethnic, multicultural, and diversity issues. Interest in how organizations can be more sensitive and culturally competent stems from several sources.

The most significant source of this interest has been the estimated demographic changes in the composition of the workforce by the year 2000. Whereas today almost half of the workforce consists of native-born White males, only 15% of new labor force entrants will be native-born White males by the year 2000 (Johnston & Packer, 1987). Approximately 85% of the net increase in the labor force will consist of women, Blacks, Asians, and other minority groups. Women will make up 47% of workers, and minorities and immigrants will hold 26% of all jobs (Edwards, 1991). Thus, 8 of every 10 new entrants to the workforce will be immigrants, women, or members of minority groups. In fact, women workers of all ethnic groups will outnumber men.

People with disabilities will also be more prominent in the workforce. Advocacy and legislative initiatives will result in a greater number of

17

workers with disabilities, especially as they are increasingly seen as an untapped labor source. The Americans with Disabilities Act passed by Congress in 1992 was a strong incentive to hire the disabled, and organizations are finding accommodations for disabled workers are not as costly or difficult as anticipated (Foster, 1993; Ledman & Brown, 1993). Older workers are also expected to be in the workforce in increased numbers, especially as they too are increasingly viewed as dedicated and valuable workers (Mor-Baral & Tynan, 1993). America's workforce therefore will become older, more female, and more ethnically and culturally diverse. Along with the demographic shifts, there are likely to be difference in lifestyles, attitudes, and work ethics that will affect work and the workplace.

The challenge of managing this diverse workforce has been a major concern for businesses and corporations. Because organizations will be composed of workers from different backgrounds, values, and perspectives, businesses and corporations are now asking, "How can we capitalize on the talents of the various groups and leverage these difference to give us a competitive advantage?" (Johnson, 1994). Social service agencies are beginning to realize the same challenge (Seck, Finch, Mor-Barak, & Poverny, 1993).

A second source of interest in multicultural sensitivity stems from today's litigious climate, which requires affirmative action, mandates accommodation for workers with disabilities, and prohibits discrimination. At the same time, entrenched policies and practices, as well as insensitive and inappropriate behaviors, either deliberately or unintentionally, continue to prevent equity in the workplace. Biases that influence hiring, retention, and promotion remain unnoticed while sexual harassment and ethnic humor create tensions in the workplace, hostilities among workers, and bases for legal action.

A third source of heightened interest in multicultural organizational issues is the professional concern that the service delivery system is falling short of meeting the needs of many of its clients. As Gutierrez (1992) points out, agency barriers can restrict access to services for members of minority groups, and agency practices and procedures can lead to incorrect assessments and treatment based on race or ethnicity. Fong and Gibbs (1995) remind us that traditional mental health agencies have not been successful in delivering culturally appropriate services to ethnically diverse families even when funded to serve catchment areas with specific minority populations. To effectively reach, work with, and treat families who are from diverse ethnic and cultural backgrounds, continuing attention must be given to the values and behaviors of human service workers that might, if left unchecked, become barriers to service delivery.

More, however, is called for. Agencies today must demonstrate that they value diversity, understand and respect diverse cultures, and plan and provide culturally relevant and responsive programs and services. Agencies need to examine their management and program practices at all levels to determine to what extent they are culturally competent and what steps they can take toward becoming more culturally competent. They must assess what might be less overt and more subtle ways in which they fail to provide effective services or perhaps even offer inappropriate, ineffective, and potentially damaging services to multicultural client populations.

This chapter assumes that both workers and agencies are in need of change in order to effectively provide multicultural services. It also recognizes that social service agencies generally have not been ethnically or culturally sensitive, nor have they demonstrated that they value diversity. In fact, agencies give little evidence of appreciating the need to address multiculturalism, despite their position as employers of and service providers to diverse populations and the increasing research that identifies barriers to service for people from minority groups (Gutierrez, 1992).

The chapter focuses on the two primary ways that agencies can be culturally sensitive and responsive. It begins with managing a diverse workforce, an earlier approach. It then introduces the later concept of developing culturally competent organizations and service delivery systems. In both approaches, material from outside the social work field is drawn upon liberally to identify trends and offer examples that may be useful for the field.

MANAGING A DIVERSE WORKFORCE

Because the labor market is going to look different and be different, the challenges are to attract and retain this new workforce, to utilize the strengths and uniqueness associated with these differences, and to build a multicultural workplace. Organizations that value diversity attempt to bring about qualitative changes through increased appreciation of the range of skills and values that dissimilar employees offer and through increased opportunity to include members who are culturally distinct from the dominant group (Loden & Rosener, 1991). The ultimate goal is to develop an organization that fully taps the potential of all its employees.

These challenges move beyond earlier efforts to address differences by ignoring or denying them in the interest of equality or by asking workers to abandon their cultural identity and merge into the majority in the interest of integration. Expecting minority group members to assimilate and adopt the norms and values of the majority group to survive in an organization is characterized by Cox (1991) as a *monocultural organiza-tion*. According to Cox, three types of organizations can be distinguished according to their basic attitudes toward cultural diversity. *Plural organi-zations* have a more heterogeneous workforce because they have taken steps to include diverse groups. Yet the quality of work relationships between members of different groups as well as inadvertent discrimination are not addressed. In contrast, in *multicultural organizations* differences are appreciated and uniqueness is respected, and consequently, there is a general absence of prejudice, discrimination, and intergroup conflict. Multicultural organizations are those in which the organizational culture recognizes and appreciates diversity, resources and influence are distrib-uted without regard to race or sex, and policies and practices are responsive to all workers' needs.

Another typology of organization progression in relation to cultural diversity is offered by Nixon and Spearmon (1991). Level 1 organizations are merely token *Equal Economic Opportunity (EEO) organizations*, with people of color and women clustered at the bottom of the hierarchy and a few tokens located at mid-management levels. Level 2 organizations aggressively recruit people of color and women, support them, and encour-age nonracist and nonsexist behaviors. But in these *affirmative action organizations* assimilation continues to be the key to individual success. Level 3 organizations are *self-renewing*. They are actively becoming pluralistic, examining their mission, culture, values, operations, and mana-gerial styles to include a wide range of cultural perspectives. The *pluralistic organization*, at level 4, however,

> reflects the contributions and interests of diverse cultural and social groups
> in its mission, operations, and delivery of services. It seeks to eliminate
> all forms of cultural and social oppression in the organization, and its

workforce is represented by different cultural and social groups at all levels. Even more significant, diversity in leadership is reflected in the organization's policymaking and governance. Equally important, the pluralistic organization exhibits a sensitivity to issues that affect the larger community and participates in socially responsible activities and programs. (Nixon & Spearmon, 1991, p. 158)

Today it is considered wrong to have a diverse workforce and pretend you do not. No longer are workers expected to set aside their cultural values while at work. Rather than avoid the issue of diversity, organizations are encouraged to address it (Goldstein & Leopold, 1990). We now speak of valuing diversity, that is, enabling individuals to make their maximum contribution and to succeed regardless of race, ethnicity, gender, age, or disability (Solomon, 1989).

Yet we acknowledge that many cultural differences cause miscommunication and conflicts at work, which can then further compound existing stereotypes and prejudices (Solomon, 1989). Therefore, we strive to understand diverse cultural values and beliefs and their influence on how one works and acts in the workplace. Managers and workers need to understand their own culture and how their behavior is influenced by culture. They also need to understand their assumptions about and stereotypes of other cultures in order to get past the prejudices and biases that interfere with their productively working with those who are culturally or socially different from them. To help workers develop such awareness and sensitivity, organizations have turned to training.

Multicultural Training

Cultural awareness or sensitivity training is used to help individuals gain an understanding of their own personal values, whereas cross-cultural training focuses on learning about cultures of different groups. Both have a long tradition in the field. They assume that, by learning about cultural differences, workers can learn to accept and respect differences between and among people and thus will be able to communicate more effectively and develop strategies for effective intervention (Kavanagh & Kennedy, 1992). Social agencies have used training to increase cultural awareness, to help workers better understand the attitudes and behaviors of minority persons toward their own culture and toward the majority culture, and to focus on culture commonalty and cultural specificity in working with ethnically diverse populations (Stevenson, Cheung, & Leung, 1992).

The current popularity of multicultural training programs is a direct response of the nation's major corporations to the prediction that by the year 2000 about two-thirds of the workforce will be people other than White males (Egan, 1993). Although training is not the only way they are addressing diversity, it is an early and key component of the more successful efforts to do so (Motwani, Harper, Subramanian, & Douglas, 1993; Solomon, 1989). Consequently, a new field has been spawned, with a wide array of training consultants, seminars, and videos dealing with the realities of the multicultural workforce and designed to challenge workers to examine and overcome their biases.

Training programs vary, yet there are similarities among them. For example, programs generally (1) are led by specially trained instructors; (2) combine role playing, exercises, lectures, discussion, and group experiences; (3) cover stereotypes, assumptions, cultural awareness, and sensitivity; (4) run from 1/2 to 3 days; and (5) are supported by follow-up initiatives at the workplace.

Although there is little empirical evidence that multicultural training brings about the desired productive multicultural workforce, corporations such as Digital, Hewlett-Packard, McDonald's, Xerox, Proctor & Gamble, and Avon remain committed to it (Solomon, 1989). A number of factors tend to increase the likelihood that training will be valuable. Training as an isolated project does not seem to have much impact. It works only if supported by a clear and strong commitment to diversity among top management. It must be integrated with the organization's affirmative action and equal opportunity efforts, related policy decisions, and incentives that reward workers who demonstrate culturally sensitive and appropriate behaviors. It helps if the training is seen as a process of moving from a monocultural to a multicultural organization rather than as a one-shot deal (Solomon, 1989).

Multicultural training does not always achieve its intended goals. Some critics say it is futile to try to change attitudes through workshops and seminars. Many participants resent the presumption that they are not tolerant or sensitive and that they need such training. It can often lead to greater polarization among workers and even more complaints about behaviors deemed improper (Egan, 1993; Murray, 1993).

Celebrating Diversity

Bringing together workers on a regular or occasional basis to celebrate various cultures is valuable for increasing awareness of the cultures of coworkers. These may include luncheons devoted to ethnic foods, sharing in traditional holiday events, and arranging opportunities to purchase crafts or items representing different cultures, perhaps for holiday gifts. At one agency, celebrating cultural heritage is important not only for workers but also as part of programming for clients. The intensive case management staff organizes two annual special celebrations: an African Day celebration and a Hispanic Day celebration. Both events involve families in sharing food, music, dancing, storytelling, and a history or language lesson under the leadership of the workers. In addition, workers plan and conduct a series of presentations, based on their own cultural experiences, for the program staff on working with Caribbean, Dominican, Ecuadoran, Puerto Rican, and African American families ("Multiculturalism Taking Root," 1995).

Work Groups

Corporations have also led the way with diversity work groups, also referred to as pluralism councils (Mabry, 1990). These are small focused groups or multicultural discussion sessions aimed primarily at airing grievances as they relate to biases or discrimination and improving understanding among participants. Unlike more general diversity training, these councils are targeted to specific needs of the groups' participants. For women or minorities who have felt it best to remain silent about sexism or racism, the group offers a safe and supportive context to do so. Mere exposure to and experience with members of the opposite gender and other ethnicities on this somewhat intimate level can in itself decrease bias. In this kind of setting, workers may learn how to manage the tendency to see any conflict or criticism as the result of racism. Other groups may be given organizational responsibility to plan and develop the organization's multicultural initiatives. They may identify concerns, determine if problems being experienced are associated with diversity, and propose solutions such as workshops or celebrations of various cultures. These groups usually have access to upper management, which allows their work to get translated into policy-related decisions.

Transforming Organizational Culture

The culture of an organization is reflected in the pattern of beliefs, values, and expectations shared by organization members that establish norms and rules governing acceptable and unacceptable employee behaviors. The standards against which behavior is evaluated are invariably that of the majority culture and reflect the attitude and values of the White men who hold positions of authority and power. Those who are different, outsiders, may not measure up to the standards and therefore not be allowed to participate fully in the organization and reap its benefits. For example, the standard of effective management has traditionally been based on attributes stereotypical of White men, which women have been unable to demonstrate or unwilling to emulate. Their supposed lack of suitable qualities has contributed to the gender-based glass ceiling that limits the advancement of women to top management levels. The glass ceiling is a popular metaphor from the 1980s that describes a barrier so subtle that it is virtually transparent yet so strong that it prevents women (and people of color) from moving up in the organization's hierarchy (Morrison & Von Glinow, 1990). Similarly, the standard that expects managers to work late and forfeit family responsibilities fosters the "mommy track," a channeling of women into positions with no opportunity for advancement. The double bind that Black managers find themselves in can also be explained in part by expectations of them because they are Black (Anderson & Maypole, 1986).

An organization's culture can be tolerant of behaviors that discriminate or harass, thus making the workplace inhospitable and offensive to workers who are not members of the majority group. Blatant examples of discrimination or harassment may be rare in social agencies; however, microinequities, examples of subtle discrimination, either conscious or unconscious, are abundant. Microinequities are unjust actions taken against an individual based on stereotypes about other races or members of the opposite sex. They are usually so subtle that it is difficult to know how to counter it—for example, the case of a woman who speaks up at a meeting and later finds that her remarks were attributed to the man seated next to her or the African American professional who is mistaken for a support person (Laporte, 1991).

Harassment along racial, ethnic, and gender lines has the potential to create disrupting tensions in the workplace. Although flagrant violations of the EEO laws may not occur, many situations exist in which racial slurs, jokes, and epithets are less pervasive, not necessarily directed at specific workers, and not necessarily vicious or threatening (Leap & Smeltzer, 1984). In many agencies such a culture can be functional. Humor and joking can relieve tension or frustration, reduce boredom, reinforce status levels, establish roles, and provide a means to express feelings where there are no socially acceptable outlets. However, if a work environment is polluted with such behavior or management has implicitly or explicitly condoned it, then it is likely to violate Title VII or other fair employment laws.

Agency Policies

Written agency policies can be effective in preventing racial, ethnic, and sexual harassment from taking root. A general policy should support the dignity of each employee and forbid unnecessary forms of harassment, racial tensions, and demeaning behavior. According to Leap and Smelzer (1984), the policy should recognize that

- Workers have the right to work in an environment free of undue personal harassment. stress, and interpersonal friction.
- Certain types of racially motivated remarks and harassment are contrary to federal and state civil rights laws and can impose a legal liability on the agency as well as tarnish the agency's public image and damage worker morale.
- Workers have an individual responsibility to desist from behavior that might offend the dignity and violate the personal and legal rights of others.
- Supervisors and managers are obliged to investigate incidents or complaints of harassment. Sanctions against offending workers should be imposed consistent with the agency's discipline policy.

Increasingly, agencies are developing and distributing specific policies forbidding sexual harassment and spelling out the penalties, including dismissal or personal legal and financial liability. Initially, sexual harassment was viewed in terms of threats or insinuations that a worker's submission to or rejection of sexual advances could influence personnel decisions regarding employment, wages, advancement, assigned duties, or any other condition of employment or career development. In 1986 the Supreme Court clarified its definition of sexual harassment to include subtle forms of intimidation—lingering, intimate touches; repeated sexual innuendos; and comments about aspects of a person's physique—that can create a hostile work environment.

CULTURALLY COMPETENT SERVICE DELIVERY

Just as the workforce is undergoing dramatic changes in its composition, the client populations in our social and health agencies are reflecting the same shifts. Children of color will make up an increasing portion of the country's young population. Many will have known an immigrant experience, possibly a castelike status, severe economic conditions, upheavals and losses, or ongoing civil warfare. It will be incumbent upon agencies to respond to the unique needs of these populations whose cultures are different from those considered mainstream American.

Traditional efforts to make dominant agencies and their programs more sensitive and responsive to diverse client populations emphasized hiring workers from the same ethnic and cultural populations. Indigenous bicultural and bilingual paraprofessionals were hired beginning with the Economic Opportunity Act of 1964. Even today many serve as case aids, social work assistants, and interpreters, working as team members or alongside professionals from dominant ethnic and cultural populations. Indigenous workers are expected to be better able to relate to clients as well as bridge the different cultures. In so doing they can help families understand what agencies need from them and can help the agencies understand the needs of their diverse families and communities.

Hiring professional staff of similar ethnic and cultural backgrounds as clients has rarely yielded a significant cohort in a dominant agency. Underrepresentation of ethnic diversity in staffing and programs continues to be problematic and is likely to remain so (Fong & Gibbs, 1995).

Agencies with bicultural and bilingual staff and multicultural training have made important strides, but neither assures that they are culturally competent organizations. Culturally competent agencies are those whose policies, behaviors, and attitudes combine in such a way that the agency and its workers can effectively provide services in multicultural situations. According to Cross and his colleagues (1989), a culturally competent system of care acknowledges and incorporates—at all levels—the importance of culture, the assessment of cross-cultural relations, vigilance towards the dynamics that result from cultural differences, the expansion of cultural knowledge, and the adaptation of services to meet culturally-unique needs. (Cross, Barzon, Dennis, & Isaacs, pp. iv, v)

According to Isaacs and Benjamin (1991), culturally competent organizations would (a) value diversity, (b) have the capacity for cultural self-assessment, (c) be conscious of the dynamics inherent when cultures interact, (d) have institutionalized cultural knowledge, and (e) have developed adaptations to service delivery that reflect an understanding of cultural diversity. Most important, these five elements would be manifested at every level of an organization—policy-making, administrative, and practice levels. They would be reflected in the agency's attitudes, structures, policies, and services.

Because there are many ways that agencies can further the concept of cultural competence, allowing each to cater to the particular needs and characteristics of the ethnic groups, the community, policymakers, and the agencies themselves, it is useful to examine the principles and key elements that contribute to culturally competent agencies. After examining 98 agencies in a nationwide survey of culturally competent programs, cross-cutting issues and characteristics inherent in these programs emerged, providing lessons that could be valuable to agencies striving toward greater cultural competency. Although these examples were specifically mental health programs serving ethnic and minority children and families, the principles are applicable to social service and health services in general (Isaacs & Benjamin, 1991).

Agencies that effectively serve ethnic minority groups promote access, availability, and acceptance, leading to high utilization of their programs. They do so primarily by creating a positive image of the agency and its programs in the community. At times agencies must work toward changing negative perceptions of their services or clients to encourage use. Programs that have strong linkages to the community are more likely to have good reputations and greater credibility. They maintain and use informal community resources, leaders, and networks on behalf of their clients. Even physical location, as a free-standing center or clinic in a particular ethnic minority community, is an asset. Agencies that deliver services directly in the community, in settings that are familiar and comfortable, such as home, school, church, or community center, are more easily seen as community resources, which increases access. When agency personnel play active roles in the community (e.g., members of parent-teacher associations and school or community boards) and agencies contribute to the community over and beyond their services (e.g., making their rooms or copying machines available for community groups), they create a positive image that also increases access. Participation in community events such as health fairs, parent education meetings, and Little League games helps to reinforce the notion that the agency is part of the community.

Policymaking Level

Agency policymakers can begin by building a diverse board (Rutledge, 1995). They can examine their organization's mission statement and incorporate cultural competence into it and into its long-range planning. Policymakers can establish linkages with the community and develop ways for representatives from the community's different cultural populations to make their voices heard and participate in shaping agency policy. Policymakers can set standards for multicultural services that incorporate cultural competence. They can commit resources to training board members and staff in cultural competence. They can require unbiased research and data collection on minorities be undertaken to guide their decision making. They can support efforts to design programs and provide services in collaboration with minority community groups, with the intention of eventually turning over the programs to the community groups to operate on their own behalf.

Administrative Level

At the agency's administrative level, the directors, managers, supervisors, and program or unit heads provide credence and direction for the development of cultural competence. Their commitment to cultural competence can then be communicated to all staff in goals, programs, and practices. The administrative level is responsible for spearheading some form of agency cultural competence self-assessment, ensuring that a diverse staff is recruited and retained, providing training, and adapting personnel policies to make an agency more culturally competent. Increasingly, keeping a diverse workforce may be more of a challenge than recruiting one (Deutsch 1991a, 1991b).

The provision of culturally competent services requires that the design and delivery of programs be adapted, flexibly and creatively, to fit the needs of the targeted multicultural client populations. Frequently, services are delivered from a culturally blind perspective, not taking into account cultural norms or values. Administrators can enhance service delivery to be sure that programs are accessible to minority communities. Not only must they be geographically located in community sites, but their hours and their physical facilities must be inviting and culturally sensitive. Programs must be designed so that their structures and policies do not create obstacles to their use by minority groups, even if unintended.

Practitioner Level

Workers need to be committed to providing culturally competent services and to becoming culturally competent practitioners. Workers first need to be aware of their own cultural values, accept cultural differences, and learn about their families' cultures in order to adapt their practice to fit the client's cultural context. Styles of greeting and interviewing, who is included in family interventions, and treatment goals are a few examples of the helping process that can be altered to respond to cultural differences.

Agency Self-Assessment

Cultural competence is a goal. Few organizations are at the point of cultural competency. Most are in earlier stages of a continuum building toward this goal. Some may actually be culturally destructive or culturally blind. It is important that all agencies understand where they fall on this continuum in order to appreciate how much farther they may have to move along. It is equally important that agencies begin to take the kinds of steps to modify and create service delivery systems that are more culturally sensitive and reflect the needs of various ethnic populations.

Agency self-assessments to examine how well an organization is addressing diversity and multiculturalism are attracting greater attention. A framework suggested for services in the field of aging directs diversity assessments to mission, governance and administration, personnel practices and staffing patterns, service offerings and caregiving approaches, targeting, and outreach and marketing approaches (Capitman, Hernandez-Gallegos, & Yee, 1991). The Child Welfare League's Cultural Competence Self-Assessment Instrument (CWLA, 1993) provides a valuable format for agencies to use to determine whether their policies, practices, and programs are culturally competent. It is designed to assist agencies in identifying strengths and weaknesses in their response to culturally diverse staff and client populations and in developing action steps for specific changes to become more culturally competent.

The following self-assessment questions from the CWLA instrument illustrate the kinds of issues that agencies are asked to examine in regard to delivering culturally competent services.

- Do the agency's mission statement and goals include reference to cultural diversity and competence?
- Do the policy statements and the work of the agency board of directors incorporate the agency's mission statement and goals, including reference to cultural diversity and competence?
- Does the agency's board of directors consult organizations that represent culturally diverse groups as part of the board recruitment process?
- Does the agency executive report regularly to the board of directors on progress made in the area of cultural competence and on the impact of cultural issues on the agency?
- Does the agency collaborate with culturally diverse organizations on special projects of benefit to the agency's clients?
- Does the agency have a clear process for evaluating the short-term and long-term impact of its programs and policies on culturally diverse families and/or communities?
- Does the agency provide opportunities for advancement for staff members who demonstrate, among other skills, cultural competency?
- Does the agency utilize, as appropriate, the expertise of community leaders, natural healers, elders, and other cultural resource persons in planning and delivering its agency services?
- Do agency staff members continually examine their own cultural beliefs and attitudes to better understand the dynamics of cultural difference and interaction?
- Wherever possible, do agency staff work with families in settings that are comfortable and familiar to them (i.e., home, neighborhood, reservation, community facility)?

- Do the agency's interventions make use of culturally diverse natural helping networks in the service delivery process?
- Is the agency involved in efforts to advocate for programs, policies, and services that directly or indirectly affect the cultural groups it serves?

There seems to be a consensus that managing diverse workforces and multicultural organizations, as well as attaining culturally competent organizations, is essential. Social agencies seem to be lagging behind the corporate sector, where a higher priority is placed on these goals. If there is one lesson that dominates current thinking in this area, it is that success depends on diversity, multiculturalism, or cultural competence being tied to everything an organization is doing. The goals cannot be accomplished by a one-time program, such as a staff training initiative, or by hiring bilingual or bicultural staff. They require a long-term comprehensive organizational change process. Support by executive directors and top management is key because it makes the agency's commitment to them real. It communicates the belief that diversity is valued and is beneficial to the agency and everyone in it. As has been noted, "in the absence of explicit leadership, all other efforts may appear hollow" (Capitman et al., 1991, p. 76).

REFERENCES

Anderson, R. B., & Maypole, D. E. (1986). Role stress, strain and conflict: The case of three black administrators in community substance abuse agencies. *Journal of Intergroup Relations*, *14*(2), 13–22.

Capitman, J. A., Hernandez-Gallegos, W., & Yee, D. L. (1991, Fall/Winter). "Diversity assessments" in aging services. *Generations*, pp. 73–76.

Child Welfare League of America. (1993). *Cultural Competence Self-Assessment Instrument*. Washington, DC: Author.

Cox, T. (1991). The multicultural organization. *Academy of Management Executive*, *5*(2), 34–47.

Cross, T. L., Barzon, B. J., Dennis, K. W., & Isaacs, M. R. (1989). *Towards a culturally competent system of care*. Washington, DC: Georgetown University Child Development Center.

Deutsch, C. H. (1991a, November 24). Hanging on to diversity in the 90's. *New York Times*, p. 21.

Deutsch, C. H. (1991b, December 1). Listening to women and Blacks. *New York Times*, p. 25.

Edwards, A. (1991, January). The enlightened manager: How to treat all your employees fairly. *Working Woman*, pp. 45–51.

Egan, T. (1993, October 8). Teaching tolerance in workplaces: A Seattle program illustrates limits. *New York Times*, p. A18.

Fong, L. G. W., & Gibbs, J. T. (1995). Facilitating services to multicultural communities in a dominant culture setting: An organizational perspective. *Administration in Social Work, 19*(2), 1–20.

Foster, R. S. (1993). The disabled as part of a diverse workforce. *SAM Advanced Management Journal, 58*(2), 21–27.

Goldstein, J., & Leopold, M. (1990, November). Corporate culture vs. ethnic culture. *Personnel Journal*, pp. 83–92.

Gutierrez, L. M. (1992). Empowering ethnic minorities in the twenty-first century: The role of human service organizations. In Y. Hasenfeld (Ed.), *Human services as complex organizations* (pp. 320–338). Newbury Park, CA: Sage Publications.

Isaacs, M. R., & Benjamin, M. P. (1991). *Towards a culturally competent system of care*. Washington, DC: Georgetown University.

Johnson, S. (1994, October 23). What companies have learned: Diversity affects how business recruits, trains and promotes workers. *New York Times*, pp. 4, 6.

Johnston, W. B., & Packer, A. H. (1987). *Workforce 2000: Work and workers for the 21st century*. Indianapolis, IN: Hudson Institute.

Kavanagh, K. H., & Kennedy, P. H. (1992). *Promoting cultural diversity*. Newbury Park, CA: Sage Publications.

Laporte, S. B. (1991, January). The sting of the subtle snub. *Working Woman*, pp. 53, 55.

Leap, T. L., & Smeltzer, L. R. (1984, November–December). Racial remarks in the workplace: Humor or harassment? *Harvard Business Review*, pp. 74, 75, 78.

Ledman, R., & Brown, D. (1993). The Americans with Disabilities Act: The cutting edge of managing diversity. *SAM Advanced Management Journal, 58*(2), 17–20.

Loden, M., & Rosener, J. B. (1991). *Workforce America! Managing employee diversity as a vital resource*. Homewood, IL: Irwin.

Mabry, M. (1990, May 14). Past tokenism. *Newsweek*, p. 37.

Mor-Baral, M. E., & Tynan, M. (1993). Older workers and the workplace: A new challenge for occupational social work. *Social Work, 38*(1), 45–55.

Morrison, A. M., & Von Glinow, M. A. (1990). Women and minorities in management. *American Psychologist, 45*(2), 200–208.

Motwani, J., Harper, E., Subramanian, R., & Douglas, C. (1993). Managing the diversified workforce: Current efforts and future directions. *SAM Advanced Management Journal, 58*(3), 16–21.

Multiculturalism taking root and bearing fruit at JCCA. (1995). *JCCA Journal, 21*(1), 4.

Murray, K. (1993, August 1). The unfortunate side effects of "diversity training." *New York Times*, p. 5.

Nixon, R., & Spearmon, M. (1991). Building a pluralistic workplace. In R. L. Edwards & J. A. Yankey (Eds.), *Skills for effective human services management* (pp. 155–170). Washington, DC: NASW.

Rutledge, J. M. (1995). *Building board diversity.* Washington, DC: National Center for Nonprofit Boards.

Seck, E. T., Finch, W. A., Mor-Barak, M. E., & Poverny, L. M. (1993). Managing a diverse workforce. *Administration in Social Work, 17*(2), 67–79.

Solomon, C. M. (1989, August). The corporate response to workforce diversity. *Personnel Journal*, pp. 43–53.

Stevenson, K. M., Cheung, K. M., & Leung, P. (1992). A new approach to training child protective services workers for ethnically sensitive practice. *Child Welfare, 70*(4), 291–305.

Tully, C. T., & Greene, R. (1994). Cultural diversity comes of age: A study of coverage, 1970–1991. *Arete, 19*(1), 37–45.

Culturally Diverse Families Across the Life Cycle

CHAPTER 3

The Child, the Family, and the School: A Multicultural Triangle

Carmen Ortiz Hendricks

Social work in urban public schools is one arena of multicultural social work practice in which knowledge of a client group's culture and status in society is central to service delivery. With rapidly increasing racial and ethnic diversity in cities throughout the United States, there is an urgent need to find solutions to the evident mismatch between mainstream school systems and many of those they serve. This chapter looks at the complex interplay of cultures present when inner-city families and children of diverse backgrounds interact with professionals working in public schools, each representing different values, beliefs, and histories that are generally overlooked in the process of addressing the child's learning needs. A definition of multicultural social work practice is offered with application to the school social worker's role as "cultural mediator" (deAnda, 1984), the one school professional who focuses interventions on the child while mediating the dynamics of such multicultural encounters on the family and the school. It is the school social worker, with all of her or his own personal and professional cultural identities and beliefs, who is in the best position to function as the interpreter between the culture of the family and the culture of the school.

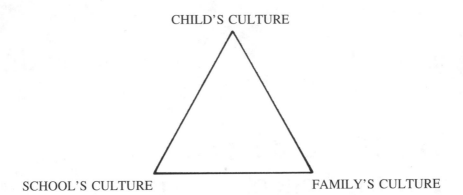

Figure 3.1

THE MULTICULTURE TRIANGLE

Multiculturally sensitive professionals recognize the importance of cultural beliefs and cultural identities in interpersonal relationships and social interactions, especially in educational institutions, a major system affecting the lives of all children and their families. Public schools have traditionally been the incubators of cultural assimilation and socialization in the United States. Schools exert an enormous impact on children whose cultural base is different from the mainstream culture, and on families whose knowledge of the school system is limited, who are faced with overcrowded and underfunded schools, and who may already feel powerless and alienated within their communities.

A multicultural triangle (Figure 3.1) invariably forms when distinct cultures come into conflict over measures of a child's ability, normalcy, or educability (Compher, 1982; Constable & Walberg, 1988). The child's family and the school each feels the tensions of differing cultural values and objectives, and each encompasses a culture that needs to be understood, separately and interactionally, in order to promote positive learning experiences for children within the educational system (Aponte, 1976). To begin with, there may exist radically different cultural understandings, assumptions, and expectations by the family and the school regarding education, as these questions suggest:

- How does a particular cultural group view children?
- What is it like to be a child of a particular cultural group?
- How does it feel to not belong to the "dominant" cultural group?
- What is it like to grow up feeling different?
- What is the particular culture of the school?
- What value is placed on the parents' role in educating children?
- How do different cultural groups measure intelligence?
- What value is placed on education by different cultural groups?
- How does one define a "normal" range of development?
- How much do we understand about different behavioral norms?
- How does one define a learning problem?
- How culture-bound are the labels and definitions of educability?

These questions also point out the interrelationship between a child's performance, the family's identity, and the school's assessments (Figure 3.2).

From a systemic point of view, what affects one part of the system has a reverberating impact on other parts of the system. Therefore, assessment of a child's school performance cannot be separate from assessment of a family's self-identity or an evaluation of a school's educational practices (Dowling & Osborne, 1985). The problems or positions of one by necessity affect the other. This triangle—like most triangles—provides many convenient and handy issues to argue about while avoiding the truly fundamental cross-cultural conflicts at hand.

For example, school programs, especially Head Start and other early childhood intervention or special education projects, frequently expect or mandate parental participation in a child's educational planning. But

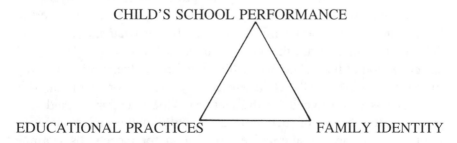

CHILD'S SCHOOL PERFORMANCE

EDUCATIONAL PRACTICES   FAMILY IDENTITY

Figure 3.2

expectations and requirements are not enough to ensure parental participation in a child's educational experiences, particularly if cultural factors are overlooked as professionals and parents focus attention on a child's educational needs and avoid examining their cross-cultural encounter (Correa, 1989). School professionals are not always able to find effective ways of ensuring a shared understanding or shared responsibility for achieving educational goals. Overburdened parents often feel alienated and unappreciated by the school and remain outside the school's sphere of influence while their confusion and doubts are misinterpreted as resistance or lack of interest (Delgado-Gaitan, 1987). However, when parents are genuinely invited and properly utilized, they are an invaluable resource and highly effective collaborators in the educational process (Aponte, 1976; Chavkin & Garza-Lubeck, 1990; Correa, 1989). Parents are in the best position to assist educators and social workers in decision making while protecting and advocating for their child.

One factor that blocks parental participation is language usage and professional jargon. There are many conflicting interpretations of such terms as *bilingual education, special education, learning-disabled, mental retardation, brain-injured, attention deficit disorder, hyperactivity, slow learner, special-needs child, speech or developmentally delayed*, and so on. These technical terms do not always translate accurately or sensitively (Bennett, 1988). Most school professionals are not sufficiently cautious in using these diagnostic categories or labels, which are based on measurements that use mainstream, middle-class, North American standards as the yardstick for evaluating intelligence across cultures and class status groups.

For example, *disability* is a term that inevitably suggests a "deficit within the individual, a lack of adequate power, strength, or physical or mental ability; incompetence; incapacity; a handicap that prevents a person from living a full, normal life" (*Random House Dictionary*, 1987, p. 560). It is common sense that caring parents will resist this "less than" categorization of their child and will seek to protect their child's identity from labels that define the child's behavior as deviant or abnormal. This resistance is compounded by the fact that little attention is paid to a parent's interpretation of such terms as *disability*, and even less attention is given to a parent's alternative explanation for the child's learning difficulties (Bennett, 1988; Harry, 1992b; Kalyanpur & Rao, 1991).

The school's traditional cultural norm is to view a child's difficulties in learning as deviance and therefore as a problem to be treated. Most school professionals are aware that diagnostic categories are based on social judgments, and they need to keep in mind that parents, especially minority group parents, will be particularly sensitive to labels that appear to stigmatize the image of the entire child or person rather than describing a particular difficulty in a particular aspect of the child's educational capacity. When a parent denies a diagnosis of learning disability, it should not be assumed that the parent is wrong, resistant, or ignorant. Rather, educational specialists need to consider whether the parent's position is a more accurate representation of the child's needs as well as the parent's experience of the world. A parent's opinion could simply be another opinion based on a different perspective. Minority group parents, who can see with their own eyes the disproportionate placements of minority group children in special education classes, may view broad categorizations as instruments of discrimination and oppression. When there is overrepresentation of minority group students in special education programs, it supports the parental perception of the arbitrary nature of designating a child as learning-disabled (Dao, 1991; Delgado-Gaitan, 1987; Kalyanpur & Rao, 1991).

Experienced school social workers are generally aware that special education may reflect social values more than objective reality and that underachievement in school encompasses a range of meanings to parents, children, and teachers (Kurtz & Barth, 1989). It is the school social worker who often hears and responds to teachers' questions: e.g., How can I make these parents understand that their child has special needs? Why do they criticize my efforts to help their child? Why are they unable to help their child with homework? What can you do to help these parents understand what we are trying to do for their child? It is the school social worker who generally hears and responds to parents' questions: e.g., Why is the school picking on my child? Why is the school criticizing my child rearing? What have I or the family done wrong? Why are they saying that my child is crazy? Why is the school discriminating against my child?

If a parent disagrees with school officials, particularly about definitions of learning problems, it does not necessarily mean that the parent is misguided or does not recognize that the child is having learning difficulties (Dowling & Osborne, 1985; Golden & Cupuzzi, 1986). For example, elementary school professionals were very frustrated and impatient with a Bangladeshi mother whose child was severely delayed in speech and language development, but the mother steadfastly refused all efforts to move the child to a remedial educational placement outside the immediate neighborhood. Then it was learned that she had lost four of her children in devastating floods that destroyed her village in Bangladesh a few years earlier. Losing a child, even to a nearby school, was too stressful for this mother, and other arrangements had to be made to meet the child's needs. This example clearly underscores the kind of multicultural misunderstandings that can arise when well-intentioned professionals and parents get mired in their own definitions of a problem (Lynch & Stein, 1987), while the child struggles alone to deal with the demands of both the school and the family. As with most triangulated communication, the goal is to stop the blaming, get the parties to hear each other, and get the focus back on the real issue at hand—how to help the child have a positive learning experience.

One way to get back on track and equalize the flow of communication is to listen to parental definitions of what is causing the child's difficulty. The parents may be interpreting or naming the difficulties in their own way, sometimes not that differently from the professionals they meet. Parents may very well be trying to help their child by reframing the issues in words that are more compatible with their cultural values and beliefs and words that do not harm the child's self-image (Harry, 1992a; McAdoo & McAdoo, 1985). A Jamaican mother, raised and educated in Jamaica, had been told by a medicine man that her son would experience many difficulties during his first year in the United States. She was convinced that after the year ended, her son's health problems and school difficulties would cease. These redefinitions and clarifications need to be respected and heard, however dystonic they may seem to Western European cultures. If parents are listened to, they will provide an explanation for the difficulties or limitations a child is experiencing in relation to learning that can be utilized in the educational assessment and plan.

Parents may use any number of phrases or narratives, as well as history and cultural lore, to describe to school officials how they view a child's difficulties.

"He's just the way my brother was at this age."
"She'll grow out of it, the way I did."
"His father was just like him."

"She is much smarter than she lets on to the teachers."
"My child has been taught not to boast about his abilities."
"Give her time. In time she'll catch on."

These perceptions can be useful in discussing genetic predisposition, developmental or maturational factors, different historical evolutions, medical and psychological progress, and family strengths rather than just pathology as indicators of prognosis.

Multicultural children who hear conflicting comments about their abilities from their parents and teachers are frequently torn between the demands of two cultures—the culture of home and the culture of school (Freeman & Pennekamp, 1988). As bicultural and frequently bilingual children, they struggle daily to live up to the teacher's demands to learn new ways of solving problems and relating to others (Bennett, 1988; Lynch & Stein, 1987), their peers' demands for mainstream behavioral responses, and their family's admonitions to remain true to their culture of origin regardless of what they see around them. Very few families recognize the child's need for "cultural brokers" who can help negotiate, facilitate, and support the child's resolution of these multicultural dilemmas and opportunities.

When school professionals and parents use different culturally based and culturally biased criteria for describing a child's behavior, it is the child who gets caught between their respective interpretations (Ryan & Smith, 1989). Before using foreign or alien criteria to evaluate a child's difficulties in school, school professionals need to pay careful attention to the parents' criteria for normalcy and ability, which holds special meaning for the families with whom they work.

An excellent case study (Harry, 1992b) of low-income Puerto Rican parents and their definitions of disability can best demonstrate this diagnostic triangulation. Ana is a 55-year-old Puerto Rican woman with many years of experience with the American educational system. When her daughter, Maria, was 8 years old, she was placed in a special education program for children who were labeled "educable mentally retarded." At age 13, Maria was mainstreamed into a regular class. Now Maria's daughter, Consuelo, is currently in a special education class for mildly mentally retarded children. This classification and a subsequent change in class assignment reached a crisis point for the family.

One day, when Consuelo was in second grade, I went to get her and as I was walking along the street, the child came running toward me screaming and crying. I was very frightened and thought that something terrible had happened to her. When she got close to me she grabbed me and threw herself on me sobbing, "Abuelita! Abuelita! They say I am crazy!" "Hay Dios mio! What happened?" She explained, "The teacher told me that I will be going to a different class. She is not going to work with me anymore because I am crazy!" So I went to the school and in my broken English I told them that Consuelo is not crazy. They calmed me down, but they put her in the special class even though Maria and I told them at the school meeting that Consuelo has a good mind, she works hard on her schoolwork, she can read and speak both English and Spanish. No person who is "retardada" can do all that. Now Consuelo does not want to go to school until they stop saying she is crazy. I don't think Consuelo has anything wrong with her mind either. She behaves well and is a good girl. The social worker tried to explain to us the meaning of "retardada" or handicapped. But for Puerto Ricans, a person who is handicapped is a person who is not of sound mind . . . is incapacitado . . . is blind or has problems in speaking, or is paralyzed or missing a leg . . . a person who is an invalid and cannot work or do anything. My Maria and my Consuelo have nothing like that gracias a Dios y la Virgen! (Harry, 1992b, p. 30)

What this family's plight points out is that there are different cultural meanings to what school professionals may believe are uniform and universally acceptable definitions of disability (Dao, 1991; Kalyanpur & Rao, 1991). Most parents are incredulous when they are first told that their child is learning-disabled or suffers from a more severe neurological impairment (Bennett, 1988). They see a healthy body, a child that can use common sense, a child who has achieved elementary academic skills in two languages, a child who has already exceeded a parent's educational attainments, a 6 1/2-year-old who speaks and reads English and Spanish. These accomplishments clearly deny a diagnosis that is designed for someone whose competence is severely impaired or who is mentally deranged. It is very confusing for parents to be asked to see their child as significantly different from their own expectations when their own education may have been at the 3rd- or 4th-grade level or they find English difficult to master (Ryan & Smith, 1989). Parents cannot view their child as anything but intellectually superior when the child's homework is harder than anything the parents have experienced in their own education (Spener, 1988). By working with the definitions offered by parents, school

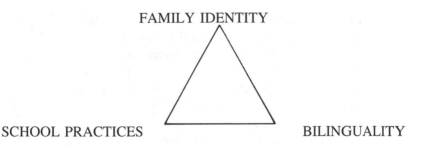

Figure 3.3

professionals can reinforce the fact that the child is not severely crippled or incapacitated. Starting from a perspective of strengths, the school may be better able to appreciate the cultural explanations for learning difficulties and to motivate children and their families to address learning needs in a less alienating and definitely more empowering way.

When examining a child's difficulties in school, experts point to several important themes that emerge as children and parents struggle to understand why a child is having trouble in school. Family identity, bilinguality, and school practices are culturally bound and culturally interwoven aspects of all school social work (Harry, 1992a, 1992b). These contribute to narrow definitions of a child's difficulties and rigid triangular communication (Figure 3.3).

Family Identity

Family identity is very important in the dynamics of interpreting a child's developmental patterns or learning needs. Wherever there is a strong cultural value placed on the family there is an equally strong emphasis on a family's identity as a group rather than as a collection of individuals. Illness is viewed as a problem that resides within the family rather than solely within the individual. This ''enmeshed'' family feels a collective disgrace when school professionals inadvertently or intentionally give the impression that the child's difficulties result from something that is wrong within the family. The child's difficulties bring shame on the family and are tied to some bad family trait or character flaw or even an immoral personality trait or immoral past behavior.

A strong family identity diffuses the stigma on a child who is having school problems. A strong family identity engenders vulnerability in the whole group, and thus family identity serves to protect an individual's identity. The child is different because he or she is just like everyone else in the family. Lynch and Stein (1987) found that Hispanic and Black children were described in terms of family traits and were often not considered to be outside the family's normal range of behavior.

A multiculturally sensitive school professional will take the family identity into consideration, recognizing that for some families group identity is paramount when a child's individual learning needs are at issue. For example, when a child is described as quiet or shy, school professionals need to include an assessment of how the family interprets the child's shy behavior. If the behavior is viewed as culturally syntonic, then the family will see shyness as an inherited aspect of family behavior, a part of the family's preferred mode of behavior, and a negative view of shyness reflects on the whole family. In the case of a hyperactive child, a mother may tell the school social worker that her child has always been hyperactive, that it is a family trait inherited by the child from the father and grandfather. She will say that the child does not have any real problem; the family will help deal with the child's behavior.

Bilinguality

Bilinguality requires an understanding of the advantages and disadvantages of second-language acquisition in a child's education. Enormous difficulties for children can arise simply from the confusion generated by changing from one language to another (Cummins, 1984; Spener, 1988). Children generally go into regular English-speaking classes until they are assessed as needing remedial English, English as a second language (ESL) classes, or bilingual education.

The point of immigration in the child's life cycle has a great deal to do with how a child adjusts to English and American schools. Parents often describe their children as having done well educationally in their country of origin, and they see their children's problems as beginning with the demands placed on them in American schools. They find it difficult to understand or are suspicious about why their children are now having problems in school. Parents will frequently criticize a teacher's intolerance and unreasonable expectations for their children. They feel that their child is being singled out because of English language difficulties and nothing more. Other parents are so proud of their child's ability to learn to read and write English that they see American teachers as overly critical of the child's accent or mispronunciations or too strict in their expectation that children speak English perfectly when they are only 6 or 7 years old (Correa, 1989).

Parents are further confused by such terms as ESL and bilingual education, and many misconceptions exist about these programs. They are viewed as holding children back rather than helping them learn. Many immigrant parents are adamant that their child must learn English even if the parents themselves are resistant to learning a new language (Dao, 1991; Spener, 1988). These same parents worry that the child, who will most likely not learn to read or write the native tongue, might forget the first language completely. To lose the ability to speak a native tongue is to lose the ability to communicate with relatives and close friends. Furthermore, the ability to speak more than one language is viewed as an advantage in their country of origin, whereas in the United States there is enormous pressure against keeping a language of origin, a pressure that often translates into a social mandate to keep the native language alive at all costs.

Educational Practices

Educational practices represent the school's culture and are central to the way in which reading is taught, changing classes are handled, and curricula are delivered. Parents frequently complain about how inflexibly reading is taught in American schools, how unstimulating curricula can be, and how frequently a child's classrooms, programs, teachers, and even schools are changed (Sarason, 1982). Parents get angry if they perceive that their child is being given repetitive, boring, or easy schoolwork that does not reflect the child's abilities or potential. They feel that their child could learn to do a great deal more if given the chance or encouraged to do so, or if the school did not discriminate so harshly against their particular cultural group. Sarason (1982) points out that many mainstream as well as immigrant parents are not able to assert their parental authority by refusing to go along with educational practices imposed on them. In most cases, parents and children are confused and become angry and frustrated when educational changes occur without their understanding or approval.

Some "experienced" parents who have struggled with public schooling in the United States arrive in this country prepared to outsmart the schools. Some parents will falsify or lose their child's class placement from their country of origin, especially if the child demonstrated any kind of learning difficulty. These parents are eager for the child to be seen as possessing normal intelligence and capacity. Other parents will insist on their child's entrance into a regular, age-appropriate grade, a "normal" grade. These parent have determined that the only way to secure adequate education for their children is to avoid school practices that hinder and obstruct this objective.

MULTICULTURALLY SENSITIVE PROFESSIONALS

The subjective nature of education is inescapable for many school professionals, and it becomes more evident with children from culturally diverse backgrounds. Each child is different and unique, but classification of learning needs is based on the cultural values and expectations of a society at a particular time in history (NYS Education Department, 1990; Sarason, 1982). In different cultures, mainstream conceptions of intelligence and normalcy may be considerably different from North American or Western ideologies. But educational laws and policies and the medical model they cling to reflect none of this diversity. Only culturally sensitive school professionals can help to ensure unbiased assessment of a client's needs for services. "Culture broker" skills are a fundamental necessity for school social workers who have to mediate between the client's culture and the agency's culture by helping to increase sensitivity and understanding of each other's values, practices, customs and beliefs, while at the same time assessing the effects of their own culture (Figure 3.4).

School professionals should become more aware of their own values in order to prevent subjective, culturally learned patterns and beliefs from interfering in their work with families (Lynch & Hanson, 1992). For example, if practitioners believe that a parent's lack of interest is partly responsible for a child's poor performance, the work with the child and family will be frustrating and will get nowhere. Parents need help, not criticism, to contribute to the educational debates, to critique appropriate instruction for their children, and to evaluate the efficacy of special education placements.

CLIENT'S CULTURE

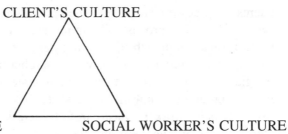

AGENCY'S CULTURE   SOCIAL WORKER'S CULTURE

Figure 3.4

More bilingual-bicultural professionals, as well as more multiculturally sensitive professionals, are needed. Recent ethnographic studies conclude that parent-professional interactions are so structured as to render parents effectively powerless as partners in their children's educational careers. Most often, parental power is undermined by culturally different ways of understanding. Parents with little formal education and a different language and culture may, through their own analysis of their children's difficulties, have a significant contribution to make to current debates in education.

Parental empowerment requires that school social workers create more rather than fewer opportunities for parents' theories about their children's learning difficulties to be heard. Social workers working with culturally diverse families and children need to find ways to culturally sensitize themselves and their assessments and interventive skills by opening themselves to new ways of defining and evaluating normalcy. First, they can begin by recognizing that there are many important ways in which the meanings of such terms as *learning* and *learning-disabled* differ along cultural lines, and they need to examine these meanings and their significance to parents. Second, they should review the parameters of what is normal in child development and integrate much broader explanations of normalcy than those utilized by the educational system. Third, multicultural parents need help to understand the distinction between measurements of intelligence and measurements of emotional or mental stability. And finally, all school professionals must listen carefully to the parents' own theories that explain how their child learns best and why the child may be having difficulties in school.

Cummins (1986) argues that only through holistic interventions that incorporate cultural, linguistic, and community needs will minority group students be empowered to achieve their potential. The input of their parents is essential in this process. Cummins calls for a collaborative versus an exclusionary approach to defining the roles of families: "Children's seeming unpreparedness for mainstream schooling is only a measure of the rigidity and ignorance of our school system which creates handicap out of social and cultural differences" (p. 70).

School social workers must carefully assess these social and cultural differences, beginning with an evaluation of (1) the family structures, including the number of children in the household, parenting and grandparenting influences, and so on; (2) the family's length of time in the United States; (3) the socioeconomic conditions confronting the family; (4) the educational history of all family members; and (5) the language proficiency, both native tongue and English, of all family members. In addition, social workers should pay attention to the parents' attitudes toward education, which initially may include having great faith in the educational system without knowing anything about what actually goes on in schools in the United States. These same parents can gradually become disillusioned, losing faith in the school system and developing a negative image of education in general. Understanding these patterns can help social workers anticipate and intervene to prevent or explain the frustration encountered by many multicultural families.

Lynch and Hanson (1992) propose a specific methodology for competent cross-cultural practice that includes appreciating the impact of cultural assumptions on the interventive process, enhancing cultural self-awareness, understanding the factors that contribute to cultural identification and acculturation, and gathering information on other cultures and guidelines for using interpreters or translators. It is equally important to understand how a particular culture views the helping relationship, how cultural traditions affect problem solving, and "what specific intervention skills and ways of thinking work more effectively with particular groups than those based primarily on the Euro-American frame of reference" (Dungee-Anderson & Beckett, 1995, p. 460).

Furthermore, practitioners should engage in an ongoing self-evaluation of their own multiculturally skills. This ensures their ability to listen to and hear different cultural perspectives, not just the prerogatives of their own cultural heritage or of the social work profession, which is in and of itself a cultural point of view. The following self-awareness inventory, an adaptation of the Ethnic-Sensitive Inventory (ESI) presented by Man

Keung Ho (1991, pp. 57–67), is presented as a useful self-assessment guide for social workers.

ETHNIC-SENSITIVE INVENTORY (ESI). When working with culturally diverse clients, supervisors, and other staff members who may be different from or similar to my own cultural background, I am conscious of the following factors:

A. I realize that my own gender and sexual orientation, race, ethnic, and class background may influence my effectiveness as a social worker.
B. I am very aware of the systemic problems of sexism, heterosexism, racism, ethnocentrism, classism, ageism, etc., and of how these factors affect social work practice and professional relationships.
C. I am quite capable of identifying the links between systemic problems and how individuals respond to power, difference, and oppression.
D. I am able to help clients understand whether practice problems are of an individual or a collective nature.
E. I am able to understand and "tune in" to the meaning of a client's gender and sexual orientation, race, ethnic, and class disposition, behavior, and experiences.
F. I consider it a professional obligation to familiarize myself with a client's culture and history and to engage clients in identifying major cultural values that may affect their problem-solving and decision-making skills.
G. I am sensitive to the fears and resistances of well-meaning helping professionals about discovering racist or prejudiced or discriminatory tendencies in their practice behaviors.
H. I resist contracting too soon, or I avoid highly focused efforts at problem solving, behavioral change, or introspection with certain client populations.
I. With some clients, I recognize the need to move slowly in my efforts to help them search for solutions to their problems or to actively "reach for feelings."
J. With some clients, I understand that the working relationship may need to be a very close one and last a long time before they can begin to trust me and the helping process.

K. I am aware of the implications of race, sexual orientation, ethnicity, gender, etc., on what is being discussed in supervision and how the differences and similarities shared with my supervisor affect our work together.

L. I clearly delineate agency functions and inform clients of my professional expectations of them in a culturally sensitive manner.

M. I am able to explain clearly the nature of the helping relationship and reconcile this with the client's cultural expectations of help.

N. I am respectful of how clients define their concerns even if they pose unique or unusual external factors at the core of their problems.

O. I am able to help clients set goals that are consonant with their perceptions of gender and sexual orientation, race, ethnic, and class diversity.

P. I frequently seek new practice approaches that may be more culturally sensitive.

MULTICULTURAL PRACTICE DEFINED

Defining multicultural social work practice is an enormously complex task, especially when the definitions proposed reinforce a broader and more inclusive attitude about diversity in the United States. Social workers, like other proponents of multicultural perspectives, are stereotyped as ethnic cheerleaders proposing hyphenated cultural identities and political ideologies that are primarily anti-Western or antiassimilationist. However it is defined, multicultural diversity is creating many new tensions in North American societies, where it is often experienced as a threat rather than as a valuable opportunity to enhance human understanding and intergroup relationships.

Social workers must appreciate diversity as an opportunity to provide leadership, support, and advocacy for the right to multiculturally diverse identities in people's lives. Social workers have used the term *multicultural* in place of such other terms as *bicultural, cross-cultural, ethnocultural,* and "minority" descriptors. Greene (1994) speaks of *cross-cultural* and *culturally diverse* as "umbrella terms for diversity of human experience that is rooted in ethnic, national, or religious identity, race, gender, and social class membership'' (p. xii). Along similar lines, the following definition of multicultural social work practice is offered for consideration:

> Multicultural social work practice encompasses a range of professional knowledge, skills, and values to address the complex cultures emerging in a society from the interplay of difference and power associated with gender and sexual orientation, race and ethnicity, religious or spiritual beliefs, social class, and developmental or disabling conditions.

This definition recognizes that all people have a cultural group identity, whether they are aware of it or not. Furthermore, many types and forms of group membership in society take on varying significance depending on the societal context. A societal context in which difference is not merely ''different from'' but is also associated with ''better than'' or ''less than'' is a society in which differences are not viewed as the norm for human behavior but rather are viewed as deviance needing to be minimized or oppressed. There is also the complex question of power— who has power, who is seeking power, and who is in the most powerful or dominant position. Unequal status relationships contribute to the oppression of many groups not considered within the mainstream of society (e.g., recent immigrant women) as well as certain groups that are a part of the mainstream society (e.g., White women) but who are relegated to inferior status by means of oppression (e.g., sexism).

Multicultural social work practice is much more than a belief in the preservation of different cultures, cultural beliefs, or cultural identities within a unified society. It is not about accumulating knowledge regarding specific cultures and then approaching clients as an expert in their culture.

> Multiculturally competent practitioners are not necessarily experts in many different cultures. Rather, they are aware of cultural values and patterns that motivate their own and their clients' behaviors. They are sensitive to differences and do not project their own internalized cultural responses onto practice situations. (Dungee-Anderson & Beckett, 1995, p. 465)

Multiculturally sensitive practice involves a dynamic, interactive assessment of a client's particular lifestyle which moves from universal categories of culture as we know them (Hispanic, Jewish American, Irish Catholic American, African American, etc.) to more specific, individualized, and complex categories of cultures within cultures. Gould (1995) proposes that a multicultural framework refutes the basic assumption that cultural identity has to be undimensional or that becoming more of something else automatically means becoming less of the original. "A multicultural framework goes beyond encouraging intercultural learning and multicultural competency to building a multicultural identity for all groups" (pp. 202–203). A specific situation can help to clarify exactly what is entailed in such a multicultural framework.

> For example, a Puerto Rican social worker encounters a client from the Dominican Republic. Each can be viewed from very broad class, racial, ethnic, or gender categorizations as Latino or Latina, but these distinctions do not do justice to the multifaceted cultures each uniquely encompasses. One client system, the Velasquez family, is composed of a 27-year-old woman who is a laboratory technician and a 28-year-old man who works in his cousin's food market. They are married and have two children, 6-year-old Nita and 4-year-old Migelito. The family has recently "re-migrated" for the third time, from a rural community in the Dominican Republic to New York City. Ms. Velez, a 42-year-old Latina school social worker, was born in Puerto Rico and raised in New York. She has no memory of the migration experience of her family and considers herself a middle-class Hispanic American professional. The case is automatically referred to the Latina school social worker because of ethnic and linguistic commonalities. The referral is made because of suspected incidents of family violence, excessive school absences, and the newly diagnosed 6-year-old's learning disability.

A multicultural framework can help this social worker appreciate the similarities as well as differences between herself and the Velasquez family. As Latinos, the Velasquez family and Mrs. Velez have shared experiences with oppression, both within and outside their countries of origin. The impact of oppression has been integral in both their lives and their cultural backgrounds. There are also some significant differences between the Velasquezes and the social worker that may need to be acknowledged by both. These differences grow out of their distinct experiences as Dominicans and Puerto Ricans in the United States, their different skin colors, distinct historical and social evolutions, immigration patterns and citizenship status, and the stress of resettlement. The social worker can best help this Dominican family and others like them by recognizing the oppression experienced by immigrant Hispanic women, men, and children who need to deal with the stress of (im)migration, resettlement, and family reorganization in addition to economic hardships and discrimination.

Together, the social worker and clients can engage in a multicultural encounter in which understanding each other's unique multicultural experiences is integral to the work that confronts them and their shared ethnic identities; bilingual skills; gender identities and sexual orientations; developmental stages; religious affiliations; abilities and disabilities; class differences; personal values, norms, and beliefs; and individual goals and aspirations. Add to this complex picture the impinging culture of an inner-city public school system, with all of its values, norms, and beliefs, and the multicultural arena can become engulfed with misinformation and misinterpretation.

CULTURAL SELF-IDENTITY

The problem for every social work practitioner is to maintain a balance between different and competing cultural identities. It is hard work and stressful for any person to maintain a bicultural or multicultural identity in the face of mainstream demands. Multicultural social work practice demands that social workers become increasingly adept at understanding and utilizing the diverse experiences of clients throughout their practice assessments and interventions. To help diverse individuals, families, and groups, social work practice requires successful integration of the worker's own unique sense of cultural identity and self-definition. Confronting discrimination and prejudice directed at others as well as oneself begins with social workers understanding and feeling good about their multicultural selves and becoming increasingly conscious of their own multicultural identities. The more ideas one has about who one is, the greater one's understanding of diversity, leading to greater opportunities to sort out those aspects that have valid meaning for the client from those that are inaccurate stereotypes. Pinderhughes (1989) asserts that "it is not possible to assist clients to examine issues concerning cultural identity and self-esteem if helpers have not done this work for themselves . . . effective service delivery requires practitioners to develop cultural sensitivity that is characterized by flexibility, openness, warmth, and empathy" (p. 19).

Aponte (1991) advocates an intensive "personal-social-clinical" (PSC) approach as preparation for multicultural social work practice. This approach "incorporates the ecosystemic realities of a family's life into the therapist's clinical framework" (p. 30).

PSC: DIMENSIONS OF DIFFERENCE. The following questions are provided to assist social workers in appreciating their PSC dimensions of difference through an intensive evaluation and assessment of cultural backgrounds and identities.

1. *What is your cultural heritage?* Include as many dimensions of your cultural heritage as possible (i.e., multiple generations, races, ethnicities, social classes, religions, sexual orientations, languages spoken, disabilities, national or regional affiliations, etc.). You might also organize this information on a genogram or family tree.

2. *What were the values, norms, beliefs, and behaviors that you grew up with?* What was your family of origin's approach to child rearing, and how were you disciplined? Were there other relatives around during your childhood? What role did your grandparents play in your family of origin?

3. *What is your primary cultural group identity at this stage of your life?* Include as many dimensions of your cultural identity as possible (i.e., age or generation, gender, races, ethnicities, social class, religions, sexual orientations, languages spoken, disabilities, national or regional affiliations, etc.).

4. *When did you first become aware of your race, gender, religion, ethnicity, sexual orientation, social class, etc., as different and unique from "the other?"*

5. *Which dimensions of your cultural identity are the most affirming and empowering aspects of your identity and why?* What do you like most about your cultural heritage?

6. *Which dimensions of your cultural identity are the most troublesome and difficult to manage and why?* Are there any painful experiences associated with your cultural heritage that continue to affect your cultural identity today?

7. *Have you ever tried to deny or reject any dimension of your cultural identity and why?* Which dimensions of your cultural identity do you think need work and why?

8. *What generalizations do people make about you that reflect their misinformation about some aspect of your cultural group identity?* What would you like to teach people not of your cultural group about your cultural heritage and identity?

9. *Which dimensions of your cultural identity are most helpful and least helpful to you as a social worker today?*

Social workers are responsible for identifying their own biases and preventing them from creeping into their work with clients. These questions can be used by social workers individually or in groups. As they struggle to answer these questions, they engage in a valuable introspection that highlights the range of diversity existing within their own immediate lives, not just those of certain cultural or client groups. The development of multiculturally sensitive skills and knowledge begins with the self. Beyond increasing self-awareness and self-knowledge, social workers should engage in a lifelong learning experience about their clients' own multicultural experiences by (1) listening carefully to clients, who will tell them everything they need to know about their cultural identities and situations; (2) taking advantage of every opportunity available to read, attend conferences, and actively work to expand multicultural social work practice knowledge and skills; (3) sharing practice concerns and dilemmas with colleagues to allow for reflection on existing biases and stereotypical blocks; and (4) recognizing how biases and misinformation about other people or groups of people (e.g., race determines intelligence, bilingualism hinders language development, assimilation is desired by all immigrant people) are systematically taught in a number of ways, and practitioners must actively guard against contaminating professional consciousness with misinformation.

CONCLUSIONS

This chapter is a beginning effort in defining a multicultural framework for social work practice that responds to the client system's diversity as well as the agency's culture, an encounter made especially complex when it is experienced between a child, a family, and a public school. As cultural diversity increases in the next century, school social workers are needed to empower families and themselves in order to guarantee that the parents' voices are heard.

Social workers and clients often belong to groups that are openly oppressed in society, generally on the basis of characteristics they have no control over—gender, skin color, sexual orientation, religion, even the neighborhoods they occupy. Therefore, appreciating and dealing with power, powerlessness, and unequal power relationships are integral aspects of multicultural encounters. Increasingly, empowerment skills are needed within the profession as well as within the communities served by social workers (Pinderhughes, 1983). The consumers and providers of social work services share diverse perceptions of themselves, and these factors influence perceptions of each other's power and powerlessness in the broader society. School professionals should recognize that it is within the parent's power to understand, address, and overcome situational problems or lifelong oppression.

"True empowerment benefits both the client system and the practitioner in that client and worker experience a sense of each other's freedom and individuality which includes a real appreciation of each other's differences and similarities" (Pinderhughes, 1989, p. 240). With empowerment of families, vast numbers of children will experience an increasingly satisfying and productive relationship with the educational system and will be able to reconcile the various cultural challenges presented by the home, the community, and the school. This is difficult work but extremely rewarding, as school professionals, children, and families educate each other for living in a multiculturally diverse society.

REFERENCES

Aponte, H. J. (1976). The family-school interview: An ecostructural approach. *Family Process*, *15*(3), 303–312.

Aponte, H. J. (1991). Training on the person of the therapist for work with the poor and minorities. *Journal of Independent Social Work*, *5*(3/4), 23–39.

Bennett, A. T. (1988). Gateways to powerlessness: Incorporating Hispanic deaf children and families into formal schooling. *Disability, Handicap and Society*, *3*(2), 119–151.

Chavkin, N. F., & Garza-Lubeck, M. (1990). Multicultural approaches to parent involvement: Research and practice. *Social Work in Education*, *13*(1), 22–23.

Compher, J. V. (1982). Parent-school-child systems: Triadic assessment and intervention. *Social Casework*, *63*(7), 415–433.

Constable, R., & Walberg, H. (1988). School social work: Facilitating home, school, and community partnerships. *Urban Education*, *22*(4), 429–443.

Correa, V. I. (1989). Involving culturally different families in the educational process. In S. H. Fradd & M. J. Weismantel, (Eds.), *Meeting the needs of culturally and linguistically different students* (pp. 130–144). Boston: College-Hill.

Cummins, J. (1984). *Bilingualism and special education: Issues in assessment and pedagogy*. San Diego, CA: College-Hill.

Cummins, J. (1986). Empowering minority students: A framework for intervention. *Harvard Educational Review, 56*(1), 18–36.

Dao, M. (1991). Designing assessment procedures for educationally at-risk Southeast Asian-American students. *Journal of Learning Disabilities, 24*(10), 594–601.

de Anda, D. (1984). Bicultural socialization: Factors affecting the minority experience. *Social Work, 29*(2), 101–107.

Delgado-Gaitan, C. (1987). Parent perceptions of school: Supportive environments for children. In H. T. Trueba, (Ed.), *Success or failure? Learning and the language minority student* (pp. 131–155). New York: Newbury House.

Dowling, E., & Osborne, E. (1985). *The family and the school: A joint systems approach to problems with children.* London: Routledge & Kegan Paul.

Dungee-Anderson, D., & Beckett, J. (1995). A process model for multicultural social work practice. *Families in Society: The Journal of Contemporary Human Services, 76,* 459–466.

Freeman, E. M., & Pennekamp, M. (1988). *Social work practice: Toward a child, family, school, community perspective.* Springfield, IL: Charles Thomas.

Golden, L., & Cupuzzi, D. (1986). *Helping families help children: Family interventions with school related problems.* Springfield, IL: Charles Thomas.

Gould, K. (1995). The misconstruing of multiculturalism: The Stanford debate and social work. *Social Work, 40*(2), 198–205.

Greene, R. R. (1994). *Human behavior theory: A diversity framework.* New York: Aldine de Gruyter.

Harry, B. (1992a). *Culturally diverse families and the special education system.* New York: Teachers College Press.

Harry, B. (1992b). Making sense of disability: Low-income, Puerto Rican parents' theories of the problem. *Exceptional Children, 59*(1), 27–40.

Ho, M. K. (1991). Use of ethnic-sensitive inventory (ESI) to enhance practitioner skills with minorities. *Journal of Multicultural Social Work, 1*(1), 57–67.

Kalyanpur, M., & Rao, S. S. (1991). Empowering low-income black families of handicapped children. *American Journal of Orthopsychiatry, 61*(4), 523–532.

Kurtz, P. D., & Barth, R. P. (1989). Parent involvement: Cornerstone of school social work practice. *Social Work, 34,* 407–413.

Lynch, E. W., & Hanson, M. J. (Eds.). (1992). *Developing cross-cultural competence: A guide for working with young children and their families.* Baltimore: Paul H. Brookes.

Lynch, E. W., & Stein, R. C. (1987). Parent participation by ethnicity: A comparison of Hispanic, black and Anglo families. *Exceptional Children, 54,* 105–111.

McAdoo, H., & McAdoo, J. L. (1985). *Black children: Social educational and parental environments.* Beverly Hills, CA: Sage.

New York State Education Department. (1990). *Parent partnerships: Linking families, communities and schools: Regents policy statement.* Albany, NY: Author.

Pinderhughes, E. (1983). Empowerment for our clients and for ourselves. *Social Casework, 64,* 331–338.

Pinderhughes, E. (1989). *Understanding race, ethnicity, and power: The key to efficacy in clinical practice.* New York: Free Press.

Ryan, A. S., & Smith, M. J. (1989). Parental reactions to developmental disabilities in Chinese American families. *Child and Adolescent Social Work Journal, 6*(4), 283–299.

Sarason, S. B. (1982). *The culture of the school and the problem of change.* Boston: Allyn and Bacon.

Spener, D. (1988). Transitional bilingual education and the socialization of immigrants. *Harvard Educational Review, 58,* 133–152.

CHAPTER 4

Working with Poor Ethnic Minority Adolescents and Their Families: An Ecosystemic Approach

Carol P. Kaplan
Manuel Muñoz

Psychodynamic theorists who have written about adolescence, including Erikson (1963, 1968), Blos (1962, 1967), and A. Freud (1958), have focused on the developmental tasks of individual adolescents: separation from the family of origin, forming intimate relationships, and forging an identity with respect to work and the larger world. Adding to this perspective, family systems theorists have taught that the family will both influence and be influenced by the young person's passage through the teen years. Family therapists believe that adolescent problems reflect conflictual or dysfunctional interactional processes within the family system and have sought resolution of these maladaptive patterns. In addition, however, the notion of context (i.e., how the family interacts with the environment), although always basic to systems theory, has garnered greater attention in recent years as family therapists have become increasingly aware of the importance of examining how families function within larger social, cultural, and economic systems. It has now become axiomatic that each family must be understood in its environmental context, and family therapy's field of attention has been enlarged to include elements such as culture, ethnicity, gender, and class.

It is the premise of this chapter that poor ethnic minority adolescents and their families are affected by the stresses of poverty, racism, and (in many cases) immigration. Hence, these social and institutional forces must be taken into consideration by helping professionals to the same extent that individual development and intrafamilial factors are. Poverty constitutes a major stressor for people in all ethnic groups. Sidel (1986) has noted that the poor (approximately 34 million people) are predominantly women and children. Also, 46.5% of African American children and 39% of Hispanic children live in poor families. For such families life is not simply like that of the middle class but with less money. Rather, constant crises concerning the basic necessities of life may lead to feelings of helplessness, hopelessness, and powerlessness. Because they have limited resources, poor families are more vulnerable to environmental demands and changes than are more affluent families. For example, the closing of an after-school program in a middle-class neighborhood may well require that parents be resourceful in finding alternative arrangements for children's care and recreation. However, in a poor community, where few services are provided and parents must cope with multiple problems, including neighborhood violence, this kind of program closure may become a crisis for the whole family by limiting the options for parents' employment.

ECOSYSTEMIC FAMILY THERAPY

Ecosystemic family therapy approaches derive from the meshing of family systems theory with ecological perspectives. Among the authors whose work has contributed to ecosystemic family therapy are Aponte (1976), Auerswald (1968, 1971, 1987), Boyd-Franklin (1989), Combrinck-Graham (1989, 1990), Congress (1994), Falicov (1982, 1988, 1995), Hansen and Falicov (1983), Hartman and Laird (1983), McGoldrick, Pearce, and Giordano (1996), and Minuchin (1974). According to this perspective human beings are in constant interchange with all aspects of their environment, with the result that human needs and problems are generated by the transactions between individuals, their families, and the larger systems within which they function. As Germain and Gitterman (1980) point out, the better the "fit" between the family and the social environment, the less psychological stress the individual and family will experience and the greater the opportunities for stability will be. On the other hand, a poor fit will lead to impaired family functioning, and the family will experience dissonance with the external environment.

Individuals change and affect their environment and are influenced and changed by it through the process of reciprocal adaptation. Therefore, it is important to understand how all the systems come together and what their relationships are to each other. Ecosystemic family therapists believe that an individual or family that displays a problem may be responding as much or more to what is being communicated between systems as to something occurring in any one system alone. It may well be that the focus for intervention will be found at the points where systems touch each other or come together.

Using an ecosystemic framework, an adolescent having problems is assessed neither as a sole individual nor simply as part of a family system. Rather, another dimension must be included: it is assumed that the young person is constantly responding and adapting to the different systems that he or she is exposed to. Poor ethnic minority adolescents are "triply stigmatized" in our society by virtue of ethnicity, race, and socioeconomic status (Gibbs & Huang, 1991). They have a more threatening and less forgiving environment and may also have fewer resources with which to cope. In the context of these stressors the developmental tasks of adolescence—separation from the family of origin, forming a new identity, and intimacy—nonetheless proceed apace. However, poor minority adolescents are far more vulnerable and at risk of developing symptoms during this developmental stage than their more affluent White counterparts.

Growing up in socially isolated communities, with inferior schools and high unemployment, poor adolescents may regard the opportunities of the street as more attractive than those of the educational system (Parnell & Vanderkloot, 1989). For the ethnic minority adolescent from a poor family the question may be not *how* to make it but *whether* to bother trying to make it at all (Inclan & Herron, 1991). Thus, the clinician working with such adolescents and their families must have an understanding of the communities in which these youngsters live, especially the impact of poverty, racism, culture and ethnicity, and immigration. In addition, the clinician must address not only the nuclear and extended family systems but also such larger systems as public assistance, public housing, schools, and other community institutions.

The family therapist utilizing an ecosystemic approach to family therapy is guided by a number of principles, each of which overlaps with another. These principles include (1) the concept that there are multiple versions of reality; (2) the framing of problems in descriptive language, as deficits in the environment or in the transactions between systems, rather than labeling them as psychopathology; (3) the use of a strengths perspective; and (4) the focus on finding solutions.

Multiple Versions of Reality

The first principle influencing practice with poor ethnic minority families is that there are multiple versions of reality, all of which should be considered as potential explanations for "the problem." Because each system has its own structure, norms, and values, each will have its own special way of defining, analyzing, and explaining experiences and problems (Falicov, 1995; Pare, 1995). How a problem is defined and explained will influence the interventions one selects. The ecosystemic family therapist must first of all be aware of his or her own construction of reality and of the fact that it does not represent the only reality. He or she will attempt to view a given situation from the vantage point of as many systems as possible, including the micro- and macro-systems, in order to avoid overlooking an explanation that could potentially be helpful to the family.

In addition, the ecosystemic family therapist may utilize a cross-systems approach, by which a situation can be evaluated using the different perspectives of the various systems involved. Such a cross-systems approach has several advantages: (1) it can facilitate dialogue between systems to broaden the analysis of a problem; (2) when used with a family, it can help family members to consider alternatives as they view an issue in a different light; and (3) it helps to assess the effectiveness of interventions.

Use of Descriptive Language

The ecosystemic family therapist will avoid the use of labels and may reframe them if they have previously been applied. Instead, problems are framed—or reframed—in descriptive language as deficits in the environment or in the transactions between systems or even as adaptive strategies that are insufficient to mitigate the demands of the environment. Rather than understanding *why* something occurs, ecosystemic family therapists seek to operationalize and concretize *what* happens, *when* it happens, *who* is involved, and *how* it develops. It is assumed that individuals and families are doing the best they can; the therapist's job is to introduce new perspectives that may help facilitate the construction of new realities and new solutions (Hartman & Laird, 1983).

Use of a Strengths Perspective

In their contacts with larger social systems, poor minority families are constantly reminded of what they are doing wrong. This feeling may be exacerbated by racist, sexist, and antiimmigrant bias existing generally in the society. All too often these families come to feel that they are "different" (i.e., inferior or defective). Working from a strengths perspective, ecosystemic family therapists focus instead on what a family is doing right and what it is accomplishing (Saleeby, 1992; Wachtel, 1993). The family is supported in the view that difference does not represent deficit. This shift empowers family members to find new ways to understand and deal with their situation. Then, by developing alternative responses to problems, the family improves its overall problem solving capacity.

Focus on Solutions

Following the first three principles enumerated above—appreciating multiple versions of reality, avoiding labels, and fostering strengths—the ecosystemic family therapist will empower the poor minority family in yet another way. Rather than devoting attention exclusively to the problem, the therapist will emphasize possible solutions, including those the family may already have attempted. Working together with the family, sharing the members' realities while trying to help them understand the meaning of other people's behavior, the therapist assists them to build on solutions in order to understand and eventually to alleviate problems (De Jong & Miller, 1995; De Shazer, 1988; Hoyt, 1994). The therapist assists the family in its struggle to do the best it can, often against tremendous odds.

CASE EXAMPLES AND DISCUSSION

The Fernandez Family

Sonia Fernandez, a 13-year-old girl from the Dominican Republic, was referred for treatment by her school counselor on the grounds that she was "enmeshed" with her mother and as a result would not be able to "separate" and assume an "independent lifestyle." According to the counselor, the girl had been missing school to accompany her mother to appointments. The counselor felt that the mother was taking advantage of her daughter and placing her in a "parentified" role. The counselor described Sonia as generally well liked by classmates and teachers, a good student who could do even better, and presenting no significant behavioral or management problems in school although she was friends with several of the "tougher" girls in her grade. The counselor further explained that she had seen many situations like this before and did not want Sonia to become "another student who did not live up to her potential."

The counselor had felt so strongly about this that she had had several meeting with Sonia and her mother, Luz, to "educate" them on how they should relate to one another. At the time of the referral for family therapy the counselor was no longer meeting with Luz, who had refused to continue these sessions, but she was still seeing Sonia in order to "support her independence." Feeling she had done all she could, the counselor made the referral so that the mother would stop interfering with her daughter's development.

In the first family session, Luz spoke openly about her adversarial relationship with the counselor, who she felt was "putting bad ideas into my daughter's head." As a result, she said, she had begun having problems with Sonia, who was now challenging her and testing limits. Luz said that she did not want her daughter to miss school, but she needed Sonia's assistance to negotiate other systems (e.g., public assistance, medical clinics) because "Sonia knows English better." She had begun limiting some of Sonia's privileges because of her daughter's disrespectful attitude and her violation of curfew, which strained their relationship. The mother worried that her daughter was growing up too fast and did not want to "lose her to the streets," a concern that led her to believe that Sonia needed increased supervision rather than more freedom.

The family therapist contacted the counselor, and they discussed her experience with similar situations in the past. The therapist agreed with her about the frustrations of working with children when resources are limited, while clarifying her criteria for a successful intervention. This dialogue enabled the clinician and the counselor to express their beliefs and hopes about what could be done, which charted the initial course of treatment. With this clarification of expectations the counselor felt less isolated and more focused in her role, which was reconceptualized as "monitoring" the student's attendance and adjustment to school but not requiring her to solve the problem. She was to pass on information to the mother, either directly or through the family therapist.

The counselor also modified her approach to Sonia in that she did not push the mother-daughter dyad to reach any solution. In time this contributed to a shift in the adversarial relationship with Luz, who no longer perceived the counselor as being against her. Simultaneously, Sonia and Luz were engaged in several family therapy sessions to help them understand the intensity of their interactions. They learned how to negotiate more effectively the demands and inevitable changes in their relationship as Sonia grew older, with due regard to the reality of Luz's concerns for her daughter.

Discussion: The Fernandez Family

Clearly, the school counselor initially intervened with Sonia according to her own construction of reality, involving certain beliefs about adolescent and family life cycle development as well as her own vantage point in relation to the school, including prior experiences with other teenagers in that system. Defining the problem from a microsystem perspective as a separation-individuation issue, she had tried to persuade Luz Fernandez to give her daughter increased freedom to develop as an individual.

The family therapist, using an ecosystemic approach, took the position that there were multiple versions of reality. He understood that for this immigrant family the school counselor's middle-class notions of separation and independence might not be considered desirable. He recognized that Sonia's accompanying of her immigrant mother to appointments, which represented a sense of responsibility for her family, might actually constitute a healthy adaptation, as opposed to enmeshment or a lack of independence (Inclan & Herron, 1991).

In addition, the therapist focused his attention not only on the mother-daughter dyad but also on the dyad's transactions with the counselor and the school system. He intervened with the counselor in order to improve the quality of the relationship between the mother and the school. If he had been unable to connect with the counselor, he might have engaged the family in speculating about her intentions or concerns in an attempt to broaden *their* understanding of multiple systems and multiple realities.

Finally, the therapist engaged Luz and Sonia in a dialogue about their relationship in the context of their inner-city neighborhood, the dangers that lurked on the streets, and the benefits to Sonia of continuing with her education. In the process he emphasized their strengths, including Sonia's sense of responsibility for her family and Luz's love for her daughter. He supported their current actions that reflected their mutual love and concern, and he engaged them in seeking additional solutions that would address as many of their needs as possible, including Sonia's need to attend school.

The Diaz Family

Maria Diaz, a 35-year-old Puerto Rican woman and single parent of two teenagers—Roberto, age 15, and Amanda, age 13—sought help at the suggestion of her son's school principal. Roberto had been diagnosed with attention deficit hyperactivity disorder at age 5 and had attended special schools ever since. Currently, the school was complaining that his aggressive behaviors were presenting significant management problems for the school staff. He had been medicated in the past for his hyperactivity, although he had not been on medication for the past several years. Now the school staff were questioning whether more needed to be done to cope with his behavior.

The precipitating cause of the referral was an incident in which Roberto, who had poor impulse control, retaliated against another student who had been taunting him. The school expressed concern that his impulsivity could get Roberto into trouble in situations that were less well supervised and protected. It was felt that he was at risk for involvement in all aspects of negative street culture, especially if he did not learn some self-control. According to Maria, Roberto had become more disrespectful to her of late and more overtly testing of limits. She shared many of the same fears for her son that had been expressed by the school staff but felt powerless and at a loss regarding solutions to the problem.

Maria's concerns were exacerbated by the fact that Amanda had also begun to act out; she felt she was being pulled in many different directions. Amanda's grades had dropped dramatically during the past months, and she had begun hanging out with the "wrong" kind of peers, although she continued to maintain a close relationship with her best friend of many years. Amanda had begun answering her mother back, provoking conflict between them. Maria reported that whenever she approached her daughter to talk about a problem, Amanda rejected her by refusing to listen or participate in a discussion. All of these behaviors were tempered with periods of good communication and understanding, but Maria's attempts at discussing things when they were not going well had been unproductive.

As a single parent, Maria felt isolated in managing the demands of her children. Their father had been in and out of jail and had not been a resource for the family for over 11 years. Maria's own extended family had offered support by providing child care when the children were younger but were less willing to do so as they became older and more challenging of authority. The paternal extended family had been decimated by drug addiction and incarceration. Despite her isolation and her sense of powerlessness and frustration, Maria told of several incidents in which she had followed her children to see exactly where they were and what they were doing. She had even gone so far as to request a leave of absence from her full-time job to supervise the children more vigilantly. By the time the first session took place, she had not been working for several weeks and was beginning to feel financially strapped. Roberto and Amanda were also worried because, aside from her increased vigilance and the family's economic stress, they perceived their mother as going through a depression.

In the early sessions with the Diaz family the therapist concentrated on assessing needs and establishing a contract for treatment. Initially, the children maintained that they had no problems and did not think counseling would help. They spoke about the numerous helping professionals they had encountered in the past; Roberto even mimicked questions he had been asked in previous counseling experiences. Maria, although depressed and feeling hopeless, clearly believed that her children needed supervision to prevent problems in the future. However, this conviction was tempered by the fact that friends and family members had criticized her for leaving her job, telling her that she would not be in such a predicament had she been doing things right in the first place. This resulted in her becoming defensive, which only served to give more credibility to her detractors, confirming her low self-esteem and increasing her sense of uncertainty about whether she was handling the situation appropriately—a vicious cycle.

Rather than addressing the pros and cons of Maria's leaving her job, the family therapist emphasized her commitment to her family. Whereas others had told her that her determination to make supervision of the children a priority was mistaken, he framed this decision as a strength and as an indication of her love for them. This provided an entry point to join with Maria in her attempts to provide for her children, and all three family members were encouraged to express their wishes about what type of family they envisioned. With this line of exploration the atmosphere of the sessions changed, as the blaming that usually characterized their interactions decreased. The focus was not on what was wrong but on what was right and what might be possible.

Simultaneously, the children were engaged, not in efforts to change them but to explore what it was that the other counselors were trying to fix and how this fit in with their perceptions of what they needed. They reported that they were always made to feel that there was something wrong with them, a view they vehemently rejected because they thought they were just like all the other kids they knew. In fact, they were confused and angered by this negative perception of them because they knew many other youngsters who had already dropped out of school and were selling drugs or in other ways presenting far greater problems for their families and the community.

The family therapist shared with the Diaz family his experience that once teenagers had left school it was often much harder to figure out how to help them and their families. Roberto and Amanda thus were enabled to see that they had better prospects than some of their friends who had dropped out because of problems such as pregnancy or involvement with the law or with drugs. This discussion then helped Maria to realize that her children had goals that were consistent with hers: graduating from high school and attending college. This made her feel more secure about how she had raised them and about her parenting in general. At the same time, Roberto and Amanda were able to understand Maria's "intrusiveness" as her way of caring for and protecting them, something they knew could have made a difference in the lives of some of their friends. Thus, a process of negotiation between Maria, Roberto, and Amanda was facilitated, without the blaming and defensiveness that so often had resulted in the polarized positions that prevented a workable compromise.

The dialogue described above led, finally, to a powerful experience for the Diaz family, as the children told stories of "casualties" among their peers and Maria's anxiety increased regarding the dangers and negative influences in the community over which she felt she had no control. The family therapist clarified the contrast between their visions of the future and what they were witnessing in their neighborhood. As the family discussed the other families living in their housing project and what percentage of the children were attending school successfully and responding to limits set by their parents, they were better able to identify the obstacles inherent in a variety of systems that ran counter to their goals. The family felt both challenged and empowered as they began to make sense of their individual and collective struggles with a difficult environment containing limited resources. As their perceptions shifted and they became less blaming of one another for their situation, they were better able to confront intrafamilial processes to seek solutions productively. Both Amanda and Roberto became more cooperative and less hostile toward their mother, and Amanda's behavior and grades improved. Subsequently, Maria and Roberto were able to utilize the help of the family therapist in working to negotiate appropriate supports at school for Roberto, who came to be seen as less problematic in that setting.

Discussion: The Diaz Family

Using an ecosystemic approach, the family therapist reviewed all systems involved with the family as he sought a point of entry into the family system. To begin with, Maria was depressed. Many within her support network disapproved of her decision to stop working, which reduced their availability to her in her current crisis. The perspective of multiple realities pointed to beliefs that she might have been a bad mother in the past, that adolescents are old enough to fend for themselves, that by the time children become adolescents there is nothing one can do to change them, or even that she was using the children's behavior as an excuse. The therapist was able to point out to Maria that, regardless of these beliefs, her decision represented the best solution she could think of to help her family in their current crisis. She was doing the best she could. The use of such a solution orientation and the framing of her decision as a strength significantly reduced Maria's depression.

Roberto and Amanda were both initially resistant to therapy. For his part, Roberto was dealing with the stigma of having been labeled as a difficult youngster over many years by the school system. Amanda, in turn, was increasingly receiving negative feedback from a variety of adults in her environment. It was clear to the therapist that all members of the Diaz family, in one way or another, felt criticized and blamed by other individuals and systems, including friends, extended family, and the school. In turn, they had adopted a hostile stance toward one another and in the case of the children, toward the larger systems as well. By engaging the family in describing their goals and their vision, the therapist was able to focus on their mutual desire for improvement, an important strength. In addition, the process of comparing themselves with others in their community who had more serious problems defused the inherent shame, confusion, and disqualification of their problem-solving abilities that many families experience when referred for family counseling.

The ecosystemic framework provided the Diaz family with a way of understanding their experiences from different perspectives. With their strengths supported, Maria, Roberto, and Amanda were able to share their opinions, hopes, and fears with each other and to work together in arriving at practical solutions to improve interactions within the family. As the family functioned better as a unit, their relationships with members of the extended family also improved. The family therapist also assisted Roberto and Maria by helping them negotiate with the school, resulting in an improved fit for Roberto with this system. In sum, the family was strengthened in its overall ability to adapt flexibly to the complex problems they were facing in their transactions with a multiplicity of systems.

CONCLUSION

Parnell and Vanderkloot (1989) have described how poor inner-city neighborhoods may at first seem not only unfamiliar but also frightening and negative from the perspective of the stranger who is White and middle class. With time, however, the vitality and resilience of the residents will begin to emerge, as will their strength of purpose and their values and sense of morality. Similarly, the family therapist who works with poor ethnic minority families may at times feel as though he or she is struggling against overwhelming forces. This is especially true at present, as the already fragile, yet vital, network of services and resources for these families is taken away. Therapists often need to struggle against their own sense of helplessness as they work with families to enhance their strengths and their resiliency.

Adolescents, for their part, often pose a particular challenge because of their vulnerability to negative peer group influences and their tendency to act out within the family system, the school, and the community in the course of their search for identity. In poor ethnic minority communities this challenge becomes even greater. Adolescence may constitute a critical crossroads: one direction may lead to the dead ends of substance abuse, crime, early pregnancy, and school dropout, while the other leads to more resilient functioning and survival. One way to conceptualize the task of the family therapist with poor minority adolescents is that he or she either guides young people to a positive developmental track or assists them in continuing along one that they have already begun.

This chapter has demonstrated that an ecosystemic approach to family therapy, although applicable to work with all families, is especially useful with poor ethnic minority adolescents and their families because it empowers them. These families may have greater needs and be involved with multiple helpers while at the same time experiencing stress because of a lack of "fit" with the larger systems they interact with. Four overlapping principles of ecosystemic family therapy have been delineated: the concept of multiple realities, the use of descriptive language that focuses on the transactions between systems, a strengths perspective, and a solution-oriented approach. Two case illustrations have been provided, demonstrating how ecosystemic family therapy was utilized with two families that included adolescents. The authors believe that, because the family therapist's interventions with the Fernandez and Diaz families improved both the intrasystemic functioning of each family system and the family system's transactions with other systems, youngsters were enabled to proceed with their development in a more positive manner. These and many other examples make it clear that ecosystemic family therapy offers the possibility of support and empowerment to vulnerable populations at a crucial moment in the family life cycle.

REFERENCES

Aponte, H. (1976). The family-school interview: An eco-structural approach. *Family Process, 15*(5), 303–311.

Auerswald, E. (1968). Interdisciplinary versus ecological approach. *Family Process, 7*(2), 202–215.

Auerswald, E. (1971). Families, change, and the ecological perspective. *Family Process, 10*(3), 263–280.

Auerswald, E. (1987). Epistemological confusion in family therapy and research. *Family Process, 26*(3), 317–330.

Blos, P. (1962). *On adolescence: A psychoanalytic interpretation.* New York: Free Press.

Blos, P. (1967). The second individuation process of adolescence. *Psychoanalytic Study of the Child, 22*, 162–186.

Boyd-Franklin, N. (1989). *Black families in therapy: A multisystems approach.* New York: Guilford.

Combrinck-Graham, L. (Ed.). (1989). *Children in family contexts.* New York: Guilford.

Combrinck-Graham, L. (1990). *Giant steps: Therapeutic innovations in child mental health.* New York: Basic.

Congress, E. (1994). The use of culturagrams to assess and empower culturally diverse families. *Families in Society, 39*, 531–540.

De Jong, P., & Miller, S. (1995). How to interview for client strengths. *Social Work, 40*, 729–736.

De Shazer, S. (1988). *Clues: Investigating solutions in brief therapy.* New York: Norton.

Erikson, E. (1963). *Childhood and society.* New York: Norton.

Erikson, E. (1968). *Identity: Youth and crisis.* New York: Norton.

Falicov, C. (1982). Mexican families. In M. McGoldrick, J. Pearce, & J. Giordano (Eds.), *Ethnicity and family therapy* (pp. 134–163). New York: Guilford.

Falicov, C. (1988). Learning to think culturally. In H. Liddle, D. Breunlin, & R. Schwartz (Eds.), *Handbook of family therapy training and supervision* (pp. 335–357). New York: Guilford.

Falicov, C. (1995). Training to think culturally: A multidimensional comparative framework. *Family Process, 34*, 373–388.

Freud, A. (1958). Adolescence. *Psychoanalytic Study of the Child, 13*, 255–278.

Germain, C., & Gitterman, A. (1980). *The life model of social work practice.* New York: Columbia University Press.

Gibbs, J., Huang, L., & Associates. (Eds.). (1991). *Children of color: Psychological interventions with minority youth.* San Francisco: Jossey Bass.

Hansen, J., & Falicov, C. (1983). *Cultural perspectives in family therapy.* Rockville, MD: Aspen.

Hartman, A., & Laird, J. (1983). *Family centered social work practice.* New York: Free Press.

Hoyt, M. (Ed.). (1994). *Constructive therapies.* New York: Guilford.

Inclan, J., & Herron, G. (1991). Puerto Rican adolescents. In J. Gibbs, L. Huang, & Associates (Eds.), *Children of color: Psychological interventions with minority youth* (pp. 251–277). San Francisco: Jossey Bass.

McGoldrick, M., Pearce, J., & Giordano, J. (1996). *Ethnicity and family therapy* (2nd ed.). New York: Guilford.

Minuchin, S. (1974). *Families and family therapy.* Cambridge, MA: Harvard University Press.

Pare, D. (1995). Of families and other cultures: The shifting paradigms of family therapy. *Family Process, 34*(1), 1–19.

Parnell, M., & Vanderkloot, J. (1989). Ghetto children: Children growing up in poverty. In L. Combrinck-Graham (Ed.), *Children in family contexts* (pp. 437–462). New York: Guilford.

Saleeby, D. (Ed.). (1992). *The strengths perspective in social work practice.* New York: Longmans.

Sidel, R. (1986). *Women and children last.* New York: Viking.

Wachtel, P. (1993). *Therapeutic communication: Principles and effective practice.* New York: Guilford.

CHAPTER 5

Multicultural Dimensions of the Third Shift: Employee, Mother, and Student

Susan Bair Egan

The multiple roles of women have been explored from many vantage points. As women have increasingly entered the workforce, much research has focused on the impact of the role of employee on women's roles of wife and mother. As daughters are more likely than sons to care for their elderly parents, the multiple demands on women caring for parents while parenting young children has been studied. However, the role of student, a role that many women have taken on, has received less attention in the literature. Perhaps because the role of student is seen as voluntary, the added stress of the role is overlooked. Yet as colleges and universities are creating more flexible programs for employees and mothers on both undergraduate and graduate levels, and because it is important for women to be competitive in the job force through education, more women have become students in addition to their other roles.

Hochschild (1989) found that even when women are employed outside the home, they are also largely responsible for homemaking and child care obligations, therefore working a "second shift." This extra shift takes a toll on women's psychological and physical health, their marriages, and their children. Therefore, women who are employees, mothers, and also students in essence work a "third shift." How these women manage their multiple roles, what they find stressful, and where they find support are important factors to understand. Mental health professionals must be aware of all of the roles a woman has and how she experiences each role. This chapter looks at some of the implications of the student role for women, with particular attention to ethnic and cultural factors.

It is generally accepted that students experience stress. The research on women in higher education largely relates to institutional responses to assist the nontraditional or the "new traditional" student adjust to the transition to the role of student along with her other roles. Support groups, workshops, special orientations to include family members, and mentoring programs are often suggested to assist the adult female student adjust to the student demands. A review of this research can assist the mental health professional in awareness of the issues that women in school face.

REVIEW OF THE LITERATURE

Leavitt (1989) studied midlife married women living with their husbands and children to see how their return to school affected their relationships with family, friends, household tasks, emotional and physical health, and self-perception. The study affirmed the importance of women's returning to school and the positive contribution to their lives both internally and at home. The women largely performed well academically, and all reported increased self-esteem. Marital relationships remained strong, even enhanced, and husbands were viewed as supportive. The greatest stress was in the management of household responsibilities. The women in this study feared that their increased role strain would adversely affect their children, but in fact it was seen that there was a gain in their children's school performances. These women were clear about how to meet the demands of each of their roles separately; it was when the roles competed for their energy that they had increased stress. The women in this study were all full-time students and all were White.

Redding and Dowling (1992) conducted an in-depth study of a small number of reentry college women who were married and had children. They found that the women made great efforts to preserve the spousal and maternal roles and used a wide range of coping behaviors. The women, as well as their families, were assisted in their transitional role by rites and ceremonies that were not recognized by traditional university rituals.

Social work researchers in particular have studied stress and the multiple roles of social work students. Several of the studies found that students did not experience much stress from their student role. Sales, Shore, and Bolitho (1980) examined the characteristics of a group of women with children who had completed a graduate program in social work. They found that most of the women adapted easily to the role of student and had a smooth transition into the social work profession. It should be noted, however, that the women in this study with the highest satisfaction in their roles were older women with older children, and they had husbands who supported their decision to attend school. Also, only half of the women in this study were employed full-time in addition to their roles of student and mother.

In another study of social work students, Munson (1984) found that the subjects actually reported low levels of stress and that no major differences in stress were seen on the basis of gender or marital status. Although the majority of the students in this study were women, almost all were full-time students and only half had children. Supporting this, a study of female social work students by Fortune (1987) found that students with multiple roles do not experience greater stress than do students who do not have added responsibilities. In fact, Fortune found that multiple-role students may avoid role strain by assuring that one of their roles is successful.

Sturges, Bombyk, and Chernesky (1989) looked at the older female social work student in terms of the developmental issues they face in returning to school and how they cope with stress. These women had positive feelings about their decision to pursue higher education and their performance in school. Their stress came from the demands of balancing personal and academic responsibilities. The women in the study were predominantly White; half were married, and their youngest children ranged from adolescent to young adult.

It would seem from these studies that in fact stress is not an issue when a woman has the additional role of student. However, in another study of social work students, Kramer, Mathews, and Endias (1987) found that part-time students who were likely to be employed full-time were found to have higher levels of stress than full-time students. Koeske and

Koeske (1989) also studied working and nonworking students, emphasizing the importance of the work role and social supports. They found that full-time social work students with part-time jobs experience greater stress than did full-time students with no jobs and part-time students with full-time jobs. Social support was associated with the reduction of stress symptoms. Brennan and Black (1986) studied the multiple roles of the part-time student and found that they best juggled the demands of employment, family, and school through bridging the boundaries between role responsibilities.

Only one study was found in the literature that specifically looked at minority female students. Gibbs (1984) identified some of the sources of stress and psychological conflicts experienced by minority women in their roles as students. Gibbs found that there were four sources of stress typically mentioned by the minority female graduate students she studied. They were academic stress, competing demands from family and community, male-female relationships, and the choice of a career. She also pointed out that those students who were also wives and mothers had a fifth source of stress—role complexity. She stated:

> Marriage per se adds another role and another dimension to the graduate student's life. It can be more stressful or less stressful, depending on whether the husband is a student or a wage earner, whether the wife and husband have a satisfactory division of labor in their home, and whether they have mutual goals and aspirations for their careers. However stressful the marital relationship, the wife-student can deal with her husband as another adult who is able to manage his own life. Such is not the case with dependent children. The student-mother who has to work out child care arrangements, monitor the child's psychosocial and health needs, and participate in the child's school and recreational activities often must place the needs of her child before her own needs as a student, particularly when the child is ill or when child care arrangements break down. All of these stresses are exacerbated for those graduate students who are single mothers without regular partners. (pp. 29–30)

Gibbs (1984) found that how minority female students coped with stress depended on learned family and cultural patterns, personality attributes, previous methods of dealing with stress, use of support systems, and perceptions of alternatives in the environment. Maladaptive coping was seen when women strove to overachieve or became overinvolved, disengaged, immobilized. Those who were also wives and mothers often attempted to cope by becoming superwomen. Although White female graduate students also experience similar stresses and coping mechanisms, it is Gibbs's belief that maladaptive coping is intensified for minority female students. "These strategies are more threatening to the mental health of minority women because they are inextricably tied to the women's perception of their abilities and competence and how their professors and fellow students view them" (p. 33).

As seen from the literature, research on the combined roles of employee, mother, and student is scarce, and only one study included ethnicity as a factor in women in their multiple roles. This author did a study to gain insight in this area.

RESEARCH STUDY

This study was conducted in a large graduate social work school with an urban and a suburban campus. The sample was graduate social work students who were known to have at least two roles, full-time employee and full-time student. When social supports and coping with stress were explored, a pattern of ethnic differences as well as similarities was seen. The influence of cultural factors is the main contribution of this study to the current literature on women students in multiple roles.

Data were collected through a questionnaire with closed- and open-ended questions as well as interviews with students. Of the 111 students in this study, the age range was 22 to 58 years; 48% were White, 28% African American, 22% Hispanic, and 2% Asian. Women of color were younger than the White women in this study. Half of the students were in a couple relationship; 57% did not have children. Of those with children, almost all had at least one child living at home.

Students were asked about their motivation to attend graduate school. Responses were similar among groups. They wanted to gain more clinical skills and theoretical knowledge, advance their careers, help others, and promote self-growth and professionalism. Hispanic women made particular reference to planning to work with the Hispanic community. Students were asked about their social supports when they were considering attending graduate school. Differences were seen in reference to the ethnicity

of the women. The White women ranked their spouses as the most supportive, then friends, supervisors, and therapists. The African Americans
ranked spouses first, then mothers, relatives, and friends. The Hispanic
women ranked supervisors first, then spouses, mothers, and co-workers.
It is significant to note that the African American women in this study
found family in general to be their source of support, whereas Hispanic
women found their support in the workplace. When asked about their
supports while in graduate school, the answers were similar, but in addition, women from each group made friends in the graduate school program.
Also, whereas supervisors were ranked as the most supportive to the
Hispanic women at the time of consideration for graduate school, they
were not ranked as a main support while the students were in school.

Interviews with some of the Hispanic women revealed that although
they received support from role models in the field, they also received
discouragement from family members. When asked if there was anyone
who was particularly discouraging to her when she was considering graduate school, one Hispanic woman stated that her parents were; and when
asked if anyone was particularly discouraging now that she was in graduate
school, she answered that her husband was. Another Hispanic woman
stated,

> I feel disappointed in my family that they don't help me and my kids. I
> have no support from them. I'm the one who has to be supportive of them.

Although few women indicated that their children were sources of their
support, when asked about them, they indicated that they felt that their
children were proud of them, and they were pleased that they were positive
role models for them. The women of color particularly expressed how
important it was that they set examples for their children regarding the
importance of education. Some of these women had older adolescents or
young adults still at home who were not planning to attend college. They
hoped that they would change their minds after seeing that their mothers
could accomplish a graduate professional education.

The students in this study were also asked to rank-order their most
stressful role while in school. The White respondents ranked the student
role as the most stressful (38%), then the employee role, then the role of
mother. The African American respondents ranked the student role as
most stressful (53%), then the employee role, then being a spouse/signifi-
cant other. The Hispanic respondents ranked the student role as the most

stressful (58%), then the employee role, then being a spouse/significant other. Although all respondents experienced the student role as their most stressful, the women of color saw this to a much higher degree. Also, whereas being a mother was the third-ranked response for White women, only one Hispanic woman and no African American women indicated that mothering was their most stressful role. These responses were for all women in the study.

When the most stressful roles were looked at only for the group of women who had children at home, the student role was still ranked first, then employee, then wife/significant other. It would appear that having children at home is not a significant factor in how these women view their most stressful role. Also, dichotomizing the respondents into groups of those in married and living-together relationships against those who were single found no change in how the students in this study ranked their most stressful roles.

In spite of the stress experienced by the women of color in their student role, they were clearly happy about being in graduate school and had no intention of terminating their studies. They felt that they were accomplishing what they had hoped to and that the sacrifices they were making would be worthwhile. One Hispanic woman expressed her feelings about graduate school in an interview:

> I've become a more independent, responsible, caring and loving person. I am happy to say that returning to school makes me feel that I've accomplished a goal. I am a very good role model for my daughters, a smarter person, a much better person.

The women were asked to wish for things that would facilitate their competency and comfort with their roles and responsibilities. Again, similarities as well as differences were seen in relation to ethnic groups. The modesty of these respondents in terms of their wishes is impressive. Most women wished for more money but did so in relation to their schooling. That is, they wanted to make their lives easier to complete their studies. No one wished that she would never have to work again, just that she could have the luxury of being a full-time student or that she wouldn't have to take out loans. Most women wished for more time for family and for studying. White women wished for housekeepers; the Hispanic and African American women wished for child care. White women were the only group indicting a wish for more time for leisure or vacations.

One African American respondent wrote:

> I would only wish for one thing. That would be for everyone that I relate
> to in each role (minus mother role) to realize that I do perform in other
> roles and that I need more time and less demands to be as productive as
> I can be.

A Hispanic respondent wrote:

> My number one wish would be that my husband would also start his
> master's degree education so that we can both be economically secure.

In the interviews women were asked what has suffered since they began
school. Most women mentioned housework and social life. One White
woman, who during the interview said that she felt she was surprisingly
managing everything, called back later in the afternoon to say she had
just opened her mail and found a disconnect notice from the electric
company. She laughingly said she guessed she wasn't as on top of things
as she had thought because she had forgotten to pay the bill.

Because the literature on adult female college students calls for institutional responses to meet the needs of these women, the women who were
interviewed were asked if the faculty or administrators in the graduate
school could do anything for them to make their lives more manageable.
Several of the women stated that they wanted the individual attention of
faculty regarding their academic and career concerns. The White women
were more amenable to the idea of support groups than the women of
color. One African American woman stated:

> I have enough resources on the outside. I don't need a group to discuss
> how tough it is being a single mother or working full-time or having a
> teenager. In terms of educational support, maybe yes.

A Hispanic woman also did not feel a need for a support group, saying
they all know each other anyway and always ask how the kids are.

This study of social work students would indicate that even when a
female student has multiple roles, she views the role of student as the
most stressful, regardless of the student's ethnicity, whether or not she
is married, and whether or not she has children at home. The study also
challenges previously held assumptions about the needs of social work

students. Although the literature on students and stress and the literature specific to multiple roles recommends that these students be targeted with special support groups or programs, this study revealed the ethnocentric bias of those ideas. A support group based at school may be appealing only to White women, and although attempts to culturally diversify such a group may assuage liberal conscience, the group might be regarded as an irrelevant use of time by women of color who are working mothers.

Role models were important in the lives of Hispanic women. Although the African American women did not receive as much support for professional training from social work supervisors as the Hispanics in this study did, their belief in the importance of supporting others in the future was evident in the interviews. One African-American woman clearly stated:

> With all of my other roles I have an added responsibility to be supportive to the black community. To be a minority in the school and trying to get a degree says that we have a point of view that should be looked at. I feel the pressure.

Although this study was done to demonstrate to the faculty, administrators, and advisors the importance of their roles in the lives of every student, the implications are certainly helpful for clinicians as well. Interventions must effectively meet the needs of culturally diverse students based on differential assessments of issues relevant to each group and on the suggestions of the individuals. An understanding of particular needs of the women in relation to their cultural diversity enhances the satisfaction they have about their educational experience and their experience in clinical treatment.

CLINICAL AND MULTICULTURAL IMPLICATIONS

When a woman is seen in treatment, whether individually, in a couple, or in a family, it is important that the clinician include in the assessment how the woman is adjusting to her multiple role responsibilities. Because the issues can be so complex, many women may be unable to verbalize their problems or to request help in resolving them. Being a student may be viewed as a luxury, and because the role is usually time-limited, related problems may be overlooked by both the client and the clinician.

When the woman seen in treatment is a student, several aspects pertaining to that role must be understood by the clinician. First, the circumstances under which the added role of student was taken on should be determined. Some women must enroll in school to retain employment and therefore experience added pressure in that a job depends on success in the student role. Some women who attend school are hopeful for job advancement, or they may be planning a career change. In these cases the role of the student is more voluntary, but it still carries the pressure of an expectation that the added role will have a quantitative outcome.

Second, it is also important to know if the woman has the support of her family and to know how education is viewed by her immediate as well as extended family. If she is the first woman in her family to earn a college or graduate degree, this may put added pressure on her. In some cases the family members may be proud of her; in others they may view the time spent away from her husband and children as selfish or unnecessary. The time needed to study may be resented by her husband. If the degree earned puts her at a higher educational level than her husband, this may cause him to feel threatened, particularly if the wife will become the higher wage earner. The cost of tuition may be incurring a financial burden. Children need to understand why she is in school, as her availability to them may lessen.

Third, it is important that the woman's own perception of the role be assessed. She may resent the added pressure. She may feel guilty about the time away from family responsibilities, or she may, in fact, enjoy the time away from her more traditional roles. Fourth, the clinician should explore how the woman is adjusting to the student role. Some women may feel uncomfortable if they are in a minority in the classroom because of gender, ethnicity, or age. If the woman is enjoying the challenge of term papers and tests or if she is feeling fearful and incompetent needs to be understood.

Multiple roles do not always lead to role overload or stress, yet the potential is certainly there. Certainly, many woman thrive when they have multiple roles. They may experience greater independence, a more positive sense of self, and an expanded support network. Yet when there is conflict among the roles, depression, anxiety, anger, or dissatisfaction can result. In treatment, the clinician must approach these women from a strength perspective. We must be sensitive to the experience of the individual woman as well as to the individual-family fit and the family-to-community fit. Efforts must be made to assess the advantages of multiple roles, not just their disadvantages (McBride, 1990).

Freeman, Logan, and McCoy (1987) emphasize that the clinical assessment of working women should focus on theoretical concepts that deal with role performance and problem solving in the work and family environments. This can pertain to the adult female student as well. They suggest a structured interview guide, a stress questionnaire, and an explicit contract. As the stress women experience in their multiple roles often becomes evident only later in treatment, it is important that they be evaluated in the initial assessment. They recommend an action-oriented as well as an ego-supportive approach. They also point out that counseling may impose additional demands of time and commitment on these already overburdened women and therefore recommend brief treatment with specific goals. Gibbs (1984) found that the female minority students in her clinical work responded to an ego-supportive approach that helped them identify their conflicts, evaluate their behavioral consequences, and work out coping behaviors that reduced their anxieties and promoted positive functioning.

Certainly, clinicians must be aware of how the role of student is viewed in the context of the adult female student's ethnicity and culture. This author's study showed that there are differences in how women of different ethnicities experience the stress of their student role and in where they find support. McGoldrick, Garcia-Preto, Hines, and Lee (1989) find that role overload is a common deterrent for the African American women's engagement in treatment. Because they typically have so much to do that unless they really understand how therapy can be helpful it is hard to commit themselves. They suggest that it helps for the therapist to emphasize the woman's sense of being a survivor, her strength, and her ability to find her own solutions. Also, because African American women tend to underrate the complexities of their lives because their older female relatives had it so much harder, clinicians must help them validate their experiences.

Hispanic women are expected to be responsible for taking care of their home and children, often feel obligated to sacrifice themselves in order to accomplish this, and are glorified when they put their children's needs above everything else. Although many Hispanic women also work outside the home, they are still expected to be submissive and passive in comparison to men (McGoldrick et al., 1989). As their roles expand outside the home, in the workplace or in school, they may find unhappiness in their traditional role prescriptions but not be able to verbalize this in treatment.

A culturally sensitive, ethnically competent clinician must have the personal attributes, knowledge, and skills to work with minority persons. Gallegos (1984) states that clinicians must be able to see their clients from a dual perspective—as part of two systems, the larger societal system and their immediate environment—and to assess the degree of congruence or incongruence between the two systems. He states:

> The achievement of congruence for ethnic minorities, in a society that devalues their immediate environmental system, is difficult. Yet, when congruence is found, it is likely that the strengths of the systems can be identified. Whether the systems are congruent or not, useful cues for intervention can be discerned, and it is this aspect that makes the dual perspective uniquely suited for working with ethnic minorities. (p. 5)

Although there is conflicting thought about women's multiple roles and how they affect mental health, it is clear that the clinician must consider each one of these roles—how each affects the woman, her family, and her larger community. This can be done effectively only when an understanding of the woman's ethnicity and culture is an integral part of the assessment and treatment. As more and more women are working a "third shift," we must be responsive to them.

REFERENCES

Brennan, E. M., & Black, E. A. (1986). On finding a workable balance: The multiple roles of the part-time student. *Journal of Continuing Social Work Education, 19*, 43–46.

Fortune, A. E. (1987). Multiple roles, stress and well-being among MSW students. *Journal of Social Work Education, 23*, 81–90.

Freeman, E. M., Logan, S., & McCoy, R. (1987). Clinical practice with employed women. *Social Casework: The Journal of Contemporary Social Work, 68*(7), 413–420.

Gallegos, J. S. (1984). The ethnic competence model for social work education. In B. W. White (Ed.), *Color in a white society* (pp. 1–9). Silver Spring, MD: National Association of Social Workers.

Gibbs, J. T. (1984). Conflicts and coping strategies of minority female graduate students. In B. W. White (Ed.), *Color in a white society* (pp. 22–36). Silver Spring, MD: National Association of Social Workers.

Hochschild, A. (1989). *The second shift: Working parents and the revolution at home*. New York: Viking.

Koeske, R. D., & Koeske, G. F. (1989). Working and non-working students: Roles, support and well-being. *Journal of Social Work Education, 25*, 244–256.

Kramer, H., Mathews, G., & Endias, R. (1987). Comparative stress levels in part-time and full-time social work programs. *Journal of Social Work Education, 23*, 74–80.

Leavitt, R. S. (1989). Married women returning to college: A study of their personal and family adjustments. *Smith College Studies in Social Work, 59*, 301–315.

McBride, A. B. (1990). Mental health effects of women's multiple roles. *American Psychologist, 45*, 381–384.

McGoldrick, M., Garcia-Preto, N., Hines, P. M., & Lee, E. (1989). Ethnicity and women. In M. McGoldrick, C. M. Anderson, & F. Walsh (Eds.), *Women in families: A framework for family therapy* (pp. 169–199). New York: W. W. Norton.

Munson, C. E. (1984). Stress among graduate social work students: An empirical study. *Journal of Education for Social Work, 20*, 20–29.

Redding, N. P., & Dowling, W. D. (1992). Rites of passage among women reentering higher education. *Adult Education Quarterly, 42*, 221–236.

Sales, E., Shore, B. K., & Bolitho, F. (1980). When mothers return to school: A study of women completing an MSW program. *Journal of Education for Social Work, 16*, 57–64.

Sturges, P., Bombyk, M., & Chernesky, R. (1989). Social work education and the older woman student. *Women and Aging, 1*, 119–131.

CHAPTER 6

The Aging Family: Ethnic and Cultural Considerations

Irene A. Gutheil
Lynn M. Tepper

Older persons constitute the only age group in our society frequently discussed in both professional and popular literature as if it were composed of individuals with little relationship to families. Even the family therapy literature has to a large extent overlooked the relationship between older people and their families. In 1988, Anderson noted that family therapists had little to say about older people, relegating them to the role of filling spaces in genograms in order to clarify the problems of younger generations. As a result of the tendency to see older persons primarily in individual terms, the interrelationships between older persons and their families have at times received insufficient attention. One striking reflection of this is the durability of the myth that older people are abandoned by their families and thrust into nursing homes when they become infirm. The reality is that most older persons are very much a part of their families, whether they are married, widowed, or never married; healthy or infirm; ethnic minority or White middle class.

Acknowledgment: We are grateful to Debra Greenberg, MSW, and Patricia Kolb, PhD, for contributing case materials for this chapter.

In large part because of increases in life expectancy, the population of the United States is aging. The older population itself is aging as well; the fastest-growing segment of our population is persons aged 85 and older. The older population is also becoming more culturally diverse as greater numbers of disadvantaged groups gain access to a higher standard of living and the accompanying better health care. In addition, many people who came to this country in their youth or earlier adulthood have now reached old age. Increasing numbers of foreign-born older persons can be anticipated as more recent immigrants (e.g., Vietnamese) grow old (Myers, 1990). The proportion of non-White older persons is expected to rise, reaching a projected 20% of all elders by the year 2050 (Myers, 1990).

FAMILIES AND AGING

With the aging of the population, came the aging of the family; older persons are increasingly part of four, even five-generation families (Bengston, Rosenthal, & Burton, 1990). However, with recent decreases in marriage and fertility rates there is greater likelihood that younger generations will be smaller (Hines, 1992). Another interesting phenomenon has occurred in the American family. Time spent as an adult child of aging parents has increased, and average time spent as a parent of a child under 18 years old has decreased (results of living longer and having fewer children). Consequently, the number of years spent with parents over age 65 is greater than that spent with children under 18 (Bengston et al., 1990).

In the past the tendency was to view older persons in terms of their potential as burdens to their adult children, but a more balanced view has now emerged. There is clear evidence that older persons are frequent supports to their children, especially those who are coping with stressful life events (Greenberg & Becker, 1988). This is not surprising given that most older persons are in frequent contact with their children, are healthy, and live productive lives.

A striking example of older persons as resources for their families is the increasing phenomenon, especially prevalent in inner cities, of grandparents acting as surrogate parents for their grandchildren. Historically, many African American grandparents assumed this role. Burton (1992) notes that, although the reasons grandparents take on a parenting role have changed over the years, a number of grandparents continue to parent grandchildren. The African American grandparents she studied played a vital role in their families. Not only did they care for grandchildren, they were caregivers to other family members as well, often putting their own needs second to those of the family.

When older persons are infirm, frail, or otherwise in need of assistance, families generally perform heroically in their efforts to meet these needs. The family is the primary source of caregiving and support to older persons. This support comes primarily from spouses and adult children. The myth that older persons are abandoned by their families is tenacious but simply inaccurate. Most older persons are integral parts of their families, serving as resources when they can and being cared for when they need care. Literature addressing the influence of ethnicity on caregiving points to the supportiveness of families in various ethnic groups. However, there is no clear evidence that families of ethnic older persons meet their elders' needs more consistently than do other families (Chappell, 1990). There may be differences, however, in the manner in which caregiving norms are defined and culturally reinforced.

ETHNICITY AND AGING

As the older population grows increasingly ethnically diverse, it becomes even more important to recognize the influence of this diversity. As Gelfand (1982) noted, ethnicity refers to "a variety of groups that have a distinctive sense of personhood" (p. 14). This may come from

- Common heritage.
- Memories of a shared historical past.
- Cultural focus on one or more symbolic elements they view as central to their identity as a people. Examples are kinship patterns, living patterns, religious affiliation, common physical features, or other "differences" from the larger society.
- Social differentiation based on cultural criteria such as common language, customs, and voluntary associations (Gelfand, 1994).

There is wide diversity within ethnic groups. Some of these differences are related to length of time in the United States and socioeconomic status,

both of which affect assimilation and the relative degree of cultural identity.

Gelfand and Fandetti (1986) noted that several factors affect the degree
of a family's ethnic affiliation. Among those they discuss are the following:

- Socioeconomic status. Stronger ethnic ties may be maintained by
  persons of low socioeconomic status as a consequence of their limited
  social mobility.
- Language fluency. Inability to speak English limits opportunities
  for acculturation.
- Religion. A nationality-based religious community also limits opportunity for acculturation.
- Residential pattern. Living in a homogeneous area reinforces traditional cultural values and norms and may limit interaction with other
  ethnic groups.
- Generational succession. Because second-generation members of ethnic groups generally strive for better conditions than their parents
  had, they become more integrated into the larger society. This results
  in greater acculturation and an erosion of cultural patterns.

People who immigrated to this country often have a stronger connection
to their cultural heritage than following generations who have been more
"Americanized." These older persons, a rich link to their families' cultural
heritage, may also be out of sync with following generations, especially
when their values regarding child rearing and filial responsibility conflict
with mainstream values.

Many of the oldest of the ethnic elderly were part of the largest migration
of immigrants to the United States in the early 1900s. These people and
others who followed came to the United States for varying but distinct
reasons, which have helped shape their behavior and attitudes. Persecution
in their country of origin and the economic incentives of the United States
are among the major reasons for immigration. Their children, referred to
as the "new old" (Butler & Lewis, 1986), still possess much of the
culture and traditions of their parents but have, for the most part, adopted
more of the mainstream American identity than their parents did. Until
the 1970s, the "melting pot" ideal of blending into the mainstream culture
was strongly held by many of this generation. It was not until the 1970s

that an emphasis on identity based on the cultural origin of many groups emerged, and terms such as Afro-American, Asian American, and Mexican American were heard. New boundaries based on ethnicity were drawn and maintained, with increased patterns of in-group identity and interaction.

Many of the ethnic elderly have strong roots in their neighborhoods of origin. The poorest of this group may still reside in neighborhoods that have deteriorated, coping with the difficulties related to changing inner-city urban areas (crime, violence, drugs, etc.). Because they also tend to live in their original ethnic communities, many of them retain their original cultural values and beliefs (Congress & Johns, 1994). Many of the rural elderly who also remained in their homes may be having other types of difficulties: isolation from families and friends who have moved away and geographic barriers to needed services.

THEORETICAL PERSPECTIVES

An understanding of the aging process as it relates to specific ethnic and cultural aspects of development is basic to acknowledging the similarities and differences among diverse groups. It is important to acknowledge the effects of minority group membership and its resultant outcomes, including the impact of exclusion, discrimination, and racism. These outcomes may include lower lifetime income, lack of education, and perhaps lack of access to social welfare programs that could improve quality of life. On the other hand, it is equally important to recognize the tremendous strengths of people who, given these extreme hardships and conditions, have survived to old age and late old age, possibly reflective not only of superior genetics but of a psychological status that contributes to their longevity (Gelfand, 1994). Such triumph over adversity should be seen as a potential source of empowerment.

Several theories of aging have emerged to identify patterns that contribute to an understanding of the ways psychological and social factors influence how people age. These theories did not initially address ethnic differences but can be expanded to include the influence of ethnicity on patterns of aging and on older persons and their connections to their families. Two conflicting social theories emerged in the early 1960s. Both sought to explain how people may respond to old age and how these responses influence the attainment of success and satisfaction in later life.

Disengagement theory (Cumming & Henry, 1961) contended that it is normal and inevitable as people begin to age that they give up specific roles, activities, and interests and slowly withdraw from participation in society. Society, it was held, mutually disengages from the older person because it requires people with new energy and skills. This idea was later expanded to include psychological disengagement (withdrawal), known as "interiority of personality" and evident by increasing self-preoccupation and decreased emotional ties to persons in the outer world (Neugarten, 1973). This self-preoccupation was considered beneficial for successful aging.

This theory has been highly criticized by gerontologists, as it supports social myths and stereotypes related to aging and the aged. Among these are that social withdrawal is inevitable and the elderly welcome it, that high activity results in low morale, that life satisfaction in old age is associated with fewer roles, and that disengagement is usually mutually welcomed. Self-preoccupied behavior, which has been observed by families and those working with the elderly, can be attributed to the need for self-reflection in later life, when older people review their lives and relationships in an attempt to come to terms with their lives as they have lived them, a necessary prerequisite for accepting mortality. Disengagement theory continues to be under attack. Although some of the research generated by the controversy supports social and psychological disengagement, most does not.

Activity theory, conversely, states that continued social interaction and productivity are essential to a sense of well-being and life satisfaction in old age. It suggests that it is healthy for older people to continue roles that were held in middle age for as long as possible. The more active an older person is, the more likely he or she is to experience a higher level of satisfaction with life. This may be true as a general rule, but activity is certainly not a predictor, in and of itself, of life satisfaction for everyone. Nonetheless, a well-known study investigated the controversy of engagement versus disengagement (Neugarten, Havighurst, & Tobin, 1968) and demonstrated that involvement and activity were, more often than not, associated with life satisfaction.

Substitution theory (Tepper, 1994) has emerged from the activity and disengagement theories to consider the pros and cons of activity and disengagement. It is based on factors such as previous personality, likes and dislikes, physical and mental health, attitudes toward former and current social and work roles, and identities that have been especially rewarding to the older person. It acknowledges activity and involvement as important for life satisfaction but recognizes that certain social and work roles are disengaged from either voluntarily or involuntarily because of predetermined rules (such as retirement), chance (such as marriage and parenthood), economic reasons (such as retirement, insufficient social or private pension income, and recession), or health factors (such as sensory losses, arthritis, and reduced energy levels). Substitution theory suggests that as individuals age, they substitute new activities, interests, involvements, and people for those from which they have disengaged. It suggests that a certain level of activity be maintained (i.e., not increased or decreased) that will ensure a continuation of life satisfaction and not compromise quality of life.

A *continuity theory of aging* (Kahana & Kahana, 1982) focused on the efforts of adults to maintain the basic structures of their lives as they grow older. This involves applying familiar strategies to daily life and using past experiences as a guide, keeping stable some aspects of the external environment such as neighborhood, friends, and rewarding activities. Atchley (1989) views continuity as a preferred strategy for dealing with aging. Both internal continuity (a sense of competence, integrity, and identity) and external continuity (continuing one's ongoing roles in the family and community, thereby affirming self-esteem by positive long-term relationships and associations) help older people focus on and maintain their strengths and minimize the effects of deficits that are part of normal aging. Strong ethnic identity certainly fits into this theory as a source of positive self-image and ego integrity, which can translate into good mental health.

When some of these theories were initially postulated, "the elderly" were seen as a representative group with only chronological age as a requirement for membership. As there is no theory of ethnic aging or of family relationships among aging families in various ethnic groups, do the four theories have equal application to all ethnic groups? What role do families of ethnic elders play in influencing patterns of aging? Do ethnic and cultural identity influence the aging pattern one follows in later life and its effects on families as they age?

The older person's ethnic identity may lend support to the assumptions of activity theory. For example, many older African American women continue to play a caregiving role to grandchildren and great-grandchildren as a result of family role expectations. For some older persons, activity levels may actually rise because of renewed interest in ethnically based religious and community functions. The new role of passing on specific cultural history, attitudes, and values may be a source of status. Continuity theory may be demonstrated by the older person's need to maintain a meaningful role within the family. When opportunities for family role continuity become less available, many elders volunteer in settings where family-like ties can be substituted, such as hospitals and public schools. New caregiving roles may also be substituted for old ones within families, as when providing care to a spouse or elderly parent or to grandchildren after the death of an adult child.

One positive effect of ethnic identity in later life can be seen in the context of the "age as a leveler" concept (Rose, 1965). An early idea in the field of gerontology, it states that, as we age, all of our prior individual differences become less important. Being "elderly" becomes the primary determinant of identification. Not recognizing differences among older people in values, norms, temperament, and skills, this concept may lump them together into one stereotyped image of a frail and less capable group (Gelfand, 1994). Ethnic identity certainly counteracts this concept, drawing attention to the diversity between older people. Families may need help in understanding that they should not stereotype an older family member as "just another old person," thereby disengaging those members from important family roles with their concomitant expectations.

Adaptation to the many losses related to aging is one of the primary determinants of mental health in later life. These losses include a shrinking social world, with established networks of friends and relatives lost through geographic mobility and through death; loss of income and possibly economic security resulting from retirement; loss of heath status and physical functions; and loss of status due to the negative stereotypes related to aging and being old in American culture. Coping and the ability to substitute new activities and associations for some of those lost as a result of aging (Tepper, 1994) may be enhanced through ethnic identity. Gelfand (1994) believes that an ethnic background may provide an "alternative compensation" through association with ethnic organizations and involvement in social issues that affect the ethnic community. Well-defined roles for older people are provided by many ethnic groups by increasing family and community responsibilities, including the passing on of values, morals, and traditions of their culture to younger generations.

WORKING WITH
CULTURALLY DIVERSE AGING FAMILIES

Man Keung Ho (1987) reviews dimensions of cultural value preferences that are particularly helpful in understanding and working with older families. For example, time orientation differs for White middle-class Americans, who are future-oriented; Asian and Hispanic Americans, who are past-present-oriented; and Native Americans and African Americans, who are present-oriented. As a consequence of these differences, most ethnic minorities will be more concerned with solving specific, immediate problems than with working toward future-oriented goals (Ho, 1987). This may conflict with the longer-range planning a White middle-class worker may have in mind.

Regarding relations with people, whereas the White middle class tends toward individual autonomy, ethnic minorities embrace collectivity (Ho, 1987). Ethnic minority families generally feel a strong responsibility to care for aged family members, sometimes making it difficult to seek or accept outside help they desperately need. Because ethnic minorities have more extended family ties than does the White middle class, which tends to be oriented around the nuclear family (Ho, 1987), the extended-family network may be both a source of help and an impediment when help is needed. Adult children, especially daughters, may feel responsible for providing for parents, and their failure to do so may reflect badly on the entire family.

In work with aging families, the worker must consider the diversity both among and within different cultures and the potential differences between generations in a single family.

Changing work and family roles may influence family relationships. Retirement often reduces the individual's work identity and in many instances lessens social contact as well. Although family relationships tend to continue, family role changes influence the intensity of these relationships. Middle age is marked by one's children becoming increasingly independent, starting their own families and developing their own careers. This often results in a reduction in actual contact and direct family responsibility for parents. As parents grow old, both retirement from work and changing family roles may contribute to a need to return to more familiar and socially rewarding relationships. Ethnically sponsored organizations, ranging from church or synagogue sponsorship to private organizations, are a source of attachment and satisfaction for many ethnic elderly.

They may also be a source of services when the need arises. Sponsorship of services often influences whether those in need take advantage of them. Within the past decade there has been increasing attention in community services, such as senior services, nutrition sites, health-related programs, and case management, to ethnically diversified programming and provision of workers and resources that are representative of the cultures to be serviced and ethnically sensitive to their needs.

Ethnicity may influence intergenerational issues when resulting in differences between generations that are related to becoming acculturated or assimilated. Each successive generation may achieve its own personal identity by adapting values and behaviors that may conflict with the Old World values and behaviors of past generations. The first generation of an ethnic family may be bound together by very close ties. The second generation, however, is expected to become "successful" in the majority culture and to retain strong ties with their cultural heritage. Some may feel conflicted in these expectations; some may be able to balance both expectations. The third generation may feel that the ethnic identifies may actually interfere with American cultural identity and expectations and reject ethnic ties to the older generation. These largely Americanized children of first-generation American-born parents may be part of the inevitable mass of the "superassimilated," who have little if any ethnic ties to the past. This may change caregiving roles, resulting in the use of more formal (outside) caregivers, which may create tensions between generations.

The worker must always be cognizant of the family's cultural heritage and the potential for differences in how this heritage influences various family members. In addition, offering services to persons from different cultures demands of the worker a knowledge of and sensitivity to how the family's understanding of their situation, their definition of the problems, and potential solutions to problems are perceived and experienced. Both cultural and family history must be taken into account. The worker with aging families must be sensitive to issues related to both ethnicity and aging as they are currently played out and in a historical context as well. The following two cases demonstrate the impact of cultural history on current practice with culturally diverse clients.

CASE EXAMPLES

Mrs. Smith

A 76-year-old African American woman, Mrs. Smith was brought to a hospital clinic by her son for diagnosis of a breast mass. Mrs. Smith was born in a small town in the South, where there was no access to traditional medical care. Her mother was the community midwife and healer, and Mrs. Smith had practiced herbal medicine all of her life, as did her ancestors. She had always been in good health. When she married, she moved to a large northern city, where she raised her four children and worked as a home attendant. Thirty years ago, Mrs. Smith was hospitalized after a serious accident, needing extensive surgery. During this hospitalization she was treated disrespectfully, and she has not turned to traditional medical care since that time. Since her retirement 10 years ago, Mrs. Smith has lived with her son and has been a caregiver for her grandchildren.

Mrs. Smith was reluctant to come for traditional medical care after having had such a demeaning experience many years ago. However, her efforts to treat her breast mass for a year had been unsuccessful, and her children prevailed upon her to go to the hospital.

The social worker recognized that Mrs. Smith's health care beliefs, strongly rooted in the culture in which she grew up, and her history of a dehumanizing experience with the health care system were factors that needed to be recognized and respected. Mrs. Smith had clearly been successful in her efforts at self-care, needing to use traditional medical care only once before in her 76 years. She was also clearly an independent woman who had continued a role of great responsibility in her family. Her son, more accustomed to mainstream medical care, encouraged Mrs. Smith to seek help but was respectful of her hesitancy.

With the son's support, the social worker discussed the doctor's recommendation of a biopsy as offering an opportunity for Mrs. Smith to gather more information about her condition so that she could make an informed decision about her care. Mrs. Smith expressed concern that the mass was cancer and agreed that a biopsy would answer this question. The social worker emphasized that if this was the case, Mrs. Smith was the one who would then decide what to do. From the information she had obtained about Mrs. Smith and her family, the social worker was able to identify the son who had brought Mrs. Smith to the hospital as the primary decision maker in the family. Consequently, she was careful to engage the son's support in her approach while at the same time respecting Mrs. Smith's expertise about her own health care and her control of this decision. Mrs. Smith agreed to have the biopsy.

Mr. and Mrs. Rubenstein

Mr. and Mrs. Rubenstein, he in his early eighties and she in her late seventies, are Holocaust survivors who met after they came to the United

States following the war. They were the only ones from their respective families to survive the Holocaust, and they spoke very little about their war experiences with anyone. Mr. Rubenstein worked as a tailor in this country and was able to provide a modest but comfortable lifestyle for his family. The couple's two children are well educated and financially secure.

Over the past 4 years, Mr. Rubenstein had been exhibiting symptoms of Alzheimer's disease and had become increasingly dependent on his wife. The couple's two children initiated the request for help when it became clear that the stress of caregiving was taking a tremendous toll on Mrs. Rubenstein. Mrs. Rubenstein was receptive to the idea of respite, although she did not want her husband cared for by non-Jewish caregivers. Initially, a referral was made to a Jewish agency, and Mr. Rubenstein attended their day program. After a year, however, Mr. Rubenstein's condition had deteriorated to the point that he was incontinent and increasingly disoriented, and he wandered if he was not closely watched. In addition, he had become so suspicious that it was difficult for his wife to leave him.

At this point the children raised the possibility of placement in a nursing home. Mrs. Rubenstein was adamant about not "incarcerating" her husband. She felt a strong sense of obligation to her husband and to the memory of their families. Having survived the Holocaust, she felt that keeping her husband out of an institution gave meaning to her survival. Her felt need to honor her memories, do her moral duty, and maintain her financial legacy to her grandchildren all blocked her ability to accept or even consider nursing home care.

The social worker involved in the case at this time recognized and honored Mrs. Rubenstein's strong commitment to her husband and her history. Issues of past loss had to be addressed before Mrs. Rubenstein could even consider planning for the future. Work with these issues was slow and painful. Over time, as Mrs. Rubenstein became more accepting of help, a patchwork of services was put together to help her maintain her husband in the home until such time, if ever, as she could consider placement.

Mrs. Rubenstein was encouraged to attend a support group for caregivers, which she did eventually join. Neither of her children was willing to attend the support group. The social worker worked with the adult children to help them understand their mother's decision to keep her husband at home, a decision they strongly disagreed with. They were able to find ways to be of assistance to their mother through providing emotional and financial support. Mrs. Rubenstein's children had a view of the best solution to this family crisis that was very different from their mother's, but they were helped to see that the decision was out of their hands.

As the cases of Mrs. Smith and Mr. and Mrs. Rubenstein demonstrate, frequently the request for help comes not from the older person but from concerned family members. The worker has a dual responsibility in such instances: ensuring that the older person's wants and needs are recognized and respected and ensuring that the family members, who may view the situation quite differently, are involved in the work and helped to understand their older relative's perspective.

The following two case examples demonstrate the importance of considering ways in which a family's cultural background affects decision making and receptiveness to services.

The Ruiz Family

Mrs. Ruiz, a 78-year-old Puerto Rican widow and mother of three, had lived for several years with her middle-aged daughter Louisa in her daughter's third-floor walk-up. Her other daughter and her son, married and with children of their own, lived some distance away but visited Mrs. Ruiz regularly and maintained close family ties. In recent years, Mrs. Ruiz had become increasingly infirm and feeble and required considerable care. During her mother's hospitalization for a respiratory infection, Louisa and the hospital social worker arranged nursing home placement. This occurred despite the pressure put on Louisa by the rest of the family to bring her mother back to her home after discharge.

Louisa told the nursing home social worker that even though she no longer felt able to continue caring for her mother, her siblings expected that she, as the single daughter, would do so. She felt ongoing pressure to take her mother home. The difficulty was compounded by the fact that Mrs. Ruiz spoke no English, and none of the residents or staff on her floor spoke Spanish. Consequently, she was unable to communicate her needs and became depressed and withdrawn.

The nursing home social worker advocated getting Mrs. Ruiz transferred to a floor where there were some Spanish-speaking staff and residents. She developed a good relationship with Louisa and, at Louisa's request, arranged a family meeting when her siblings were in town. At this meeting the social worker and one of the floor nurses explained their perceptions of the extent of Mrs. Ruiz's needs and how the nursing home could meet these needs. Louisa's brother and sister were relieved to see that their mother was no longer withdrawn and was interacting with the Spanish-speaking residents. They seemed to feel better about their mother's placement as the meeting progressed. However, after the meeting, Louisa's sister questioned how her mother could be happy living in a nursing home and how the family could live with this outcome.

The social worker identified two ongoing tasks in her work with this family. First, she would continue supporting Louisa as she dealt with the pressures from her siblings generated by their ambivalence about nursing home placement. In Puerto Rican families children are expected to care for their aging parents (Garcia-Preto, 1982). Louisa had gone against the family's strong cultural expectations that she, the unmarried daughter, would continue providing her mother's care. The family remained deeply involved with their mother, visiting regularly and maintaining ongoing contact with nursing home staff by telephone, but they continued to pressure Louisa to take her mother home.

The second task the worker faced was working within the nursing home to help all levels of staff develop a greater sensitivity to Puerto Rican culture. This nursing home was not oriented to a Hispanic population but, as the neighborhood in which it was located changed, Hispanic residents had been admitted. The facility had not yet developed procedures for ensuring that Hispanic residents' needs were immediately recognized and addressed.

The Paltesevic Family

The Paltesevic family had emigrated from Albania to the United States 3 years before they came to the attention of the school social worker. Grandfather, grandmother, father, mother, and 6-year-old Merlin all lived together in a small but adequate apartment. The senior Mr. Paltesevic was a strong, dominant man, clearly the head of the family. His son, also a strong man, deferred to his father. The grandmother spoke very little English and always dressed in a long black dress and a babushka. The mother, although less traditionally dressed than the senior Mrs. Paltesevic and more conversant in English, was very quiet and deferred to the men in the family.

Merlin's grandparents often picked him up after school. The grandfather developed a good relationship with Merlin's first-grade teacher, and whenever he saw her, he asked of his grandson, "Is he good?" Although doing well in school, Merlin was not learning as quickly as he could, given his natural intelligence. The teacher sensed that he felt a great deal of pressure to do well and became paralyzed by this. As the year progressed, he became quiet and appeared sad, and his schoolwork began to suffer. The teacher was hesitant to let the grandfather know that Merlin was experiencing difficulties as she was afraid this would result in more pressure at home. According to Merlin, his grandfather sat with him while he did his homework and made him redo it until it was perfect.

The teacher turned to the school social worker, who invited Merlin's parents and grandparents in for a meeting. All four adults, clearly concerned and committed to the child's welfare came in. The men in this family were in charge of everything except the running of the household, and the senior Mr. Paltesevic clearly was the most powerful force in the family. Recognizing this, the social worker directed her attention to engaging him in helping her puzzle out the best way to help Merlin. In their discussion it became clear that the grandfather felt he was responsible for his family's well-being in all areas, and this was, to some extent, a burden for him. Because Mr. Paltesevic had a good relationship with the teacher, the social worker worked toward helping him see the teacher as a partner in Merlin's schooling. His important role in the family was recognized and respected, but he was also offered a way to be relieved of some of his responsibility by suggesting that he let the teacher be more responsible for helping Merlin learn.

CONCLUSION

As the older population increases in size and diversity, social workers should keep several factors in mind. First, older persons are generally integral parts of their families, often providing help and care to other family members or receiving care themselves. Second, older people's ethnicity and cultural heritage may have a strong influence on how they and their families experience and cope with aging-related changes. Third, ethnicity and cultural heritage may also affect the way help is sought, interpreted, and received. Finally, members of different generations within the family may have very different views of the nature of aging-related difficulties and the best solutions to these difficulties.

To effectively serve culturally diverse older families, social workers draw primarily on two knowledge bases: aging and diversity, always being sensitive to the interactions between the two. The four cases considered here offer examples of the range of situations workers may find themselves dealing with. In each case, the worker was effective because she understood and worked within the cultural context of the client. This is the key to successful work with the aging family.

REFERENCES

Anderson, D. (1988). The quest for a meaningful old age. *Family Therapy Networker, 12*(4), 17–22, 72–75.

Atchley, R. (1989). A continuity theory of normal aging. *Gerontologist, 29,* 183–190.

Bengston, V., Rosenthal, C., & Burton, L. (1990). Families and aging: Diversity and heterogeneity. In R. H. Binstock & L. K. George (Eds.), *Handbook of aging and the social sciences* (pp. 19–44). San Diego, CA: Academic.

Burton, L. M. (1992). Black grandparents rearing children of drug addicted parents: Stressors, outcomes, and social service needs. *Gerontologist, 32,* 744–751.

Butler, R., & Lewis, M. (1986). *Aging and mental health: Positive psychosocial approaches.* New York: Mosby.

Chappell, N. L. (1990). Aging and social care. In R. H. Binstock & L. K. George (Eds.), *Handbook of aging and the social sciences* (pp. 438–454). San Diego, CA: Academic.

Congress, E., & Johns, M. (1994). Cultural diversity and practice with older people. In I. A. Gutheil (Ed.), *Work with older people* (pp. 65–84). New York: Fordham University Press.

Cumming, E., & Henry, W. E. (1961). *Growing old: The process of disengagement.* New York: Basic.

Garcia-Preto, N. (1982). Puerto Rican families. In M. McGoldrick, J. K. Pearce, & J. Giordano (Eds.), *Ethnicity and family therapy* (pp. 164–186). New York: Guilford.

Gelfand, D. E. (1982). *Aging: The ethnic factor.* Boston: Little, Brown.

Gelfand, D. E. (1994). *Aging and ethnicity: Knowledge and services.* New York: Springer.

Gelfand, D. E., & Fandetti, D. V. (1986). The emergent nature of ethnicity: Dilemmas in assessment. *Social Casework, 67,* 542–550.

Greenberg, J. S., & Becker, M. (1988). Aging parents as family resources. *Gerontologist, 28,* 786–791.

Himes, C. L. (1992). Social demography of contemporary families and aging. *Generations, 17*(3), 13–16.

Ho, M. K. (1987). *Family therapy with ethnic minorities.* Newbury Park, CA: Sage.

Jackson, J. (1980). *Minorities and aging.* Belmont, Ca: Wadsworth.

Kahana, B., & Kahana, E. (1982). Environmental continuity, futurity, and adaptation of the aged. In G. Rowles & R. Ohat (Eds.), *Aging and milieu: Environmental perspectives on growing old* (pp. 205–228). New York: Academic.

Myers, G. C. (1990). Demography of aging. In R. H. Binstock & L. K. George (Eds.), *Handbook of aging and the social sciences* (pp. 19–44). San Diego, CA: Academic.

Neugarten, B. (1973). Personality change in later life: A developmental perspective. In C. Eisdorfer & M. P. Lawton (Eds.), *The psychology of adult development and aging* (pp. 311–338). Washington, DC: American Psychological Association.

Neugarten, B., Havighurst, R. J., & Tobin, S. (1968). Personality and patterns of aging. In B. Neugarten (Ed.), *Middle age and aging* (pp. 173–177). Chicago: University of Chicago Press.

Rose, A. (1965). The subculture of the aging: A framework in social gerontology. In A. Rose & W. Peterson (Eds.), *Older people and their social worlds.* Philadelphia: Davis.

Tepper, L. (1994). Developmental theories in the second half of life. In I. A. Gutheil (Ed.), *Work with older people* (pp. 29–41). New York: Fordham University Press.

SECTION **THREE**

Selected
Culturally Diverse Populations

CHAPTER 7

Motherless Children:
Family Interventions
with AIDS Orphans

Kathleen Romano
Luis H. Zayas

By the end of this century, about 100,000 children and adolescents are expected to have lost their mothers to HIV infection and AIDS in the United States (Michaels & Levine, 1992). New York, the hardest-hit city in the nation, will account for some 30,000 of these youngsters. More than 80% will be ethnic minorities, primarily Latino and African American (Levine & Stein, 1994), from inner-city communities such as the South Bronx, the epicenter of heterosexual HIV in New York City.

The Centers for Disease Control and Prevention (CDCP), the World Health Organization (WHO), and the United Nations Children's Fund (UNICEF) currently define *orphan* to mean children whose mothers have

Acknowledgment: Support for Luis Zayas's work on this chapter was provided, in part, by the Cultural and Economic Diversity Award of the American Family Therapy Academy. Partial support for Kathleen Romano's work on this chapter was provided by grant number BRH 970165-02-0 from the Health Resources and Services Administration. Its contents are solely the responsibility of the authors and do not necessarily represent the official views of HRSA.

died. This is particularly the case when referring to orphans of the AIDS epidemic in the United States. Though exact statistics are not known, the majority of families affected by HIV infection and illness are headed by women, with fathers or fathering figures present only intermittently.

Most of the children who are or will be orphaned by AIDS are not HIV-infected themselves. In many ways, they are similar to other grieving children who have lost their parents (Altschul, 1988), and they are also similar to those in their communities who have been exposed to poverty, discrimination, and violence. Unlike other children who have suffered parental loss, however, AIDS orphans must deal with the stigma, secrecy, and isolation that comes from being affected by an illness that provokes so much open hostility and misunderstanding in the country at large.

Mental health care, including bereavement counseling, for these children heads the list of services recommended by the Orphan Project, a research study designed to explore policy options to meet the needs of HIV-affected children and young adults (Levine & Stein, 1994). Because children are rarely the most powerful members of their families, nearly all the interventions that improve their lives are family interventions. This is true even when all or most family members are not directly engaged in the treatment effort. In discussing her multisystems approach to African American families in therapy, Nancy Boyd-Franklin (1989) says that it is not unusual for one person to be sent for therapy while the rest of the family watches and waits. In our experience this one person is often a child or adolescent. If family members notice positive changes in this youngster, others can then venture in, either individually or in conjunction with the original patient.

The families we deal with in our practices come in many different configurations and stages of development. One, of course, is the one most commonly thought of as "the family," with mother, father, and children. More common is the single mother with children, sometimes with a male or, less often, a female step-parent, with or without extended family input and support. Children may also be living with one or more grandparents, aunts, uncles, or other extended-family members who may or may not be related by blood. They may be in foster families or adopted by people who are not connected to the family in any way. Finally, they may be in a stage of transition from one type of family to another. Assessing bereaved children requires that we weigh the interaction among individual factors of childhood bereavement with family (nuclear and extended) factors, death-related factors, and the child and family's social, religious, and cultural background (Papadatou & Papadatou, 1991; Wass & Corr, 1982; Webb, 1993).

In this chapter we discuss children's and adolescents' reactions to parental HIV and AIDS; the way families deal with AIDS and death, focusing particularly on African American and Latino families; and interventions that have proved helpful in assisting children and their families through these difficult times.

BEHAVIORAL REACTIONS
AND PSYCHOLOGICAL NEEDS

The impact of the announcement that a parent is HIV-positive, and to the loss that that announcement immediately conjures up almost invariably leads to depression. Depression can be manifested as withdrawal, isolation, moodiness, argumentativeness, irritability, changes in appetite and sleep, and problems in concentration. The painful feelings can also be masked by more externalized behaviors, such as risk taking and provocativeness. Fighting in school and on the street is not uncommon.

> Kamal's mother died of AIDS when he was 15. In a group workshop with the authors, Kamal told how he had taken care of his mother before she died. Her medical status inevitably worsened. On the night of her death he had gone to sleep with her, as he had often done before, to be near her, both for his own comfort and to be available to help her if she needed him. In the early hours of the morning, Kamal awoke to find his mother dead. Her body was, as he said, "crazy cold." Frightened and panicked, he ran into the street, not knowing what to do, and punched the first person he saw.

An associated manifestation of depression may be the initiation of or increase in drug and alcohol use for their numbing effects. Easy access to these substances, combined with unremitting emotional distress, can turn use to abuse rather quickly in a youngster. In addition, early adolescence can begin a more actively self-destructive phase, with the possibility of suicidal ideation, gestures, and acts, in reaction to parental HIV infection or AIDS.

> Twelve-year-old Maria, who expressed suicidal ideation after learning that her mother was HIV-positive, said that she didn't think she could tolerate her

mother's dying and didn't think she could live if that happened. A very intelligent girl, Maria often got into trouble in school for arguing with teachers or administrators and was expelled for 5 days for a fight with another classmate over how Maria's mother got AIDS. That weekend Maria was hospitalized for her first suicidal gesture.

Acting-out disorders in school and complaints of disciplinary problems at home are most likely to emerge in the preadolescent to adolescent years, but they can occur at any age.

Yvette was little more than a year old when her mother, Carol, gave birth to a very sickly boy with AIDS and also learned of her own HIV-positive status. The next 2 years were chaotic for Yvette, tagging along with her mother to frequent medical appointments for the baby and moving four times as a result of her mother's efforts to find decent, stable housing for her family (which also included Yvette's older sister and sometimes their father). As her mother's health deteriorated, neighbors became concerned about her ability to care for her children and called Child Protective Services. For a year, Yvette and her sister stayed in a foster home, and their brother was placed in a residence for young children with HIV/AIDS. A few months before Carol died, Yvette's paternal grandmother took custody of the girls, allowing them more contact with their dying mother and their intermittently drug-abusing father. The grandmother was involved in a custody battle for the 5-year-old grand-niece she had raised since the age of 2 weeks but whose mother's parental rights were never terminated. Yvette was brought for therapy with the complaint of school behavior problems at the end of kindergarten year, after school officials had determined that Yvette would not be allowed to attend any field trips with her class because of behavior dangerous to herself and others.

Concern may be expressed as anger or as feelings of guilt and responsibility toward the parent, as in Kamal's story. The acting out may be confirmed by teachers, counselors, and adult family members around the youngster, or the described behavior may be a distortion filtered through the dying parent's own pain and suffering.

At the extreme of acting-out behaviors may be anger that leads to violence and criminal activities within the community. Bobby's case is an example of this behavioral reaction.

Bobby was a 15-year-old Puerto Rican boy whose mother had AIDS. Through the emotional and physical pain of her illness, his mother projected onto him her own poor self-image and hatred for Bobby's incarcerated father. She belittled Bobby as she had always done and expressed disappointment in him, saying that he was bad and that she had always thought so. Bobby's depression and his lifelong tendency to stay out of the house for long hours and out of his mother's "line of fire" converted to even longer hours out of the home and increased risk taking (e.g., carrying bullets or holding guns for his friends and associating with peers who were known to be armed drug dealers). Bobby was arrested three times in a period of 2 months, each time as an accessory or "being in the wrong place at the wrong time." He was once stabbed in the arm when held up by rival neighborhood drug dealers.

Another reaction often seen in middle childhood and adolescence is that of overcompensation for the loss of parental functioning by assuming caretaking roles for the parent and siblings. Adolescents may be called on to make adult decisions and to be responsible for household chores and child care while also attending school. Some children respond to such demands by becoming "superchildren" who immerse themselves in these activities to keep busy and avoid facing the painful reality of the impending loss (Zayas & Romano, 1994). A secondary motivation may be to get the attention and approval of the ill or dying parent, who may have been too involved with drug use in the past to pay much attention to the child. The behavior may also convey a sense of readiness to take on life's tasks in the absence of the parent.

José, 12, came to New York City 2 months after his mother died of AIDS in Puerto Rico, where he had spent his entire life until then. The youngster told his therapist how he and his older brother took care of their mother when she was strung out on crack cocaine and prostituting to make money for her habit. In sessions he talked about the many times he had prepared dinner when he was only 8 years old and had left the food warming while he went into the street to search for his mother. His brother and he would find her high on drugs, bring her home, and, together, would wash her, dress her, feed her, and put her to bed. He spoke with pride of his ability to cook modest Puerto Rican dishes.

For many months prior to his mother's death, both José's extended family and his friends' parents invited him to stay in their homes, some even offering him a permanent home. Each time, José insisted that he had to remain with his mother despite her severe drug problems and worsening illness. He said that, in retrospect, he knew she had AIDS and refused the many offers because he knew someone had to take care of his mother. As his mother became sicker and weaker and the realization of her illness broke through José's denial, he sought the refuge of friends' and relatives' homes, moving from home to home but finding little solace. Now he says, with a disquieting but poignant maturity, "I have got to be prepared for anything in life."

At the opposite end of the spectrum from the superchildren are the adolescents who distance themselves from the fact of the presence of HIV in a parent. Running away or simply staying out of the house for extended periods during the day are coping responses that may be developmentally related. Distancing not only allows for time and space away from the parent and the pain, but it may also bring the child or adolescent closer to uninfected persons, such as a friend's parents (a form of adopting a new, uninfected family).

Healthy denial may be interpreted as distancing, but it is not. Some denial helps maintain involvement in daily routine. It may be adaptive over a long illness but if overused can leave the youngster unprepared for the parent(s)' death and can add to the confusion and distress of the terminal phase.

The stress of dealing with a parental diagnosis that positively connotes death can cause regression to earlier developmental levels of functioning. Younger children may develop enuresis and encopresis after years of adequate control. A common reaction among teenagers is to go back and forth between adult and child behavior. Unlike younger children, however, adolescents often have a more realistic idea of death. They are curious about its biology, and their desire for details may seem macabre to adults. Normative developmental fantasies of parents' deaths take on a grim reality.

FAMILY REACTIONS

In some families stigma and secrecy make children's and adolescents' adjustment to HIV and AIDS very difficult (Tasker, 1992). The stigma attached to HIV and AIDS remains, despite nearly two decades of knowledge about it. This stigma comes from the history of HIV and AIDS being first reported in a group that was already highly stigmatized— homosexuals. Intravenous drug users, the second group associated with the disease, have never been held in very high regard either. The fact that the virus can be transmitted sexually adds to the difficulty of talking about it because of a general societal discomfort about discussing sex.

Add to this the anxiety raised by any terminal illness (Jewett, 1982). As Becker (1973) pointed out, this anxiety causes those not directly affected to withdraw from the dying person and his or her family. The silence of this isolation engenders a feeling of shame in those affected, particularly in children and adolescents, who do not have the sophistication to realize that others are responding to their own fear of death.

Many persons affected by HIV/AIDS feel a need to hide their diagnosis from their families and communities. Children are excluded by parents, and the secret is kept from them, or they are included in the conspiracy of silence surrounding the illness. This tends to isolate the family and the children within the family from possible sources of support in both the extended family and the community. Often, this secrecy leaves the adolescent without anyone outside the family, whose members are already involved in the emotional turmoil, with whom to share and discuss the illness and its anticipated aftermath of death, family disruption, feelings of abandonment, loss, and fear.

> Willie, a good-looking 14-year-old boy, was the family's sole bearer of his mother's secret. They both said that they had seen family members use disposable plates and utensils when there was a chance that they were dealing with someone with HIV, and they didn't want to become victim to that sort of discrimination. Willie seemed to do well in all areas of his life but had difficulty sleeping and had become nervous and irritable during the day. When psychotherapy was offered, he could not explain what he thought it was or how he would use it, but he knew he wanted it. With a place to be free to ask his questions and vent his feelings, he relaxed and resumed the hypersomnia of a teenage boy.

Among the reasons families keep HIV infection a secret from their children is the parents' own sense that they are abandoning their children. HIV and AIDS forces an erosion of the parents' idealization of their importance to the child. Consciously or unconsciously, dying parents recognize that someone else will parent their child once they are dead, eclipsing their presence in the child's life and their effect on the child's values, development, maturity, growth, and behavior. In many ways, HIV/AIDS is linked to thoughts such as "I have not been a good parent" and "I am abandoning my children by dying." This can lead to an overprotection of the children, with a myriad of rationalizations about why the diagnosis cannot be disclosed.

Although secrecy and denial are potent mechanisms used by parents to protect themselves and their children from the overwhelming feelings they face, the physical deterioration forces a confrontation with the illness as a family matter that is undeniable. Having to keep the secret deprives the child of the opportunity to discuss the situation with the parents and prepare for future bouts of illness and the prospect of the parent's death. When the secret is kept from adolescent children, parents often find that the youngster has known all along and has been keeping that secret to protect the parent. This is especially true when the parent has been battling HIV-related illnesses requiring lengthy hospitalizations and frequent clinic visits. Once the diagnosis is out in the open, however, the chances of helping children deal with it increase. Younger children are aware, on some level, of some danger to the parent but generally cannot verbalize it too clearly.

FAMILY INTERVENTIONS

Here it is important to restate the rationale for our broad qualifications for a family intervention. Even when we are working individually with a child or adolescent, the family is involved. For the child that involvement is fairly direct, if only in the need for an adult family member or guardian to take responsibility to ensure that the child gets to the clinic for therapy appointments. Frequently, that adult will meet with the therapist to report on the child's progress and/or discuss new issues as they arise.

With teenagers, the adult is not necessarily that involved. Teenagers, after all, can usually be expected to be responsible for keeping their own clinic appointments. They do not usually want their parents or guardians informed about what goes on in their therapy. The standard therapy with teens, however, involves exploring their relationships with the adults in their lives, with an eye to identifying those who will listen and advise and on whom they can rely.

Interventions with some families take place periodically over several years, focusing on different issues as the illness develops and its consequences become clearer. Interventions can also take place many years after the death of the parent. Frequently, in cases involving child and adolescent orphans, adult family members and therapists must make decisions that are intended to be in the best interest of the child when the child cannot or will not participate in decision making. Often, the therapist becomes involved with the family—something like an unofficial elder—and works with different configurations of family members on numerous issues over the years of involvement.

The final section of this chapter presents case examples of the four types of interventions mentioned above.

Example 1: Periodic Interventions

Segunda brought her daughter, Frieda, then age 14, to therapy shortly after Segunda, 35, tested positive for HIV infection and disclosed her status to her daughter. Jessenia stayed in therapy for a couple of months, getting over the shock of her mother's announcement and encouraging her mother to disclose the information to Frieda's father, who lived in New Jersey with his wife and two children. Frieda was supported in her attempts to connect with her father so that he would be emotionally available to her in the years to come. With her connection to her father more obvious and her mother's health improving, Frieda decided to leave therapy.

Several months later, Frieda called her therapist to talk about her mother's brother, who was then dying of AIDS. During the next few months, Frieda again attended therapy sessions to talk about her uncle, her mother, and her concerns for herself. After Frieda felt that she had sufficiently processed her uncle's death and funeral, she requested another pause in the sessions. Her mother's health was still relatively good.

Now 17, Frieda has been attending weekly individual therapy, with an occasional mother-daughter session, at her own request; this was precipitated by an organically induced psychotic episode in her mother 5 months ago. Early sessions in this most recent series dealt with helping Frieda understand what had happened to her mother and what was being done to prevent it from happening again. Frieda, motivated by what she had seen happen to her mother, was helped to think about and decide whom she most wanted to be with if her mother became incapable of caring for her and was supported in communicating her wishes to her mother. Segunda was then assisted in filing the necessary paperwork with the courts.

In therapy, Frieda has come to terms with her father's inability to be there for her in the way that she would like. Her struggle to compose a letter to him, at the encouragement of her therapist, has sparked a desire in Frieda to write. She now includes poetry in her repertoire and uses it to express the pain and fear she feels when she thinks about her mother's death.

Example 2: Post-Loss Intervention

Domingo was 9 years old and halfway through fifth grade when his grandmother brought him to therapy. His mother had died just before his first birthday, and his grandmother had raised him as her own child. He called her Mommy and her boyfriend Daddy. Domingo was never told how his mother died, but he had his suspicions, and he was pretty sure that his father was dead too. This was the third year that his behavior was reported as a problem in school, and the principal of his parochial school said he would not be allowed to register for the sixth year unless there was big improvement before the fifth year ended.

Domingo's grandmother refused all attempts at a family intervention. She was committed to keeping him, but she wanted him to start behaving in school and to stop causing her stress and inconvenience. In individual play therapy, Domingo learned to channel his anxiety and confusion into fantasy aggressive reenactments and structured games. He explored his ability to nurture and take care of himself, as well as his ability to persevere and follow through.

School behavior, good through most of sixth-grade year, did not improve in time to save the fifth-grade year, and Domingo transferred to another parochial school. When the behavior did get better, though, Grandmother wanted to end therapy, citing convenience as an issue. The therapist recommended against it, and Domingo, then 10, requested that he be allowed to continue. Grandmother acceded to this request, but she no longer maintains much contact with the therapist. Domingo, who never misses a session, has begun the transition from play therapy to the more adolescent one of learning how to negotiate with the adults in his environment.

Example 3: Making the Decisions

As family-oriented therapists, we find that providing a child with some continuity to his past, present, and future families is an important part of our work with AIDS orphans. Because personal identity is closely tied to one's family history, it becomes essential for families and therapists to create opportunities for AIDS orphans to rediscover and rework their family past. These opportunities can come in many ways. As the following case shows, the therapist and adoptive father collected objects from the child's family of origin to provide this necessary continuity despite the child's current lack of interest in maintaining a tie to his parents and sister.

Tomas, 8, and his standby guardian and prospective adoptive father, Jeff, were referred by their caseworker to prepare them for the adoption. Tomas had lost his mother several months before coming to therapy and a 5-year-old sister a year earlier—both to AIDS. His father was now hospitalized for AIDS and was not expected to be discharged from the hospital alive. There were no known surviving relatives. Tomas often refused to visit his father in the hospital; when he did visit, Tomas sat on the end of the bed with his back toward his father. The guardian asked for help in the transition to the adoption, which would come at his father's death.

Tomas told the therapist that he did not look sad or ask about his family but said that ''I mainly get sad in my head.'' Tomas would often ask Jeff if he would be removed from Jeff's house someday. Tomas hoarded food and objects in Jeff's house, symbolic of his need to maintain some continuity in his life and prepare for the inevitable day in which he would be removed from Jeff's home. Tomas was worried with ''not bothering'' Jeff so that he would not be asked to leave Jeff's home; Jeff assured him that they would remain together. Numerous other incidents indicated Tomas's distress and worries about his future, including asking to take Jeff's surname as his. In a session with the therapist it was agreed that Tomas could keep his own and add Jeff's surname.

As a new father, Jeff was sensitive to Tomas's need for some continuity in his identity, although Tomas did not wish to talk about his family, preferring to deny his past. In spite of this present denial, both the adoptive father and the therapist agreed that in some future time Tomas might want to revisit his past, after he had gained some stability in his new family. The two adults felt it their responsibility to at least preserve some vestiges of the past for Tomas. Later in life, Tomas could make his own decisions about whether to preserve that past or not, but at least the therapist and father would have provided him with that option.

Upon Tomas's father's death, Jeff and Tomas worked with the family therapist to collect family mementos (e.g., pictures, heirlooms, videos, letters, report cards, etc.) from his parents' apartment. Although Tomas was not ready to discuss his past, this approach enabled Jeff to keep materials for Tomas that could someday help him in his search for identity related to his family. At this point in his life, as his father died and the last vestige of his family's past was lost, Tomas was unable to do this himself.

Example 4: Multiple Interventions over Time

The following case study, with many interventions over a long period, illustrates how the stigma and fear of HIV and AIDS that comes from cultural and familial beliefs may lead to avoiding discussion of the illness. Also, the behavioral indicators of children's and adolescents' awareness of the presence of a family secret are evident in this case. Finally, the case shows the impact on therapists' interventions and the need to remain closely allied with the family despite the frustrations brought about by not disclosing.

Martina, a 43-year-old Dominican woman, and Julio, a Dominican man about 10 years her junior, were both HIV-positive. The primary care physician referred them for treatment of Julio's depression and the couple's refusal to inform Martina's two children by a previous marriage about their HIV status. The oldest child, Carmen, 15, was a friendly, affectionate, impulsive, and outspoken adolescent. A year earlier she had made a suicide attempt after Martina forbade her to see a married man in his late 20s. Carmen was seen by a therapist for a brief period and then stopped attending. The second child, Carlos, 13, had speech and learning problems; he seemed sad, angry, and puzzled a great deal of the time. Both children were very close and affectionate with Julio, the man they considered their father. Carlos was very close to his mother, who he felt understood and cared for him more than anyone else did.

In couples' sessions, Martina disclosed that Julio blamed her for infecting him because she had been raped by an ex-brother-in-law. Martina accepted the guilt stoically, but medical tests later suggested that Julio, not the rapist, had probably infected Martina. Through joint and individual sessions, Julio acknowledged that he had infected Martina. He was reticent about how he contracted the virus.

Julio was the one who decided that their HIV status would not be disclosed to anyone. Martina appeared more open to discussing the possibility of disclosing but deferred to Julio's requests. Julio and Martina feared that if the children were told, Carmen might attempt suicide again and that both kids would suffer serious psychological trauma. Martina and Julio also felt that they would live long enough to see Carmen and Carlos graduate from high school. At an older age, the parents reasoned, their children could weather the disclosure with greater equanimity.

Julio was also concerned about his extended family's reaction to his HIV status. He felt that even if the kids were sworn to secrecy, his family in the Dominican Republic would know immediately, shaming Julio and driving his family from him. His position as elder son and provider for his aging parents was a great source of Julio's self-esteem, and he feared jeopardizing his stature. Julio, more than Martina, felt that Carmen and Carlos could not be trusted to keep the secret from family and friends.

When little movement was apparent in their sessions, Martina and Julio raised their concern with Carmen's moody defiance at home. Family sessions followed that gave Carmen a chance to voice age-appropriate concerns about her autonomy. Martina and Julio listened carefully and agreed to some concessions that enabled Carmen to feel that she had been listened to by her parents in a way they had not been able to listen to her before. Carmen apologized, and within three sessions the conflicts had diminished.

Several weeks later, Carlos was brought in because of defiance that occurred in school but not at home. Because of scheduling conflicts, Carlos could only be seen alone or with Martina, not in family sessions. In individual sessions, Carlos was elusive and silent, though he enjoyed playing checkers. Joint sessions with his mother were livelier, Martina often nurturing Carlos.

It was apparent to the therapist that both Carmen and Carlos were responding to the emotional atmosphere created by the secret of the parents' HIV infection. The children gave hints of their awareness of a family problem. For example, when the children asked why Martina had to go to the clinic so often, they were told that Martina had a serious liver problem and that Julio had some serious kidney ailment. On another occasion, when the children were watching television and a public service announcement about AIDS was aired, Carlos asked his mother, ''Mami, if you had AIDS, would you tell us?'' Martina answered that she would.

When confronted by the therapist with the paradox of her response to Carmen and Carlos and the reality that she was withholding information, Martina looked blankly away, conveying her awareness of the problem that had been created and maintained. The therapist gave sensitive warnings of the children's potential sense of betrayal, at a later date, when the secret would have to be revealed. He urged Martina and Julio to allow the children the opportunity to participate fully at this important point in their parents' lives. Finally, the therapist emphasized the importance of allowing the children to have the experience of giving to their parents emotionally, physically, and spiritually during the illnesses that would inevitably occur as the disease progressed. Julio held firm to his convictions, and Martina deferred.

The effects of HIV and AIDS and the complicated familial and cultural constraints to disclosure were extremely powerful in opposition to the therapist's interventions to help this family. Despite their steadfastness, Julio and Martina and their children maintained their connection to the therapist. This connection, which subsequently consisted of intermittent family or individual sessions, seemed to provide hope to Martina and Julio for their children, who would be orphans some day. By remaining involved with the therapist, Martina and Julio felt that, as their illness took its course and made the presence of HIV and AIDS undeniable, the participation of the therapist in the family's life would provide some stability and continuity. The family's willingness to integrate the therapist as a helping, caring, integral part of its system and as a link to the medical system they depended on would help reduce the potential negative psychosocial outcomes for the children. For the therapist it meant working with patience, paced by the family.

GENERAL RECOMMENDATIONS

Youngsters need to be encouraged to communicate what they are feeling and helped to express it in nondestructive ways. At times they may require gentle, loving confrontation to help them understand that, although they have a right to their own feelings of sadness and anger, they do not have a right to mistreat others because of their feelings.

Adolescents need physical comfort as much as younger children do but may be uncomfortable with physical expressions of affection and condolences by others. Embarrassment may appear in the guise of emotional distance or separation and may push away those able to give affection when the teen most needs it. Sensitivity to this conflict requires asking for the adolescent's permission before giving a hug, for instance, to allow the youth some degree of control about closeness and distance.

In the course of our clinical work we have learned that children and adolescents generally move in and out of sorrow and loss, sometimes rapidly. They are distractible in their grief. Adolescents especially may even find reassurance as an indication of rejection of their emotions when adults try to reassure them too soon, preempting the adolescents' desire to grieve in safety, or when adults try to tell them how to feel or how not to feel. Clinicians must proceed with caution. Parents and clinicians can allow children to comfort the adult, whether that adult is the ill parent, the surviving parent, or some other adult.

Psychologists and social workers in HIV care should provide individual, family, and group therapies expressly for dealing with issues of disclosure. Often it is the clinician who understands why it would be helpful for the child to know the parent's diagnosis and can help the parent appreciate the child's needs in an atmosphere of concern for the family. However, the rationales that parents and other family members give for concealing HIV status may be powerfully ingrained in the family system.

Maintaining order, predictability, and stability in the child's life as much as realistically possible is important. Clinicians and other adults must remember that children tend to idolize the dead and need gentle help to regain balance and perspective. One 10-year-old, who told her therapist that her mother was an "angel," also thought that something was terribly wrong in the way her family avoided talking about her dead mother. "You can't trust grown-ups," she said. The struggle to reconcile the idealized image of her mother with her unconfirmed speculations left the child feeling so angry that she voiced suicidal feelings, first to a friend and then to a school counselor.

CONCLUSION

In this chapter we have presented principles and approaches for family-centered interventions with inner-city minority children and adolescents whose parents are HIV-positive, have AIDS, or have died of AIDS and

AIDS-related illnesses. Our perspective on family work with AIDS orphans is that interventions aimed at individuals, dyads, family subsystems, or the entire family are worthy of consideration as family interventions.

Recognizing that developmental aspects affect youngsters' reactions to the parental diagnosis, illnesses, and death, we have reviewed the kinds of reactions by children and families that we have witnessed in the course of our clinical work in urban primary care and mental health settings, using clinical examples to illustrate our points. Finally, four more-detailed case examples were used to portray the work involved in helping youngsters and their families navigate the choppy waters of family transition brought about by the presence of HIV/AIDS.

REFERENCES

Altschul, S. (Ed.). (1988). *Childhood bereavement and its aftermath.* Madison, CT: International Universities Press.

Becker, E. (1973). *The denial of death.* New York: Free Press.

Boyd-Franklin, N. (1989). *Black families in therapy: A multisystems approach.* New York: Guilford.

Jewett, C. L. (1982). *Helping children cope with separation and loss.* Boston, MA: Harvard Common.

Levine, C., & Stein, G.L. (1994). *Orphans of the HIV epidemic: Unmet needs in 6 U.S. cities.* New York: The Orphan Project.

Michaels, D., & Levine, C. (1992). Estimates of the number of motherless youth orphaned by AIDS in the United States. *Journal of the American Medical Association, 268,* 3456–3461.

Papadatou, D., & Papadatou, C. (Eds.). (1991). *Children and death.* New York: Hemisphere.

Tasker, M. (1992). *How can I tell you? Secrecy and disclosure with children when a family member has AIDS.* Bethesda, MD: Association for the Care of Children's Health.

Wass, H., & Corr, C. A. (Eds.). (1982). *Helping children cope with death: Guidelines and resources.* New York: Hemisphere.

Webb, N. B. (1993). Assessment of the bereaved child. In N. B. Webb (Ed.), *Helping bereaved children: A handbook for practitioners* (pp. 19–42). New York: Guilford.

Zayas, L. H., & Romano, K. (1994). Adolescents and parental death from AIDS. In B. Dane & C. Levine (Eds.), *AIDS and the new orphans: Coping with death* (pp. 59–76). Westport, CT: Auburn House.

CHAPTER 8

Working with Immigrant Families in Transition

Ana Paulino
Jeanette Burgos-Servedio

Immigrant families encounter multiple stressors when they first arrive, and later they experience stress if family members acculturate at different rates. This chapter discusses family-centered practice for assessing and identifying interventions that may be used with families experiencing cultural conflicts.

Family-centered practice as a therapeutic framework, proposed by Hartman and Laird (1983), provides a challenge to clinicians who may intervene with various systems, thereby reducing stressors that may affect the immigration and acculturation processes of immigrant families. Canino and Canino (1982) contend that any family therapy approach is more effective than individual or group therapies in treating Latino families. Family therapy is the treatment of choice for family members who are

---

Note: A shorter version of this chapter was presented at the conference "Multicultural Perspectives in Working with Families," Fordham University Graduate School of Social Service, New York, November 5, 1993.

experiencing life transitional difficulties, especially family members exhibiting a ''deep sense of family commitment, obligation, and responsibility'' (Garcia-Petro, 1982). Professionals must recognize that the traditional health and mental health services do not always address the needs of the immigrant families in a culturally sensitive and competent manner. Lack of appropriate integration of valuable culturally specific information places the immigrant family at risk of being misdiagnosed and inappropriately served.

This chapter focuses primarily on Dominican immigrants, a group whose rapid growth in the United States has taken place during the past three decades. Currently, over 1 million Dominicans reside in this country. Dominicans comprise the second largest Hispanic group in New York City after Puerto Ricans (U.S. Bureau of Census, 1991). Professionals must see learning about this group's culture as an integral part of their professional development if effective services are to be developed and delivered.

Dominican immigration has been mainly directed to New York City. The reason for this is unclear, but New York City is strongly advertised in the Dominican Republic as the most desirable place for immigrants to seek work. Dominicans are also found in substantial numbers in Florida, Washington, DC, Puerto Rico, Massachusetts, Rhode Island, and Connecticut.

An analysis of the immigration flows of Dominicans to the United States identifies three distinct groups of families. These groups of Dominican immigrants share similar adjustment problems with other immigrants residing in the United States, but they also have unique needs and varying attitudes toward seeking help from human service professionals. For example, the Trujillo* era (1930–1961) group are established professionals, many of whom are too proud to seek help. The post-Trujillo era immigrants, middle-class to working-poor Dominicans, might seek help from a social service agency as a result of a referral from their child's school. The third group, who immigrated to urban areas from 1982 to 1986, is composed of the very poor ''flotilla'' people and ''jodedores,'' who might be seen in inpatient units with a dual diagnosis: substance abuse and either mental illness or HIV-positive status. These three groups of Dominican

---

*Rafael L. Trujillo, the president of the Dominican Republic, ruled the country for 30 years. His regime ended with his assassination in 1961.

immigrants have unique needs and varying attitudes toward seeking help from human service professionals (Paulino, 1994).

IMMIGRATION PROCESS

Drachman and Ryan (1991) identify three critical stages affecting individuals' immigration experience. These stages are (1) premigration and departure, (2) transit, and (3) resettlement (Drachman, 1992). For Dominican immigrants the premigration and departure stage includes the selection of caretakers for those family members who are staying on the island, especially the children and the elderly. The transit phase of migration refers to the period in which the immigrants initiate their travel experience. This stage of migration has different legal and psychological implications than for immigrants coming from Eastern Europe or Southeast Asia, who might be expected to wait in refugee camps for proper governmental clearance before they can proceed with immigration. Dominican immigrants experience the transit phase while they await a change in legal status. For example, if they enter the United States with a tourist visa, it is not unusual for them to request permanent status as their visa expiration date approaches. If renewal or a change of status is denied, they might choose to go underground or they might return to their country of origin.

The third stage of immigration is referred to as the resettlement phase. In this phase social workers must assess the impact of sociopolitical and cultural factors on immigrants' coping styles and the community resource systems they may utilize in their efforts to acculturate effectively to their new environment. When a client does not speak English, professionals should explore the sociopolitical context affecting the immigration process of that individual. It is possible that what appears to be resistance to learning English might instead be a symptom of a deeper conflict or fear of losing their Dominican identity and being associated with the "dominant group." Similarly, if an immigrant shows ambivalent feelings about becoming a naturalized citizen of the United States, human service providers must explore individual, family, and immigration history, all of which may influence the decision to give up Dominican nationality. Both issues, language and naturalization, require a thorough assessment of the effects on the immigrant's self-concept and identity.

The adjustment process is difficult for some Dominicans, who find themselves disappointed with the reality that awaits them, namely, lack of proficiency in English, and lack of community supports. Many of these immigrants struggle to survive on low incomes and live doubled up with grandparents or other relatives for several years until they are settled. When the children finally arrive, they too must make an enormous adjustment, learn a new language, reacquaint themselves with their parents and make the transition to the new environment and its school system. Often, those who come from rural settings have an even greater adjustment to make. Immigrants retain their belief systems, which may include a different orientation to life and the way they see themselves in relation to the wider social structure (Giordano & Giordano, 1977). Social workers and other helping professionals have their own biases and therefore need to examine their ignorance regarding ethnicity and its importance in shaping the individual's self-concept and perception of others (Green, 1982; Pinder-hughes, 1989).

Women who assume multiple roles within the family system encounter role confusion as they attempt to act independently and carry the same burdens as their male counterparts do. They cannot cope effectively if adherence to traditional Dominican family roles and values are in immediate conflict with the demands of the wider society. Dominican women remain ambivalent about returning to their motherland (Pessar, 1987). While in the United States, they learn that they have more legal rights and better financial, educational, and social opportunities than when they lived on the island. By returning to the Dominican Republic they might lose some of the privileges gained in the United States.

Often, Dominican men experience equal or perhaps more value conflicts than do women. For the first time their sense of manhood might be challenged by a culture that seems to encourage women to share equal opportunities with men. Women can apply for welfare benefits without having to depend on their husbands for financial support. Dominican men view this governmental help as a threat to their roles as caretakers and providers. Practitioners must be sensitive to this issue of fear of loss of control experienced by Dominican men.

INSTITUTIONAL SUPPORT

In a period of adjustment, such as occurs during immigration, the family as a social institution undergoes many changes in both structure and function. In the motherland, Dominican immigrants benefit from the support of the extended family system. This serves the purpose of setting standards and expectations for the next generation. In times of stress, Dominicans, like other Latino groups, turn to their families for help. Their cultural expectation is that when a family member is experiencing a problem, others in the family are obligated to help, especially those who are in stable conditions/positions (Ghalis, 1977). Human service providers must actively reach out to family members during such times of adjustment and crisis. The families need assistance with referrals to appropriate agencies that will provide positive reinforcers to self-esteem, such as educational programs to begin to learn English, job skills programs, and help in obtaining better housing.

Societal supports are required as stress mediators to prevent family disruption. As it relates to a lack of institutional support, human service professionals must develop consciousness that institutional racism exists (Jones, 1974). It is deeply rooted in the socioeconomic structure. Institutional racism, as a source of stress on the lives of family members' during the process of acculturation and adaptation, must be critically assessed by human service providers. Drachman and Ryan (1991) suggest that social workers are in a position to help immigrant families during their process of adjustment and adaptation to the host culture. Professional interventions must take place as soon as the immigrant families or the service providers recognize a need for securing therapeutic assistance.

IMPLICATIONS FOR SOCIAL WORK PRACTICE

Case Example: The Gonzalez Family

The Gonzalez family consists of Mr. Pedro Gonzalez, age 41; Mrs. Elisa Gonzalez, age 40; Wanda (identified client), age 19; Peter, age 15; Kenny, age 12; and John, age 11. The Gonzalez family is primarily financially supported by Mr. Gonzalez, who is employed as a short-order cook in a cafeteria located in midtown Manhattan. Mrs. Gonzalez also receives public assistance for the children. The family lives in a four-bedroom apartment in the Washington Heights section of Manhattan. Washington Heights is an area predominantly populated by Dominican families who have immigrated to this country within the past 20 years. The majority of the families have low incomes, and a disproportionate number of them are receiving public assistance. This immigrant group falls into the third wave of Dominicans arriving in the United States, as described earlier in this chapter.

Background Information and Major Themes

The Gonzalez family has been in treatment at a community mental health agency for 5 years. Family treatment has been recommended for all family members. In addition, individual sessions have been provided as they have become therapeutically indicated. The focus of the family sessions has been on issues affecting all family members, with hopes to improve communication patterns and to strengthen intergenerational boundaries. A major issue in treatment included conflicts stemming from different rates of acculturation achieved by family members. Another area needing family intervention centered around Wanda's disclosure of incest.

The family was originally referred in 1988 following a school referral of Peter. The nature of the referral at that time included poor behavioral and academic issues. Peter's individual sessions addressed his conflicts over his learning difficulty and its impact on his sense of self. Concurrently, Mrs. Gonzalez was seen individually about parenting issues. It was through her treatment that conflicts in the home were revealed. She identified having parenting conflicts with her husband, who seemed to undermine her role and disciplinary efforts. The entire family was engaged in the treatment process within a short time of the referral. Workers proceeded with the family as a unit until the children's symptoms diminished and Mr. Gonzalez's involvement in the family increased. Mr. Gonzalez was initially reluctant to participate in treatment. It was clear that he did not have any awareness of what psychotherapy was or why he needed to be involved. Mrs. Gonzalez reported that Mr. Gonzalez felt that they should be able to solve their own problems. Once these issues were dealt with, he engaged well in treatment and demonstrated the potential for improving his role within his family system.

As the conflicts concerning parenting were resolved and communication between family members improved, marital conflicts began to surface. Thus, the focus of treatment shifted to the couple. Mr. and Mrs. Gonzalez are currently seen jointly on a weekly basis combined with family sessions every other week.

Mr. Gonzalez

Mr. Gonzalez was born in the Dominican Republic. He came to New York City shortly after marrying Mrs. Gonzalez, leaving her in the Dominican Republic until he established himself here and was able to send for his family. Mr. Gonzalez came to this country in the hope of working and of living a better life than in his native country.

Mr. Gonzalez is a recovering alcoholic who has been abstinent for 6 years. Reportedly, Mr. Gonzalez used to drink on a daily basis. Incestuous acts with Wanda took place during periods of intoxication. For the most part, Mr. Gonzalez was an isolated, noncommunicative man. As he put it, "I worked all day and drank whenever I was free." Mr. Gonzalez was severely physically abused by his father throughout his upbringing. He describes himself as having been a very angry man for many years. He reported that "he could not talk because he feared that he would lose control over his angry feelings." Occasionally, he was physically abusive toward his children. His drinking created many marital conflicts throughout the years, resulting in some separations. In both Mr. and Mrs. Gonzalez's extended families there are generations of alcohol abuse.

Mrs. Gonzalez

Mrs. Gonzalez was born in the Dominican Republic. When she began treatment, she was unable to communicate her thoughts or feelings. She was easily brought to tears and always reported feeling guilty for whatever it was she was dealing with that was not right. Mrs. Gonzalez also reported having difficulties expressing love to her husband and children, in addition to having difficulties in communicating appropriately with them. She exhibited a very poor sense of self-worth; this was manifested in her inability to give herself anything or to allow others to give her anything (i.e., she would reject gifts from Mr. Gonzalez or the children). Mrs. Gonzalez is functionally illiterate. She was physically and sexually abused as a child. She had to work from the time she was 8 years old to help the family financially. Mrs. Gonzalez reports that she was never given any love. Mrs. Gonzalez and Wanda arrived in this country when Wanda was 4 months old. Mr. Gonzalez had already been here 2 years.

Wanda

Wanda is a Dominican American adolescent, 5 feet 8 inches tall and fair-skinned, with jet black hair and dark eyes. At birth she suffered a perinatal injury that limited use of her right arm, and she walks with a slight limp. Wanda was born in the Dominican Republic. She attended parochial school and since September 1991 has been attending college.

During one of the family sessions, Wanda looked particularly sad. She was asked by her worker if she would like to talk about what was troubling her. She refused to share any significant information, but later, during an individual session, she disclosed that at age 10 her father had sexually molested her. At the time of disclosure, Wanda was 15 years old. She denied any recent incidents of sexual molestation and reported that 5 years earlier there had been two incidents in which her father had molested her. Wanda reported that "all of a sudden she found herself thinking about having been molested by her father; she thought she had forgotten about it." She could not explain why she was thinking about this now but was clearly feeling distressed.

Mr. and Mrs. Gonzalez were reluctant to let Wanda separate appropriately at this stage in the family life cycle. Mr. and Mrs. Gonzalez felt Wanda was "too different from other girls in the family." This pull was creating conflicts between Wanda and her parents. Wanda was also becoming sexually active at the time, and this rekindled old feelings about sex and her father's incestuous acts. Disclosing the incest was a way of emancipating herself and declaring her independence while simultaneously rebelling and acting out her anger and anguish.

During the course of treatment between the time of the disclosure and the present time, Wanda has been able to confront her parents with her feelings toward them centering on the incest. She has been able to verbalize her feelings of anger, sadness, and guilt. Other issues that have surfaced during the course of treatment have included Wanda's poor feelings of self-worth, specifically as this has been affected by the incest and her physical handicap. A major issue Wanda is confronting at present is related to conflicts over her identity. She also reports being conflicted about her cultural identity. Repeatedly, she questions whether or not she is "Dominican or American." Wanda is experiencing tremendous distress in making the transition from adolescence to adulthood. She reports that the "more separate she becomes, the greater the void she experiences within herself." Also she reports feeling that she is "betraying her family. I don't know who I am." The transition to college has been traumatic. Wanda is living in a college dormitory. She has experienced several depressive episodes during this period and has begun to drink alcohol regularly. Recently, there was also a suicide attempt following a breakup with a young man she had been dating. Wanda tends to develop very dependent relationships with both males and females. She reports feeling uncomfortable in group situations unless she drinks. Wanda describes herself as a loner.

Other Family Members

Peter, the oldest son in the family, was in individual treatment at the agency for 1 year prior to Wanda's request for individual treatment. As the time of his treatment he was described as rebellious and difficult to manage in the home. He was also described as having academic difficulties. Currently, he is in his first year of public high school in special education and is reported to be doing well. After 1 year of psychotherapy his behavior at home and in school improved, indicating no further need for treatment.

Kenny is described as the family genius. His grades in school are always above average and his favorite pastime is sitting home and reading or playing chess. He is a shy boy who has difficulties expressing his thoughts and feelings. Kenny has been in Catholic schools since kindergarten.

John is described as the "tough one in the family." He is the most verbal and interacts with all family members in an appropriate manner. John also gets above-average grades in school and has attended Catholic school since kindergarten.

The Gonzalez family has a very close-knit extended-family network. Extended-family members live within a 1-mile radius of each other. The family socializes within the extended-family system. The only other source of support for the Gonzalez family is the Catholic church.

Cultural Assessment and Conflicts

From the standpoint of acculturation as a process of identity reformation it is useful to note that lack of adequate acculturation by some family members has served as a major disorganizing factor for the Gonzalez family. They have not made the adaptations necessary to master the process of acculturation; Mrs. Gonzalez does not speak English and has remained marginalized from the host culture. Therefore, as a family system and as individuals in the system they are in an identity crisis and to some degree experiencing identity diffusion (Erikson, 1963). Their family life cycle has been interrupted by the process of immigration (Carter & McGoldrick, 1989). Different rates of acculturation within the family system have created much stress and cultural identity confusion for Wanda as an adolescent caught between two cultures, the Latino and the Anglo. Wanda is fearful of cultural identity discontinuity. Separation from the family has led to a sense of identity loss for Wanda. Additionally, Wanda does not have anyone in the extended family to look to for models of different behavior. In her father's family there are cousins who have gone to college and have acculturated but at the expense of rejecting their cultural identity. Mrs. Gonzalez's family is very "traditional" and adheres to similar values, as Mrs. Gonzalez does, something that Wanda rejects. The one she turns to for modeling new behavior is her social worker, who is also Latina. Psychotherapeutically, this has been a major factor in Wanda's progress in treatment. It has been important for her to know that others have survived similar conflicts and have been successful.

Wanda, like most adolescents, is struggling intensively with issues related to her ego identity. The process of normal identity formation was complicated and intruded on by her physical handicap, father-daughter incest, and an overall maladaptive home environment. Without devaluing the impact these experiences have had on Wanda's emotional development, in the service of brevity the major focus of discussion here is the impact that acculturation issues have had on Wanda's ability to master the task of identity formation and their implications for other family members.

Mr. and Mrs. Gonzalez are ambivalent about their cultural identities. Mr. Gonzalez has acculturated to some degree in that he is able to leave his community to go to work and has learned English. However, he notes that "I am half and half. I behave one way at work and another way at home." It is clear from this statement that he has not been able to integrate a consolidated identity. As the first one in his family system to immigrate to the United States, Mr. Gonzalez was forced to take action when he arrived here. His level of acculturation is derived as a result of his need to provide for his family, rather than as a conscious, planned action to fit into the host society. Mr. Gonzalez quickly reverts to traditional ways of behaving while in his community. His exposure to the world outside his community has served to help him integrate some of the values of the host society, but these values are held ambivalently.

Mrs. Gonzalez is in constant despair and depressed. She is traditional in her views and values. She has coped with the transition of immigration by nonacceptance of the host culture. She holds onto her ethnic identity and thus is much more stressed than her other family members and has low self-esteem. Coming from a patriarchal society, with its respect for the authority of a dominant father who rules the household, Dominican women undergo a tremendous amount of intrapsychic, interpersonal, and environmental stresses during their period of acculturation in the United States. The flexibility to modify traditional roles must be evaluated within the cultural context to avoid further family disruptions. In the Dominican culture sex roles are traditionally more rigid and demarcated more clearly. Males are granted greater independence and at an earlier age than females are. There are greater expectations for achievement outside the home for males.

Several cultural conflicts have surfaced in treatment related to different levels of acculturation achieved by family members. Although Mr. and Mrs. Gonzalez try not to restrict the process of acculturation in their children, their sense of ambivalence and fears of cultural discontinuity do not allow them to consistently support or model new behaviors for their children. As the children acculturate, Mr. and Mrs. Gonzalez are forced to shift roles. This is particularly difficult for Mrs. Gonzalez, whose self-esteem is based on her role as a parent. Additionally, of all the family members she is the least exposed to the host society. She remains marginalized and disconnected from the wider social structure. The children's differences and pull for autonomy create much despair for Mrs. Gonzalez. In treatment, Mr. Gonzalez has demonstrated difficulties being sensitive to Mrs. Gonzalez's needs; thus, marital conflicts arise.

Mr. Gonzalez's understanding of his immigration to New York City was that he would come to this country, make money, and move back to the Dominican Republic. In fact, every dollar he could spare he saved to buy a house in the Dominican Republic. Ultimately, he did buy a house, which is now for sale because Mr. Gonzalez realizes that he will not be returning to his native country.

Mr. Gonzalez struggles with his identity as a Dominican man in the United States. He says that while he is in Washington Heights he is Dominican; at work in midtown Manhattan he is "half and half" (i.e., half Dominican, half American). He reports that it is hard for him to know how to behave. Mr. Gonzalez reports feeling that it is more stressful for him to interact with his own family system because the pressures for conformity to traditional values are greater. In comparison to Mrs. Gonzalez, he has been able to achieve a greater degree of acculturation.

Mrs. Gonzalez, on the other hand, is the carrier of the traditional cultural values of her native country. Since her arrival in the United States she has basically maintained herself "community bound." Her behavior is motivated by the values and beliefs of her culture and upbringing. Until recently, she maintained rigid traditional views regarding her role of wife, woman, and parent. Shifts in her children's behavior and values have caused her to examine her position in her family structure and consider alternate adaptive strategies. Her identity has been defined by her role as a parent. As Wanda began to struggle for autonomy and behaved in nontraditional ways, Mrs. Gonzalez became more depressed. Wanda's behavior was a catalyst for Mrs. Gonzalez to question not only her views on parenting but more important, her sense of personal and cultural identity. This realization served as a challenge for all family members to reorganize their interactive modes within the system.

Wanda's cultural identity is currently undefined. Aside from Mr. Gonzalez, who is supportive of her efforts to integrate, Wanda does not have any role models in her family or community to help her through this process. Wanda identifies with Mr. Gonzalez, whom she perceives as struggling with similar conflicts but is fearful of feelings of attachment toward him. The therapeutic sessions provided her with the holding environment she so desperately needed (Graziano, 1992).

Thus far, Peter, Kenny, and John are experiencing fewer cultural conflicts than the other members in the family. The reasons for this may be that Mr. and Mrs. Gonzalez are now more receptive to their children's needs and have allowed them more autonomous functioning. The boys in the family were not as overprotected from external influences as Wanda was, giving them greater exposure to American values. It is interesting to note that Peter, Kenny, and John are more fluent in English than in Spanish. They prefer to speak English at home and in the therapy sessions. Mrs. Gonzalez is the only one in the immediate family who does not speak English.

Overall, Mrs. Gonzalez is able to provide a stable, supportive environment for her children, although she is also depressed and has not allowed herself to fully mourn the process of immigration and the losses of all familiar and known faces left behind in the Dominican Republic. The process of immigration throws a person into a period of mourning that is similar to the death of a loved one. What such persons are mourning is the loss of part of themselves. A major part of one's identity is being given up; one must mourn not only what was physically and concretely familiar but also that part of oneself that one has left behind. As Mrs. Gonzalez works through her unresolved mourning regarding issues associated with separation and loss, she will be more in tune with her children's needs and be able to make the necessary adjustments expected of their developmental life cycle. For Wanda, this means being able to make an adequate transition from adolescent to young adult. For the boys, it means not feeling guilty if they do not speak Spanish fluently. Bowlby (1960) and Fulmer (1983) stress the importance of recognizing and assisting families in working through grieving issues before they can establish other meaningful attachments.

Fulmer's (1983) conceptualization of unresolved grief suggests that Mrs. Gonzalez's depression is a special problem in the treatment of family members who are experiencing an impending loss. In this case, Mrs. Gonzalez is responding to Wanda's need to separate as an individual. This emotional and physical loss is having an adverse impact on Mrs. Gonzalez's self-worth as a mother. Mrs. Gonzalez's inability to resolve her own mourning regarding her separation from significant others and homeland interferes with Wanda's achieving an accurate perception of what is really going on within herself as an individual. Wanda needs validation and reassurance that her feelings are welcomed and encouraged, that they are real.

Wanda needs to talk about her unresolved feelings of loss (e.g., attachment to her mother). Wanda's depression may be seen as resulting from unresolved mourning that is maintained by the family system. Some techniques of structural family therapy are proposed in a specific order to facilitate mourning in such families. A successful mourning experience requires a restructuring of the family that provides energy for the remainder of the therapy.

Following Minuchin and Fishman's (1981) model of structural family therapy, Fulmer (1983) demonstrates the following techniques, which are effective in working with families to facilitate and promote their working through unresolved mourning. These techniques were used successfully in the Gonzalez family to change the rules of the system so that mourning could be promoted:

1. *Joining.* The clinician's initial efforts should be directed toward developing an atmosphere in which the family can experience a sense of trust. Mrs. Gonzalez should be allowed to merge with the clinician so that a therapeutic alliance may be formed. By doing this, the clinician will bond more closely with Mrs. Gonzalez so that she will not have to perceive her daughter's separation as a narcissistic injury. In other words, because Mrs. Gonzalez experiences Mr. Gonzalez as not providing the necessary support needed by her in regard to her disciplinary role, the therapist functions as the transitional object for Mrs. Gonzalez to rely on.

2. *Framing and reframing.* The clinician should make an effort to universalize mourning as a normal process following the loss of a loved one. Mr. and Mrs. Gonzalez need to recognize that they and other family members have experienced psychological as well as environmental losses resulting from their immigrant status and other life transitional issues. The process of normalizing their immigratory experience while reflecting on previous losses and attachments to new objects will allow them to master difficult transitions that must be made during the process of acculturation to the host society.

Through the process of immigration, the family's coping mechanisms are put through the most difficult test of a lifetime because they must try to function in a new environment. Immigrant families must try to cope with differences not only in language, food, values, and beliefs but also a very different physical environment. There is little in the new culture to connect to. Immigration creates a disruption in the person's and/or family's identity. The manner in which the family or individual copes with the process of immigration will set the stage for future developmental growth or crisis. Sometimes family members feel relieved to hear the clinician identifying such issues and feelings as universal and thus normal.

3. *Transformation through enactment.* The clinician works on the client's maladaptive pattern of behavior and the explicit rules of the family system (i.e., Mom cannot cry, so she acts out her feelings to cover or to avoid expressing painful feelings; consequently, she will distract herself from expressing mourning). In this stage, which is labeled "construction of a mourning ritual," Mrs. Gonzalez is allowed to verbalize her fear, fantasies, guilt, and pain regarding the loss of her daughter's dependency on her. Mrs. Gonzalez might be experiencing this separation as a desertion of her beloved object.

4. *Drawing boundaries*. The clinician reinforces rules that allow mourning. The clinician must intervene so that family members will not reassure themselves too prematurely. For example, Mrs. Gonzalez may be encouraged to mourn, recognizing at times that different family members might have different abilities in working through mourning process.

5. *Restructuring*. The family members should be helped to become more involved with peers. In a transitional structure the clinician can be the peer. The following suggestions can be included as part of this family's treatment goals: (a) to help Mrs. Gonzalez to mourn apart from family members, (b) to reassure Wanda and siblings that Mrs. Gonzalez is okay even though she is sad, and (c) to increase peer support for Mrs. Gonzalez and other family members by arranging for the family to visit the Dominican Republic. During this phase of the treatment, it became evident that Mrs. Gonzalez was involved with religious groups in her community. Indeed, Mrs. Gonzalez and the clinician discussed her use of that network. Boyd-Franklin (1989) notes that religion has long been recognized as an extremely important institution utilized by many families in times of stress.

CONCLUSION

Community leaders and human service providers must advocate for and assume an active role in helping Dominican and other immigrant families to negotiate bureaucratic organizations that are identified as stressors in the acculturation process. Social workers who are knowledgeable and sensitive to these issues can certainly function as culture brokers for these families. The culture broker is the individual who negotiates the challenges posed by living in an ethnically diverse, sometimes hostile society. The mental health professional carries out this role during daily routines with the client and the agency. The concept of the culture broker refers to the notion of relationship, interaction, and linkage between the individual within the family and between the family and the broader social environment.

This chapter has discussed family-centered practice as a conceptual framework in which clinicians conduct culturally sensitive assessments and develop appropriate interventive strategies in their work with immigrant families experiencing cultural conflicts. A case example is offered to illustrate the identification of interventive strategies and application of family-centered practice in work with a Dominican family in crisis. Functioning as a culture broker, the social worker involved in the Gonzalez case was able to assume multiple therapeutic roles in her efforts to assist each family member to reduce cultural conflicts and develop a greater sense of personal coherence within the context of the mainstream society. Family-centered practice provides a step-building process leading to an effective and empowering model of service delivery for immigrant families, with implications regarding knowledge building in the areas of curriculum development and social work training programs.

REFERENCES

Boyd-Franklin, N. (1989). *Black families in therapy: A multisystems approach.* New York: Guilford.

Bowlby, J. (1960). Grief and mourning in infancy and early childhood. *Psychoanalytic study of the child, 15,* 9–52.

Canino, I., & Canino, G. (1982). Culturally syntonic family therapy for migrant Puerto Ricans. *Hospital and Community Psychiatry, 33,* 299–303.

Drachman, D. (1992). A stage-of-migration framework for service to immigrant populations. *Social Work, 37*(1), 68–72.

Drachman, D., & Ryan, A. S. (1991). Immigrants and refugees. In A. Gitterman (Ed.), *Handbook of social work practice with vulnerable populations* (pp. 618–646). New York: Columbia University Press.

Erikson, E. (1963). Eight stages of man. *Childhood and society.* New York: Norton.

Fulmer, R. H. (1983). A structural approach to unresolved mourning in single parent family systems. *Journal of Marital and Family Therapy, 9*(3).

Garcia-Preto, N. (1982). Puerto Rican families. In M. McGoldrick, J. K. Pearce, & J. Giordano (Eds.), *Ethnicity and family therapy* (pp. 164–186). New York: Guilford.

Ghalis, S. (1977). Cultural sensitivity and the Puerto Rican client. *Social Casework, 58,* 459–468.

Giordano, J., & Giordano, G. P. (1977). *The ethno-cultural factor in mental health.* New York: Institute on Pluralism and Group Identity.

Graziano, R. (1992). Treating women incest survivors: A bridge between cumulative trauma and post traumatic stress. *Social Work in Health Care, 17*(1), 69–85.

Green, J. W. (1982). *Cultural awareness in the human services.* Englewood Cliffs, NJ: Prentice-Hall.

Hartman, A., & Laird, J. (1983). *Family-centered social work practice*. New York: Free Press.

Jones, T. (1974). Institutional racism in the United States. *Social Work, 19*(2), 218–225.

Lazarus, R. S., & Folkman, S. (1984). *Stress, appraisal and coping*. New York: Springer.

McGoldrick, M. (1989). Ethnicity and the family life cycle. In B. Carter & M. McGoldrick (Eds.), *The changing family life cycle: A framework for family therapy*. New York: Gardner Press.

McGoldrick, M., Pearce, J., & Giordano, J. (Eds.). (1982). *Ethnicity and family therapy*. New York: Guilford.

Minuchin, S., & Fishman, H. C. (1981). *Family therapy techniques*. Boston: Harvard University Press.

Paulino, A. (1994). Dominicans in the United States: Implications for practice and policies in the human services. *Journal of Multicultural Social Work, 3*(2), 53–65.

Pessar, P. (1987). The Dominicans: Women in the household and the garment industry. In N. Forner (Ed.), *New immigrants in New York*. New York: Columbia University Press.

Pinderhughes, E. (1989). *Understanding race, ethnicity, and power: The key to efficacy in clinical practice*. New York: Free Press.

U.S. Bureau of the Census. (1991). The Hispanic population in the United States: March 1990. Washington, DC: U.S. Government Printing Office.

CHAPTER 9

Working with Soviet Jewish Immigrants

Robert Chazin

The past two decades have witnessed a sharp increase in the number of emigrés into the United States from countries around the world. One group that has shown a particularly significant increase in immigration is from the former Soviet Union. As reported in the 1990 census, well over 300,000 persons born in the Soviet Union now reside in the United States, according to the 1990 census. Of this population, experts note that a majority are Jewish (Gold, 1994). The Hebrew Immigrant Aid Society, an organization that assists Jewish emigrés in their resettlement, reports that by the end of 1993 it helped resettle 289,719 Soviet Jews (Gold, 1994). This includes only those assisted since the United States liberalized its immigration laws in 1965.

Social work has always acknowledged that workers and the agencies in which they work must understand the special needs and cultures of the various ethnic groups they serve (Congress, 1994; Drachman & Halberstadt, 1992). Translating this tenet into practice is difficult with Soviet emigrés because of the diversity of their origins and cultures. These immigrants are not a homogeneous group; they come from 15 different republics that once constituted the Soviet Union. Immigrants from these different communities vary considerably in their lifestyle, coping mechanisms, and hopes and expectations for their new life in the United States. The task of understanding these emigrés is only slightly eased by the fact that 80% of them came from only three republics: Ukraine, Russia, and Belarus (Gold, 1994). However, there are significant differences among these three. Further, the remaining 20% of immigrants originate from a broad spectrum of other Soviet republics and therefore vary widely.

Regardless of differences in origin and culture, Soviet Jewish immigrants share some common characteristics. Family structure is one. Typically, the Soviet family was a close-knit, emotionally connected, interdependent three-generation unit. Grandparents often resided with and were fully involved in the family. They cared for their grandchildren, performed various household chores, and contributed to the family financially. Gender roles of husband and wife were clearly defined and differentiated. Although both husband and wife worked, the wife carried additional responsibility for the household and the children. Recognition of the wife's contribution is seen in the use of two family names, the husband's and the wife's.

In summary, although the husband's main role was as breadwinner, the wife also was a wage earner, with additional responsibilities as homemaker and mother. The family's burden was eased by its dependency on and involvement of older adult parents. Because the citizens were supported by the state, they had few financial worries. Regarding children, parents were responsible for their care and protection, and the school was responsible for their socialization. Older parents significantly contributed to the family and remained the responsibility of their adult children.

In addition to family structure, Soviet emigrés also shared a common motivation for leaving their homeland. Anti-Semitism and increased discrimination in higher education, employment, and social life all pressured Soviet Jews to leave. Although many chose to resettle in Israel, many more preferred the United States, where they felt that there would be greater economic opportunity, better national security, noncompulsory military service, and a comfortable secular and pluralistic society (Gold, 1994).

In considering the Soviet Jewish immigrant experience, a framework that views migration as a process of stages provides a fuller understanding (Drachman & Halberstadt, 1992). This framework underscores the necessity of understanding more than the resettlement experience. The emigrés' life in their native lands, the culture they carry with them, and their experience in traveling from their homeland to the United States also must be understood. This view considers immigration as comprising three phases: premigration, transit, and resettlement. All three phases are discussed here, as well as some case examples of immigration difficulties and implications for social work practice with these immigrants.

PREMIGRATION

The premigration experience of Jewish Soviet immigrants is similar in some respects and different in others. These emigrés generally were the targets of anti-Semitism in the form of restricted social, educational, and occupational opportunities. This was the primary reason for migration. However, significant differences exist among Soviet Jewish emigrés as to decision making regarding emigration, time of immigration, and region of origin.

The Decision to Emigrate

Immigrant families must go through a decision-making process regarding whether or not to surrender a known lifestyle for one that is unknown in a foreign land. This is stressful for most families, particularly for those consisting of three generations with close emotional and functional ties. The presence of three generations creates a greater possibility for disagreement about emigrating. In cases of disagreement families may separate, some members remaining behind while others emigrate. In this scenario both those left behind and those who depart feel the pain of the family breakup. Even if differences are resolved and the family emigrates as a complete unit, the initial dissension may later haunt the family. Adjustment difficulties may evoke the earlier reluctance of some family members, resulting in bitter recriminations and blame for their emigration and present predicament.

Time of Immigration

The Soviet emigrés can be divided into three groups according to the time of immigration. The earliest group, the refusniks, were followed by those emigrating between the years 1980 and 1988; a third group has arrived since then. The refusniks of the first period suffered great hardship. They were denied permission to leave by the Soviet government and forced to wait for years. During their wait the government punished them for their attempt to emigrate by denying them state benefits such as employment and housing. In addition, their fellow citizens would frequently harass and humiliate them.

In 1980, under pressure from the United States government, the Soviets opened the door for Soviet Jews to emigrate. Simultaneously, the United States granted this group refugee status, further easing their immigration by granting them various entitlements. In 1988 the United States again changed its immigration policy, leading to a still different experience for emigrés. These differences will be discussed in the "Transit" section below.

Generally, those who emigrated since 1980 (and particularly since 1988) benefited from more humane Soviet governmental policies. Although their leaving was easier, the reasons for migrating remained painful: growing anti-Semitism and threats of pogroms by an anti-Semitic grass-roots movement. Other factors, such as fear of Chernobyl radiation, political turmoil, and increased economic hardship, also contributed to the recent emigrés' decision to migrate. Despite this stress, many emigrés were less motivated than the earlier refusniks; they left the USSR reluctantly, fearful of changing their homeland (Chazin, 1995; Drachman & Halberstadt, 1992).

Regions of Origin and Cultural Differences

Considering the vast expanse of the former Soviet Union and the fact that emigrés came from some 15 different republics, it is not surprising to find significant regional differences in social class, occupation, and education that influence their relationships with one another and their adaptation. These emigrés are sensitive to such differences. To understand a particular client family, the worker must be similarly sensitive. A worker must know of the client's cultural, historical, and geographical origins.

Urban Centers and the Intelligentsia

Many of the Soviet Jewish immigrants originate from the urban centers of Moscow and Leningrad, which had the largest concentration of educational and cultural institutions. Although Jews found these institutions difficult to enter, many successfully pursued higher education. The urban centers generated a large number of the elite intelligentsia, including professionals, scientists, artists, and musicians, as well as many craftsmen and dissidents. These emigrés shared a rich involvement in the cultural life of their cities—the concerts, operas, theaters, and museums, a cultural life offered primarily in big cities. As metropolitan residents they are flexible, accustomed to the complex lifestyle characteristic of city life, and more verbal and articulate.

Another characteristic of families from urban centers is their close family ties. Often, both parents worked, with child care provided by housekeepers or grandparents. The poor quality of child care available fostered involvement of grandparents and family interdependence. The low wages paid professionals continued the children's dependency on their parents. Young couples often remained dependent on their parents, further strengthening family ties and interdependence (Bentsianov, 1995; Drachman & Halberstadt, 1992). Such particularly close family ties give rise to postemigration difficulties.

Provincial Towns in Ukraine and Belarus

Emigrés from the towns of Ukraine and Belarus differ sharply from the urban centers' cultured intelligentsia. They are more like blue-collar workers or tradesmen in culture, lifestyle, and expectations. Their communities of origin offered limited social and cultural opportunities. Jews in these smaller communities typically knew many of their brethren. Their cultural life centered on the "palace of culture," which included movie theaters, a sports stadium, and some musical offerings but nothing comparable to the cultural life of the urban centers (Bentsianov, 1995).

It is noteworthy that many provincial immigrants speak the universal language of Yiddish and are more likely to be familiar with Jewish traditions than the intelligentsia are. However, because of their small-town origins they are less prepared for the demands of big-city life and for the loss of their extended families.

Odessa

In addition to the urban center and small-community subcultures discussed, a third group of Soviet emigrés are those from Odessa. Odessa was one of the largest cities within the former Soviet Union and contained the largest Jewish population in the region. Although located within the Ukraine, its inhabitants considered themselves Odessans. These Jewish emigrés created a special bond, with their own unique folk language, songs, and especially their own brand of humor. They developed a separate society with its own class structure (Bentsianov, 1995).

The Baltic Republics: Latvia, Estonia, and Lithuania

Still another subculture within the Soviet immigrant population is that of the Baltic emigré. The Baltic republics were not annexed by the Soviets until 1940, then occupied by the Germans in World War II, and incorporated into the Soviet system in 1945. Consequently, these emigrés lived in the Soviet system for a relatively short time, with ample opportunity to develop and preserve their own culture. They had enjoyed an active Jewish cultural life—religious center, political parties, and youth organizations. The small number who survived the Holocaust faced both governmental and civilian anti-Semitism, which produced large-scale emigration. Understandably, these immigrants hold a stronger Jewish identity than those from other sites.

Although the emigrés from the Baltic republics come from agricultural rather than industrialized societies, they more comfortably identify with the citizens of the industrialized Central European countries such as Germany and Poland. Consequently, the Baltic Soviet Jewish immigrant brings a mix of European, Jewish, and Soviet cultures.

Other Cultures

Finally, Soviet Jews from the Caucasian and Asian areas, such as the Bukharan Jews from Uzbekistan and those from Georgia, Armenia, and Azerbaijan, also must be acknowledged. These republics differ in culture, so emigrés from these lands also differ from each other as well as from those already noted. The Bukharans, the largest immigrant group from this general population, have a history of some 2,000 years of acceptance within a Muslim society. Their culture includes both Jewish and Muslim elements and is steeped in a rich history of Jewish values that differ from contemporary Judaism. Because this group was accepted by their Muslim neighbors, they did not assimilate but preserved their own Jewish identity and culture.

Culturally, they dress like their ancestors and have large families and close ties with extended family. Young couples often live with their in-laws. Values include a positive Jewish identity and financial rather than educational achievement. Status is dependent on one's age and the number of children one has. There is a double standard in sexual relationships and an acceptance of extramarital affairs for men.

TRANSIT

Effects of Soviet Emigration Policy

More recent emigrés have had an easier transit experience in some ways and a more difficult one in others. The relaxed Soviet emigration policies and the granting of refugee status in the United States eased the Soviet Jews' relocation after 1980. The more recent Soviet policy of permitting emigrés to return to visit family and friends, as well as allowing family visits to those who have emigrated, has further eased emigration. Allowing those asking to emigrate to maintain their apartments and their employment until the time of emigration also provided relief.

However, the resultant rise in the number of Soviet immigrants created new problems. In 1988, Soviet immigrants reached the refugee quota limit and stretched the resettlement funds available for refugees. Consequently, the United States limited the number of Soviet Jews applying for refugee status. Many now faced a difficult decision while waiting in American resettlement facilities located in Austria and Italy. Those not offered refugee status were given the option of entering the United States as "parolees," without the entitlements accompanying refugee status. This shift in immigration policy was particularly traumatic for those families in which some members were offered refugee status and others only entrance as parolees. Many rejected parolee status, recognizing that without benefits survival would be difficult. Families split in this way—some granted refugee status, others either having parolee status or being forced to wait—often suffered increased intergenerational, marital, and intrafamilial conflict. The separation of members was particularly painful for Soviet families because of their usual pattern of close family ties and three-generational interdependence (Bentsianov, 1995; Drachman & Halberstadt, 1992).

In 1989 another change in American immigration policy further affected the transit experience of the Soviet immigrants. The United States closed its resettlement facilities in Austria and Italy and transferred its headquarters to its Moscow embassy. Emigrés still waiting in the resettlement facilities were both positively and negatively affected by this change. A positive consequence was that they had more time to learn about their new homeland and to heal the wounds caused by their losses. Also, many of them had family and friends who had emigrated earlier and were now settled in the United States, willing and able to provide support and assistance. Negatively, they were now forced to wait in the discomfort of the resettlement facilities, with little to do.

Those who now came to the United States directly from Moscow also gained in some ways and lost in others. They were spared the transient wait in the Austrian and Italian resettlement facilities and permitted to keep their Soviet jobs and apartments until their departure. However, the direct move from the USSR to the United States increased the likelihood of culture shock. Also, there was little opportunity to learn about their homeland. Nor was there time to heal the wounds caused by loss, sometimes of family members, always of homeland and lifestyle.

Expectations

Whatever else they have in common, it is likely that all immigrants carry their own special baggage of motivation, aspirations, and expectations about achievement in the new world. Those Soviet emigrés who held unrealistic and idealized expectations of this new society (e.g., that all of its citizens are wealthy and that its high level of technological development would assure them well-paying jobs) were subjected to abrupt and painful disillusionment. Most emigrés settled in urban centers, where their expectations of high quality of life often were dashed by the reality of unemployment, crime, and a high cost of living. Exacerbating their adjustment to their new home was the sense of special entitlement that many had. Although the Soviet government had for many years prevented their emigration, American Jewry's active support conveyed the promise of special status once in the United States. Instead, they were faced with the same adjustment difficulties that all immigrants face—learning a new language, finding suitable employment and housing, and adjusting to a new culture and environment.

RESETTLEMENT

Having discussed the Soviet Jewish emigrés' preimmigration and transit experience, we now consider their resettlement. All immigrants confront the loss of home and lifestyle and the necessity of coping with acculturation demands in their new home, and Soviet Jewish immigrants faced the same challenges. This section discusses common resettlement circumstances and the resolution of issues. Several case vignettes are included to illustrate various adjustment difficulties.

Choice of Community

The Soviet Jewish emigrés chose to reside in communities inhabited by family, friends, and those from their cities and regions of origin. Their choice of neighborhood was influenced by their comfort with the neighborhood's character, climate, and job opportunities. They selected neighborhoods that replicated their original communities, geographically and socially. This clustering is especially visible in areas with large concentrations of Soviet emigrés. A city's neighborhoods of immigrants often have their own distinct populations and culture. New York City is one example of this phenomenon. One neighborhood is populated primarily by the intelligentsia of Moscow and Leningrad. Another, consisting largely of Odessans, is known as "Little Odessa." Yet a third neighborhood is composed of Bukharans with their own unique religion, language, and culture (Barber, 1987; Gold, 1994).

Culture Conflict: Dependence versus Independence

Immigrants generally experience the stress of uprootedness, vulnerability, and loss. The Soviet emigrés' difficulty in resettlement is heightened because of the dramatic difference between the Soviet and American social and economic systems, particularly as they relate to government's responsibility for its citizens. The Soviet system provided for the basic needs of its citizenry in employment, housing, and medical services. Through its pervasive care, it fostered dependency. In contrast, the United States values independence; one is encouraged and expected to make one's own way. For the Soviet emigrés, welfare is a familiar and acceptable form of state care. Despite welfare's stigma in our society and the pressure to gain employment, some Soviet immigrants prefer welfare to the American way of starting at the bottom of the economic ladder and working one's way up. This is particularly true of emigrés with higher educational and occupational status (Belozersky, 1990).

Loss of Occupational and Social Status

The close-knit, interdependent, three-generational Soviet Jewish family unit that had been functional in the USSR often is problematic in the United States. All Soviet family members—the children, their adult parents, and the parents' older adult parents—face difficult adjustment problems. Middle-aged couples with children often have a difficult time on two fronts: their loss of status in the family and in the outside world.

In the Soviet system these adults generally had achieved some level of social status accompanied by feelings of competency and value. They were at the peak of their earnings in their occupations and had authority within the home. In their new land they experienced limited skills in language, technology, and knowledge of their occupational fields. Unemployed emigrés have lost a major source of identity and a symbol of successful acculturation. They also have lost entry into an economic network that facilitates continued success. Further, their children often mastered the English language more readily than they did and adjusted more quickly. Their simultaneous loss of status in both the community and the home was painful.

The following two cases illustrate the dilemmas of middle-aged adults from two different backgrounds: the large city and the provincial town. The case of Mrs. Y highlights the anguish of middle-aged adults from large cities. Immigrants frequently do not qualify for the same high-level career position they achieved in the Soviet system. They often find themselves rejected for entry-level positions in their fields of expertise because they are judged as overqualified. At the same time, their age often blocks them from beginning the education needed to gain American credentials comparable to those achieved in the Soviet system. Many thus face only the choice of unemployment or beginning in a new or related but lower-status career at entry level. This drop in status is particularly painful for those who achieved higher degrees in the USSR and belonged to the intelligentsia. The decline in occupational status is often exacerbated by loss of the cultured life once treasured.

The Case of Mrs. Y

Mrs. Y's experience illustrates the dilemma of many large-city Soviet emigrés. A woman in her mid-50s, Mrs. Y sought help from a mental health clinic. In Leningrad, she was a PhD and a medical doctor, a significant achievement. Her ancestors had lived in Leningrad for many generations and had enjoyed the cultural life of the intelligentsia, with its rare books, art, antiques, opera, and the like. While atypical of the Soviet emigré, it was typical of this elite. In the United States her husband, who also had held a Soviet PhD and had a high-status occupation, was unemployed. Her married son was a medical student, her married daughter studying computer programming. All three families were now on welfare.

Lost was the culturally rich, high-status life she had led back in the USSR. Her professional status as a high-ranking professor in a medical school had further enhanced her status. Because of this status and her social connections she had enjoyed access to literature not readily accessible to the general public and to the best of the cultural life available. Despite Soviet anti-Semitism and social pressures, she had created her own insulated society. In a sense, her world was like the Ivy League world in our own society: in the Soviet system, the intelligentsia constituted a social and cultural elite, lacking only economic status.

At the mental health clinic, Mrs. Y presented as a depressed client with some psychosomatic symptoms. The worker was sensitive to the enormity of her loss—her cultural life, social support system, and occupational status. Because of the client's age and the lower value placed on her credentials, there was no opportunity to begin her career again. In subsequent sessions the worker learned that Mrs. Y's emigration was motivated by the virulent anti-Semitism of the time and her fear for the safety of her children and grandchildren. Having lived in a close-knit family unit and not wanting to be separated from her family, she had decided to sacrifice her life in Russia for the safety of her family.

At first, Mrs. Y was comforted by the physical closeness of the three families and her active and influential role as homemaker. However, her grandchildren, adjusting quickly, with their greater language facility and school contacts, lost respect for her. Her children, involved in their own adjustment, had less time for her. Her initial comfort changed to an acute awareness of her loss and a sense of futility, depression, and betrayal. She obsessed about having sacrificed everything, with no family appreciation or substitute gratification.

In their work the social worker focused on Mrs. Y's loss and her unrealistic expectations. The loss of her social system, cultural life, and occupational status were explored, as well as her expectations of re-creating them. Her expectations that her children would remain a part of the same emotionally connected family she once had and would serve as a substitute for whatever loss she had to endure also were dashed by the reality of adjustment.

The social worker's understanding of the unique experience of this client both guided and facilitated the therapy. The worker understood the client's loss as well as her special resources. Because of her cultural and educational background, Mrs. Y was more verbal and articulate and comfortable in using her intellect in problem solving. Consequently, she was able and eager to use a cognitive, analytical therapy. Having resided in a large city, she also was more flexible and accustomed to the lifestyle characteristic of a big city (e.g., how to negotiate a complicated transportation system).

The worker's understanding of this client's cultural background and her special resources enabled her to see that Mrs Y could experience therapy as a means of regaining a piece of her lost intellectual life. The worker used her understanding to assist this client to work through her depression and to regain some of what she had lost. She helped Mrs. Y recognize that, as a major city, New York had a rich cultural life of its own. The client was encouraged and aided in becoming active in the cultural life of her new home in the United States.

The Case of Mrs. G

A second case illustrates the typical adjustment problems of another Soviet immigrant group discussed above, namely, those from the provincial towns of Ukraine and Belarus. Here the most painful aspect of adjustment is not the loss of a cultural life shared with a select elite but loss of a kinship network and loss of value in her family.

Mrs. G sought social work services because of depression. Her family, including a husband and two young children, had emigrated from a small Ukrainian town. At her parents' urging she had obtained a professional degree at an easily entered regional institute. Her degree led to an engineering position at a local factory, providing higher social status than possible without the degree. Her satisfaction came not from her work but from her homemaker role and her family, which included her husband and a son and his wife and children. She had few interests outside her home and little involvement in any cultural life.

Her relatives who had emigrated to the United States wrote about the miraculous freedom and economic opportunity in the new land. She had arrived with few resources, to encounter a reality very different from what she had anticipated. Neither she nor her husband could find employment, resulting in welfare status, with some supplemental income derived from sporadic housekeeping and bookkeeping jobs. Her 25-year-old son easily gained employment as a cab driver. Having held only a low-status position in the USSR, this represented no drop in status and yielded enough earnings to provide for his family's needs.

Unlike Mrs. Y, this client experienced no painful loss of social status and cultural network. Nevertheless, her loss was equally painful. With the independence of her son and his family, her homemaker role was sharply curtailed. Further, she experienced an economic reality markedly different from her high expectations.

It was important for the social worker to understand Mrs. G's losses as the basis of her depression. Further, the worker accepted Mrs. G's limited ability to articulate her suffering and disbelief in a talking therapy. The worker also understood that Mrs. G's somatic distress brought secondary gains in the form of increased family attention. Working in a limited time frame and using a supportive therapy approach that focused on concrete problems and services, the worker assisted Mrs. G with the family's economic problems. She also helped Mrs. G to redefine her homemaker role to fit her present reality and to find a circle of friends. This was accomplished by introducing husband and wife to the nearby Jewish community center, which offered a variety of social and cultural programs. Most important, the center offered a supportive network of understanding fellow immigrants.

Marital Conflict

Various intrafamilial problems arise because of the Soviet emigrés' loss of their family lifestyle. One area of conflict is the husband-wife relationship. Because the husband has so much invested in his role as breadwinner, his job loss is especially painful for him. His pain then affects the marital relationship and all family relationships. Although the Soviet wife also is a worker, her loss of job in the United States often is less painful. She is not only a breadwinner but, as parent and homemaker, retains other significant sources of gratification. The case of Mrs. T, a 42-year-old, married, Russian-speaking woman illustrates the marital tension that develops when a husband is unable to find employment while his wife succeeds. In this case the wife not only succeeds in becoming the breadwinner but maintains all three roles—wage earner, parent, and homemaker.

There are two additional pressures on adjustment in this case. One is the initial conflict about emigrating. The husband carried his reluctance and resentment about emigrating to his new home. It then became a weapon of blame as he attacked his wife for his adjustment difficulties. A second obstacle is the husband's definition of mental health service as appropriate only for those who are "crazy." This Soviet view contributes to resistance to use of mental health services, allowing problems to escalate unnecessarily.

The Case of Mrs. T

Mrs. T requested consultation for emotional disturbances with which she was unable to cope. She complained of sadness, nervousness, increased irritability, poor sleep, frequent headaches, and other physical symptoms. Two years earlier, Mrs. T arrived in the United States from Kiev, accompanied by her husband, her son and daughter, and her husband's parents. She reported no history of psychiatric disorders and presented a consistently good physical health record. She first experienced her symptoms about 4 months before entering therapy. After failing to resolve her problems she realized that she needed professional help. She described herself as having been a "normal" woman with a "normal" family. She now felt her family was splitting apart, and she was deeply concerned about her husband and their relationship.

In Ukraine, Mrs. T had been an accountant at a large factory where her husband had been chief of the engineering department. Their income was above average, and their lives were satisfactory. They enjoyed long-time friends and regularly attended social events, parties, concerts, and theater. Their two children were good students, and they had little difficulty as parents. The marital relationship had been warm, supportive, and friendly. Mrs. T reported that their problems began when they first considered emigration.

She had initiated the idea because she feared for the family's safety in the social and economic instability of the time. She particularly feared anti-Semitism, always present in Ukraine but particularly virulent during unstable times. Her children had been very enthusiastic about relocating in the United States, but her husband and his parents had agreed only reluctantly. He maintained that they both had stable work and income and were in no immediate danger. He feared that because of his age he would be unable to begin a new life and reach the occupational level he had attained in their homeland. His parents also were against relocation, fearing its numerous demands. Despite these concerns, Mrs. T had her way, and they emigrated.

In the United States, Mrs. T and her children successfully overcame major adjustment challenges. The children continued their education in public school, performing satisfactorily. After a few months of learning English, Mrs. T completed training in a business school and received a certificate in office management and bookkeeping. She soon found a job as assistant manager at a trade company, with a salary and medical insurance sufficient to cover her family's needs.

Mrs. T's husband fared poorly. He gained the support of an organization that helped former Soviet scientists and engineers start their new careers. He attended English class and classes to prepare for searching for employment. He prepared and mailed his résumés. Despite a number of interviews, however, he failed to secure a position. Gradually, his enthusiasm, motivation, self-confidence, and hope dwindled. By the time his wife found a job, he was depressed, spending most of his time lethargically at home; he was bad-tempered and jealous of other family members' successes. His relationships with his wife and children deteriorated. He was irritated and angry with his wife, blaming her for the family's emigration and his current failure. His subsequent loss of all sexual interest in his wife was particularly painful for Mrs. T because this had always been a source of mutual pleasure.

Mrs. T's success in the work world afforded her some small solace for her painful marital situation. Aware of her male co-workers' attention and compliments, she paid more attention to her grooming, acknowledging in sessions that she now felt even more "female power" than in her youth. Her acceptance of some co-workers' dinner invitations further lifted her spirits. However, her husband, noticing the change, became even more jealous and angry. Their marital tension increased until, frustrated and frightened by her loss of interest in her husband, she considered divorce. Aware of their long, pleasurable marriage and blaming herself for having forced the family to emigrate, she remained unable to resolve their predicament, developing her presenting symptoms.

After a few individual sessions with Mrs. T, the social worker invited Mr. T in to discuss the family's situation. Although initially resistant, insisting he was not "crazy" and had no need of professional help, Mr. T reluctantly agreed to marital therapy.

The work with this couple lasted several months and included both individual and joint sessions. The worker helped each of them explore their respective psychological difficulties and the origins of their problems. Therapy afforded each partner a better understanding of the other and the dynamics of their relationship. In joint sessions the couple learned to communicate effectively, share their feelings, identify common problems, and search for optimal solutions.

By treatment's end both Mr. and Mrs. T expressed willingness to remain together and to continue joint work on their problems. Mr. T regained his motivation to begin a new professional career. Through cognitive restructuring and behavioral modification he developed the skills he needed for success in job interviews. His self-esteem and self-confidence significantly improved so that by treatment's termination he had completed three job interviews and was awaiting decisions. Mr. T was more comfortable with his wife's success at work and encouraged her to pursue further professional advancement. Their relationship improved further with the resumption of a satisfying sexual relationship. Treatment terminated with marital and family relationships greatly improved and both partners better able to identify their issues and work together on their resolution.

Middle-aged adults are not the only family members at risk for marital conflict. Young married couples also may experience difficult relationship problems. On the one hand, emigration helps some young couples to separate from the family enmeshment typical in Soviet families. Often these young couples possess occupational knowledge and skills and greater language facility than their elders have, which affords them quicker social and occupational adjustment. However, other young couples, separated from their families by emigration, have difficulty with resettlement. Having relied on their parents for assistance in decision making and child rearing, they may lack skills in both areas. This situation may be particularly true in the intelligentsia families discussed above. Such young couples may fight, blame each other, voice regrets about marriage and emigration, and even talk of separation and divorce. Their lack of awareness of the impact of their acrimony on their children only exacerbates family difficulties (Halberstadt, 1994).

Adults and Their Parents

Another area of conflict is the relationship between adults and their parents. In the Soviet system older adults often played a valued role in the family, contributing to its welfare by providing child care for grandchildren and contributing to family income. In the United States, however, although these older adults may continue to provide some relief from parenting responsibilities, they may create an entirely new set of problems for their adult children. Older adults living with their adult children may interfere in their offspring's problems, making matters worse. The older generation also suffers from its own adjustment problems. Difficulty in finding gainful employment weakens their position and status in the family in this new world, adding to the family's stress. Older adults have a much harder time mastering English than do the younger family members. Because their grandchildren speak English better and know more about this new culture through their contact with peers and their school experience, older adults lose their authority to the younger generations, and their status in the family diminishes further. This new family structure, with the oldest generation given little respect and value, more closely resembles the American family system.

The case of Mrs. M illustrates some typical problems older adults face. It demonstrates the breakup of the three-generational family, the adults relinquishing responsibility for their older parents, and the anguish of older Soviet immigrants.

The Case of Mrs. M

Mrs. M, a 66-year-old Russian-speaking woman, emigrated from a mid-size Baltic republic some 3 years ago. She presented with symptoms of depression, insomnia, and multiple psychosomatic complaints. She explained that her problem was her painful loneliness.

Mrs. M had emigrated with her daughter's family, including a husband and two children aged 13 and 9 years. Her daughter and son-in-law were computer programmers, and she had been a high school Russian language and literature teacher. Her husband died in 1979, after which she moved in with her daughter's family. Mrs. M described her relationship with her deceased husband as "friendly" and her relationship with her daughter as always "very close."

During the first 2 years of resettlement, Mrs. M continued to reside with her daughter's family. She helped them by baby-sitting the grandchildren, cooking, and doing housework. Approximately 1 year prior to seeking therapy, her daughter and son-in-law received and accepted a very good job offer out of state. Because the new city lacked a Russian community and social life for Mrs. M, the family decided she would remain in New York.

Although anticipating some difficulty with the family's separation, Mrs. M experienced more pain than she expected. Despite having established satisfying relationships with Russian-speaking people her age, her major satisfaction had derived from her role in the home, particularly as a grandparent. She had taken much pleasure in her close relationships with her grandchildren and in feeling a part of their successful assimilation into American life. They, in turn, had given her the love and respect common between Soviet grandparents and their grandchildren. Mrs. M reacted to her loss with depression, withdrawing from social activities with her peers and becoming increasingly isolated at home. Her initial frequent communication with her family by mail and telephone gradually declined to a rarity. To avoid worrying her daughter and son-in-law and impeding their professional careers and family adjustment to their new community, she maintained secrecy about her predicament. Eventually, her frustration, isolation, and hopelessness about finding a solution led her to therapy.

Early in treatment the social worker referred Mrs. M to a psychiatrist for evaluation and treatment. He prescribed antidepressants to relieve her depression and facilitate psychotherapy. The social worker assisted Mrs. M in understanding the source of her depression and in identifying and disputing the irrational beliefs contributing to it. Despite her resistance, Mrs. M was helped to accept and resolve her issues of separation with her daughter and grandchildren. She was supported in regaining her lost sense of self-confidence and self-esteem and in functioning independently so that she was able to live alone supported by a network of her peers.

After several months of treatment, Mrs. M showed significant improvement in mood and increased participation in daily life and special social events. She rebuilt positive relationships with her former friends and participated in activity groups at her local community center. She initiated communication with her daughter and her family, sharing her concerns without intruding in their lives. Finally, she stopped her medications and terminated treatment with a good prognosis.

Parent-Adolescent Problems

Emigré's also struggle with relationship difficulties between parents and their adolescent children. Although generational conflict exists among all immigrant families, the adult Soviet emigrés' protectiveness adds to the problem. The Soviet emigrés' parental protectiveness was born out of a desire to protect their children from the Soviet Union's anti-Semitism. Their protectiveness, however, conflicts with the adolescent's typical struggle for independence and use of the peer group as guide and mentor. Parental unemployment, difficulty with English, and inability to understand their children's struggle with acculturation in their peer group and school create a deeper chasm between parent and child. One consequence is an erosion of the parents' authority over their adolescent children.

The case of B illustrates some of the difficulties Soviet immigrants confront with their adolescent children. The parents' limited ability to assist B is partly due to their lack of understanding of his acculturation experience. As an aside, it is interesting to note that B reported no academic difficulty at school. Soviet education does not parallel ours, and some youths find themselves academically ahead of their grade, experiencing boredom at school.

The Case of B

A 14-year-old Russian-speaking boy, B is the only son of a family who emigrated from Moscow 1 year ago. His parents took him to a mental health clinic, complaining of his increased irritability and poor communication with them, as well as misbehavior, withdrawal, and failing school grades.

A good student in Russia, B initially was motivated and enthusiastic in public school. Because he had attended a specialized English school in Russia, he was accepted into a regular eighth-grade class in the United States. His early work produced good grades and positive teacher evaluations. After several months, however, B's attitude and behavior changed, his grades dropped, and he withdrew at home. In their effort to help, his parents used habitual methods of suggestion and criticism, prohibiting activities and limiting relationships. Finally, accepting their failure, they sought therapy.

After working through B's resistance and establishing a therapeutic alliance, the social worker elicited his concerns about his physical changes, his growing interest in sexual issues, and his difficulties in adjusting at school. He was ashamed to discuss his sexual concerns with his parents because sex was never discussed in the home. He was interested in girls, but they liked "cool" guys. In his effort to become one of them, B copied their appearance, attitude, and behavior, losing interest in his studies. He finally found himself an outsider at school, with neither a reputation as a good student nor as "cool." He did not discuss his frustration and disappointment with his parents, believing they could not possibly understand and help. He insisted he still loved them but could not respect them because they remained Russian, whereas he desperately wanted to become "American" as soon as possible.

The social worker's treatment plan included two main elements: one focused on B, the other on his parents. With B, the worker sought to help him understand the physical and psychological changes he was undergoing and their effects, to clarity his strengths and support his efforts to use these to cope, to support his self-esteem and self-confidence by developing skills of positive self-evaluation and self-acceptance, and to help him better understand his parents' difficulties and reestablish communications with them. With his parents the worker sought to reframe their son's experience as a normal part of the adolescent's struggle for independence and to educate them as to more effective means of communicating with their son, using more approval and understanding and less criticism.

Treatment was successfully completed in about 5 months. Family relationships and B's school grades improved. He developed new interests in tennis and the computer. At school, although not fully accepted by the class leaders, he was less the outsider and formed his own circle of friends. His relationship with girls remained difficult, but it was now in the range of normal adolescent difficulty, and he was better able to cope with the stress of social relationships.

IMPLICATIONS FOR SOCIAL WORK PRACTICE

Social work has a long history of serving many different groups of immigrants. To assess and intervene effectively with resettlement problems, the worker must be sensitive to the experience of each particular immigrant group and individual. This sensitivity necessitates individualizing each client and having a sound understanding of the emigré's resettlement difficulties. The worker must also be sensitive to the emigré's homeland culture and lifestyle as well as his or her transit experience. Efforts to move too quickly into work on adjustment issues without first understanding the client's culture and transit experience may well prove self-defeating. Because emigrés are a heterogeneous population with considerable diversity, individualizing them is crucial to understanding each immigrant's unique experience. Sensitivity to this issue is also necessary to help Soviet emigrés overcome their learned distrust of social service workers. We now consider these elements and others and their practice implications.

Soviet-American Cultural Differences

In practice with Soviet Jewish immigrants, the social worker must be aware of Soviet-American cultural differences. As is true of all immigrants, cultural differences cross all facets of life, including mental health as well as family and social relationships. The relationship of the Soviet government to its citizens is one particularly significant factor to consider. The Soviet government provided its citizens with a range of welfare services, so the emigrés consider government subsidy a normal part of life. Understandably, given the choice of a low-status job or welfare, the emigré will opt for the familiar and acceptable welfare. Despite the American view of welfare as a stigmatizing alternative to employment, the emigré views it as an acceptable option. Without fully understanding the Soviet emigré's previous experience and perception of welfare, the worker may find it difficult to understand and accept the emigré's choice of welfare in the United States.

The Soviet emigré also may have difficulty with social service personnel because of cultural differences in service delivery. In the Soviet system the government and its bureaucrats provide service. Often, bureaucrats must be manipulated in order to gain benefits. In the United States, voluntary agencies play a significant role in the delivery of social services, and manipulation of the social worker is not a normal part of the transaction. The emigré who treats the social worker as a bureaucrat who must be manipulated in order to obtain service may initiate an unwanted interaction. The worker, ignorant of the customary Soviet transactions in securing services, risks misperceiving the emigré as psychologically disturbed, inappropriately demanding, and manipulative. The emigré then sees the worker as not understanding and, worse, uncaring.

Furthermore, social workers must be attuned to the emigré's mistrust of strangers and sense of entitlement. The Soviet system, through its persecution of Jews, fostered in them a distrust not only of governmental bureaucrats but of strangers in general. Soviet emigrés have learned to speak intimately only with family and a select group of trusted friends. Their mistrust of strangers impedes the social worker's efforts to establish rapport and a therapeutic alliance. Compounding the problem of establishing a therapeutic relationship is the emigrés' sense of entitlement. Their identification as victims, combined with American Jewry's promise of a better life in the United States, led to their sense of entitlement and unrealistic expectations of assistance and benefits.

Another general cultural difference worthy of special note is the emigrés' view of mental illness. The Soviet emigré is likely to view mental illness as biologically caused and best treated with medication. The talking cure at the heart of much of American therapy is understandably viewed as peculiar. Their difficulty in seeing the connection between talking and solving concrete problems adds to their confusion. The social worker's use of communication as a healing tool evokes in these clients a lack of confidence and trust in the worker who seeks to help (Drachman & Halberstadt, 1992).

To overcome the Soviet emigré's difficulty in using social services requires sensitivity to all facets of the emigré's experience and personality. The social worker must devote time to empathic listening and understanding. What was this emigré's unique native land circumstances? When and how did he or she travel from the USSR to the United States, and did he or she enter as a refugee or a parolee? What has he or she experienced in resettling? The worker's effort to understand empathically each emigré's full experience aids in healing the wounds of loss and in resolving resettlement problems. The social worker's most helpful role is as surrogate parent, providing the client with genuine interest, empathic caring, and some advice, direction, and counseling.

The emigrés' difficulty in using American mental health services, with their emphasis on communication, has other practice implications. It is more than coincidence that, although the case vignettes presented above cover a range of problems, they all involved short-term approaches. Time-limited, highly focused counseling seems most appropriate, given the Soviet emigrés' views and experience.

The Immigrant as Service Provider

One aid in overcoming these cultural differences is the use of bilingual fellow Soviet immigrants. Social work has a history of involving indigenous people in helping their fellow compatriots to acculturate. Their own experience as emigrés uniquely qualifies indigenous people to assist professionals in bridging the cultural gap between social worker and emigré. Bilingual Soviet emigrés trained as social workers in the United States are especially qualified to work with this population. Their personal experience and professional training make them ideally equipped to overcome the cultural obstacles discussed above. They possess the empathic understanding and language skill that facilitates the development of trust and understanding. One way of serving these emigrés, then, is to provide social work training and assistance to professional colleagues serving Soviet emigrés.

Soviet Emigrés' Communities

Trained in a systems perspective, social workers are uniquely prepared to take a comprehensive view of clients and their problems. They are well aware of the need to consider their clients' history and culture. They also are committed to understanding the broader social systems within which clients function. This particularly applies to Soviet emigrés, who often settle in communities with family, friends, and those of similar origins. Social workers must be aware of clients' relationships with existing neighborhood networks that can provide needed information and practical assistance. Some community networks may be informal, including family, friends, and neighbors. Others may take the form of business or professional associations and social and cultural organizations. To intervene effectively, the social worker must be aware of these resources in the client's own community.

CONCLUSION

Several themes emerge in considering the Soviet Jewish immigrant presence in the United States. One theme is that there are areas that are common to all the groups. One significant common element is their close-knit, emotionally connected, multigenerational family structure. Another is the anti-Semitism they experienced in the form of restricted social, educational, and occupational opportunities.

A second theme is their exceptional heterogeneity. They are diverse in origin and culture. They come from some 15 different Soviet republics, with very different cultures and lifestyles. They also significantly differ in the circumstances of their transit from the USSR to the United States. On arrival in the United States, they formed distinctly separate communities, replicating the social and geographic character of their original communities. They are aware of their differences and cluster with family, friends, and those from their homeland towns, cities, and regions.

A third theme is that despite their differences in origin, the emigrés share the experience of dealing with the challenge of relocating in a foreign land. Coming from a system that fosters dependency, they encounter one that demands independence and self-sufficiency. The loss of occupational and social status poses other hardships. The breakup of the traditional family unit constitutes further stress, particularly for the elderly.

Finally, there is the theme of a cultural mentality that presents special problems for the social worker seeking to serve the emigrés, namely, their distrust of social service delivery systems. Though this population may pose a considerable amount of difficulty for the social worker, it is important to remember social work's long and honorable history in assisting other immigrant groups to acculturate. The profession has developed generic knowledge and skills that can be as useful in serving these immigrants as it was with so many preceding groups. To be effective with this immigrant group, social workers must call on their skills of empathy, sensitive understanding of the client's problem and needs, and appreciation of the uniqueness of the emigré's cultural background.

REFERENCES

Barber, J. (1987). The Soviet Jews of Washington Heights. *New York Affairs, 10*, 34–44.

Belozersky, I. (1990). New beginnings, old problems. *Journal of Jewish Communal Service, 67*, 124–131.

Bentsianov, E. Director, New Hope Guild Russian Program. (1995). Interview with author.

Budner, S., Chazin, R., & Young, H. (1973). The indigenous nonprofessional in a multiservice center. *Social Casework, 54*, 354–359.

Chazin, R. (1995). *Chernobyl and Its Aftermath.* Unpublished manuscript.

Congress, E. (1994). The use of culturagrams to assess and empower culturally diverse families. *Families in Society, 75*, 531–540.

Drachman, D., & Halberstadt, A. (1992). A stage of migration framework as applied to recent Soviet emigrés. In A. S. Ryan (Ed.), *Social work with immigrants and refugees* (pp. 63–78). New York: Haworth Press.

Gold, S. J. (1994). Soviet Jews in the United States. *American Jewish Year Book, 94*, 1–57.

CHAPTER 10

Redefining the Family: The Concept of Family for Lesbians and Gay Men

Stephen McFadden

One of the first tasks that social workers learn in their training is how to make an accurate assessment of the person-in-situation. Indeed, what distinguishes assessment from diagnosis is the appraisal of how the presenting problem interrelates with the biological, psychological, and sociocultural features of the person and his or her world (Northen, 1987).

Two important aspects of an assessment are the individual's internal sense of himself or herself and the individual's interaction with the social systems of his or her world. For clients who are lesbian or gay, this presents a paradox. First, the lesbian or gay person's sense of self has often been developed out of a recognition that it is at odds with the larger society. Second, because of this fact lesbian or gay persons often have to make choices about how open and honest to be about their homosexuality in relation to the larger sociocultural institutions that they participate in.

Although family is but one of our sociocultural institutions, it is perhaps the most important one. The family is the first social institution most of us experience. Conformity with familial and gender norms plays a role in how we interrelate with other social institutions (education, employment,

167

legal, government, religion). For all gay and lesbian persons the process of relating to these larger systems necessitates redefining the self and often redefining the concept of family.

This suggests the need for a different framework in working with lesbian and gay persons, because by definition such persons view themselves as differing from dominant familial and gender norms. In this chapter, I discuss how the process of redefining the family occurs for lesbian and gay persons throughout the life cycle. It begins with family of origin and, through the process of coming out, leads to the creation of a new sense of family and community that is separate from yet interactive with one's family of origin and the larger heterosexual world.

WHAT IS A FAMILY?

In the current political climate, with the renewed emphasis on traditional "family values," it is pertinent to ask, what is a family? The answer, for all our institutions, is socially constructed and culturally determined. Yet the traditional nuclear family configuration is in flux, if indeed it ever was truly the norm (Coontz, 1992). In terms of contemporary social work practice, Hartman and Laird (1987) present what they call

> an inclusive, self-determining, or phenomenological definition of the family . . . created when two or more people construct an intimate environment that they define as a family, an environment in which they generally will share a living space, commitment, and a variety of the roles and functions, usually considered a part of family life. (p. 576)

If using this definition, most lesbian and gay couples and the families they create could easily see themselves as family. But it is rarely that simple. The very act of identifying oneself as lesbian or gay involves making a break with traditional gender norms in the larger society, usually learned within a heterosexual family constellation. In looking at how lesbian and gay persons construct a sense of family, we must first look at the process of coming out, identifying as homosexual to oneself and to others.

HOMOSEXUAL IDENTITY: COMING OUT

Over the past 15 years a number of models have been developed by lesbian and gay social scientists to describe the process by which homosexual persons come to an acceptance of themselves as lesbian or gay and assume an identity as such. The best known of these are the models developed by Cass (1979), Coleman (1982), and Troiden (1989). All the models share some common characteristics.

First and foremost, the models are all progressive, emphasizing that the individual goes through stages in developing an identity as lesbian or gay. First, the individual becomes aware of feeling different from same-sex peers, generating dissonance, confusion, and inner turmoil. There is a gradual tolerance and then acceptance of oneself as being different. Next is the exploration and assumption of a homosexual identity in the larger world. This exploration can occur through initial contacts with the homosexual world but eventually involves the decision of whether to disclose one's homosexuality to heterosexuals, including one's family of origin. Finally, the individual develops a commitment to a homosexual identity, involving pride in oneself, development of committed relationships, a sense of community, and an integration of the lesbian or gay self within the larger heterosexual world.

Second, the models not only reflect internal processes but are relational as well. Because of societal sanctions against gender nonconformity and homosexuality, the individual first feels very alone in her or his difference. As lesbian or gay persons accept themselves as different, there is a subsequent need to establish a relationship with other lesbian and gay persons and to redefine oneself vis-à-vis the dominant social systems one participates in. This necessarily involves questioning social norms, including those of the traditional heterosexual family.

Questioning and redefining oneself in relation to established social norms involves both losses and gains. Lesbian or gay persons need to come to terms with the fact that the families they develop are not the families accepted and sanctioned by the dominant culture. This is reinforced repeatedly and in countless ways. However, this can be balanced by a sense of belonging and community in the lesbian and gay world and by developing a sense of pride rather than shame. Kimmel (1978) believes that, because this challenge and redefinition occurs early in their lives, most lesbians and gay men develop a sense of "crisis competence" that helps them confront later challenges that are part of being different in the world.

The process of coming out continues through the life cycle and presents different challenges at different developmental periods, from adolescence

(Hetrick & Martin, 1988) through old age (Friend, 1991; Kimmel, 1978). It always involves defining oneself and one's sense of family in relation to the dominant culture. Although the coming-out models described above apply to both lesbians and gay men, there are some differences in how each experiences coming out. Reflecting gender role expectations, lesbians often emphasize and act on their emotional attachments first, whereas gay men will often act first on their sexual attractions. Lesbians may also come out via involvement with the women's movement and through an identification with gender issues as well as issues of sexual orientation (de Monteflores & Schultz, 1978). Likewise, lesbian and gay people of color struggle with the issue of multiple identifications and finding a fit between an identification with the lesbian and gay community and an identification with their own ethnic/racial community (Chan, 1989; Espin, 1987; Loiacano, 1989).

RELATIONSHIP TO FAMILY OF ORIGIN

By definition, coming out as lesbian or gay to one's family of origin involves changing rules and roles. All parents have gender-specific expectations of their sons and daughters that relate to their role in the family, so the disclosure that a child is lesbian or gay creates a family crisis. Dealing with a son's or daughter's homosexuality necessarily involves losses for parents involving their expectations and assumptions for their child.

There is also a need for education about homosexuality in light of the myths, shame, stigma, and misinformation that surround the subject. Often, the family member best equipped to educate and inform the family is the lesbian daughter or gay son because their disclosure often is preceded by their own coming-out process. This can create a bind for the family due to the conflicted feelings of each party. Lesbian and gay clients can provide their parents with a book on the topic (Fairchild & Hayward, 1989) or refer them to support groups such as Parents and Friends of Lesbians and Gays (P-Flag).

Redefining oneself to family of origin involves two challenges: (1) there is wide variability in families' degrees of acceptance, and (2) reminders of the difference recur at different family developmental points. The shame and societal stigma associated with homosexuality may lead families to deny or avoid the topic, even after it has been raised (bringing to mind the current policy in the U.S. military: "Don't ask, don't tell"). The lesbian daughter or gay son may be presented with the uncomfortable choice of repeatedly confronting the family's defenses or of colluding with secrecy and shame. A compromise that many lesbians and gay men learn to live with is accepting some level of loss of full acceptance from the family of origin and addressing needs unmet by the family through involvement with a lesbian or gay family within that community.

Lesbians and gay men internalize the strong societal injunction not to disclose, and it is only by dealing with their own coming-out process that they gradually share who they are with the world. Many leave home and come out in the lesbian and gay world prior to coming out to their families of origin. Thus, the family and the adult child are often at different levels of comfort and awareness in their dealings with homosexuality.

The issue of homosexuality is raised not only at the initial time of coming out but again and again, at different developmental points for the adult child and for the family of origin. Families that were able to ignore or minimize a daughter's or son's homosexuality are not able to do so as easily when the adult child forms a committed relationship or establishes a family with children of his or her own. Relationships with extended family and with children (nieces and nephews) in the family, as well as observance of family rituals and celebrations (such as holidays, weddings, and funerals) all have the potential to highlight the family's attitude toward the lesbian or gay member. In working with lesbian and gay clients and their families, the social worker must remember that dealing with being gay is a normative and ongoing process for the entire family and must treat it as such.

Finally, the issue of an adult child's homosexuality can arise out of a family crisis, such as the dissolution of a marriage or an AIDS diagnosis. For differing reasons, often having to do with struggles with identity and coming out, some lesbians and gay men come out after forming a heterosexual marriage and family. The complex issues of redefining the self to one's spouse, children, in-laws, and family of origin draw on the same themes as coming out for all lesbian and gay persons but involve exploring the feelings of betrayal, hurt, anger, and confusion that are evoked by all parties (Buxton, 1994). Each family member has his or her own process and time frame for integrating this information and usually needs some separation to sort out the issues, as well as education and support from others.

Family shame, stigma, and difficulties with coming out also occur in situations where a family must concurrently learn of a member's homosexuality at the time they learn that he has AIDS. As with coming out after a marriage, family members need to have their complex emotions heard, need accurate information to educate and assist them, and need some time apart as well as some guidance in communicating their feelings and needs to the person with AIDS. Although both situations initially present a crisis to the families involved, I have worked with families in which the outcome has drawn the family together in improved caring and cooperation, whereas before there had been secrecy and hurt, confused feelings.

THE COMMUNITY AS A FAMILY

Unlike racial and ethnic communities, where parents elders, and older siblings share norms, traditions, and skills for coping as members of a subordinate group, lesbians or gay persons start off completely on their own. Even when there is a personal acceptance of one's gay identity, the lesbian or gay person is hesitant and sometimes fearful of seeking guidance from parents because of shame, fear of rejection, and an expectation (usually accurate) that the family will be ignorant or misinformed about the homosexual world.

For many, the lesbian and gay community becomes a substitute family, providing socialization, setting norms and guidelines, and taking over functions that are usually the province of family. The first involvement in a gay environment, whether it is through the bar/club scene, a women's music festival, or a political or social group, is a powerful experience for most lesbians and gay men, evoking a sense of belonging, as distinct from often feeling different and marginalized. Indeed, immersion in a lesbian or gay environment is often a stage in the development of a homosexual identity.

Friendship with other lesbians and gay men can provide the support and sense of belonging often missing in interactions with the family of origin. The camp use of "sister," "girlfriend," and "auntie" by some gay men is interesting in this context. Questions about whom one is dating, about an ex-lover, about how one reacts to homophobia in society may be tactfully avoided at celebrations with one's family of origin but are easily raised in gatherings with other lesbian and gay friends. Friendships are highly valued and may serve as the prelude to a romantic/sexual relationship, and romantic/sexual relationships, once ended, may continue on as deep friendships (Vetere, 1983).

The definition of family is thus expanded, with relational aspects such as love, support, and commitment emphasized more than legal or biological family structure (Benkov, 1994). This becomes increasingly important throughout the life cycle, especially with older lesbians and gay men, for whom children and other relatives may not be available to help with issues of bereavement, physical disability, and other losses (Kimmel, 1978). Instances of friends and community supports providing functions usually assigned to the family have been most striking in the case of AIDS (Shernoff, 1984). Hospital and AIDS service workers can provide multiple examples of friends, "buddies," ex-lovers, and community volunteers caring for their own in the midst of crisis. This expanded definition of family also leads to expanded rituals, such as the increasing practice of commitment ceremonies and anniversaries for lesbian and gay couples, gay pride celebrations, and AIDS memorial services and vigils.

LESBIAN AND GAY COUPLES

All couples, heterosexual or homosexual, must define their relationship over time. But lesbian and gay couples do this without the gender norms, parental and family models, and legal structures that heterosexual couples have. Like coming out to oneself and others as gay, defining the couple presents both a challenge and an opportunity.

Because people of the same gender provide a common pool of potential friends and romantic partners, lesbian and gay persons must first define their status with each other, whether as friends, dating partners, or sexual partners. For some, these roles can change over time, with ex-lovers remaining close friends and friends having some initial or later sexual involvement.

The issues that arise for the lesbian and gay couple are tied into their identity as homosexual, that is, different from the heterosexual norm. What do they call each other (partner, lover, spouse, husband, wife, companion)? What do they date as the anniversary of their relationship?

How do they define themselves to their respective families of origin, to their co-workers, and to their neighbors? How do they differentiate household chores, finances, and child rearing? How "out" is each partner to the outside world?

It is clear from these questions that lesbian and gay couples must continuously define themselves to each other and to the outside world. Without the legal structure of marriage and the assumption of traditional gender roles, couples have the freedom to create their own norms. They also run the risk of locating problems that develop in their relationship solely within themselves and their partners if they do not take into account the impact of the special challenges of being lesbian or gay.

One challenge arises from joining with a partner of the same gender. Both partners experienced the same gender socialization, including gender expectations of how to behave in a relationship. Gender socialization and expectations influence how same-sex couples react when problems develop: lesbian couples tend to come together (fusion) in response to relationship problems, whereas gay men reactively distance. These reactions are not only determined by socialization but also by the couple's isolation as a lesbian or gay couple (Krestin & Bepko, 1980).

Jealousy is experienced differently by same-sex couples because they often socialize in a lesbian or gay environment, where people meet not only to socialize but to find romantic and sexual partners. The couple's sexual relationship also needs to be negotiated. Many lesbian and gay couples are monogamous, but others opt for more open sexual relationships over time (Berger, 1990). Gay male couples often must contend with the prevalence of AIDS in their community, involving a host of challenges such as negotiating a safer sexual relationship, dealing with differences in HIV status, and the not uncommon occurrence of one partner having lost a former lover to death from AIDS (Mattison & McWhirter, 1994).

The lack of legal safeguards and gender role expectations results in the couple's struggling with issues of finances, career, work, and child rearing without the presumed guidelines married couples have. Couples are advised to seek legal guidance concerning joint property, wills, health care proxies, and child custody agreements.

A couple may be at different stages of identification as lesbian or gay and may be at different stages of coming out. This can generate conflict, as well as differing levels of acceptance, in the partners' families of origin. As stated earlier, the very fact of being in a couple can cause a family to revisit its homophobia. Unspoken family "contracts" on dealing with homosexuality need to be reexamined by the couple as they form a unit (Decker, 1984).

Another difference for lesbian and gay couples may arise from the fact that there seems to be more variability in age, class, income, race, and ethnicity than in heterosexual couples. There are reasons for this: First, there is a smaller pool of choices, and lesbian and gay persons of all types often come together socially due to limited opportunities to meet others, especially outside large cities. Second, the primary identification of each partner may be based on being lesbian or gay, rather than on class, age cohort, or ethnicity. A difference in group membership or status does, however, bring its own set of challenges (Carl, 1990).

Several developmental models have been proposed for lesbian and gay couples (Berger, 1990; Carl, 1990; Falco, 1991; Forstein, 1986; McWhirter & Mattison, 1984; Murphy, 1994; Peplau, 1991). All have in common the fact that lesbian and gay couples must develop their own norms and stages based both on being different (from the heterosexual marital model) and on being the same (gender). As is clear from the preceding discussion, this presents both opportunities and challenges.

PARENTING AND CHILDREN

Although some lesbian and gay persons have always been parents, there is a new emphasis in the community (and in the media) on lesbian and gay individuals and couples forming their own families with children. In our discussion of redefining the family, this is one area that is most challenging for lesbians and gay men and for the straight world.

We first need to define two types of lesbian and gay parents. First are lesbians and gay men with children from past heterosexual involvements that they are now bringing into their gay family, whether that is defined as a couple or a community. Especially important are lesbians and gay men who come out after a marriage. The issue of disclosure predominates here; a parent's decision to disclose his or her homosexuality to a child is tied into the parent's own identification and coming-out process (Buxton, 1994; Matteson, 1987). In making the decision about whether and when to come out to a child, lesbians and gay men need to be alert to custody issues, as the courts have been inconsistent and often biased in their responses to lesbian and gay parents in child custody cases (Falk, 1989).

Second are lesbians and gay men who decide to have children after coming out. This sometimes occurs in the context of a couple and sometimes in the case of an individual. Unlike heterosexuals, who are expected and often pressured to have children when married, lesbians and gay men come to this decision after a deliberate and usually thought-through process that may involve giving oneself permission to see oneself as a viable parent (Martin, 1993). Having made the choice, lesbians and gay men should next consider the various methods available to them in becoming parents (adoption, foster parenting, artificial insemination, donors and surrogacy, and co-parenting). Each method entails legal, medical, financial, emotional, and support issues, which must be examined in advance (Benkov, 1994; Bozett, 1987; Martin, 1993; Shernoff, 1996).

Once again, the issues of identifying oneself as homosexual and of how open one is become a critical part of each choice. On a legal and practical level, many lesbians and gay men becoming parents must conceal their sexual orientation or their having a partner. This is especially true in adoption and foster parenting, where state guidelines vary and can change over time. Even when using procedures that enable one to be openly lesbian or gay, there is the potential to face renewed homophobia in dealing with pregnancy, parenting, and child-centered agencies and services.

Becoming a parent invariably leads to more dealings with the heterosexual world and sometimes less with the gay world and the gay family one has created. There may be renewed contact and redefinition of oneself (and one's partner) with families of origin. Issues of internalized homophobia can arise as the lesbian or gay person takes on the dual identities of homosexual and parent, which are not at all linked in a traditional view of the family. Fortunately, in larger cities there are now support groups and even agencies (such as Center Kids, at New York City's Lesbian and Gay Community Services Center) where lesbian and gay parents and would-be-parents can get help with information and legal and other resources, as well as joining other parents dealing with the same issues.

Once the child arrives, the issues center on raising the child in a nontraditional family. As with defining the couple, the issues now focus on defining parenting roles without traditional gender norms that heterosexual parents accept as a given, even when they challenge them. Questions arise regarding naming and defining the role of each parent, defining the legal status of the nonbiological or nonadoptive parent, and choosing how to relate to families of origin, peers, and the surrounding gay and straight community. Of special concern is educating the child over time about homophobia, which the child will have to confront in dealing with peers from heterosexual families and with the straight world in general (Bozett, 1987; Pennington, 1987).

As is the case with the lesbian and gay couple, the lesbian and gay family with children must define and redefine itself at different developmental points: the birth of the child, the entry into school, dealing with extended families, the child's adolescence and sexual development, separation of the couple, or the death of one parent. All of these developmental points bring specific dynamics that necessarily interact with the family's status in society as a lesbian or gay family.

IMPLICATIONS FOR PRACTICE

The preceding material makes clear that clinicians working with lesbian and gay clients must reach for a different conception of "family," a new conception that is informed by the client's identity as a lesbian or gay man and by how she or he has dealt with this in the larger world. This is important not only for clients who are self-identified as lesbian or gay and who see themselves as part of the gay community but also for clients who are not out and are struggling with identity issues. The latter group of clients needs even more assistance in considering an expanded definition of family as they develop a social identity in the world in which they live.

Clinicians are advised to remember that, just as taking on a lesbian or gay identity is a process, so is the method by which lesbian and gay persons create and define their family. Replacing a genogram with a sociogram can be useful in helping clients define their family; a sociogram explores the client's interactions with both the gay and the straight world and how well these two are integrated (Shernoff, 1984).

Families of origin also struggle with a new definition of family in their approach to a lesbian or gay member, involving shifts, changes, and cut-offs. Even when the family of origin rejects the lesbian or gay person, the issue of homosexuality forces family members to confront their own parameters of what should constitute a family. This occurs at different developmental points for both the family of origin and for lesbian or gay persons as they create their own families.

As with any subordinate societal group, clinicians of the dominant group (in this instance, heterosexuals) must be willing to acknowledge their bias in working with lesbians and gay men and be open to learning more about the experience of being homosexual from the voices of those who constitute the subordinate group. Especially with lesbians and gay men, whose struggle for self-definition and self-determination informs identity, we must ask what their conception of family is and what their familial needs are and must work with them to actualize this in the complex world that belongs to both homosexual and heterosexual persons.

REFERENCES

Benkov, L. (1994). *Reinventing the family: The emerging story of lesbian and gay parents*. New York: Crown.

Berger, R. M. (1990). Men together: Understanding the gay couple. *Journal of Homosexuality, 19*(3), 31–49.

Bozett, F. W. (1987). Children of gay fathers. In F. W. Bozett (Ed.), *Gay and lesbian parents* (pp. 39–57). New York: Praeger.

Buxton, A. P. (1994). *The other side of the closet: The coming-out crisis for straight spouses and families*. New York: Wiley.

Carl, D. (1990). *Counseling same-sex couples*. New York: Norton.

Cass, V. C. (1979). Homosexual identity formation: A theoretical model. *Journal of Homosexuality, 4*(3), 219–235.

Chan, C. S. (1989). Issues of identity development among Asian-American lesbians and gay men. *Journal of Counseling and Development, 68*, 16–20.

Coleman, E. (1982). Developmental stages in the coming out process. In J. C. Gonsiorek (Ed.), *Homosexuality and psychotherapy: A practitioner's handbook of affirmative models* (pp. 31–43). New York: Haworth Press.

Coontz, S. (1992). *The way we never were: American families and the nostalgia trap*. New York: Basic Books.

Decker, B. (1984). Counseling gay and lesbian couples. *Journal of Social Work and Human Sexuality, 2*(2–3), 39–52.

de Monteflores, C., & Schultz, S. J. (1978). Coming out: Similarities and differences for lesbians and gay men. *Journal of Social Issues, 34*(3), 59–72.

Espin, O. M. (1987). Issues of identity in the psychology of Latina lesbians. In Boston Lesbian Psychologies Collective (Eds.), *Lesbian psychologies:*

Explorations and challenges (pp. 35–55). Urbana: University of Illinois Press.

Fairchild, B., & Hayward, N. (1989). *Now that you know: What every parent should know about homosexuality*. San Diego, CA: Harcourt Brace Jovanovich.

Falco, K. L. (1991). *Psychotherapy with lesbian clients: Theory into practice*. New York: Brunner/Mazel.

Falk, P. J. (1989). Lesbian mothers: Psychosocial assumptions in family law. *American Psychologist, 44,* 941–947.

Forstein, M. (1986). Psychodynamic psychotherapy with gay male couples. In T. S. Stein & C. J. Cohen (Eds.), *Psychotherapy with lesbians and gay men* (pp. 103–138). New York: Plenum.

Friend, R. (1991). Older lesbian and gay people: A theory of successful aging. *Journal of Homosexuality, 20*(3–4), 99–118.

Hartman, A., & Laird, J. (1987). Family practice. In A. Minahan (Ed.), *Encyclopedia of social work* (18th ed., pp. 575–589). Silver Spring, MD: National Association of Social Workers.

Hetrick, E. S., & Martin, A. D. (1988). Developmental issues and their resolution for gay and lesbian adolescents. In E. Coleman (Ed.), *Integrated identity for gay men and lesbians: Psychotherapeutic approaches for emotional well-being* (pp. 25–43). New York: Harrington Park Press.

Kimmel, D. C. (1978). Adult development and aging: A gay perspective. *Journal of Social Issues, 34*(3), 113–130.

Kresten, J. A., & Bepko, C. S. (1980). The problem of fusion in the lesbian relationship. *Family Processes, 19,* 277–289.

Loiacano, D. K. (1989). Gay identity issues among Black Americans: Racism, homophobia, and the need for validation. *Journal of Counseling and Development, 68,* 21–25.

Martin, A. (1993). *The lesbian and gay parenting handbook: Creating and raising our families*. New York: HarperCollins.

Matteson, D. R. (1987). The heterosexually married gay and lesbian parent. In F. W. Bozett (Ed.), *Gay and lesbian parents* (pp. 138–161). New York: Praeger.

Mattison, A. M., & McWhirter, D. P. (1994). Serodiscordant male couples. In L. A. Kurdek (Ed.), *Social services for gay and lesbian couples* (pp. 83–99). New York: Harrington Park Press.

McWhirter, D. P., & Mattison, A. W. (1984). *The male couple: How relationships develop*. Englewood Cliffs, NJ: Prentice-Hall.

Murphy, B. C. (1994). Diversity and difference: Gay and lesbian couples. In L. A. Kurdek (Ed.), *Social services for gay and lesbian couples* (pp. 5–31). New York: Harrington Park Press.

Northen, H. (1987). Assessment in direct practice. In A. Minahan (Ed.), *Encyclopedia of social work* (18th ed., pp. 171–183). Silver Spring, MD: National Association of Social Workers.

Pennington, S. B. (1987). Children of lesbian mothers. In F. S. Bozett (Ed.), *Gay and lesbian parents* (pp. 58–74). New York: Praeger.

Peplau, L. A. (1991). Lesbian and gay relationships. In J. C. Gonsiorek & J. D. Weinreich (Eds.), *Homosexuality: Research implications for public policy* (pp. 177–196). Newbury Park, CA: Sage.

Shernoff, M. J. (1984). Family therapy for lesbian and gay clients. *Social Work, 29*(4), 393–396.

Shernoff, M. J. (1984). Lesbian and gay families in the 1980s. In M. Shernoff & F. Schwaber (Eds.), *Sourcebook on lesbian/gay health care* (pp. 57–59). Washington, DC: National Lesbian/Gay Health Foundation.

Shernoff, M. J. (1996). Gay men choosing to be fathers. *Journal of Gay and Lesbian Social Services, 4*(2), 41–51.

Troiden, R. C. (1989). The formation of homosexual identities. *Journal of Homosexuality, 17*(1–2), 57–73.

Vetere, V. A. (1983). The role of friendship in the development and maintenance of lesbian love relationships. *Journal of Homosexuality, 8*(2), 51–65.

CHAPTER 11

Machismo, Manhood, and Men in Latino Families

Yolanda Mayo

"I want to be in America." These familiar words from the musical *West Side Story* reflect the popular notion that newcomers to the United States are usually ecstatic with life in America, the land of milk and honey. This popular belief also helps to camouflage the limited understanding the population at large has of immigration and its devastating toll on individuals and families. The immigrant experience—of differences and sudden changes in once-familiar areas of physical, social, psychological communication and relationships—challenges the very core of personal identity. The immigrant is forced to shed traditional behavior patterns and attitudes and to adapt to new ones in as brief a period as possible.

For the majority of Latino families the move is from a traditional agricultural and paternalistic environment to a technological, postindustrial society, with an aggressive, individualistic, competitive culture (Shorris, 1992). Migration, acculturation, and adapting to a new and markedly different culture often begin an erosion of native-bound, natural support systems and values, such as the extended family. These changes are particularly significant for Latino men who have been socialized in an extended patriarchal and positively enmeshed system (Canino & Canino, 1980) that designates the man as head of household and family leader.

The traditional patriarchal role of the Latino father has thus become one of the most misunderstood aspects of Latino male gender experiences. Latinos (to use the more encompassing definition for a population that blends Iberian/Luso, African, and Indian roots) bring to the United States marked differences in culture, language, lifestyles, and value systems, all of which in turn differ considerably from the American core culture (Michener, 1989). It is in deference to this rich and complex cultural blend that I have chosen to use the term *Latino*, as reflective of an identity that comprises the diversity and multiculturalism of Latin Americans in the United States. As a concept, *Latino* expands the Spanish cultural legacy emphasized in the term *Hispanic*.

Latino cultural practices and behavior patterns in the United States are often in direct opposition to those of the host society. Preferred styles of action, such as "speaking with your hands," behaving more animatedly, and choosing specific foods and colors (McGoldrick, Pearce, & Giordano, 1996), often lead to cultural misunderstanding and at times misdiagnosis (Fitzpatrick, 1971). Such is the fate of machismo, the manifestation of male superiority attributed to Latino males by a host society that often misunderstands both its etiology and its function (Inclan, 1985; Mayo, 1994; Ramirez, 1992; Wells, 1968).

This chapter explores the impact of machismo on the lifestyles and role behavior of Latino men living in the United States. Emphasis is placed on how this concept needs to be examined professionally, looking at both its positive and its negative elements, as well as at its organizing function in structuring Latino male identity and its potential as a tool for the engagement of Latino men in treatment. This chapter thus presents an etiology of machismo, a review of its component parts, a discussion of Latino family structure, an overview of Latinos in the United States, and a consideration of implications for treatment.

AN ETIOLOGY OF MACHISMO

Few things have become as perfectly assimilated to American core culture as the Spanish word *macho*. A term that describes male animals and specific types of hardware related to husbandry, it has been Anglicized into a descriptive term for Latino men and Latino male behavior, as noted in *Diccionario de la Lengua Española* (1947; Monfort Tomas, 1985).

The word *machismo* is found in the 1984 edition of this dictionary, defined as *actitud de prepotencia de los varones respecto de las mujeres* (an attitude of supremacy by men regarding women). The inclusion of *machismo* in the Spanish-language dictionary in recent years suggests a move toward its common usage in the Spanish vernacular. Within its new cultural definition in the United States, *machismo* is best known in the context of the Hollywood "tough leading man." It has become a catchall term for all aspects of male physical, sexual, and authoritative patriarchal behavior. In a collection of essays on American machismo, Kriegel (1978) equates American manhood with the control of and adaptation to the environment (e.g., the American frontier). Pete Hamill discusses American manhood as exemplified in literature by "Hemingway, who became the central figure in American *macho* style"; and in politics by Theodore Roosevelt, who depicted American machismo through his imperialistic political exploits (Kriegel, 1978, p. 395). Machismo in this expanded cross-cultural form, identifiable in Anglo as well as Latino societies, is presented as a universal concept that is reflected differently by men in different cultures. Machismo is supported by most major social systems and by cultural value premises reflected in family lifestyles.

In Latino families and in Latino societies, machismo, or manhood, takes shape and form from the Spanish *varon* or *hombre* (male or man). A definition of *varon* in Spanish, contrary to the definition of *macho*, refers to "a rational being of the male sex. A man who has reached an age of virility—a man of respect, authority and other attributes—of God—a holy man of special spirit or virtues" (*Diccionario de la Lengua Española*, 1947, p. 1276). The birth of a male child is therefore announced by joyous cries of "*Es varoncito*"—a little male, or simply stated, "It's a boy." *Ser varon* (to be a man) is a matter of character; *ser macho* (to be macho) is a matter of behavior.

The roots of the traditional cultural conceptualization of machismo can be traced to the quixotic idealism and the distinctive cult of chivalry that developed in the Iberian peninsula, an idealism and a cult that viewed males as strong warriors and protectors of womanhood. Once transplanted to the new world, machismo was assimilated and blended with the multicultural and ethnic populations that shaped the men of the "Indies" (Las Indias), as Spain had historically referred to its former colonies.

In Latin America, machismo takes still another turn. Although described by some authors in the United States as reflecting a behavior pattern characteristic of Latino men from countries bordering the Caribbean (e.g., Cuba, Santo Domingo, Puerto Rico, and Venezuela) (Stevens, 1973), the term has also been used to describe all Latino men in Spanish-speaking countries. Repudiating machismo as a cultural trait reflective of Latin men and the North American focus on machismo, Latin America has also begun to explore this concept in relation to families and gender roles. Monfort Tomas (1985) suggests that the popular view of machismo in Venezuela, if it exists at all,

> would present an individual governed by his passions and sexual appe-
> tite . . . such an animal of the masculine sex, whose resemblance with a
> man is purely coincidental . . . would be therefore abnormal. (p. 17)

Ramirez (1993) notes that in Puerto Rico, as far back as 1922, machismo was perceived as a negative characteristic of men who refused to see women in their separate and culturally emancipated roles. Quoting Neme-sio Canales, a Puerto Rican newspaperman and well-known humorist, Rameriz identifies machismo as "a negative attitude shown by some men who refused to see women other than in their 'soulless' role of 'Dresden china dolls' " (p. 17).

As described in the media, in countries like Argentina (characterized by a Eurocentric society) and Peru (with its large indigenous population) it is the women's movement that has been active in addressing the issue of machismo ("Influencias del Machismo," 1994. Argentinean and Peruvian women, together with women's movements in Brazil, the Caribbean, Central America, Colombia, and Venezuela, have joined in a Latin American effort to publicly address machismo, male dominance, and patriarchy and their impact on daily life.

STRUCTURE OF MACHISMO

This chapter also focuses on culture, specifically traditional values as tools for empowerment. Machismo, or male superiority, is viewed as a key concept in the engagement of Latino men in social work intervention. This chapter emphasizes the need to include men in the assessment of the total extended family system. Further, we note that the engagement and outreach of the Latino family in service delivery rests on the engagement of the patriarchal head of household. Machismo is thus viewed in its dual context. We often recognize the negative influences that the concept of machismo can and does exert, particularly in regard to women and children as they function in an American environment that encourages more inquisitive, participatory, and independent roles on their part. But the concept is two-sided, and there is an overlooked aspect to machismo. As an organizing concept that determines male attitudes, behavior, and relationships, machismo must also be viewed as positive (De La Cancela, 1991; Mayo, 1994). Viewed in its appropriate cultural context, machismo is an important element in defining Latino male self-image and self-esteem as well as identity. Machismo as defined in American pop culture—like its cousin, the stereotypical Latin lover—is virtually unknown in traditional Latin cultures (Carrera-Damas, 1980; Ramirez, 1993). Rather, machismo encompasses the totality of attitudes and behaviors that make up Latino gender identity in society. This is much broader than the popularly accepted, albeit inaccurate, notion that machismo primarily connotes aggressiveness and sexualized behavior. As posited here, machismo is crucial and pivotal in determining individual male role behavior, shaping attitudes, determining styles of action, and influencing family roles among Latino men. As described by Wells (1968) and discussed by De La Cancela (1985), machismo includes all male behavior and action patterns within the family and the larger society. Machismo, within its cultural definition, connotes "manly behavior." A male stands, sits, talks, uses hand motions, and walks in a specific style. Deviations can raise suspicions of homosexuality. A real man must *responder como hombre* (respond like a man) when confronted by a variety of situations, most often seduction. To avoid or deny an overt sexual provocation, particularly before other men, causes the man to lose face before his peers and risk suspicion that he is not "all man."

Paradoxically, machismo also has a hidden side, best characterized by the term *varon*. This side reflects characteristics not often associated with men seen as macho. It is most often seen among leaders (for example, *el presidente* (the president), *el caudillo* (the leader), *el jefe* (the chief). In bringing this side of machismo into focus, this concept is seen as a desirable value, of critical importance to the family head of household. Wells (1968), in his study of political power in Puerto Rico, lists the attributes of a leader as a man who can be artistic and appreciate the arts, who is fatherly and caring, who can be close and familiar and yet stand apart and protect the weak. He must be a strong decision maker. Wells quotes a popular Spanish proverb that every *caudillo* (leader) must be a *macho*, but not every *macho* is a *caudillo*. In noting the complexity of machismo and the difficulty of being a "real man" in Latino culture, Ramirez (1993), quotes a well-known poem by the Chilean poet Pablo Neruda: *Resulta que a veces me canso de ser hombre* (It happens that at times I tire of being a man) (p. 37).

Machismo thus encompasses related value systems that guide how appropriate and manly behavior is exercised in public and within the family system. Machismo thus becomes a role-set that defines the cultural status of the male, or *varon*. It encompasses not only the traits of other traditional values but the do's and don'ts of cultural systems that define maleness. It encompasses *dignidad* (dignity), which delineates the parameters of what a man can accept or must respond to. *Dignidad*, in turn, sets the boundaries of *respeto* (respect) and *relajo* (playfulness) (Lauria, 1964). What language shall be used before ladies or in jest with one's peers? What is the proper deference due those of higher status or to older persons? Machismo encompasses *amor propio* (self-love, or self-respect). It rests on *personalismo* (personalism), which governs styles of action. Depending on the family's adherence to traditional structures, children and younger women might lower their eyes when speaking to others. A man, in contrast, must be comfortable looking into someone else's eyes and giving a firm handshake. He must be as comfortable and appropriate when "holding his liquor" as when protecting a lady.

The popularity of machismo as a definition for Latino male behavior has also led to increased attention to this concept in Latin America (Diaz Guerrero, 1979; Monfort Tomas, 1985; Ramirez, 1993), as well as by researchers in the United States (De La Cancela, 1981; Mayo, 1994; Ruiz, 1975; Torres, 1974). In Latino cultures machismo embodies the essence of traditional systems that see the male as head of family, as decision maker, and as protector of the more vulnerable family members—women, children, and the elderly. Machismo gives Latino males sanction and support for carrying out gender-appropriate actions and activities (i.e., manly behavior). Not only must the man be strong, often autocratic, when making decisions and bearing responsibility for the total family; he must also be protective, caring, and understanding. With such a blend of characteristics, the man must be as sensitive as he is assertive (Diaz Guerrero, 1979).

In Anglo (i.e., non-Latino) culture in the United States, machismo is most often viewed simplistically, with limited evaluation of its multiple and complex characteristics. In both popular and professional literature, machismo is linked to aspects of physical and sexual power and prowess. It is this latter view of machismo that has been adopted by American society; the Latino male is described with disregard to the defining role that machismo plays in determining male identity.

LATINO FAMILY STRUCTURE

The Latino family structure, with its roots in an age of colonialism and in Spain's Latin ancestry, is generally accepted as being traditionally extended and patriarchal. Patriarchy places the male head of household not only at the helm but also in possession and control of the wife and children (Canino & Canino, 1980; Garcia-Preto, 1984; Ghali, 1977; Rodriguez, 1992; Sotomayor, 1991). Roman Law and Judeo-Christian religious traditions, in their overt support of male superiority, ensure the continuation and endurance of a patriarchal structure. The Latino family system, in contrast to the American middle-class family structure (DuBois, 1955), can be conceptualized along a perpendicular line, with the father at the top, the wife in the middle, and the children at the bottom. It is to be noted that Roman law not only legally designates the male as head of household but also gives ownership of the wife and children to the man. This system gains significance as men in countries with this legal system use the law to uphold the battering and even the killing of women under the rubric of "crimes of passion" (United Nations, 1995). In countries where the essence of the law is best shown in lifestyle and action, it is interesting to note how little attention is paid to rituals such as the marriage ceremony, in which the proceedings are begun by the question, "Who gives this woman away?" In both legal and religious traditions the woman symbolically goes from being a daughter (belonging to the father) to being a wife (given to the husband).

Similar examples of status differences in traditional families are seen in the role of a male child. A male child has special privileges, particularly if he is the oldest child. He is not assigned housework, which is for women. Instead, he enjoys greater freedom of action outside the family, and he often enjoys greater attention from the extended family, particularly from the mother. The other side of the coin shows a harsher set of expectations for the male child. Male children bear greater responsibility to become providers and caretakers for the mother, the sisters, and the elderly. The caretaker role often includes economic and social responsibility for other female members of the extended family and for those unable to care for themselves. For the male child, learning to be a man is often a "hands-on" experience, with limited opportunity for role modeling. In this context, expectations for men and boys in a traditional Latino family closely resemble those of the broader Latin family systems, which include all cultures of Roman origin. Should the father be absent from the home, a male child (usually the eldest) most often becomes the designated father figure and thus the parental child, *el hombre de la casa*.

An additional example of role differences can be found in the employment patterns of men and women in the garment industry. Men, most commonly from Central and South America, are often employed in the garment industry as sewing machine operators. Caribbean Latinos have consistently shown stronger resistance to this "unmanly" work. Questions would need to be raised regarding appropriate cultural male work roles in a new environment where employment for new, unskilled immigrants is difficult to find.

In contrast to Webster's definition of a family as a group of people united by convictions held in common (e.g., religious or philosophical) or a group united by a common ancestry, the *Diccionario de la Lengua Española* (1947) describes family as "1. People who live in a house under the authority of its master (el señor); 2. servants belonging to him, even if they do not live under the same roof." As such, Roman law at the base of legal systems in Latin countries legalizes and supports the traditional patriarchal structure. These opposing definitions of family perhaps best signal the differences between two cultural views. The English version moves toward a more generalized and egalitarian view; the Spanish clearly sets the male at the top of a vertical structure that defines the man in the home as the decision maker and guide to the functioning and relationships of the total extended family. The woman in this system conceptually plays a subjugated role, acting as the executive and administrator of the home.

Familia (family) in the Latino world extends beyond the dictionary definition of family described above. It connotes the complex relationships and bonds in the extended family, which include consanguinal, marital, and at times *pura amistad* (plain friendship) members. Among Puerto

Ricans, for example, it includes *agregados* (literally, "added to"), who are also considered extended family members. An example is seen in the case of the Gonzalez family, which includes the Cruz family as aunts and uncles of the children. In explaining to the children how the two families come to be one, the parents tell how the grandmothers in each of the two families grew up in adjoining houses in the same town.

To be told to consider yourself *que estas en familia* ("one of the family") is a sign of total acceptance into the family's extended system. At the head of this system, described as positively enmeshed (Canino & Canino, 1980), is the complexity of the male role as head of household and the privileged position of the Latin paterfamilias.

LATINOS IN THE UNITED STATES

In a world accustomed to generalizations, we become accustomed to thinking broadly. This often leads to the application of labels, terms, and theories to total populations. With reference to Latinos, distinct populations are narrowed, and generalizations are confined to those men who by birth, blood line, or migration are now living in the United States. Latino men come from a wide variety of cultural, ethnic, national, and racial backgrounds. They carry a legacy of Spanish culture, often supcrimposed on African and Indian cultures. In addition, Asian (e.g., Chinese and Japanese) and other European groups have also contributed to the total composition of what is today called Latino culture (Shorris, 1992).

Viewed in this context, Latino men are part of a culture that not only defines them as persons by their cultural background but also prescribes expected attitudes and public and private (*en familia*) behavior. As such, a man can hug a male friend (*abrazo*), signifying total acceptance and brotherhood, yet touch is very much restricted when the friend is a woman. A woman might be kissed on the cheek but never on the mouth, which signals romantic involvement. Of interest is that women do not kiss on the mouth, although it is a common practice in the United States. The rules of deference and accepted styles of action very much rule the lives of Latinos in everyday functions. Also notable is the difference between public and private behavior. A man would find it disrespectful for his wife to contradict him in public. Yet in the privacy of the home, the woman can and does exert herself and express her opinion. It is how she says it, not what she says, that must comform to the rules of *respeto*. These public and private roles, when interpreted by a host culture, have earned most Latin wives the label "submissive." Another area to be noted in the family, particularly for immigrant men, is the difficulty encountered in meeting the responsibility for support of the family. This has been a growing concern as the employment market worsens (U.S. Census Report, 1990), and the number of single families has increased (Olmedo & Walker, 1990). For a Latino man who responds to two extended-family constellations, his own and his wife's, the failure to meet cultural expectations as head of household can be devastating.

THE LATINO FAMILY IN AMERICA

Migration has often proved complex for Latino families. With some exceptions, the American dream has not been a reality for the majority of immigrant families (U.S. Census Report, 1990). The larger number of Latino families in the United States live in poverty (Olmedo & Walker, 1990). The stresses of social ills—which include a disproportionately high incidence of AIDS and other health problems, mental and physical; school dropout; substance abuse; and unemployment among Latinos—have been all too well documented (Mayor's Report, 1987). Adding the stress of migration to cultural changes and challenges and the culture clash between the family's coping and value systems and those of the host culture, Latino families in the United States are under a state of siege. A large proportion of these families are considered at risk by service delivery professionals and marginal to mainstream society.

Nonetheless, the Latino family has survived. In many ways it has even thrived. It has adapted to its new environment and made significant contributions. Sotomayor (1991) presents an alternative view of the Latino family that focuses on the family's positive attributes. This model counteracts popular views of the Latino family as dysfunctional, based on the magnitude of social ills that Latinos have faced upon migration. Sotomayor suggests a view of the Latino family role "as the 'keeper' of traditional values, as a self- and mutual aid system, and as a source of strength for individual members, and shelter for the more vulnerable ones, such as the aged" (p. xiv). This view is supported by the American Psychological Association, which suggests that "the onslaught of social movement, while increasing the negatives: teen pregnancies, inter-generational conflict and single-parent households, may also have served to strengthen ties of inter-dependence in the family'' (Olmedo & Walker, 1990).

It is this transitional, paradoxical family, with its multitude of positive and dysfunctional traits, that sees its many members adjusting to new roles, especially the Latino man who is called upon to lead this new family structure. Latino men in their new environment may find it difficult to obtain the needed *respeto*. Whereas it is easier for women to find work, albeit often at low wages and in the service professions, men, when work is available, commonly earn even less than women. Too often, the work available clashes with cultural expectations. An East Harlem project in the 1970s sought to train men in the fashion industry, which involved sewing. It became extremely difficult to find students, although the rate of unemployment in the area, particularly for youths, was and has remained exceptionally high (Mayor's Report on Hispanic Affairs, 1987). The omission of cultural attitudes about proper male employment (e.g., sewing is for women) left few subjects available for training. Mizio (1974) notes that in the United States the man's role as head of the household is seriously challenged when he cannot obtain proper *respeto* as his role changes, and he cannot meet family expectations as provider.

Rogler (1972) noted that attempts to undermine the traditional male role are likely to meet with resistance. Ghali (1977) stresses the importance of machismo as Latino men attempt to secure *respeto* and *dignidad* within Anglo society. Mizio (1974) notes the emotional impact brought about by role reversal in homes where the woman becomes the primary bread-winner or an equal breadwinner. In such situations machismo becomes a buffer against the loss of self-esteem that follows the man's inability to fulfill his expected family role. As such, machismo may indeed be considered a positive cultural value, maintaining *respeto* and providing social and emotional support.

Another interesting paradox is found among Puerto Rican men who reported that they were on welfare (Mayo, 1994). In a study of machismo and acculturation, in which men on welfare were expected to show less machismo than men who reported employment, the welfare group tested higher on a machismo scale than those men who reported that they were employed. The expected results would have been a finding of low machismo among men who had to request economic aid, i.e., loss of self-respect with economic dependency (Mayo, 1994). The data suggest ways to reframe the understanding of machismo and expectations of Latino men. It would seem that welfare serves as a compensatory ideology: The high *macho*, low acculturation characteristics of the public assistance recipient are a way of rejecting a society that has stripped the man of his manhood and forced him into dependency. Among Puerto Rican men this process may be related to the cultural understanding of *mantengo* (a local term for government public welfare grants) and to the continuing legacy that government subsidies have developed for the island of Puerto Rico. The acceptance of public welfare, a cultural negative for men because of its undercurrents of loss of self-esteem and self-determination, may thus be one of many unexplored coping systems found by Latino men to survive in an often hostile environment that has rendered their survival skills dysfunctional.

IMPLICATIONS FOR PRACTICE

The literature presented suggests that, when defined within its cultural parameters, machismo, contrary to its more usual negative image, is a normative cultural value system that defines public, private, and family relationships and roles for Latino men (De La Cancela, 1991; Ramirez, 1993; Wells, 1968). Machismo ideology mandates that the male perform as head of household, respond to the social roles exacted of women and children in the culture, and show forcefulness of personality and strength of will. He must be assertive and self-confident. But machismo also values affection, love, self-respect, and the protection of the less fortunate members in the family and in society at large.

Findings on the relationship of machismo and service utilization by Puerto Rican men suggest that machismo can preclude the utilization of social and mental health services (Mayo, 1994). A request for service can be considered an open admission of weakness by the male client, which in turn violates the norms of paternalism and patriarchy. It is an admission that he lacks the strength of will to overcome problems without help from others. Thus, seeking services is a violation of the idealized image of machismo. An additional finding of this same study suggests that Latino men are most likely to seek help when this help is related to the family's needs. Their role as head of family also mandates that they do everything possible to secure help when needed. Agency systems that serve the family rather than the individual are thus more likely to see male participation in the treatment process.

Machismo is a significant factor in all aspects of the intervention phase with individuals, groups, and communities. Its ideology and impact cut across all levels of practice and social systems. Left alone in the context of family and in a traditional social system, machismo ideology would probably not have to interface with service professionals. Immigration to the United States has brought about not only the previously described cultural clash for Latinos but also a loss of extended family supports in the community and changes in the traditional patriarchal role. Thus the man is left vulnerable to emotional and physical distress (U.S. Bureau of the Census, 1989).

The close relationship between machismo and the helping professions—social work in particular—is seen in the strong adherence by both systems to such organizing principles as maintaining the dignity of the individual (*dignidad*), respect for human rights (*respeto*), and an emphasis on self-determination (*personalismo*). The importance of machismo cannot be underestimated, nor can the concept be dismissed as unimportant in the treatment process.

Practitioners often view machismo as a negative element, to be eliminated in the family's best interest. Research evidence on the multiple functions of machismo suggests that this value is part of the individual's total identity. Its close relationship to the pivotal values of dignity and respect as culturally defined also suggests that machismo should be retained by the individual. Eliminating machismo implies that the component values would also be diminished. A man without machismo would also lack self-respect. Practitioners in the treatment process would find it difficult to empower the male client toward self-determination and fulfillment or use his cultural sense of self-respect to engage him in self-reflection. Machismo can thus be conceptually viewed as an interactive subsystem of the total personality structure (Aramoni, 1972; De La Cancela, 1991; Torres, 1974).

Also of crucial importance to the practitioner is the role of *personalismo*. Not to be confused with the American value of individualism, *personalismo* rests on the innate self-worth of the individual (Wells, 1968). It is often interpreted in the realm of self-disclosure. The practitioner's verbal recognition and expression of how difficult it might be for a man to express emotion can, therefore, actually convey to the male client that he is understood and has the worker's empathy, without the need for him to put his feelings into words. In addition, this recognition often facilitates verbal communication by personalizing the relationship at a culturally accepted level—the person-to-person recognition of common human feelings as found in the Latin value of humanism (Wells, 1968). In working with a family the practitioner might symbolically (verbally) change places with the father and speak to the family: "If you will pardon me, it seems that Mr. Gonzalez has very strong feelings and emotions about this point."

The selection of skills from a variety of practice methodologies (i.e., eclectic practice) allows the practitioner to remain open to respond to nonverbal and emotional messages. A real man is a "man of few words." He should be able to express himself clearly with a look (Maldonado-Sierra, Trent, & Fernandez-Marina, 1958). Openness on the part of the worker to the man's nonverbal behavior demonstrates sensitivity and understanding of the man's cultural experience, motivates him toward verbal expression, and begins the building of trust in the professional relationship.

Social stratification, as seen in the value of *ascripcion*, which defines the hierarchy of authority and power among the many roles that people play in their daily lives, brings social stratification to the treatment process. The worker's early attunement to the man's feelings—albeit unexpressed when he is "asking for help" from a professional who carries greater authority than he, including authority over his family—ensures the development of a working relationship in the early phase of treatment. In considering the issue of uneven power within the treatment relationship, the practitioner faces an additional challenge (Pinderhughes, 1989). A simple rule that ensures proper role deference is to make every effort to address the father first, eliciting his thoughts on the issue at hand.

Notable in work with Latinos is the question of professional distancing that is called for in practice. Culture-appropriate behavior dictates that some personal amenities be exchanged; the client often asks how the practitioner's children, husband, mother are, requiring a direct, genuine response. Self-disclosure within the boundaries of professional and cultural *respeto* becomes prerequisite to the engagement process. As the development of trust grows, so does *afecto*. Affection, often expressed as "being *simpatico*," is thus as much a component of machismo as it is of the treatment relationship. In the latter part of treatment the client often brings gifts—for the most part an act not usually seen as appropriate behavior by the practitioner. Although the worker's assessment of the situation and motivation is always necessary, the gift should be considered as the client's attempts to also give to the worker. Such giving symbolizes the client's attempt to maintain pride and some equalizing control in the treatment relationship. Most often, the gifts are food—never money—or special treats or crafts made by a mother, a wife, or some other female relative.

SUMMARY

Machismo has been popularized in the United States as a negative concept that presents a stereotypical and often dehumanizing view of Latino men. The term *machismo* is commonly used in all aspects of American life to connote forcefulness, power, and often autocratic and violent behavior. This chapter has presented an additional side to machismo when viewed within its Latin cultural context. Considering machismo from a cultural perspective, one that presents a conceptual framework for understanding its positive and negative demands, we have sought to present an expanded arena for assessment and intervention with Latino men and their families. Recent focus on diversity in the United States highlights the need to explore individual subgroups in the larger population. This would allow for a broader understanding of cultural nuances in the development of multicultural intervention.

REFERENCES

Aramoni, A. (1972). Machismo. *Psychology Today*, 5(8), 69–72.

Canino, I., & Canino, G. (1980). Impact of stress on the Puerto Rican family: Treatment considerations. *American Journal of Orthopsychiatry*, 50, 535–541.

Carrera-Damas, F. (1980). *Es usted un macho? El machismo en Venezuela*. Caracas, Venezuela: Publicaciones Seleven.

De La Cancela, V. (1985). Toward a socio-cultural psychotherapy for low-income ethnic minorities. *Psychotherapy*, 22, 427–435.

De La Cancela, V. (1991). *Working effectively with Puerto Rican men: Professional and personal reflections*. New York: Haworth Press.

Diaz-Guerrero, R. (1979). *Estudios de psicologia del Mexicano*. Mexico City: Editorial Trillas.

Diccionario de la Lengua Española, 27th ed. (1947). Madrid: Talleres Tipograficos de La Editorial Espasa—Calpe.

DuBois, C. (1955). The dominant value profile of American culture. *American Anthropologist, 57*, 1233.

Fitzpatrick, J. (1971). *Puerto Rican Americans: The meaning of migration to the mainland.* Englewood Cliffs, NJ: Prentice-Hall.

Garcia-Preto, N. (1984). Puerto Rican families. In M. McGoldrick, J. K. Pearce, & J. Giordano (Eds.), *Ethnicity and family therapy* (pp. 164–186). New York: Guilford.

Ghali, S. B. (1977). Cultural sensitivity and the Puerto Rican client. *Social Casework, 58*, 459–468.

Inclan, J. (1985). Variations in value orientations in mental health work with Puerto Ricans. *Psychotherapy, 22*, 324–334.

Influencias del machismo. (1994, November 2). *Diario La Nacion* (Buenos Aires).

Kriegel, L. (Ed.). (1978). *The myth of American manhood.* New York: Dell.

Lauria, A. (1964). Respeto, relajo and inter-personal relations in Puerto Rico. *Anthropological Quarterly, 37*(2), 53–67.

Maldonado-Sierra, E. D., Trent, R. D., & Fernandez-Marina, R. (1958). Three basic themes in Mexican and Puerto Rican family values. *Journal of Social Psychology, 48*, 167–181.

Mayo, Y. Q. (1994). *The utilization of mental health services, acculturation and machismo.* Unpublished doctoral dissertation. Adelphi University School of Social Work, Garden City, NY.

Mayor's Report on Hispanic Affairs. (1987). *Puerto Rican New Yorkers: Socioeconomic characteristics and trends, Part II.* New York: Department of City Planning.

McGoldrick, M., Pearce, J. K., & Giordano, J. (Eds.). (1996). *Ethnicity and family therapy* (2nd ed.). New York: Guilford.

Michener, J. A. (1989). *Caribbean.* New York: Random House.

Mizio, E. (1974). The impact of external systems on the Puerto Rican family. *Social Casework, 55*(2), 76–83.

Monfort Tomas, E. (1985). *Machismo: El macho latino.* Barquisimeto, Venezuela: Editora Boscan.

Olmedo, E., & Walker, V. (Eds.). (1990). *Hispanics in the United States: Abstracts of the psychological and behavioral literature, 1980–1989.* Washington, DC: American Psychological Association.

Pinderhughes, E. (1989). *Understanding race, ethnicity, and power: The key to efficacy in clinical practice.* New York & Toronto: Free Press.

Ramirez, R. L. (1993). *Dime capitan: Reflecciones sobre la masculinidad.* Rio Piedras, PR: Ediciones Huracan.

Rodriguez, C. (1991). *Puerto Ricans: Born in the U.S.A.* Boulder, CO: Westview.

Rodriguez, C. (1992). *Hispanics in the labor force: Issues and policies.* New York: Plenum.

Rogler, L. (1972). *Migrant in the city: The life of a Puerto Rican action group.* New York: Basic Books.

Ruiz, J. S. (1975). *Clarifications of the concepts of machismo and hembrismo: Significance for social work practice with Chicanos.* Unpublished doctoral dissertation, Graduate School of Social Work, University of Denver.

Shorris, E. (1992). *Latinos: A biography of the people.* New York & London: Norton.

Stevens, E. P. (1973). Machismo and marianismo. *Society, 3*(6), 57–63.

Sotomayor, M. (1991). *Empowering Hispanic families: A critical issue for the '90s.* Milwaukee, WI: Family Service America.

Torres, J. (1974). *Acculturation and psychosocial adjustment among Puerto Rican men in a midwestern community.* Unpublished doctoral dissertation. University of Wisconsin, Milwaukee.

United Nations. (1995). *Violence against women: Fourth World Conference on Women.* New York: Author.

United States Census Report. (1990). Washington, DC: U.S. Government Printing Office.

Wells, H. (1968). *The modernization of Puerto Rico: A political study of changing values and institutions.* Cambridge, MA: Harvard University Press.

Challenging Practice Issues

CHAPTER 12

The Impact of Ethnicity and Race on the Treatment of Mothers in Incest Families

Virginia C. Strand

Sexual abuse of children has been a subject of numerous professional publications since the beginnings of the 1980s, but only recently has attention been paid to the cultural context in which sexual abuse takes place (Ima & Holm, 1991; Lindholm & Willey, 1986; Rao, DiClemente, & Ponton, 1992; Tjaden & Thoennes, 1992; Wyatt, 1988; Yap, 1986). The impact of culture has, of course, enormous implications for intervention and on-going treatment. As noted by Finkelhor (1984) and others, social and cultural norms influence the behavior of adults who molest children. The enormous variety of different racial and ethnic groups in this culture make it important for clinical social workers to be aware of these in their interventions.

The purpose of this chapter is to highlight ethnic differences and to show how sensitivity to those differences, as well as knowledge about the dynamics of child sexual abuse, can enhance the ability to engage in a meaningful way with the family, particularly the mother in the incest family. The focus is specifically on engagement of the mother at the time immediately following a report of child sexual abuse. The chapter explores some of the dynamics that emerge as one works with families from other than mainstream American culture. Before looking specifically at three distinct ethnic or racial groups, two issues are addressed. The first involves that of common transference reactions for clients of color working with White therapists, and the second notes dynamics characteristic of the mother in the incest family.

THEORETICAL CONSIDERATIONS

Common Countertransference Reactions

When the clinician is White, it is important to assume that racial and ethnic barriers will exist between the therapist and a client of color due to the social context in which we all live and work. The author presumes that clients of color, to a greater or lesser degree, experience a White therapist as a member of a dominant group and themselves as members of a subordinate group. Social class, educational background, and life experiences will, of course, mediate the degree to which an individual experiences being part of a subordinate group.

   In practice, there are significantly more mental health professionals who are White than otherwise. The formal mental health system is staffed primarily by nonminority clinicians who do not share the same ethnic and racial characteristics of the clients they serve (Vargas & Willis, 1994). This is also true in the subspecialty of those working in the area of child sexual abuse. The work of Jean Baker Miller (1991) sheds some light on issues regarding the relationship between dominant and subordinate groups in general. Although she was writing in the context of males to females, her principles are applicable to the situation under discussion. Dominant groups tend to act in particular ways with subordinate groups. There is (1) a tendency to act destructively to subordinate groups, (2) a tendency to restrict the range of activities and even reactions of subordinate group members, (3) discouragement of the full and free expression of their experiences, and (4) a tendency to characterize members falsely and then to describe the situation as normal (Miller, 1991, p. 183). One impact for members of the subordinate group is to engender anger, which often must be suppressed or deflected. The subordinate often develops complex psychological reactions and tendencies, including self-perceptions that one is weak and unworthy and has ''no right'' to be angry. To appease a member of the dominant group a subordinate may also act especially compliant, submissive, or passive.

The implication for the White therapist working with women of color is the need to recognize not only that the therapist may hold typical stereotypes regarding clients from different racial and ethnic groups but also that clients will bring a particular transference reaction to the work based on their life experience in mainstream culture dominated by norms and values affiliated with being Caucasian (Abney, Yang, & Paulson, 1992). It would not be unusual for clients of color to bring feelings of anger and mistrust or passivity and dependence, based on their subordinate group experience to the encounter. It is the job of the clinician to be careful not to misconstrue these as abnormal and mislabel as pathological what may be a very multidetermined response.

In addition, women of color have unique needs, encumbered as they are with the double burden of racism and sexism (Gutierrez, 1990), being members of two subordinate groups in American society. When the con-founding variable of incest is added to the mix, the situation becomes incredibly complex for the woman of color who is also the mother of a sexually abused child. It becomes crucial for the therapist to be sensitive to the multiple forces at work in her life, particularly at the time of the crisis of disclosure, and to take these into consideration when making an assessment and developing an intervention plan.

Secondary Victim Dynamics in the Mother in the Incest Family

As noted above, the focus of this chapter is on working with the mother or nonoffending parent in the incest family. To that extent it is helpful to have a conceptual framework by which to understand the mother's reaction. As the author has outlined elsewhere (Strand, 1990, 1991), there exists a useful conceptualization in the literature (Finkelhor & Browne, 1985) regarding the impact of sexual traumatization that is helpful in understanding the mother's reaction. Finkelhor and Browne (1985) have outlined four dynamics as being typical of the response of the child victim. These are traumatic sexualization, betrayal, stigmatization, and powerlessness. The mother is affected similarly to the child. In terms of sexual traumatization the mother often experiences the disclosure as a threat to her sexual identity. Because sexuality is such a core aspect of self-esteem and of personality, this threat is significant. In the author's experience, mothers typically blame themselves for the offender's sexual contact with a child, especially if they have been living with the perpetrator until the intervention by an outside authority. They tend to view the cause of the incestuous relationship as their own sexual inadequacy, rather than as an inadequate and destructive response by their partner.

The mother's feelings of self-blame may be only partially conscious at the time of interface with initial investigative staff and rarely articulated because of the mother's sense of guilt. If one considers that the disclosure of sexual abuse outside the family results in an intervention by child protective services and/or law enforcement agencies, the mother is by definition in crisis. The response of initial investigative staff, usually paraprofessionals who are ill-trained and lacking in understanding of incestuous family dynamics, is often to blame the mother. This then feeds into the self-derogatory attitude the mother is already experiencing.

The guilt and self-blame experienced by the mother, not only for the reasons outlined above but also because of her feelings of failure as a mother (particularly if the child has made a clear and factual disclosure to someone outside the family) contributes to the dynamic of stigmatization identified above. The author has known of many situations in which the mother, following a disclosure that has also been made public (e.g., through a newspaper report), will not shop at her usual places, will change banks and churches, and avoid close friends and family whom she would be ashamed to confide in lest they also blame her. Mothers often talk about being afraid to confide in close friends or family members because they worry that they will not understand, will question the child's truthfulness, or will attack the mother for failure to "see what was going on."

Therefore, at a time of crisis, when crisis theory teaches that support and the opportunity to verbalize the details surrounding the crisis are vital, the mother may isolate herself from her major sources of emotional support. The lack of opportunity to process the trauma contributes to her being immobilized. She may appear unable to take actions outsiders feel would be "normal" for a "good mother" to undertake under the circumstances. It is no wonder the mother often appears, particularly to the untrained observer, as if she is ineffective, unproductive, or dependent. From the author's point of view, this is often the result of feeling overwhelmed by events swirling around her and the lack of time to process information that has upset the foundation of her existence.

In addition to the sexual traumatization and stigmatization, the mother often feels betrayed as well. To learn that her partner, with whom she may have been sexually active until the time of the disclosure (or even after), has been involved sexually with her child engenders an enormous sense of anger. She is often then struggling internally with the two emotions of self-blame (as noted above) and rage. For women, who have been socialized to turn rage inward, the feelings of guilt and self-blame often win out. The rage, when it is expressed, may be deflected to secondary sources such as the intervention system, as Solin (1985) has written about, or to the child or children who made the disclosure.

The child may additionally become a target for the mother's rage because she feels betrayed by the child for telling someone outside the family. This heightens the mother's sense of failure as a mother—''Why didn't my child tell me?''—and in her confusion and inability to process the material flooding her, she may communicate her rage to her child(ren) out of this sense of betrayal.

The last dynamic, powerlessness, is usually present for the mother as well as for the child. She may feel as if the foundation on which her life was built has collapsed. Many mothers have been struggling with problems in relationships with their partners, but rarely do they know or expect that he will be sexually involved with their children, particularly at the same time that he is sexually involved with them. This sense of helplessness is exacerbated by an intervention that forces her to choose between having her child(ren) placed in out-of-home care and separating from her husband. In fact, some control over her life has been taken out of her hands, and she feels appropriately powerless.

These dynamics are viewed as guidelines for the therapist in engagement, assessment, and treatment planning. Implicit in this framework is the premise that the disclosure of sexual abuse by a spouse or partner is a crisis and that all four dynamics will operate in the woman's life to some extent regardless of her preexisting personality structure. The mix will be different for each woman, and the degree to which one or more of the dynamics become salient will depend on the woman's psychological vulnerabilities and the nature and duration of her relationship with her child and partner. If the woman is a survivor of childhood sexual abuse herself, the traumagenic dynamics noted above may be particularly significant, as she may be dealing both with her own history and with the issues as a mother of a sexually abused child.

IMPLICATIONS FOR WOMEN OF COLOR

The author's thesis is that the dynamics of stigmatization and powerlessness is often heightened for women of various ethnic and racial backgrounds because of a somewhat different relationship between men and women in other cultural groups and because of their relationship to the mainstream culture. As McKinley (1987) points out, the expectations and orientation of a White therapist and a client of color (in this case a Hispanic client) may be very different. For example, for women of Hispanic (particularly Puerto Rican) background, the double standard for men and women may be even stronger than it is in the mainstream culture (Comas-Diaz, 1987). The family is held in great esteem, and the role of men and women is culturally prescribed. For example, a "good" women is patient and forbearing, and the home is viewed as the appropriate center of her world. Men are the economic providers, and men need to prove their virility through domination of women. Women are supposed to show respect to men, and there is an emphasis on what is good for the family rather than good for the individual. Children are taught to respect their elders and to show deference in all social situations. Family members do not like to take problems outside the family, and informal solutions are often preferred over the interface with formal organizations (Comas-Diaz, 1987; McKinley, 1987).

Consequently, one can see how a woman who learns of suspected incest on the part of her spouse or partner would be particularly vulnerable to a sense of shame. Disclosure threatens the entity of the family, threatens the alleged perpetrator's "manhood," makes family matters public, and places the child in the position of challenging an elder's authority. All of these are counter to the role expectations for the Hispanic family member.

The Asian woman is vulnerable for many of the same reasons. As with the Hispanic family, the Asian woman is viewed as the nurturer and caretaker, and she assumes responsibility for what happens to the children (Chin, 1983). The man is seen as the head of the family, and his authority would be viewed by the child as paramount. A difference is the emphasis on the community and family, as opposed to the individual, as the organizing principle of society. This accentuates the sense of belonging and obligation to the family and concomitantly the sense of personal obligation to the family. This is manifest in the desire to maintain family harmony (Bradshaw, 1994). In addition, Asian families tend to have wide kinship networks, and their reactions will influence the mother's response, making her sensitive to criticism and to taking actions that might invoke a negative reaction from the family.

Saving face is an important part of the culture (Sato, 1980), and seeking mental health services may be avoided out of a desire not to shame the family (Sue & McKinney, 1975; Tsui, 1985). The motivation to save face would mitigate against revealing a secret as shameful as sexual abuse, especially if it was the woman's sexual partner who had molested her child. In addition, reticence to seek outside help may be influenced by the belief that distress is caused by a failure of will (Sue & McKinney, 1975) as well as by adherence to the cultural mandate to suffer in silence (Sue & Morishima, 1982).

African American mothers, with the particular history of Black Americans in this culture, bring their own sense of vulnerabilities, which may make it difficult for them to trust mental health providers. As Boyd-Franklin (1989) has pointed out, the White therapist often has to earn the trust of Black clients. Unlike other groups, attribution of trust and respect for an authority figure such as a therapist is not as typical because of the specific history of oppression and racism for Black Americans.

There is some evidence that African American families already utilize formal mental health systems less often than Whites when referred specifically for treatment of sexual abuse (Haskett, Nowlan, Hutchinson, & Whitworth, 1991). It has also been documented that African American subjects are more likely to use informal helping networks for personal problems, rather than turning to professionals (Chatters, Taylor, & Neighbors, 1989; Neighbors & Jackson, 1984).

It is more likely that an African American mother will encounter a White therapist than not. At some level there is mistrust of the dominant group, which will tend to increase the woman's inclination to keep her thoughts and feelings to herself and avoid being shamed in front of a group member who she may feel does not understand her. This guardedness and suspicion about whether the White therapist can really be helpful should be understood as a healthy adaptation to the reality of living in a racist society (Jones, 1979). Greene (1994) identifies this as a process of "armoring," a psychological mechanism manifest in both behavior and cognition whereby the African American woman prepares herself for interaction with another if there is the potential for racism. The therapist who is sensitive to this possibility can address the issue and may be able to prevent the mother from cutting herself off from a source of support where she can process her feelings. As noted above, if she does not allow herself to verbalize her reactions, it may increase her sense of shame, guilt, and stigmatization.

CASE EXAMPLES

The following examples illustrate how some of these dynamics were played out in three different cultures. The cases are based on those in the author's practice, and particulars have been changed to protect the identity of the clients. In some instances different circumstances have been coalesced into one case to highlight a particular dynamic.

A Hispanic Family

The first case involves a Hispanic family. Mr. and Mrs. L were recent immigrants from El Salvador. Mr. L had come first to the United States, shortly after the birth of his second child, Joseph. At the time of the report to Child Protective Services, his oldest daughter, Victoria, was 5 and his son, Joseph, was 3 1/2. Mrs. L had not been married to Mr. L until after the birth of Victoria. She had come to the country only about 1 year before the report and did not speak English, although she understood the language somewhat.

A day care provider made the initial report, based on observations of Victoria's behavior in day care. She was exhibiting age-inappropriate sexual behavior and language. Upon investigation and evaluation, both Victoria and Joseph made statements about their father's having molested them. He had reportedly fondled their genitals and inserted his finger and penis into the rectums of both children.

Following the disclosure, the children were removed from the home, as Mrs. L did not believe the accusations against her husband. Her children did not make any statements to her, and her husband denied the abuse. She was therefore unwilling to separate from him. The question becomes, was there anything about her cultural background that might contribute to the apparent inability to be protective? On closer examination, one can see how her background as well as her recent immigrant status in this country might make her hesitate to contradict her husband.

Mrs. L had grown up in a traditional Catholic family. She was the youngest of five children. Her mother had been the primary caretaker and was respectful and obedient to her father, a dominant and hardworking man who was rarely home due to his job responsibilities. Mr. L was much like her father. Mrs. L stayed home with the children, and as noted above, had not learned English. Neither did she know how to drive. Her relationship with Mr. L was characterized by deference to him and his opinions. Because sexual contact with children was a taboo subject and certainly counter to how a man like her husband would exhibit virility, the thought of his having been sexual with her children was beyond her comprehension.

Mrs. L, therefore, was understandably dependent on her husband for emotional support and social direction. She was not independently mobile and could not even manage the logistics to buy groceries and other necessities. She was also suspicious of formal organizations, and the family's brief encounter with the local social services department when they had been receiving income maintenance support at an earlier time had made her particularly suspicious of this agency, as it had handled the family in a bureaucratic and impersonal fashion.

In addition, Victoria and Joseph were not talking to her or repeating the statements they had made to the intervention team, and Mrs. L was suspicious of that team's accurate understanding of her children. Much as she did not want to lose custody of her children, she felt that she had no choice.

In this case the children were out of the home for a number of months, until the family court had intervened and adjudicated Mr. L as a sexual offender. He had agreed to go to treatment, and in the early work with the father and mother their therapists set up a dialogue between them. In these sessions, Mr. L was helped to tell Mrs. L specifically what he had done to the children. Hearing this directly from him enabled Mrs. L to move beyond her denial. She separated from him while he completed treatment, and the children were allowed to return to live with her.

An Asian Family

The second case involves an Asian family. Mr. and Mrs. N had been in this country for about 7 years when their oldest daughter, age 11, made a statement to her guidance counselor at school about her father touching her sexually. In addition to father, mother, and Kina, there was also a 7-year-old son, Rin. Mrs. N's mother lived with the family, and Mr. N's brother and sister-in-law owned and jointly operated the family business. The brother and sister-in-law, who did not have any children, often ate meals with the N household.

Upon disclosure, Mr. N was asked to leave the house, which he did. Mrs. N and her family were in a panic. Kina's initial statements had been that her father fondled her vagina, buttocks, and breasts under and on top of her clothing. After the first disclosure to the guidance counselor, she began to minimize the actions and only made statements to the Child Protective Services (CPS) worker about her father touching her buttocks. She began to say that he only slapped her buttocks on the top of her clothing. The family insisted that this kind of touch was typical of their culture and also minimized the possibility of disclosure.

Mrs. N, like Mrs. L, did not speak any English, and CPS had to rely on interpreters in their conversations with her. She appeared very frightened and unsure of herself. She denied to the worker that her husband could have been capable of the behavior he was accused of, saying that he worked late almost every night and sometimes slept over at the business if he was very busy. Because she did not work, she was home with her daughter and believed that she would have known if there were any inappropriate contact between her daughter and her husband.

Later in treatment a different story would emerge concerning the mother's awareness of a problematic relationship between the husband and daughter, but at the time of disclosure and in the period following, she had difficulty admitting this to herself and was not about to confide in a stranger. It is significant that early on in the intervention the relevance of cultural dictates overrode other considerations. For example, in her culture, the importance of saving face at all costs contributed to her siding with her husband against the outside, bureaucratic organization at the time of the initial report. Her husband had initially denied the allegations, and the importance of respecting his authority made it difficult for her to question him, let alone share such a shameful event, if true, with someone not only outside the family but outside the culture.

In addition, her wide kinship network, on whom she was used to relying at times of crisis, discouraged her from believing the allegations. They insisted that even if Kina had made some statements, it was because she did not get along with her father. They pointed to the sibling rivalry and her jealousy of her younger brother, whom the father did in fact favor. The fact that Kina withdrew the more serious allegations after the CPS intervention that resulted in the removal of her father added to the mother's ability to deny the allegations.

An African American Family

With the third mother, Mrs. M, one sees how traditional values in the African American family interacted with the reaction to a report of suspected child sexual abuse. Ms. M was 28 at the time that her 11-year-old daughter Tamara made a disclosure at school about her mother's fiancé, Mr. F. He had been living with the family for about a year and was the father of Ms. M's youngest child, who was 7 weeks old at the time of the report to CPS. In addition to Tamara and the baby, Ms. M also had three other children, a girl aged 6, a girl aged 4, and a boy aged 2. She was living on public assistance and not working.

The report to CPS had come about because Tamara had left a letter at school that her teacher found. In this letter she had written about how she did not like Rupert (her mother's fiancé) because of the way he talked to her and touched her. She wrote that he bought her clothes, sneakers, and other things she wanted that her mother could not afford. The letter said that Rupert had promised to buy her a kitten, and she really wanted that, but she did not want him to keep coming into her bed at night and bothering her.

Tamara and her mother did not have a good relationship. Tamara resented the pressure that her mother put on her to baby-sit and was tired of taking care of her siblings and doing housework. She had been skipping school, which infuriated her mother, partly because the school kept calling her and she felt that the school held her responsible. She was worried that they would file a neglect petition because of Tamara's absence from school. Tamara denied that anything inappropriate was happening when she was questioned by CPS. Ms. M, already stressed by the birth of a new child and anticipating, finally, the security that marriage would bring, was particularly reluctant to entertain the suspicions of sexual abuse brought against Rupert.

Like many African American women, Mrs. M had experienced a truncated life cycle (Hines, 1989), beginning her parenting in her teenage years (age 17), before she had completed her own adolescence or had

had a chance to form her own sense of identity. Three different men had fathered her first four children, none of whom had been employed and two of whom had been serious substance abusers. The fact that the father of her newest baby was employed and offering marriage was an enormous opportunity for her. It was also typical of a pattern for lower-income African American families, in which the woman first marries after having children and not necessarily the father of all of her children, resulting in the formation of a step-family (Fulmer, 1989). When Tamara denied the allegations, it was easy for Mrs. M to ignore them, given her poor relationship with her daughter and the stronger relationship with her fiancé. This case illustrates how Mrs. M's dependence on her partner, poor relationship with her daughter, and suspicion of the intervention systems interacted to create suspicion on her part about the validity of the alleged sexual abuse.

SUMMARY OF IMPLICATIONS FOR TREATMENT

The discussion and case examples suggest the following treatment implications for therapists working with women of color who are also mothers of sexually abused children. For all women of color, it is important to attend to the match between the therapist's orientation and expectations of therapy and those of the client. Because Hispanic, African American, and Asian clients tend to rely as much, if not more, on informal systems of helping, it is incumbent on the professional to take time to orient the client to the formal helping structure and to reach for conflicts for the woman in using the formal structure. It is also important to underscore that sharing emotional problems outside the family, especially for Asian women but also for Hispanic and Black Americans for some of the reasons noted above, may be uncomfortable. Because of this and the shame attached to being involved in mental health treatment, therapists may need to use restraint in initial exploration and history gathering (Lorenzo & Adler, 1984).

The therapist should be careful not to view reluctance necessarily as resistance. It is also helpful to remember that Asian American cultures, the Chinese in particular, tend to view emotional difficulties as having a physical cause and may want to seek alternative remedies (e.g., assistance from a herbalist) for the emotional difficulties they or family members are experiencing (Crystal, 1989). Again, it is wise to be cautious about immediately viewing this as resistance.

As Jones (1979) has noted, the ethnocentrist view of most White middle-class clinicians may lead them to mischaracterize reactions of African Americans generally. The tendency to label actions as a consequence of poor impulse control may reflect a lack of awareness on the part of White clinicians of the extent to which stimuli operating in the lives of average urban Black Americans constantly test self-control. Additionally, institutional racism has devalued African American women while at the same time idealizing their White counterparts (Greene, 1994).

Another variable at work for many women of color is their immigration status. This may play a part not only in fear of connection to formal systems if they are undocumented but also in the degree to which they are acculturated. Because many Asian, Latin American, and Caribbean countries hold more rigid sex role orientations than does mainstream American culture (Comas-Diaz, 1987; Jones, 1979; Lorenzo & Adler, 1984), a newer immigrant may hold more traditional views. This will affect the degree to which she feels she can accept a challenge to her husband or partner, as well as the degree to which she feels comfortable being engaged with the formal helping system.

Certain strategies that have been found to be helpful with women of color mesh with what has been found helpful in working with mothers of sexually abused children. One such strategy is that of an empowerment approach, where strengths are emphasized and validated (Vasquez, 1994). Gutierrez (1990) and Comas-Diaz (1987) both stress that the promotion of competence, adaptation, and flexibility in role relations are helpful. For the mother in an incest family, who may be separated from her husband as a result of CPS intervention and/or dealing with the world of work for the first time, this emphasis, particularly in expanding role flexibility, is also important.

Although extended-family members may be extremely helpful, some authors (Keefe & Casas, 1980) stress the importance of the carefully planned involvement of such members, keeping in mind that many extended families may discourage the use of mental health agencies in general. For an issue like sexual abuse that may be regarded as shameful not only for the individual mother but for the family, this advice is especially pertinent.

One strategy that has been especially useful for both women of color and mothers of sexually abused children is that of group therapy. McKinley (1987) describes the successful use of group psychotherapy for Hispanic women. The benefits include the ability to learn self-reliance, which may help to counter a culturally induced norm toward passivity and dependency. It can also support the development of self-assertion and provide for a correctional emotional experience. Similarly, Olarte and Masnick (1985) found group therapy helpful for Hispanic women for issues surrounding acculturation, family conflicts, and children's performance. The latter issue is often a salient one for mothers of sexually abused children, who are struggling to parent children who may be exhibiting emotional and behavioral disturbances. The power of the support and guidance gained from such a group can be invaluable.

In conclusion, it has been suggested here that mothers of sexually abused children face common dilemmas and manifest common reaction patterns in response to the crisis of disclosure of sexual abuse by a partner or spouse. For women of color, certain of these typical reactions, especially those of stigmatization, shame, and powerlessness, may be heightened by their status in mainstream American culture. For the therapist, White or non-White, it is important not only to be familiar with the dynamics presented by mothers of sexually abused children but also to value cultural differences, examine theoretical approaches for congruency with a specific culture, and incorporate culturally sensitive interventions into practice.

REFERENCES

Abney, V. D., Yang, J. A., & Paulson, M. J. (1992). Transference and counter-transference issues unique to long-term group psychotherapy of adult children molested as children. *Journal of Interpersonal Violence*, 7, 559–569.

Boyd-Franklin, N. (1989). *Black families in therapy*. New York: Guilford.

Bradshaw, C. K. (1994). Asian and Asian American women: Historical and political considerations in psychotherapy. In L. Comas-Diaz & B. Greene (Eds.), *Women of color: Integrating ethnic and gender identities in psychotherapy* (pp. 72–113). New York: Guilford.

Chatters, L. M., Taylor, R. J., & Neighbors, H. W. (1989). Size of informal helper network mobilized during a serious personal problem among Black Americans. *Journal of Marriage and the Family*, 51, 667–676.

Chin, J. L. (1983). Diagnostic consideration in working with Asian Americans. *American Journal of Orthopsychiatry, 53*(1), 100–109.

Comas-Diaz, L. (1987). Feminist therapy with mainland Puerto Rican women. *Psychology for Women Quarterly, 11*(4), 461–474.

Crystal, D. (1989). Asian Americans and the myth of the model minority. *Social Case Work, 70,* 405–413.

Finkelhor, D. (1984). *Child sexual abuse: New theory and research.* New York: Free Press.

Finkelhor, D., & Browne, A. (1985). The traumatic impact of child sexual abuse: A conceptualization. *American Journal of Orthopsychiatry, 55,* 530–541.

Fulmer, R. (1989). Lower income and professional families: A comparison of structure and life cycle processes. In B. Carter & M. McGoldrick (Eds.), *The changing family life cycle* (2nd ed., pp. 545–578). Boston: Allyn and Bacon.

Greene, B. (1994). African American women. In L. Comas-Diaz & B. Greene (Eds.), *Women of color: Integrating ethnic and gender identities in psychotherapy* (pp. 10–29). New York: Guilford.

Gutierrez, L. M. (1990). Working with women of color: An empowerment perspective. *Social Work, 35,* 149–153.

Haskett, M. E., Nowlan, N. P., Hutchinson, J. S., & Whitworth, J. M. (1991). Factors associated with successful entry into therapy in child sexual abuse cases. *Child Abuse and Neglect, 15,* 467–476.

Hines, P. M. (1989). The family life cycle of poor Black families. In B. Carter & M. McGoldrick (Eds.), *The changing family life cycle* (2nd ed., pp. 513–544). Boston: Allyn and Bacon.

Ima, K., & Holm, C. F. (1991). Child maltreatment among Asian and Pacific Islander refugees and immigrants: The San Diego experience. *Journal of Interpersonal Violence, 6,* 267–285.

Jones, D. L. (1979). African-American clients: Clinical practice issues. *Social Work, 24*(2), 112–118.

Keefe, S. E., & Casas, J. H. (1980). Mexican Americans and mental health: A selected review and recommendations for mental health services delivery. *American Journal of Community Psychology, 8,* 303–326.

Lindholm, K. J., & Willey, R. (1986). Ethnic differences in child abuse and sexual abuse. *Hispanic Journal of Behavioral Science, 8*(2), 111–125.

Lorenzo, M. K., & Adler, D. A. (1984). Mental health services for Chinese in a community mental health center. *Social Casework, 65,* 600–614.

McKinley, V. (1987). Group therapy as a treatment modality of special values for Hispanic patients. *International Journal of Group Psychotherapy, 37,* 255–268.

Miller, J. B. (1991). The construction of anger in women and men. In J. V. Jordon, J. Kaplan, A. Miller, J. Stiver, & J. Surrey (Eds.), *Women's growth in connection.* New York: Guilford.

Neighbors, H. W., & Jackson, J. S. (1984). The use of informal and formal help: Four patterns of illness behavior in the Black community. *American Journal of Community Psychiatry, 12,* 629–644.

Olarte, S. W., & Masonik, K. (1985). Benefits of long-term group therapy for disadvantaged Hispanic outpatients. *Hospital and Community Psychiatry, 36,* 1093–1097.

Rao, K., DiClemente, R. J., & Ponton, L. E. (1992). Child sexual abuse of Asians compared with other populations. *Journal of the American Academy of Child and Adolescent Psychiatry, 31,* 880–886.

Sato, M. (1980). Concept of shame and the mental health of Pacific Asian Americans. *Exploration in Ethnic Studies, 3*(1), 3–11.

Solin, C. A. (1986). Displacement of affect in families following incest disclosures. *American Journal of Orthopsychiatry, 56,* 570–576.

Strand, V. (1990). Treatment of the mother in the incest family: The beginning phase. *Clinical Social Work Journal, 18,* 353–366.

Strand, V. (1991). Mid-phase treatment with mothers in incest families. *Clinical Social Work Journal, 19,* 377–389.

Sue, S., & McKinney, H. (1975). Asian Americans in the community mental health care system. *American Journal of Orthopsychiatry, 45,* 111–118.

Sue, S., & Morishima, J. (1982). *The mental health of Asian Americans: Contemporary issues in identifying and treating mental problems.* San Francisco: Jossey Bass.

Tjaden, P. G., & Thoennes, N. (1992). Predictors of legal intervention in child maltreatment cases. *Child Abuse and Neglect, 16,* 807–821.

Tsui, A. M. (1985). Psychotherapeutic considerations in sexual counseling for Asian immigrants. *Psychotherapy: Theory, Research and Practice, 22,* 357–362.

Vargas, L., & Willis, D. (1994). New directions in the treatment of ethnic minority children and adolescents. *Journal of Clinical Child Psychology, 23,* 2–4.

Vasquez, M. J. T. (1994). Latinas. In L. Comas-Diaz & B. Greene (Eds.), *Women of color: Integrating ethnic and gender identities in psychotherapy* (pp. 114–138). New York: Guilford.

Wyatt, G. (1990). Sexual abuse of ethnic minority children: Identifying dimensions of victimization. *Professional Psychology: Research and Practice, 21,* 338–343.

Yap, J. G. (1986). Philippine ethnoculture and human sexuality [Special issue: Human sexuality, ethnoculture, and social work]. *Journal of Social Work and Human Sexuality, 4*(3), 121–134.

CHAPTER 13

Multicultural Practice and Domestic Violence

Patricia Brownell

> She looked like a woman who had seen the worst of life. . . . "My husband bates me, sir," and she pointed to a bruise on her cheek. (Brace, 1872, p. 44)

Domestic violence has been a concern of social workers and social reformers since the early days of the social work profession, as this quote from Charity Organization Movement worker Charles Loring Brace (1872) notes. In the late 19th century, the social response was to attempt to remove children from families where there was wife battering. Since then the social work profession has incorporated or evolved a repertoire of responses to the problem of family violence.

SOCIAL WORK AND DOMESTIC VIOLENCE

Domestic violence is defined as a social problem in which one's property, health, or life is endangered or harmed as a result of intentional behavior by another family member or significant other (Barker, 1995). The purpose of this chapter is to examine domestic violence and social work practice within a multicultural context.

The social work profession began with charity organization and settlement house workers assisting poor urban immigrants (Gordon, 1988). This mission to assist people of diverse cultures obtain needed resources, services, and opportunities remains with the profession today, as reflected in the NASW Code of Ethics (NASW, 1980).

The U.S. Bureau of the Census (1990) reports that the number of immigrants in the United States has increased significantly within the past two decades. It further estimates that by the year 2015 more than half the people in the United States will be from a non-Western European background (U.S. Bureau of the Census, 1988). This dramatic increase in immigrants from developing countries has spurred an interest on the part of the social work profession in developing assessment tools and intervention techniques to facilitate ethnic-sensitive practice.

A notable example is the culturagram developed by Congress (1994), a family-assessment tool for use by social workers to individualize families from diverse cultures, assess the impact of those cultures on family members, facilitate empathy, and empower culturally diverse clients. Although professional social workers have increasingly acknowledged the growing cultural diversity of the client population (Congress, 1994), this has not always translated into the development of specialized interventions for clients with socially unacceptable problems such as domestic violence.

Three main types of interventions have evolved out of social work practice with victims of domestic violence: social interventions, clinical interventions, and empowerment-oriented interventions that often utilize the criminal justice system as part of their strategy. Each present special problems for immigrant women and women in communities of color.

Social Interventions

Mrs. L, who emigrated from China a year ago, was kept a virtual prisoner in the home by her husband and her mother-in-law, who forced her to do housework and care for all the family members as well as her children. She was beaten by her mother-in-law as well as her husband if she refused to comply with their demands.

Mrs. S, who is Jewish and recently emigrated from Russia, sought medical attention from a clinic after receiving a beating from her husband. When the social worker at the clinic suggested that she consider a shelter, she refused because none was available that enabled her to keep a kosher kitchen. She stated that the loss of her family and her ability to observe her faith would be worse than the beatings she received.

Social interventions for victims of domestic violence focus on practical problem solving for battered women and their families. Short-term interventions are crisis-oriented; longer-term interventions are intended to assist the victim to live independently apart from the abuser. Examples include both residential and nonresidential services.

Residential services encompass all the shelter service models that have evolved to provide temporary safe havens for victims of domestic violence and their families fleeing a battering situation. They are considered the most extreme of the victim-centered interventions: victims entering a shelter system must not disclose their whereabouts to anyone, not even their closest relatives. They are also considered to be the most effective in protecting women and children who are threatened by harm from their batterers. Currently, specialized shelters are primary resources for women and children seeking protection from domestic violence (Dziegielewski, Resnick, & Krause, 1996).

Case management services are available for domestic violence victims through the shelters, which provide a maximum amount of time-limited security for residents, or in the community. Nonresidential services for victims of domestic violence may include emergency hotline services, assistance with relocation, accessing emergency cash and other resources, and crisis counseling (Loring, 1994; Walker, 1994).

Longer-term social interventions may include income support for battered women and their children, rehousing, and job training. Public assistance is an important resource for some battered women and their families; it remains to be seen if welfare reform initiatives that include block grants to states will eliminate this important safety net.

Most social interventions have built-in barriers for domestic violence victims from nondominant cultures. Shelters may not include multilingual staff. Those that are funded by public dollars may exclude nondocumented immigrants. Nonresidential programs may not offer culturally sensitive services or hire workers who are multilingual, although this is deemed essential for effective shelter-based interventions (Coley & Beckett, 1988). Victims of domestic violence from immigrant communities may not know about available services or understand how to obtain access to them.

Nondocumented immigrants could have an even more difficult time using long-term social interventions. Public assistance is not an option for them, housing may be too expensive to afford, and employment is difficult to obtain without exploitation. Social workers who work with immigrant women may find it useful to know how to make referrals to organizations serving discrete immigrant communities. For example, in New York City, the New York Agency for New Americans (NYANA) serves Russian and Central European immigrants, SAKHI specializes in working with South Asian and Indian Women, and the New York Asian Women's Center serves the Chinese community. One dimension of multi-cultural practice with victims of domestic violence is an in-depth knowledge of resources available to immigrants of all ethnic groups in the geographic area served.

Clinical Interventions

> Mr. and Mrs. D sought counseling from an Indian therapist in their community. Mrs. D complained that Mr. D had become abusive, both emotionally and physically, since they emigrated from India. Mr. D countered that Mrs. D had changed since coming to the United States. In India she had been compliant and a good and respectful wife. In America she began to become more independent and to demand greater freedom and autonomy.

Traditional psychoanalytic interventions have not been found to be effective with victims of domestic violence. Classical psychoanalysis defines victims of domestic violence as masochistic: they are assumed to be receiving some gratification from the battering situation. Critics suggest that the traditional psychoanalytic approach to treatment of domestic violence victims promotes a ''blame the victim'' approach that encourages self-blame in victims.

Although some feminist practitioners, such as Shainess (1984), have reframed it to be more applicable to women who are victims of domestic violence, psychoanalytic thinking is also grounded in Western European culture and thought. As such, it may have little meaning for domestic violence victims from developing countries, Eastern cultures, or communities of color.

Family therapy is a controversial treatment modality for couples experiencing domestic violence. According to the American Medical Association, couples' counseling or family intervention is generally contraindicated in the presence of domestic violence and may increase the risk of serious harm (National Center on Women and Family Law, 1993).

Family systems theory has been criticized as being inappropriate for use with couples if there is active battering (Rodning, 1988). In this approach the family is looked upon as a system and battering as a symptom of a dysfunctional system. No member is assigned blame: the victim is viewed as an active participant in the abusive situation. The abuser, in this model, can avoid responsibility for the abusive actions by claiming provocation or a desire to maintain the homeostasis of the family system. For immigrant families from cultures that emphasize the responsibility of the woman to maintain family stability at all cost, this approach could reinforce internalized cultural values demanding that she should remain in the abusive situation for the good of the family.

However, some therapists have claimed success in using conjoint family therapy to treat couples together in cases where domestic violence results from marital conflict (Geller, 1992). The premise for this is that when a couple is seen together, they are treated "as a dynamic unit whose pattern of reactions are interdependent" (Geller & Wasserstrom, 1984, p. 35). Further, cultural background and ethnic identity can create barriers to help seeking, particularly for immigrant couples experiencing domestic violence; and once a decision to seek help has been made, conjoint family therapy may be the only form of intervention the couple is willing to accept.

Crisis intervention models of treatment are utilized in domestic violence shelter settings as well as in community-based treatment for victims (Dziegielewski et al., 1996). In a crisis people respond to traumatic events according to their individual personality traits, coping mechanisms, and cultural values. The crisis intervention model suggests that in the face of the emotional and physical abuse that constitute battering, victims can learn new coping mechanisms and problem-solving skills.

Cognitive and behavioral approaches have been identified as effective short-term treatment modalities for victims of domestic violence (Dziegielewski et al., 1996). They can also be utilized to assist the victim in addressing the abusive situation within the preferred cultural context. One example of a cognitive-behavioral approach is rational–emotive therapy (RET), which seeks to assist clients to address emotional disturbances and improve life situations by targeting irrational belief systems.

According to Robin, DiGiuseppe, and Kopec (1994), RET is the treatment modality of choice when doing cross-cultural therapy or counseling. RET encourages clients to maintain their cultural reality and provides a basis for examining and challenging long-cherished cultural assumptions when they lead to dysfunctional emotions, behaviors, and consequences. It also provides clients with the tools to comprehend the link between beliefs, emotions, and behaviors but does not force clients to think, feel, or behave like members of the dominant culture in order to change (Robin et al., 1994).

Feminist therapy models have been developed specifically to address the empowerment of women (Bricker-Jenkins & Hooyman, 1986). Survivor therapy, developed by Walker (1994) is an example of an intervention model intended to respond to the problems of battered women. It is based on the treatment approaches of both feminist therapy theory and trauma theory. By analyzing power and control factors in an abusive relationship, survivor therapy treats victims of violence by focusing on their strengths, a practice known as strengths-based therapy utilized by social workers.

This model takes into account the woman's sociopolitical, cultural, and economic context, reflecting the dimensions of the nested ecological theory proposed by Dutton (1994). It also explores victims' coping strategies and assists them in building new ones, using many techniques from cognitive and behavioral therapeutic models. As a feminist model of psychotherapy, it explicitly incorporates the feminist therapist's goal of uncovering and respecting each client's cultural and experiential differences as an ethical guideline (Lerman & Porter, 1990).

Objectives of feminist therapeutic intervention models include the empowerment of clients using strategies to assist the abused partner to redefine herself or himself as a survivor (not a victim). They also seek to enhance feelings of competence, strength, self-worth, and independence from the abuser (Walker, 1994). The feminist therapeutic models, as well as crisis intervention and cognitive-behavioral models like RET, seek to assist victims of domestic violence with the immediate crisis, as defined by the client, as well as developing a new life philosophy that is based on empowerment and strength, not victimization.

A contextual perspective that recognizes the impact of cultural variables on a battered women's response to battering, as well as other situational factors, is essential to effective assessment and intervention strategies (Petretic-Jackson & Jackson, 1996). In addition, the effectiveness of clinical interventions depends in part on the ability of social workers and clients to communicate verbally. Even if clients can understand English, misinterpretations of meanings—mediated by cultural values—can result in the failure of the social worker to assist a client with whom she or he does not share a common culture.

Criminal Justice Interventions

Mrs. G was referred to a family service agency by a local church pastor, who had been counseling her regarding her abusive husband, from whom she was hiding. A nondocumented immigrant, Ms. G explained to the social worker that if her husband found her, he would arrange for her deportation. She is from Nigeria, which has laws sanctioning wife abuse by husbands.

Since the 1960s, the family court system has provided some protection and redress for victims of domestic violence through orders of protection and adjudication of family disputes. In addition, federal, state, and local funding has been appropriated for services to domestic violence victims and their families obtained through the criminal justice system.

To date, most domestic violence service dollars have targeted victims and their families, but increasingly, attention is focusing on treatment for batterers as well. These treatment modalities range from mandatory arrest and court-ordered counseling to peer group support similar to the Alcoholics Anonymous (AA) model. Success with any of the available modalities for batterers has been intermittent at best and subject to mitigating circumstances.

For example, although mandatory arrest policies appeared initially to have a positive impact on recidivism, subsequent studies found that they had no effect when the batterer was unemployed. Some practitioners support couple therapy for families in which domestic violence is a factor, but most therapists are adamantly opposed to counseling couples together when there is active battering. Reasons include the danger posed to both victim and therapist and the concern that the hope of a "cure" will dissuade the victim from heeding danger signs or seeking protection when necessary.

The criminal justice intervention may not be useful in working with all battered women. In immigrant communities both husband and wife may be unaware of laws that prohibit abuse of one spouse by another. The nondocumented domestic violence victim may not want to utilize the criminal justice system, out of concern for exposure to the Immigration and Naturalization Service. The court system may be intimidating or confusing to new immigrants, who may have difficulty communicating in English.

IMMIGRANT COMMUNITIES
AND DOMESTIC VIOLENCE

New immigrants remain as vulnerable today as they were a century ago. In spite of the growing interest and understanding of the need to ensure culturally competent and sensitive social work practice, there is still a dearth of knowledge about the incidence and prevalence of domestic violence among immigrant women and communities of color. Even more essential is a systematic study of the impact of existing services and interventions on victims of domestic violence from cultures other than the dominant European-American culture, and there is a need for changes in the service delivery system.

The data currently available are largely anecdotal and descriptive. However, case examples from the available literature may provide some ideas for more systematic study of the relationship various ethnic groups and services to domestic violence victims.

Many immigrants are from developing countries with cultures and languages significantly different from those of mainstream America. The influx of immigrants from Asia (including South Asia), Africa, the Caribbean, and Spanish-speaking countries such as Puerto Rico and those of Central and South America represent communities of color that are often marginalized in American society.

Case examples of battered women from Asia, Eastern Europe, India, and Africa, as well as the nondocumented in general, illustrate the difficulties of their obtaining needed services in the United States. An understanding of how different immigrant communities view domestic violence can help social workers begin to formulate effective responses to assist battered immigrant women.

Asian Battered Women

The Asian immigrant community may experience isolation because of language barriers. In addition, Asian women, according to Pat Eng, Coordinator of the New York Asian Women's Center, are socialized to be obedient to the men in their lives: fathers, husbands, and brothers. Failure in marriage within the Asian community represents not just an individual humiliation but shame against the entire family, according to Ching Louie (1991).

Stress and cultural conflict in the United States, as a part of the immigration experience, can exacerbate existing familial tensions. Although no correlation was found between socioeconomic status of the families involved or the employment status of the women, there were strong correlations between domestic abuse and language problems, rigid sex-role attitudes, and social isolation (Ching Louie, 1991).

Complicating the barriers preventing battered Asian women from seeking shelter and other protective services is the issue of immigration. Many Asian immigrant women were sponsored by their husbands, and they are forced to live with in-laws who may refuse to protect them from abuse (Ching Louie, 1991). They may also experience the added stress of threats of deportation and separation from their children. Asian women, including those from Indonesia, Cambodia, Japan, China, the Philippines, and Korea, are especially vulnerable to economic, physical, and emotional control of husbands who preceded them to the United States and fail to file their wives' immigration papers (Ching Louie, 1991).

Cases of spouse abuse within the Asian community prompted Asian women advocates to found the Asian Women's Shelter (AWS) in San Francisco. According to AWS director Beckie Masaki (Ching Louie, 1991), the issue of domestic violence within the Asian immigrant community has galvanized an expanding network of services, including hotlines, shelters, and counseling services in cities such as Chicago, New York, Honolulu, and New Brunswick, New Jersey.

This network has begun to link with the emerging Indian and South Asian domestic violence service system to form both national and local coalitions, conduct multilingual education on domestic violence and existing services to the Asian communities, and assist with services, jobs, relocation, legal advocacy, and English as a second language (ESL) and other educational services. The philosophy underlying the services, according to Masaki (Ching Louie, 1991), is to support Asian women in challenging the traditional notions that men are entitled to control women as property and women are required to accept this role within the family.

Eastern European Battered Women

Russian Jewish immigrants were granted asylum in large numbers during and after the cold war. This recent large-scale immigration parallels that of the 19th century and has resulted in newly created ethnic enclaves in large urban centers like New York. Judaism teaches that the Jewish home is a Mikdash Me'at, a holy space, and traditionally, Jewish women are responsible for domestic tranquility (Cramer, 1990).

One identified barrier preventing battered immigrant Jewish women from seeking help is a deep sense of shame, leading them to minimize or redefine the abuse to avoid humiliation. Another is the lack of services that meet the specific needs of Jewish battered women: shelters with kosher facilities, arrangements with Jewish educational institutions where children can continue their education, and observance of non-Christian holidays.

Lack of multilingual staff and fear of anti-Semitism by non-Jewish staff may also create reluctance on the part of Jewish women to seek services in battered women's shelters. Alternatively, they may also feel constrained in seeking services from a Jewish agency, out of fear that their community will find out they have been battered.

Effective service delivery to this population includes some provision for kosher cooking utensils, access to a rabbi, and the opportunity to select a Jewish or non-Jewish counselor if desired. Advertising services for victims of domestic violence through temples, sisterhoods, or women's organizations in temples, Hadassah, B'nai B'rith, Rabbis, Hillel, and Jewish community centers can be useful for outreach.

It is important to recognize that the actual dynamics of battering in Jewish families is the same as in non-Jewish families, although there is some evidence that Jewish women tend to stay in battering relations longer than non-Jewish women do, and those seeking shelter may be older than non-Jewish women. According to Cramer (1990), key factors in serving Jewish victims of domestic violence is understanding the meaning of family in Jewish life and the deep humiliation Jewish women often feel about being battered.

Indian and South Asian Battered Women

Domestic violence against women is an issue that many Indian Americans refuse to acknowledge as a problem within their community by contending it occurs only within poor, uneducated families (Gupta, 1992). Women advocates within the Indian immigrant community suggest that this is not the case. The story of Sita, heroine of the Indian epic *Ramayana*, mythologizes the self-immolating woman who becomes the "ideal woman" through her continuous efforts to prove herself worthy of her husband, Ram (Gupta, 1992). It is this feminine model of subjugation that female Indian children are taught to emulate.

Although the dynamics of domestic violence are not unique in the Indian immigrant community, Indian battered women face additional problems due to immigration status, level of acculturation, and culturally insensitive mainstream organizations that create barriers to obtaining needed assistance (Gupta, 1992). Traditional arranged marriages create patrilocal joint family households that make Indian women vulnerable to abuse by extended family members as well as spouses. Often her family of origin will not extend assistance once she is married, as she is not considered their concern anymore.

According to Gupta (1992), social stigma and pressure from the larger Indian community not to break up her family constitute significant deterrents to a wife's reaching out for assistance through the formal service network. In recent years a number of Indian and South Asian women have organized their own service network, including shelter services, to assist battered women in their community. SAKHI, a New York–based women's support group, is one of a number of organizations that have formed out of the Indian and South Asian communities to assist battered women and their families; others include APNA GHAR (Chicago), ASHA (Washington, DC), and MANAVI (New Jersey).

BATTERED WOMEN
WHO ARE NONDOCUMENTED IMMIGRANTS

Even feminist therapists may sometimes work with immigrant couples, particularly those who are self-referred. According to Lipchik (1994), if the identified problem is a lack of understanding of the laws governing family violence and both members of the couple are willing, the abusive husband may be referred to a batterers group as a way to learn about male-female relations in American culture and the legal ramifications of spouse abuse. This may be included as part of an intervention strategy if an assessment finds the couple is not knowledgeable about this country's laws against physical abuse.

This represents part of a solution-focused approach that can assist the special needs of some immigrant families whose members are in different stages of assimilation and acculturation. For other family violence situations, particularly for those involving a nondocumented partner who is the victim of abuse, the issues are much more problematic.

Many nondocumented women refuse to seek help for fear of being deported, according to the National Women's Abuse Prevention Project (1988). This may be because the country of origin has laws protecting husbands who beat their wives (as in the case of Mrs. G), and the threat of deportation may place the woman at risk of further abuse by family members, on whom she would be dependent for support. It may also be because of the felt need of the victim to protect the interests of her family.

> Maria married an American citizen and left an impoverished life in South America to live with him in the United States. She and her husband had three children, who were provided with advantages they would not have had in her country of origin. Her husband never applied for citizen status for her, however, and continually abused her. Maria refused to press charges or leave him out of fear that she would either lose her children to him or be forced to return to her country of origin with them, where they would live the same impoverished life she had escaped from.

In this case the fact that Maria's husband never petitioned for her green card permitted him to keep her in virtual slavery. She is in a vulnerable position if she tries to leave her husband and he reports her to the Immigration and Naturalization Service. Her status also precludes her from receiving public assistance and creates barriers to her obtaining a job that could enable her to support herself and her children.

Nondocumented battered women are among the most difficult to assist. In addition to the psychological problems such women may have to address, formidable social problems can create practical difficulties as well. Resources such as the National Center for Immigrants' Rights are available to provide information for social workers who are assisting nondocumented women to address issues of domestic abuse. Social interventions, in addition to clinical interventions and education, are critical to the success of nondocumented women in freeing themselves from battering situations.

AMERICAN BATTERED WOMEN:
SPECIAL POPULATIONS

Women born in the United States may also represent ethnic or cultural minorities. Social workers serving communities of color may encounter difficulties in identifying adequate or appropriate service interventions for their clients who are battered women. Case examples illustrate some of these difficulties and potential barriers:

Latina Battered Women

> Mrs. L complained to members of her parish that her husband was using her household food money for drugs and alcohol and that he threatened her and the children when intoxicated. Her family was in Puerto Rico and could not assist her. Parish members advised her to try appeasing him because her primary responsibility was to be a good wife and mother and respect the sanctity of the marriage bond.

A comparison of Anglo and Latino family values and structure reveal major differences that have important implications for effectively serving Latina battered women (Rios, n.d.). In the Latino culture individuals are seen first and primarily as members of the family, and family members are expected to work actively toward its unity and preservation. However, the Latino culture is also characterized by a patriarchal family structure and the expectation that traditional gender roles will be strictly adhered to.

Consequently, the Latina woman is expected to be family-identified: her sense of identify and self-esteem are linked to her perceived ability to fulfill the ideal of the self-sacrificing mother and wife. These factors, according to Rios (n.d.), make it difficult for the Latina battered woman to take action against the abuse by seeking judicial or police protection or assistance through a shelter or family service agency. She is accustomed to subordinating her needs on behalf of her family, even at the risk of her own personal safety. Also, her sense of identity is so linked to her role of wife and mother that she may consider herself a failure if she takes action to break up her family.

These concerns may be supported and reinforced by family, friends, and community, and the victim may be urged to give the relationship another chance. Religious beliefs in the sanctity of marriage can be another barrier. Service providers must acknowledge the conflicts engendered by a Latina woman's decision to confront the battering situation. This is compounded by Latinos' historical experience of oppression by the police and criminal justice system, which are viewed with suspicion. The lack of bilingual and culturally sensitive social workers can further alienate the Latina victim of family violence, should she choose to reach out for assistance in spite of the internal and structural barriers she faces in doing so.

In her paper titled *Double Jeopardy: Cultural and Systemic Barriers Faced by the Latina Battered Woman*, Rios (n.d.) stresses the need for domestic violence workers to understand and respect the cultural differences presented by the Latina battered woman and to advocate at the community level against institutional factors such as lack of social justice that negatively affect the Latino community, as well as other communities of color.

African American Battered Women

> Mrs. B called the police after a violent attack by her estranged husband that left her with bruises, cuts, and a broken tooth. When the police suggested that she enter a shelter, she refused, stating that she would lose her apartment and would no longer be able to care for her elderly mother and both her and her sister's children.

According to crime statistics, African Americans report domestic violence episodes to law enforcement in proportionately larger numbers than other ethnic groups (U.S. Department of Justice, 1984). In spite of this, only recently has a body of scholarship begun to develop that focuses on domestic violence within the African-American community (Coley & Beckett, 1988; Williams, 1994).

Coley and Beckett (1988) examine six areas that relate to culturally sensitive practice with Black battered women: community outreach, shelter services, shelter environment, shelter policies, staff training, and counseling. They emphasize that Black women are less likely to utilize formal social services than are White women and may be less knowledgeable about them. Disseminating information about available services to women within the Black community, through Black churches and organizations, beauty parlors, community centers, and housing projects, is important.

Black women may have reservations about seeking shelter services because they may associate them with the White feminist movement and believe that the value orientation of shelter staff may be alien to them. Efforts to broaden the value base of shelter programs and staff may be essential to encourage utilization by Black women (Coley & Beckett, 1988). Efforts should be made to ensure that shelter staff and residents are ethnically and racially diverse and that this is made known to the community served.

Owing to limitations in domestic violence shelter facilities in many localities, particularly in low-income states with large Black populations (e.g., Mississippi), social workers should consider providing community-based alternatives. The Black tradition of self-help groups, particularly linked to the church, may be a more acceptable source of assistance to Black battered women than more formal agency services.

There is some evidence that women of color had been excluded from the initial planning and implementation of shelter services by domination of these activities by the White women's movement (Schechter, 1982). Including representation from the Black community on shelter and domestic violence advisory boards and planning groups could serve to ensure that service delivery is culturally sensitive to Black families experiencing domestic violence (Williams, 1993). Within shelters, toys, books, and magazines that reflect Black as well as White norms create a more comfortable environment for the Black family seeking protective services.

Racism and oppression experienced by the Black community in general and by Black men in particular may complicate a Black battered woman's feelings toward her abuser. This could have an alienating effect on Black women and limit their ability to benefit from counseling and other services provided within both shelter and community-based settings (Schechter, 1982; Stovall, personal communication, October 21, 1994). Staff should be sensitive to these possibilities and ensure that Black women do not isolate themselves by supporting their participation in groups and sharing of communal space.

Shelter policies that prohibit residents from communicating with family members could have the unintended consequence of making minority residents feel estranged from their support network; allowing a call to assure loved ones of their safety (without revealing one's whereabouts) could address this concern. Cultural differences in child discipline could also run counter to established shelter policies, which generally prohibit physical discipline of children.

Staff training can prepare staff to respond appropriately to all residents and prevent the premature departure of a battered woman and her family from a shelter or community-based service setting (Coley & Beckett, 1988). This includes information on cross-cultural differences and the impact of race/ethnicity on perceptions of problems, coping behavior, and help-seeking, as well as appreciation for diversity.

IMPLICATIONS FOR SOCIAL WORK PRACTICE

The cultural diversity of American society has stimulated the growth of social work models of practice since the inception of the profession in the 19th century. Service delivery to victims of domestic violence was an integral part of family services among the profession's forerunners in the charity organization and settlement house movement. Charity organization agents serving the urban immigrant communities not infrequently were required to address problems of domestic violence, although in the early days of social work, this often was done as part of the prevailing "child saving" mission.

Early social work reformers were also maternalists and advocated against domestic abuse and for prohibition and women's pensions in order to achieve their (White middle-class) goal of assisting women to remain in the home caring for their children (Gordon, 1994). Their "clients" of the day were immigrant women, often from rural areas, who were forced to cope with the harshness and uncertainties of urban industrial life. Early social workers rarely attempted to empathize with the subjects of their ministrations; instead, they projected values that were often quite alien to their female clients and advice that was often counterproductive.

However myopic these early reformers were regarding the problems facing immigrant families of the progressive era, they fought hard for solutions to social problems that affected all women. As social work started to turn inward in the 1920s, it began to look for solutions to social problems in psychotherapeutic techniques. The civil rights era and the women's movement of the 1960s and 1970s brought social workers back to a politicized and structural perspective in relation to social problems, including that of domestic violence.

As the profession faces the beginning of the 21st century, the globalization of social issues and the widespread immigration of families from cultures significantly different from the dominant European-American culture are moving social workers to develop multicultural approaches to working with clients. To address the problem of domestic violence within a multicultural context, social workers must develop a multidimensional understanding of the victims in relation to their family, community, and culture of origin, as well as their intrapsychic processes.

The ecological model of social work practice suggests intervention strategies that represent a synthesis of social and psychological techniques. It also requires a broad knowledge base and understanding of domestic violence victims from different cultures and their responses to new and existing service systems and modalities.

Since the 1960s social work has been struggling toward a multicultural model of service delivery that better reflects the basic tenet of social work practice: begin where the client is. The 20th-century feminist movement, although begun by White middle-class professionals, has also reached communities of color.

Research by social workers into domestic violence as a multicultural phenomenon can yield important information about characteristics of abuse in immigrant communities, barriers to service utilization, and successful practice models. Lack of funding and of access to informants has made this a difficult area of study. One such study of battered women in the Indian immigrant community is currently being undertaken in New York City (Baig-Amin, personal communication, 1995). The findings should significantly add to the body of knowledge in this area.

The elimination of domestic violence by one adult family member against another, a key issue in the 20th-century women's movement, has challenged activists and social workers alike to evolve culturally sensitive models of service delivery. This reflects a new respect for diversity, as well as the commitment to reach underserved populations that have been isolated by language and culture. In doing so, social work is challenged to continually incorporate culturally sensitive values and techniques in order to remain vital, relevant, and effective into the 21st century.

REFERENCES

Barker, R. L. (1995). *The social work dictionary*. Silver Springs, MD: National Association of Social Workers.

Brace, C. L. (1872). *The dangerous classes of New York, and twenty years' work among them*. Silver Spring, MD: National Association of Social Workers.

Bricker-Jenkins, M., & Hooyman, N. R. (1986). Grounding the definition of feminist practice. In M. Bricker-Jenkins & N. R. Hooyman (Eds.), *Not for women only* (pp. 25–33). Silver Spring, MD: National Association of Social Workers.

Ching Louie, M. (1991, March/April). Hope for battered Asians. *New Directions for Women*, p. 9.

Coley, S. M., & Beckett, J. O. (1988, October). Black battered women: Practice issues. *Social Casework*, pp. 483–490.

Congress, E. (1994). The use of culturagrams to assess and empower culturally diverse families. *Families in Society: The Journal of Contemporary Human Services, 75*, 531–540.

Cramer, L. (1990, Fall). Recommendations for working with Jewish battered women. *National Coalition Against Domestic Violence (NCADV)*, pp. 4–5.

Dutton, D. G. (1994). *Domestic violence*. Manitoba, Canada: University of Manitoba Press.

Dziegielewski, S. F., Resnick, C., & Krause, N. B. (1996). Shelter-based crisis intervention with battered women. In A. R. Roberts (Ed.), *Helping battered women: New perspectives and remedies* (pp. 159–171). New York: Oxford Press.

Geller, J. A. (1992). *Breaking destructive patterns*. New York: Free Press.

Geller, J. A., & Wasserstrom, J. (1984). Conjoint therapy for the treatment of domestic violence. In A. R. Roberts (Ed.), *Battered women and their families: Intervention strategies and treatment programs* (pp. 33–48). New York: Springer.

Gordon, L. (1988). *Heros of their own lives: The politics and history of domestic violence*. New York: Viking.

Gupta, V. M. (1992, June). The weakest link: Domestic violence in our community. *The Indian-American*, pp. 42–44.

Lerman, H., & Porter, N. (1990). The contribution of feminism to ethics in psychotherapy. In H. Lerman & N. Porter (Eds.), *Feminist ethics in psychotherapy* (pp. 5–13). New York: Springer.

Lipchik, E. (1994). Therapy for couples can reduce domestic violence. In K. Swisher & C. Wekesser (Eds.), *Violence against women* (pp. 154–163). San Diego, CA: Greenhaven.

Loring, E. (1994). *Emotional abuse*. New York: Free Press.

National Association of Social Workers. (1980). *NASW code of ethics*. Washington, DC: Author.

National Center on Women and Family Law. (1993). *Couples counseling and couples therapy endanger battered women*. (Item No. 62). New York: Author.

National Women's Abuse Prevention Project. (1988). Special issues facing the undocumented woman. *The Exchange, 2*(1), 10–12.

Petretic-Jackson, P. A., & Jackson, T. (1996). Mental health interventions with battered women. In A. R. Robers (Ed.), *Helping battered women: New perspectives and remedies* (pp. 88–121). New York: Oxford University Press.

Rios, E. A. (n.d.). *Double jeopardy: Cultural and systemic barriers faced by the Latina battered woman*. Unpublished manuscript.

Robin, M., DiGiuseppe, R., & Kopec, A. M. (1994). *Using rational–emotive therapy with culturally diverse clients*. Paper presented at the Third European Congress of Psychology, Tampere, Finland, July 7, 1993.

Rodning, S. A. (1988). Victim: Family systems and feminist perspective. *Affilia, 3*(3), 83–97.

Schechter, S. (1982). *Women and male violence: The visions and struggles of the battered women's movement*. Boston: South End.

Shainess, N. (1984). *Sweet suffering: Woman as victim*. New York: Bobbs-Merrill.

U.S. Bureau of the Census. (1988). Projection of the population of the United States by age, sex and race, 1988 to 2080. *Current Population Reports* (series P-25, No. 1018). Washington, DC: U.S. Government Printing Office.

U.S. Bureau of the Census. (1990). *Statistical abstract of the United States, 1990*. Washington, DC: U.S. Department of Commerce.

U.S. Department of Justice. (1984). *Family violence: Special Report*. Washington, DC: U.S. Government Printing Office.

Walker, L. (1994). *Abused women and survivor therapy*. Washington, DC: American Psychological Association.

Williams, O. J. (1993). Developing an African American perspective to reduce spouse abuse: Considerations for community action. *Black Caucus: Journal of the National Association of Black Social Workers*, No. 2, pp. 1–6.

CHAPTER 14

Working with Culturally Diverse Substance Abusers and Their Families

Sandra Turner
Marlene Cooper

An ethnic group or cultural group is generally composed of those who conceive of themselves as alike by virtue of their common ancestry. Cultural differences explain the different value systems and beliefs of, for example, Haitians and Black Americans, or Puerto Ricans and Argentineans. It is culture that plays a major role in determining what we eat, how we work, how we relax, how we celebrate holidays, and what our beliefs are about life, death, illness, health, nutrition, and so on (McGoldrick, Pearce, & Giordano, 1996).

Cultures and families that have enforced norms and rituals about drinking practices tend to have less alcoholism than those who do not. For example, it is commonly believed that the reason there is a low rate of alcoholism among Jews and Italians is that there are strong cultural guidelines for the ritualistic use of alcohol that people tend to adhere to. In Irish and Russian cultures drinking is done in a nonritualistic fashion, and the traditional and generally accepted cultural pattern of drinking is to the point of intoxication (Segal, 1986).

At a conference in 1994 on multicultural perspectives in working with substance abusing clients, the keynote speaker, Judson Hixson, stated that culture provides the framework within which we define ourselves and interpret and make sense of the world, and guides how we interact with, respond to, and influence people, events, and conditions.

Effective cross-cultural or multicultural work with individuals or families requires an understanding of the value systems of other cultures and how those values influence the behavior of the family members (McGoldrick, Pearce, & Giordano, 1982). It also requires an understanding of one's own cultural values and beliefs. An in-depth recognition of what the practitioner considers most desirable about his or her own culture and what is least admired is very helpful in developing an understanding of and appreciation for values and practices of other cultures. Hines and Boyd-Franklin (1982) refer to this essential process as the practitioner's own soul searching.

This chapter examines the substance abuse research on Blacks, Hispanics, Asians, and Native Americans in the United States. Although these ethnic minorities represent the multicultural perspective of this country, they have been underrepresented in the substance abuse literature. A case of substance abuse in an African American family illustrates the various cultural issues that are faced when working with this particular problem. Suggestions for an effective, culturally sensitive method of family practice also are presented.

SUBSTANCE ABUSE AND CULTURE

There are cultures that are viewed as "wet" or "dry." France and Spain are typically viewed as wet. Cantonese, Bedouin, and Hopi cultures and Israel and India are dry. Austria and Germany are beer cultures; France and Portugal are wine cultures. Gaelic, Eskimo, Japanese, and Swedish are considered "spirits" cultures. Some major religions are recognized as being relatively permissive or prohibitive with respect to drinking. Catholicism and Eastern Orthodoxy tend to be relatively permissive, in contrast to the restrictive doctrines of Islam, Buddhism, and some branches of Protestantism. Nationalities are often stereotyped as having distinctive patterns of alcohol use, such as German boisterous group drinking, Russian bingeing on vodka, and French incessant wine drinking (Heath, 1990–

1991). McQuade (1989), writing about the significance of the "fiesta" to Hispanics, states: "Life is seen as an unfolding tragedy wrapped in an intermittent 'fiesta' which becomes compensation for life's suffering. With this cultural predisposition to the 'fiesta,' the Hispanic has learned to accept other deprivation. Alcohol and drugs infiltrate the 'fiesta' " (p. 30). It is important to be aware of different cultural values and beliefs to be able to determine whether a particular family is acting in accordance with its own cultural norms or is behaving in ways that are considered deviant in its culture.

Different immigrant groups bring different ethnic cultures to the host society, which may contrast with the mainstream culture. For example, heavy drinking among Irish immigrants may be associated with the "bachelor group ethic of hard drinking in the Irish culture" (Stivers, 1985, cited in Cheung, 1990–91). The low rates of alcohol consumption among the Chinese may be associated with their physiological reaction of flushing (Reed, Kalant, Gibbons, Kapur, & Rankin, 1976; Sue & Nakamura, 1984, cited in Cheung, 1990–91). It may also be associated with the Chinese philosophy of moderation and the habit of drinking only at mealtimes (Singer, 1972; Smart & Ogborne, 1986).

Cultural beliefs may affect not only immigrants' use of substances but also their utilization of treatment and other health care services. In traditional Chinese culture, mental illness of a family member is a disgrace to the whole family. For face-saving reasons, the person is likely to be concealed within the family. The head of the family would decide which treatment modality to take—usually herbal medicines. This health-seeking behavior coupled with other barriers such as language problems and lack of information about public services tends to hold back the Chinese from obtaining psychiatric help. The same may be true for use or lack of use of treatment facilities for alcohol and drugs for Chinese addicts.

When acculturation occurs, the ethnic person's perception and use of substances may gradually resemble those of the larger society. Caetano (1987) found a strong association between acculturation and increased drinking, although the association is stronger and more consistent for women than for men. Adlaf et al. (Adlaf, Smart, & Tan, 1989) reported that among students of Eastern European, Black, Jewish, Oriental, and Mediterranean descent, those who speak English at home, which is an indicator of acculturation, have greater drug involvement. Adaptation problems cause emotional stress, and many migration studies have shown that acculturation problems can produce certain physical illnesses or mental disorders (Hull, 1979). In the light of the literature on stress and alcohol and drug addiction (e.g., Crutchfield & Gove, 1984; Gottheil et al., 1987) there are reasons to believe that some immigrants would rely heavily on alcohol and drugs as a way of coping with stress.

The longest-term prospective study that has been conducted on the natural history of alcoholism traced a large sample of adolescents for more than 40 years. Ethnicity turned out to be the single most predictive factor for alcoholism, even though the researchers had expected that psychological factors would have more prognostic value (Kopstein & Roth, 1993; Vaillant & Milofsky, 1982; Vaillant, 1983). The criterion of ethnicity was the national origin of the paternal ancestors. Drinking patterns among ethnic groups have a remarkable persistence over time. Greeley et al. (Greeley, McReady, & Thiesen, 1980) found that the variables of personality and family structure play only a small role in the problem drinking of boys; yet unlike Vaillant (1983), they noted that in all of the groups studied, the tendency to drink heavily is influenced most notably by the drinking behavior of mother and friends. Ethnicity is a major variable in each study, but one arrived at the conclusion by tracing paternal ancestry and the other by looking at maternal ancestry. Recent research in prevention of substance abuse has found that family variables are indeed a critical predictor of substance misuse (Hawkins, Catalano, & Miller, 1992; Turner, 1994).

SUBSTANCE ABUSE AND MINORITIES

In the United States the minority community is disproportionately affected by "hard" drug use and its attendant problems. Blacks and Hispanics, the two largest ethnic minority groups, comprised 38.1% of the clients admitted to the Client Oriented Data Acquisition Program (CODAP) clinics in 1981 despite the fact that these groups represent only 18.1% of the national population (National Institute on Drug Abuse, 1982, cited in Tucker, 1985). This situation of overrepresentation has continued over recent years, although some abatement of African American substance abuse can be noted. Recent studies have noted that although Native Americans and Whites had the highest rates of alcohol use, followed by Hispanics, Blacks, and Asians, Black adults are the most likely to be treated in emergency rooms for alcohol and drug-related problems (Johnston, O'Malley, & Bachman, 1992; Kopstein & Roth, 1993).

Asians as a whole display disproportionately low rates of drug use (Brown, 1981; Johnson & Nishi, 1976; cited in Thompson & Simmons-Cooper, 1988). However, there is evidence that drug use among the new immigrant Asian population is on the rise. As is well known in clinical practice, poverty and discrimination are critical elements in the abuse formula.

As stated, available data indicate that alcohol and other substance abuses are major health problems in Black communities (Harper, 1976; Kopstein & Roth, 1993; Watts & Wright, 1983). Research on Black adult drinking indicates that Blacks suffer as much from alcohol-related problems (e.g., homicide, violence, crime, accidents, employment problems, family disruption, and financial loss) as from the disease of alcohol itself (Watts & Wright, 1983, cited in Harper, 1988). The problem of alcoholism is of particular concern among Black adolescents. The highest consumption of alcoholic beverages now takes place among those between the ages of 16 and 20. Since 1979 the use and abuse of alcohol has increased more than 86%, with 65% of Black youth engaging in regular weekly use (Harper, 1988). Studies done in 1992 confirm that the major substance still used most commonly by adolescents is alcohol (Johnston et al., 1992; National Institute on Drug Abuse, 1992).

Recent evidence suggests that Blacks who have a high level of awareness of racial oppression and a positive view of Black people and their institutions are less tolerant than others of alcohol and drug use (Duncan & Petosa, 1994; Garry & Berry, 1985). Gary and Berry (1985) argue that health care workers should consider racial consciousness as a key variable in the development and implementation of a substance abuse prevention program.

The severity of alcohol-related problems among adult Hispanics calls for very close attention. Hispanic males suffer disproportionately from alcohol dependence and problems related to alcohol use in comparison to other Americans (Burnam, 1985; Caetano, 1985; Gilbert & Cervantes, 1986). Alcohol-related arrest rates are particularly high among Hispanics (Caetano, 1985). Among Mexican Americans specifically, cirrhotic liver death exacts an especially early and heavy toll among men (Engmann,

1976; Gilbert & Cervantes, 1986). Caetano (1985) reports that the number of alcohol-related social and personal problems reported by adult Hispanics in a 1984 national survey exceeds those reported for the White and Black populations.

Hispanic adolescents are the fastest-growing ethnic minority age group in America and are at high risk for substance abuse (Schinke, Moncher, Pralleja, Zayas, & Schilling, 1988). By the year 2000, Hispanic Americans will be our largest ethnic-racial minority group. Among Hispanic youth, alcohol use is most frequently associated with school failure. Fewer than one half of all Hispanic youths complete high school (Malone, 1985). Hispanic homicide, which is often related to substance abuse, has a rate of 88.3 per 100,000 versus 18.5 for non-Hispanic young males (Loya et al., 1986). Morales (1984) suggests that the drug use patterns of Mexican American youth may be more related to poverty factors than to cultural factors.

Substance abuse among Native American youth has been referred to as a national scandal (Pinto, 1973). The Indian Health Service (IHS) considers alcohol one of the most urgent health problems facing Indian and Alaskan native people today. Probably no other condition adversely affects so many aspects of Native American life in the United States (IHS, 1977; Johnston et al., 1992). Fisher (1987) maintains that alcohol problems among North American Indians are not due to their "Indianness" but are correlated with economic deprivation factors, including poverty, poor housing, relative ill-health, and academic failure. In a comparative study of alcohol use patterns among Blacks, Hispanics, Native Americans, and Whites, it was found that Native Americans showed the greatest disruption because of alcohol use (Wanberg et al., 1978). For ages 15–44, the IHS discharge rate from alcohol treatment facilities is four times as great (11% vs. 2.9%) as the national rate, and the alcoholic psychosis rate for ages 15–44 years is more than six times the national rate (19% vs. 3.1%). Approximately 75%–90% of all suicides among Native Americans are alcohol-related. Inhalant use is a serious problem on reservations. Some estimates show that more than one third of Native Americans eventually try inhalants. What these and other findings suggest is that the structural conditions of an ethnic group in society have a role to play in alcohol and other drug use patterns of its members (Betancourt & Lopez, 1993).

CULTURAL SENSITIVITY
AND THE TREATMENT RELATIONSHIP

Secretive behavior is associated with alcoholism and other drug abuse in many cultures, and most minority families in the United States are conditioned to having to keep secrets. One obvious reason for this is the negative history that minorities have with the welfare system and fear of being exposed for having a lifestyle that is considered unacceptable for eligibility for welfare. There are generally two kinds of secrets: those that are known by most family members but kept from the outside and those that are kept from other family members (Boyd-Franklin, 1989). Alcoholism and other substance abuse is a disease of denial and secretive behavior. This makes it more unlikely that people of color will openly discuss substance abuse when first coming for treatment. Many Hispanics do not view alcoholism as a disease; rather, it is seen as a moral weakness or character flaw that is to be hidden. Tucker (1985) talks of the need for alternative treatment and prevention models which are sensitive to the special needs of minority populations. He suggests using nonconfrontational techniques, and deemphasizing or eliminating chemical maintenance programs. The confrontational techniques so often used in therapeutic communities were condemned by some minority group representatives as being counter to the cultural orientation of their members. A more effective treatment approach is a multisystems one that combines structural and ecological approaches (Boyd-Franklin, 1989).

MULTICULTURAL ISSUES
IN WORKING WITH FAMILIES

For many counselors and therapists cross-cultural counseling presents a challenge to examine their culture-bound attitudes and beliefs about what values, customs, and behaviors are sensible and acceptable. Perhaps because of encountering culture-bound attitudes on the part of the mental health profession, Black and Puerto Rican families have traditionally turned to their extended families or to religious leaders for help and support. Because they are not accustomed to seeking help from outsiders, questions by therapists (outsiders) are likely to be felt as intrusive and prying. Sometimes this causes Black and Hispanic families to be labeled as resistant, which in fact may have more to do with how they are approached and may really be a "healthy cultural paranoia" that has been developed over generations in response to racism (Boyd-Franklin, 1989).

It is important to be able to join with the family, not only to engage them but also to be able to do a good assessment. Clients may easily detect prejudicial attitudes as well as genuine interest and concern (Boyd-Franklin, 1989). When substance abuse is involved, there is potential for more denial and secrecy; therefore, it is critical that practitioners examine their possible culture-bound attitudes and beliefs. To make an assessment of substance abuse, the practitioner needs to determine the cultural and familial attitudes toward drinking and drunkenness, the severity and duration of the substance abuse, the history of substance abuse in the family, the degree of marital conflicts due to substance abuse, the level of denial of the substance abuse, and the history of traumatic events related to substance abuse.

Many have cautioned that it is not wise to attempt to do a genogram early on in treatment when working with families who are from cultural backgrounds different from that of the therapist (Boyd-Franklin, 1989). Showing genuine interest and concern for families is what is essential; if that is done, one can gather the information necessary to make an accurate assessment of the problems that the family wants help with (McGoldrick, Pearce, & Giordano, 1982). The initial goal should be to gain enough understanding of the problem to be able to work with the family to find a solution. In general, gaining insight into why the problem occurred in the first place is not necessary (Aponte, 1991; Beck, Wright, Cory, & Liese, 1993).

Hines and Boyd-Franklin (1982) advise that when working with Black Americans it is important to remember that "the American dream was not dreamed for them" (p. 85). The survival of Black families has been attributed to their strong ties to immediate and extended family, flexibility of roles within the family, and the high value placed on religion, education, and work. There is a strong tradition among Black couples (as is true of many other cultures) of staying together for the sake of the children (Hines & Boyd-Franklin, 1982). When a family does decide to come in for treatment, it is often because one of the children is having a problem in school (Aponte, 1991). The Lee family personifies many of the characteristics of Black American families discussed above and is presented to illustrate a multisystems approach to the problem of substance abuse within a family.

Case Example: The Lee Family

The Lee family was seen at an outpatient alcoholism clinic intermittently over a period of 6 years. Mrs. Lee was initially referred to the family counseling program by the outpatient medical clinic to which she had come for treatment for high blood pressure. During an interview with a nurse she revealed that she was very concerned about her husband, an employee of the hospital where the clinic was based, who was drinking more and more heavily. She was afraid he was going to lose his job because he was calling in sick so often. She (Ann) and her husband (William) agreed to make an appointment at the alcoholism clinic. William denied that he had any problem with drinking and stated that he did not want help. His wife refused to make another appointment if he wasn't going to agree to come with her. The therapist, who is also a co-author, initially had a very positive feeling about Mr. Lee. He reminded her of an older man in her neighborhood whom she had known and liked very much when she was a young girl. Even though he flatly refused help, she made a point of periodically going to say hello to him on the floor where he was a security guard in the hospital. He seemed to respond positively to this gesture.

About a year and a half later, William Lee called and asked if he and his wife could bring in their youngest daughter, Susan. They were very concerned because she had suddenly stopped going to school and she would not tell them why. She was also doing very poorly in school when she did go. The three of them came in, and although Susan refused to talk during the session, she did agree to come back with her parents the following week. Over the course of several weeks, Susan was able to express some anger at her parents. She was angry and frightened about her father's drinking, and she was upset that her mother was often so angry at him. She was afraid to leave the house because she was frightened that they might have a terrible fight or that one of them would leave while she was gone. It soon became apparent that Susan liked coming for sessions because, as she stated, "It was the only time that her parents talked together with her," and it made her feel as though they were a family again. She soon felt safe enough to return to school and began to see the therapist individually to help her with school problems.

About 6 months later, Mr. Lee came in for alcoholism treatment and also began going to Alcoholics Anonymous (AA). He achieved sobriety after about 1 month in the clinic.

Susan came for treatment regularly for about a year and continued periodically until she graduated from high school (3 years later) and was accepted into college.

About the time that Susan stopped treatment, her unmarried sister, Phyllis, called. She reported that she was pregnant and did not know what to do. The father of the baby had left town when he found out she was pregnant. She wanted help in making the decision about whether to have an abortion or keep the baby. Her family was very supportive, and she decided to have the baby and continue living at home. Her sister Susan became a major caretaker for the baby, as did Mr. and Mrs. Lee when they were not working.

A year later a brother, James, called and asked for an appointment. He was suffering from anxiety and was frightened that he was going to be fired from his job because he was making mistakes. The therapist referred him to someone else in the clinic because she was going on leave. He did not remain in treatment, but his sisters report that he did not lose his job.

Two years after he joined the alcoholism clinic, William called and asked for an appointment. He said that he could not read or write, and now that he was sober he wanted to learn. He was referred to a vocational program and did in fact learn to read and write. He also said he wanted to come for a few sessions for help with his relationship with his wife. He could understand why she did not pay attention to him when he was drinking, but now that he was sober he wanted more communication with her. Therapy had helped improve his communication skills and become more assertive about his needs. All the years that he was drinking, he said, he would say good-bye every morning and his wife would never answer him. Now he thought that if he stopped saying good-bye, maybe she would say it first. She did. He also began to be more expressive about his needs, and Mrs. Lee gradually became more receptive. He had promised himself that if he stayed sober he would spend his holidays as he wanted. On Thanksgiving she wanted him to go somewhere although it was raining. He said he did not get sober to go out in the rain on Thanksgiving, and he refused to go.

The last time this therapist saw William was when he called to come in for a few sessions because he was sad that he was going to have to retire. He was having severe arthritis and could no longer stand or walk for any period of time. He was pleased that everything was much better at home: his granddaughter was a source of great joy to him; his daughter Susan had returned to college after having dropped out and had moved out of the house; his daughter Phyllis was promoted at work and was managing well with her young daughter; and his son James seemed to be less nervous and had moved into his own apartment. He was also pleased that he and Ann were talking more and that she always said good-bye to him when she left for work.

MULTICULTURAL TREATMENT ISSUES

As previously stated, a Black family will often come into treatment if one of the children is having a problem (usually a school problem). This was the case with the Lee family. They were not willing to address the substance abuse when they first came to the clinic, but after some trust had been established in the initial interview and subsequent encounters with Mr. Lee in the hospital, they felt comfortable enough to come back when their daughter was not going to school. The author chose to work with the part of the family that was the most available, helping Susan to feel comfortable about going back to school, rather than insisting that William deal with his alcoholism.

The strengths of this family were highlighted and enhanced. Some of their strengths are that both parents are employed full-time (Mrs. Lee is a licensed practical nurse). They both have strong ties to their extended families in Boston and North Carolina, and the children have good relationships with their grandparents, aunts, uncles, and cousins. Both parents have strong relationships with their five children. The two eldest children are working full-time and living outside the home. The two who are still living at home are also working. Most members of the family have strong religious ties, although they go to different churches. As illustrated earlier, there is a strong sense of responsibility to each other, and family members support and care for each other.

Hines and Boyd-Franklin (1982) state: "Black families are likely to be most responsive to time-limited, problem-solving, child-focused, family therapy approaches'' (p. 102). The initial stage of treatment was just that—all the work centered around Susan and helping everyone find a way that would make her feel comfortable about going back to school. In doing this she was also able to express some of her anger at her parents for fighting and not speaking to each other and at her father for his drinking. Once she could express this anger and her feeling that she had to be home all the time in case "something happened," she realized that she missed going to school.

Over time the practitioner became like an extended family member. The Lee family most likely did not think of themselves as going for therapy but rather as going to talk over a problem they were having.

The treatment described in this case approaches Boyd-Franklin's multisystems model, described earlier in this paper. Some of the multisystems involved with the Lee family were the individual family members, the subsystems within the family (focusing on sibling alliances), the ties that the parents and different siblings had to their churches, a relationship that Susan was able to build with a favorite teacher, the occupational therapist who helped William enroll in a literacy program, the medical clinic where William was treated for his arthritis and other physical problems, and AA, of which John was finally able to become a member.

CONCLUSION

We believe that the multisystems model is useful in work with many ethnic groups where a family member is a substance abuser. The multisystems approach destigmatizes the abuser; searches for internal and external strengths within the family unit, extended family, and community, which are traditional sources of help for many people of color; and provides continuity of care over time. This enables the family to develop trust in the worker's interest and ability to provide help, which decreases shame and secretiveness. Finally, because the multisystems model incorporates the value systems and practices of people of various cultures, it is particularly appropriate for working with minority populations.

REFERENCES

Adlaf, E. M., Smart, R. G., & Tan, S. H. (1989). Ethnicity and drug use: A critical look. *International Journal of the Addictions, 24,* 1–18.

Aponte, H. (1991). Training on the person of the therapist for work with the poor and minorities. *Journal of Independent Social Work, 5*(3–4), 23–39.

Beck, A. T., Wright, F. D., Cory, F. N., & Liese, B. S. (1993). *Cognitive therapy of substance abuse.* New York: Guilford.

Betancourt, H., & Lopez, S. R. (1993). The study of culture, ethnicity and race in American psychology. *American Psychologist, 48,* 629–637.

Boyd-Franklin, N. (1989). *Black families in therapy.* New York: Guilford.

Brown, B. S. (1981, September). *Misuse of drugs by ethnic minorities.* Paper presented to the International Congress on Drugs and Alcohol, Tel Aviv, Israel.

Burnam, A. (1985, May). *Prevalence of alcohol abuse and dependence among Mexican Americans and non-Hispanic Whites in the community.* Paper presented at the National Institute of Alcohol Abuse and Alcoholism Conference, Epidemiology of Alcohol Use and Abuse among U.S. Ethnic Minorities, Bethesda, MD.

Caetano, R. (1985, May). *Drinking patterns and alcohol problems in a national sample of U.S. Hispanics.* Paper presented at the National Institute on Alcohol Abuse and Alcoholism Conference, Epidemiology of Alcohol Use and Abuse among U.S. Ethnic Minorities, Bethesda, MD.

Caetano, R. (1987). Acculturation and drinking patterns among U.S. Hispanics. *British Journal of Addiction, 82,* 789–799.

Cheung, Y. (1990–91). Ethnicity and alcohol/drug use revisited: A framework for future research. *International Journal of the Addictions, 25,* 581–605.

Crutchfield, R. D., & Gove, W. R. (1984). Determinants of drug use: A test of the coping hypothesis. *Social Science and Medicine, 18,* 503–509.

Duncan, D. F., & Petosa, R. (1994). Social and community factors associated with drug use and abuse among adolescents. In T. P. Gullotta, G. R. Adams, & R. Montemayor (Eds.), *Substance misuse in adolescence.* Thousand Oaks, CA: Sage.

Engmann, D. J. (1976). *Alcoholism and alcohol abuse among the Spanish speaking population in California: A needs and services assessment.* Sacramento: California Commission on Alcoholism for the Spanish Speaking.

Fisher, A. D. (1987). Alcoholism and race: The misapplication of both concepts to North American Indians. *Canadian Review of Social Anthropology, 24,* 81–98.

Garry, L. E., & Berry, G. (1985). Predicting attitudes toward substance use in a Black community: Implications for prevention. *Community Mental Health Journal, 21,* 42–51.

Gilbert, M. J., & Cervantes, R. C. (1986). Patterns and practice of alcohol use among Mexican Americans: A comprehensive review. *Hispanic Journal of Behavioral Science, 8*(1), 1–60.

Gottheil, E., Druley, K., Pashko, S., & Weinstein, S. P. (Eds.). (1987). *Stress and addiction.* New York: Brunner/Mazel.

Greeley, A. M., McCready, W., & Thiesen, G. (1980). *Ethnic drinking subcultures.* New York: Praeger.

Harper, F. D. (Ed.). (1976). *Alcohol abuse and Black America.* Alexandria, VA: Douglass.

Harper, F. D. (1988). Alcohol and Black youth: An overview. *Journal of Drug Issues, 18*(1), 7–14.

Hawkins, J. D., Catalano, R. E., & Miller, J. V. (1992). Risk and protective factors for alcohol and other drug problems in adolescence and early adulthood: Implications for substance abuse prevention. *Psychological Bulletin, 112*, 64–105.

Heath, D. (1990–1991). Uses and misuses of the concept of ethnicity in alcohol studies: An essay in deconstruction. *International Journal of the Addictions, 25*, 607–628.

Hines, P., & Boyd-Franklin, N. (1982). Black families. In M. McGoldrick, J. Pearce, & J. Giordano (Eds.), *Ethnicity and family therapy* (pp. 84–107). New York: Guilford.

Hull, D. (1979). Migration, adaptation, and illness: A review. *Social Science and Medicine, 13A*, 25–36.

Indian Health Service, IHS. (1977). Alcoholism: A high-priority health problem. A report of IHS Task Force on Alcoholism. DHEW Pub. No. 77–1001.

Johnson, B., & Nishi, M. S. (1976). Myths and realities of drug use by minorities. In P. Liyama, M. S. Nishi, & B. Johnson (Eds.), *Drug use and abuse among U.S. minorities.* New York: Praeger.

Johnston, L. E., O'Malley, P., & Bachman, J. G. (1992). *Drug use among American high school seniors, college students and young adults, 1975–1990, Vol. 1.* Rockville, MD: National Institute on Drug Abuse.

Kopstein, A. N., & Roth, P. T. (1993). *Drug abuse among racial/ethnic groups.* Rockville, MD: National Institute on Drug Abuse.

Loya, F., Garcia, P., Sullivan, J. D., Vargas, L. A., Allen, N. H., & Mercy, A. (1986). Conditional risks of types of homicide among Anglo, Hispanic, Black, and Asian victims, in Los Angeles, 1970–1979. In T. E. Malone (Ed.), *Report of the Secretary's Task Force on Black and Minority Health: Vol. 5. Homicide, Suicide, and Unintentional Injuries* (pp. 117–133). (Publication No. 491-313/44710). Washington, DC: U.S. Government Printing Office.

McGoldrick, M., Pearce, J., & Giordano, J. (1996). *Ethnicity and family therapy* (2nd ed.). New York: Guilford.

McQuade, F. (1989, May-June). Treatment and recovery issues for addicted Hispanics. *The Counselor*, pp. 29–30.

Malone, T. E. (1985). *Report of the Secretary's Task Force on Minority Health:* Vol. 1. *Executive Summary*, Publication No. 487-637/Q13. Washington, DC: U.S. Government Printing Office.

Morales, A. (1984). Substance abuse and Mexican American youth: An overview. *Journal of Drug Issues, 14*, 297–311.

National Institute on Drug Abuse. (1982). *Annual Data, 1981: Data from the client oriented data acquisition process.* (National Institute on Drug Abuse Statistical Series, Series E, No. 25). Washington DC: U.S. Government Printing Office.

National Institute on Drug Abuse. (1992). National household survey on drug abuse: Population estimates 1991. Rockville, MD: Author.

Pinto, L. J. (1973). Alcohol and drug abuse among Native American youth on reservations: A growing crisis. In *Drug Use in America: Problem in Perspective* (Vol. 1, pp. 1157–1178). Washington, DC: U.S. Government Printing Office.

Reed, T. E., Kalant, H., Gibbons, R. J., Kapur, B., & Rankin, G. (1976). Alcohol and acetaldehyde metabolism in Caucasians, Chinese and Amerinds. *Canadian Medical Association Journal, 15*, 851–855.

Schinke, S., Moncher, M., Pralleja, J., Zayas, L., & Schilling, R. (1988). Hispanic youth, substance abuse, and stress: Implications for prevention research. *International Journal of the Addictions, 23*, 809–826.

Segal, B. (1986). Intervention and prevention of drug-taking behavior: A need for divergent approaches. *International Journal of the Additions, 21*, 165–173.

Singer, K. (1972). Drinking patterns and alcoholism in the Chinese. *British Journal of Addiction, 67*, 3–14.

Smart, R. G., & Ogborne, A. C. (1986). *Northern spirits: Drinking in Canada then and now.* Toronto: Addiction Research Foundation Books.

Stivers, R. (1985). Historical meanings of Irish-American drinking. In L. A. Bennett & G. M. Ames (Eds.), *The American experience with alcohol: Contrasting cultural perspectives.* New York: Plenum.

Sue, S., & Nakamura, C. Y. (1984). An integrative model of physiological and social/psychological factors in alcohol consumption among Chinese and Japanese Americans. *Journal of Drug Issues, 14*, 349–364.

Thompson, T., & Simmons-Cooper, C. (1988). Chemical dependency treatment and Black adolescents. *Journal of Drug Issues, 18*(1), 21–31.

Tucker, M. B. (1985). U.S. ethnic minorities and drug abuse: An assessment of the science and practice. *International Journal of the Addictions, 20*, 1021–1047.

Turner, S. (1994). Family variables related to adolescent substance misuse: Risk and resiliency factors. In T. P. Gullotta, G. R. Adams, & R. Montemayor (Eds.), *Substance misuse in adolescence.* Thousand Oaks, CA: Sage.

Vaillant, G. E. (1983). *The natural history of alcoholism.* Cambridge, MA: Harvard University Press.

Vaillant, G. E., & Milofsky, E. S. (1982). The etiology of alcoholism: A prospective viewpoint. *American Psychologist, 37,* 494–503.

Wanberg, K., Lewis, R. G., & Foster, M. S. (1978). Alcoholism and ethnicity: A comparative study of alcohol use patterns across ethnic groups. *International Journal of Addictions, 13*(8), 1245–1262.

Watts, T. D., & Wright, R., Jr. (Eds.). (1983). *Black alcoholism: Toward comprehensive understanding.* Springfield, IL: Thomas.

CHAPTER 15

HIV/AIDS:
Issues in Working with
Culturally Diverse Families

Howard J. Hess

The HIV/AIDS pandemic has infiltrated all parts of the world and exacted an enormous toll on human well-being. In the United States as of June 30, 1995, a total of 476,999 individual AIDS cases had been reported to the Centers for Disease Control and Prevention (CDCP, 1995). The actual extent of HIV infection is difficult to measure as most cases of non-AIDS HIV infection are not routinely reported to data gathering agencies. It has long been thought that for each reported case of AIDS, there are five cases of HIV infection. Although in the United States the actual number of new cases has now begun to level off, HIV infection continues to be one of the nation's leading public health problems. The impact of HIV has been particularly heavy due to the young age of those infected. Approximately two thirds of all reported AIDS cases in the United States as of June 30, 1995, occurred in those aged 39 or younger.

The impact of HIV on infected individuals is, however, only one aspect of a much more complex picture. The families of HIV-infected persons have also been very much affected by this pandemic. Due to the often long and insidious course of HIV disease, families have been called upon to provide an extraordinary amount of care and support. It is not unusual that an HIV-infected person may live 10–15 years or more following actual HIV infection. During part of this period many persons are either asymptomatic and/or mildly ill. Their HIV-related disabilities are limited and might not qualify them for income support or other forms of psychosocial assistance. For many HIV-infected persons, families have provided the vital care that was essential for their ongoing survival (Land, 1992). The multicultural impact of HIV has affected single mothers with children, families headed by grandparents, families of diverse racial and ethnic backgrounds, and families of gays and lesbians. In addition, adult siblings and extended families have provided extensive care. These many different kinds or variations of families have provided essential HIV care and in some instances, provided overall care coordination for infected persons as well. This has been true since the very onset of the HIV pandemic in this country (Helmquest, 1984).

The burdens on families have been heavy and often persistent over extended periods (Cates, Graham, Boeglin, & Tielker, 1990). Families have confronted not only the problems of HIV disease but also the experience of being stigmatized by those around them (Macklin, 1988). In addition, many families have struggled simultaneously with other problems, such as poverty, discrimination, drug use, and homelessness (Walker & Small, 1991). As the pandemic has unfolded, increasing numbers of women, children, and whole families have become infected. Care for women and their children has proved slow to develop and particularly difficult to access (Lockhart & Wodarski, 1989; Stuntzer-Gibson, 1991). In spite of these many challenges families have constituted the "first line of defense" against HIV in the United States.

This chapter first identifies several variations in families that have provided this care. The specific HIV-related needs as well as strengths of each kind of family are discussed. A general model of family support and intervention is proposed which flexibly accommodates to families' multiple needs as they move through the trajectory of HIV infection. This proposed model emphasizes the rapid deployment of multiple community-based resources as a way to protect and promote family resiliency. In conclusion, the model is applied to an extended case example for the purpose of explication and analysis. Throughout this discussion, a holistic frame of reference is assumed, emphasizing the self-determination of each family in dealing with HIV. Above all else, this chapter points to the courage and persistence of families as they have and continue to grapple with the devastating reality of HIV infection.

FAMILY DEFINED

A broad, inclusive definition of family is used in this chapter. Those families that have been providing care for HIV-infected persons do not always fit the traditional definition of "family." For the purpose of this chapter, Anderson's (1989) definition is employed: "Family . . . includes both one's *family of origin*, particularly one's parents and siblings, and one's *present family of function*." According to Anderson, the "family of function refers to those individuals who constitute an ongoing social and affectional intimate support network for one another" (p. 193). In some instances the family of function includes a person's spouse and children. In others the family incorporates a lesbian or gay male partner and/or a collection of friends who perform family roles for the HIV-infected person. This notion of family is akin to the concept "family of choice," which emphasizes the individual's right to select his or her set of most intimate relationships.

FAMILY VARIATIONS

Parents of Adult Children with HIV Infection

The majority of those infected by HIV are young persons who were in their 20s or 30s at the time of initial HIV exposure. Consequently, their parents are usually living and healthy enough to act as major resources in their care and service coordination. According to Land (1992), parents often deal with issues of blame of either their adult child or themselves relative to the HIV infection. In those situations where HIV infection has resulted from male-to-male sexual contact, parents may be learning about their son's sexual orientation at the same time they are first learning of his HIV infection (Land, 1992). The literature points to the need for some parents to have psychotherapeutic assistance in order to integrate these experiences (Tiblier, Walker, & Rolland, 1989). In many situations adult children in advanced stages of HIV disease have come home to their parents "to die." In such situations parents have often been fearful of the stigma associated with HIV/AIDS and have become socially isolated rather than risk exposing their child's HIV infection to friends and neighbors.

A major issue confronting many parents of adult HIV-infected children is the impact of the heavy burden of care. The prolonged nature of HIV infection means that parents who act as caretakers can become severely depleted. The caretaking responsibilities for adult children often exceed their parents' capabilities. The long-term burden of care is exacerbated by the emotional reactions of grief and loss that punctuate the process of care. In family generational terms the care relationship is inverted by HIV at a time when parents have anticipated freedom from caretaking and perhaps anticipated receiving care from their children. They are instead required to sustain their child.

Families of HIV-Infected Women and Their Children

Caring for HIV-infected women and children is a highly complex undertaking. In many instances an HIV-infected woman is both caregiver and patient (Macklin, 1988). The constant demands of caring for both HIV-infected and affected children results in a diminished capacity to care for oneself. Consequently, the family is in a state of chronic overload that compromises its ability to cope effectively. In addition, HIV infection often occurs in families already overburdened by other psychosocial challenges. The route of infections for a majority of women is either injection drug use or a sexual relationship with an injection drug user. Their family experiences have often been characterized by a struggle to maintain sobriety and keep their families intact. In the lives of many such families there has been a history of unmet needs and emotional cutoffs in important relationships (Tiblier et al., 1989). Consequently, HIV infection becomes another in a series of life difficulties which must be faced with limited external resources. Families often maintain themselves in the face of considerable adversities but do not have extensive social supports to reinforce their coping efforts.

Such families also struggle with issues related to shame and secrecy. Almost one-half of all female AIDS cases have reported injection drug use as their single risk factor. For them, stigma is doubled—associated initially with their drug use and later with HIV infection as well. In those instances where HIV infection occurs through bisexual behavior of a spouse, the family is at risk for loss of social supports should that information become known. The overlay of secrecy about both the HIV infection and its source makes reaching out for services in a timely manner more difficult.

Grandparents as Caretakers of HIV-Infected and Affected Children

In families in which HIV-infected adults are the primary caretakers of dependent children, a unique set of issues emerge. The literature has only recently begun to address the profound impact that HIV has had on both HIV-infected and affected children and adolescents (Hudes, 1995; Levine, 1993; Nagler, Adnopoz, & Forsyth, 1995). In many such families, grandparents assume responsibility for child care and ultimate child rearing of both HIV-infected and affected children. These children may be difficult to care for due to their own physical needs and the parental losses already experienced. The burden of child care is characterized by extensive contacts with health care resources, limitations upon the activities of HIV-infected children, and emotional demands associated with recent and impending losses. The responsibilities assumed by grandparents can frequently lead to their depletion and increased physical illness (Groce, 1995).

Families of Gay Men and Lesbian Women

Gay men and lesbians have often created unique families that consist of their partners and a range of intimate friends. These families provide safe havens within the larger context in which to validate one's lifestyle and meet personal needs. Such families have proved invaluable in caring for HIV-infected members since the onset of the epidemic. However, the extent of loss in the gay and lesbian community due to HIV infection and AIDS has been massive. The accumulated grief has made it difficult for some persons to integrate their losses before they have been called upon to care for other family members. Consequently, gay and lesbian families sustain HIV-infected members while also needing to deal with the feelings of anger and despair resulting from the death of so many relatively young members. The constancy of these demands since the early 1980s has left little emotional space for gay and lesbian families to replenish and reconstruct themselves.

Ethnically Diverse Families

From the foregoing discussion it should be apparent that the HIV/AIDS epidemic has had an impact on a diverse population. The most recent national statistics indicate that 52% of all cumulative AIDS cases are people of color. Over one-third are African American, and 17% are Hispanic (CDC, 1995), in spite of the fact that both groups combined account for only 20% of the total population. A review of data regarding more recent infections shows a skyrocketing rate of infection in both populations while a slowing among Whites and men who have sex with men. The implications of these statistics are overwhelming. Increasingly, HIV/AIDS has become an epidemic of people of color. Therefore, the challenges of preventing and treating HIV are intensified by the continuing presence of racial and ethnic discrimination. In fact, part of the difficulty in creating and maintaining humane national HIV/AIDS policies can be attributed to the general low societal regard for these populations.

In addition, the cultures of both African American and Hispanic communities have made fighting HIV particularly challenging. For example, prevention and treatment efforts in the African American community have been hampered by reluctance within the community itself to fully recognize behaviors related to drug use, homosexuality, and bisexuality. More recently, as African American churches have become more active in the battle against HIV/AIDS, efforts within the community have accelerated. Similar constraints have existed within the Hispanic community. For example, the literature attests to the impact of machismo on HIV transmission (Medrano & Klopner, 1992) and the difficulty in enlisting Latina women to use condoms due to the reactions of their male partners. Fortunately, as culturally appropriate, community-based programs have been introduced, the transmission of HIV is beginning to be more fully addressed. Such programs recognize the importance of using community-based peer counselors for outreach and follow-up. However, immediate and extended families must play a more central role in successful HIV prevention and treatment programs within ethnically diverse communities (Groce, 1995). Otherwise such programs are not likely to succeed.

A MODEL FOR SUPPORTING FAMILIES
COPING WITH HIV/AIDS

As previously stated, families of origin and families of function are the first and most important resource in the fight against HIV/AIDS. This chapter sets forth a model for support and intervention with families, drawing from the literature, reports of HIV service demonstration projects, and the author's own research (Hess, 1990; Hess, McGovern, & Plasse, 1994; Hess & O'Rourke, 1995) and practice experience and includes the following:

1. Broad-based array of biopsychosocial services/resources designed to meet the multidimensional needs of families in a proactive, flexible manner.
2. Coordinated approach to service delivery designed for appropriate and sequential service use across the entire time continuum of HIV infection.
3. Community-based model of delivery that emphasizes the placement of services in close proximity to families.
4. Approach that emphasizes the empowerment of families and re-duces unnecessary diagnostic labeling as a requirement to ac-cess services.
5. Preventive approach that supports the capacity of the family to care for itself and take full advantage of its capacity for resilient res-toration.
6. Service design that emphasizes the delivery of care by members of the families' broader community and utilizes peer counseling and support interventions.

Broad Base of HIV Services

It has long been recognized that HIV affects a family's life in multiple ways. Certainly, HIV has far-reaching implications for the family's ability to support itself financially and remain self-sufficient. When the family relies on the income generated by the HIV-infected member(s), alternative means of income support will be necessary. In addition, resources for the continued availability of appropriate housing, food, and other necessities of daily living must be ensured. The absence or insufficiency of these basic resources will compromise a family's ability to maintain itself and adapt to the ongoing challenge of HIV. These basic resources are the foundation on which the family is able to maintain a workable care plan for its HIV-infected member(s).

Other critically important services include outpatient and inpatient medical care, therapeutic drugs, home nursing care, and in some instances nursing home or hospice care. The timely introduction of those services can limit the physical deterioration of the HIV-infected member and lighten the care burden on other family members. It is vital that the health care professionals view the family members as part of the care team and include them in designing and updating care plans.

Many other services are often needed by HIV-infected persons and their families. As the disease progresses, assistance in activities of daily living and personal care supports in the home can both greatly enhance the family's quality of life and reduce unnecessary hospitalizations. Counseling and support group resources can prove useful to both the HIV-infected person and the family as a whole. For some families, legal services may be necessary to assist with HIV discrimination, will preparation, or formalizing plans for guardianship of minor children. Permanency planning services are important when one or both parents are not expected to survive their minor children.

This listing of services does not capture the full complex challenge of their coordination. HIV care coordinators must balance multiple services, maintain appropriate communication between providers, and change care arrangements when necessary. The family is often called upon to coordinate care in diverse locations, manage multiple appointments, and make difficult choices between alternate care providers. Consequently, it is most important that professional care coordination services be provided to families initially at the onset of their HIV experience. Care coordination should then remain available throughout the entire course of the HIV infection and provide ongoing assistance to the family in altering care arrangements as HIV-related circumstances change (Gordon & Dewalt, 1993; Indyk, Belville, Lachapelle). Care coordination agencies should work with the entire family as the unit of service and view their relationship with the family as a partnership. In order to support and tap into family strengths, self-determination should be emphasized. It is highly desirable that care coordination services continue after the death of an HIV-infected family member to support family coping and reintegration.

Timely Family Services throughout the HIV Disease Continuum

The time continuum of HIV disease, in contrast to many other diseases, is lengthy. It lends itself to the development of a continuum of phase-specific HIV services (Brown & Powell-Cope, 1991). It is not unusual that an individual may remain asymptomatic or mildly symptomatic for as long as 10 or more years following HIV infection. As medical treatments have advanced, it has become increasingly useful to identify HIV infection during the asymptomatic phase so that preventive treatments can be initiated. The following general scheme is designed to pinpoint those biopsychosocial issues and needs that characterize the early, middle, and late phases of HIV infection. Although in actuality HIV progression is usually divided into a larger number of categories, for the sake of simplicity three broad stages or phases are described. Although each phase has its own specific challenges, an overriding sense of guilt and hopelessness may characterize the entire experience (Atkins & Amenta, 1991; Walker, 1987). The timely provision of support services counteracts family members' overall sense of helplessness.

Early Phase of the Infection

During this period the predominant issues involve HIV testing, disclosure of HIV status, and prevention of further infection. Typically, there is almost no early evidence of HIV infection; therefore, many persons are prone to denial and avoidance of concern about their HIV status. Effective intervention with the family in this phase sets the stage for subsequent coping with HIV and can reduce the transmission of HIV to other family members. The essence of intervention at this point is to challenge the erroneous belief that HIV is a death sentence and to encourage HIV-infected persons to make positive life choices. Families will often benefit from crisis intervention during this period, to reestablish equilibrium following the initial HIV diagnosis. In appropriately timed steps the family should be provided with sound information about the nature of HIV and the ways in which both one's life span and quality of life can be improved. In addition, during this period families can profit from counseling regarding when and to whom to disclose their family member's HIV status. The overall goal is to give the family maximum control during this high stress period.

Middle Phase of the Infection

This prolonged period often includes an expanding awareness of the presence of HIV and increased pressure to accommodate to HIV-related changes. During this phase, it is not unusual for the family to vacillate between periods of denial and reprieve and deeper levels of acceptance. Medical, emotional, and family crises can punctuate this phase as the family struggles to maintain its stable organization. The role of the care coordinator often expands as new and more extensive services are needed and the coordinating role becomes more complex. Health care resources are more frequently used, and preventive treatments give way to infection control and management. As this period concludes, the family's financial status may be threatened as income producing activities are curtailed. The family lifestyle is affected by HIV in other new ways as well. More of the family focus is directed toward the HIV-infected member, and crises begin to increase in number and severity. According to Landau-Stanton and Clements (1993), this aspect of HIV disease resembles other episodic illnesses in which remission comes and goes in an unpredictable manner. The family often experiences an intense range of roller-coaster emotional reactions during this period and may well benefit from participation in support groups and/or psychotherapy. Psychotherapy models have been developed that emphasize the family's participation in all aspects of treatment (Winiarski, 1991) and the reworking of previous family losses and cutoffs (Landau-Stanton & Clements, 1993).

Late Phase of the Infection

During this phase the symptoms of HIV disease become more severe and frequent. The disease process increasingly limits the family member's mobility and ability to care for herself or himself. Consequently, the care burden on other family members increases. Daily personal care activities, including bathing, shopping, cleaning, and climbing stairs, become more difficult. The constancy of daily caretaking can overextend the family during this period. Thus, the proactive stance of the care coordinator must accelerate in order to prevent chronic depletion of the family unit.

As death becomes imminent, the family faces a set of challenges that are unique to this period. In those families with surviving dependent children, permanent care arrangements must be established. In addition the grief inherent in the impending loss of the HIV-infected family member is difficult for most families (Houseman & Pheifer, 1988), and psychotherapy and support groups continue to be important resources. After-care programs for families can prove beneficial following the death of the family member. This is important as so many HIV services are terminated at the death of the infected family member. The family usually profits from bereavement support in its efforts to reconstitute itself.

Community-Based Service Delivery

Families confront a bewildering set of challenges and service needs related to HIV infection. It is unrealistic to expect that most families will have the inclination or resources to seek care outside their home communities. The key concept to keep in mind is economy and efficiency of effort. The more effort that is required to obtain needed care, the more highly stressed the family is likely to become. The literature clearly indicates that enhancing community access greatly increases the likelihood that services will be used (Getzel, 1991; Landau-Stanton & Clements, 1993). In addition, the likelihood of use is enhanced when services can be obtained at one central location. When services are difficult to access, community-based care coordinators should provide expedited referral and advocacy.

Empowerment of Families

Many families have a natural capacity to withstand stress and disruption. One of the basic functions of the family is to buffer individuals from social pressure and to educate the young about how to survive and grow in the social environment. Given appropriate support over time, the family can provide support and care to its members more fully than any other social institution. Recognizing this, it becomes imperative to protect the family of HIV-infected persons from becoming overburdened and compromised by the exigencies of the infection. Beyond protection, families must be empowered "to have as much control as possible over their lives and the services that they receive" (Zlotnik, 1987, p. 4). The two best mechanisms toward this end are to (1) provide the family with multiple forms of support so that it can absorb the HIV-related demands for care and change as necessary and (2) provide necessary information and tangible resources so that the family can make necessary decisions and effectively fulfill its responsibilities.

In terms of support, families often require relief from caregiving and need to know that their reactions are normative and shared by others. The provision of respite care for families allows caregivers to experience periodic relief. Such relief in the form of a homemaker, day care program, or buddy system allows the family to recoup and prevents more toxic types of family reaction. A particularly effective resource is peer group support and/or counseling. Knowing that other families are experiencing similar challenges and observing how they cope can be a powerful source of resilience.

Appropriately timed information and biopsychosocial services are akin to placing the appropriate tools in the hands of a skilled worker. Information is useful in helping families anticipate, prepare for, and normalize their own reactions. The provision of needed services allows the family to feel that it is fulfilling its responsibility to care for its HIV-infected family member. The ability to obtain care could well offset the family's sense of itself as a victim and reduce the guilt and shame often associated with HIV infection.

Preventive Approach

Akin to the concept of family empowerment is the adoption of a preventive approach. The contribution of the HIV service provider is to anticipate the family's HIV service needs and engage them in an anticipatory guidance process, thereby preventing more extensive family dysfunction. Given our knowledge about HIV, it is now possible to predict service needs with a relatively high degree of certainty. This is important for several reasons. First, through predicting these needs a family can be assisted to prepare to meet them in a timely noncrisis manner. In addition, the family can be helped to integrate the HIV experience progressively as their psychosocial resources allow. Through the anticipatory guidance provided by HIV service providers, families can also be supported in countering or challenging the stigma associated with HIV/AIDS. Successful experiences in dealing with HIV can in turn lead to increased family self-esteem and enhanced coping activities.

Peer-Focused Family Interventions

The model proposed in this chapter emphasizes the natural capacity that many families possess for managing HIV/AIDS and becoming even stronger in the process. This capacity is enhanced through the experience of peer-led interventions. Particularly in African American and Hispanic communities, working with peers offsets the family's sense of shame and social ostracism. In peer situations families can explore alternative approaches to problem solving and enact those solutions under the guidance of other families facing similar challenges. The relationships that develop among peers are very powerful in their ability to sustain and to help families maintain their hopefulness during difficult periods.

Professional Workers' Relationship with Families

Working with families confronting HIV/AIDS can be a demanding, powerful, and rewarding experience. In part this is due to the unique quality of persons who are imminently facing death and making choices about the balance of their lives. There is often an increase in honesty both within the family and with others. The immediacy of the work is emphasized, and appropriate interventions can have a strong positive impact. This sense of efficacy often attracts professional workers into the HIV practice arena.

It is important to recognize that the professional worker must anticipate and prepare for the demands of this work. There are often times when the family experiences a heavy reliance on their professional helpers. Opinions differ, but most experienced HIV/AIDS professionals point to the need for a flexible boundary between the client and professional systems. For example, the professional worker might not find the notion of professional distance useful. Some families experience such distance as offputting and are more likely to seek assistance from a professional person with greater flexibility in use of self.

However, it is equally important for professional workers to limit their sense of responsibility for the family's well-being. Professionals report that their work with families facing HIV is very intense and must be balanced by appropriate supervision and support in their own lives. Otherwise the demands of this work can lead to burnout and decreased effectiveness.

Case Example: The Perez Family

The following case represents a 4-year span of community-based care coordination provided to a Hispanic family living on the north side of

Chicago. The work is divided into early, middle, and a projected late phase for the purposes of analysis and discussion.

Early Phase

Ms. Perez, age 38, lives with her five children in a second-floor walk-up apartment approximately 5 miles from downtown Chicago. She had moved to Chicago from Puerto Rico 18 years ago to improve her general life situation. Shortly after arriving she met the father of her two oldest children, Angell, 14, and Marisol, 12. They lived together for 5 years, at which time Mr. Perez abandoned the family, returning to Puerto Rico, and has not had contact with the family since that time.

Approximately 10 years ago, Ms. Perez met the father of Francesca, aged 10, and Roberto, aged 8. This relationship persisted for 2 years and was described as abusive. Approximately 5 years ago, Ms. Perez met Gorge Montoya, the father of her youngest daughter, Rosa, 4 years of age. This relationship ended conflictually 2 years ago. There is currently no contact between Ms. Perez and Mr. Montoya. It was reported that Mr. Montoya used injection drugs, but Ms. Perez is not sure if this was the case. None of Ms. Perez's extended family lives in the Chicago area.

At the time of Rosa's birth, Ms. Perez was tested for HIV by the hospital without her knowledge or permission. Before leaving the hospital the social worker referred Ms. Perez to the local community-based AIDS service organization for services. Mr. Luis Reyes, the case manager, visited Ms. Perez in the hospital and learned that Rosa had tested positive to the HIV antibody as well. At first Ms. Perez didn't want to speak with him and took the stance that the test was an error. It was impossible that she was HIV-infected because she had not slept with anyone but Rosa's father, and he was not a homosexual. Mr. Reyes gently informed Ms. Perez that the test was important and that she might want to be retested. He left his name and telephone number and asked if she would contact him after she was discharged from the hospital. She agreed but then asked him to leave.

Approximately 3 weeks after Ms. Perez's discharge, Mr. Reyes arranged for a home visit, during which he inquired both about her health and that of her daughter Rosa. What ensured was a series of monthly home visits in which Mr. Reyes learned that Rosa was not gaining sufficient weight and seemed chronically ill. Ms. Perez asked a number of questions about

HIV without acknowledging that the hospital tests might have been accurate. She did agree, however, to have Rosa retested. On being told that Rosa again tested positive, Ms. Perez experienced an anxiety attack, during which she began gasping for breath. Mr. Reyes arranged for one of the leaders of peer group of HIV infected mothers to meet Ms. Perez that evening. They spent 3 hours with her, during which she sobbed and screamed, saying that she was dying. The group leader held her and together with Mr. Reyes emphasized how much treatment and support were available for both her and Rosa.

ANALYSIS. Ms. Perez is the single parent of five dependent children. She has been cut off from her family of origin in Puerto Rico since her move to Chicago 18 years ago. She has had a series of three relationships with men, at least one of which was abusive. Her most recent partner reportedly used injection drugs prior to and during the period of their relationship. Ms. Perez is terrified at the prospect of being HIV-infected. She has multiple misconceptions about the virus, including the notion that only homosexual men could transmit HIV and that once infected a person would die rapidly. The case manager is highly skillful in his interventions. He has reached out to Ms. Perez but did not prematurely challenge her defensive denial. Instead, he established himself as a supportive figure in her life and maintained regular contact, urging her to consider retesting. With his support, Ms. Perez risked Rosa's retesting, thereby confronting the reality of her HIV infection. The ensuing crisis was ameliorated by Mr. Reyes's interventions and introduction of an HIV-infected peer counselor. With the help of both, Ms. Perez was able to move out of her denial, correct much of her inaccurate thinking, and obtain HIV medical care for herself and Rosa.

Middle Phase

In the past 6 months both Ms. Perez and Rosa have appeared to enter into a symptomatic HIV phase. Rosa continues to be very small for her age and has experienced delayed development. At 4, she cannot walk, although now she is able to sit up unassisted. She continues to wear diapers as she has never been toilet-trained. She speaks a few words but mostly points when she wants something. In the past several months, Rosa has experienced considerable difficulty in breathing. Her pediatrician is guarded in his assessment of Rosa's immediate prognosis and has begun to prepare Ms. Perez for the likelihood that her daughter will not recover from her current infection. Until the past several months, Ms. Perez has remained largely asymptomatic. Of late she has begun to experience increased fatigue and weight loss. She finds it difficult to determine whether these problems are due to HIV or her worry about Rosa's health.

Mr. Reyes has continued to confer regularly with the Perez family. During periods of crisis his contacts average twice weekly. His primary activity is referral of the family for needed services and overall service coordination. For example, he has arranged for Rosa to receive health care at the local HIV pediatric care center. Ms. Perez is seen regularly at the HIV care unit of the local neighborhood health center. As a result of a referral by the HIV pediatric care center, Rosa is being provided home care three to five times a week.

Mr. Reyes has referred the family to other HIV services as needed. For example, he has arranged for the four older Perez children to participate in sibling support groups for HIV-affected children. Ms. Perez regularly attends weekly meetings of the HIV-infected mothers' group, where she has made many close friends. She has started to participate in community advocacy for HIV/AIDS services with other mothers in the group. On one occasion she spoke at a public hearing at the mayor's office regarding the needs of HIV-infected children. Mr. Reyes has also referred Ms. Perez to HIV legal services for assistance in drawing up a will and arrangement for her children's guardianship. Thus far she has not followed up on that referral.

The family has also been referred to the clinical social worker who provides on-site family counseling services at the AIDS service organization. Mr. Reyes had suggested these sessions as a way of helping the family talk more openly about their experiences and fears related to HIV. The four older Perez children had been experiencing increased concentration and behavioral difficulties in school. When they began to talk openly about their fears and upsets, Ms. Perez quickly began to cry. As a result of those sessions, Ms. Perez initiated contact with her mother and extended family in Puerto Rico. The family's social worker assisted her in preparing for and making the actual call.

ANALYSIS. Mr. Reyes has continued to provide family case management services, varying the amount of contact with the needs of the family. As a part of the family's case plan successful efforts have been made to involve the family in an extended HIV support system and thereby reduce their social isolation. The mothers' group has opened up an entire new world for Ms. Perez and provides her with an opportunity to witness the coping skills of other HIV-infected women. Both Rosa and Ms. Perez have been referred to excellent health care programs. Home health services have prevented Ms. Perez from being excessively depleted by the care of Rosa.

The Perez family has remained relatively stable but is now heading into a more difficult stage of HIV disease. Rosa's current illness is proving very difficult to treat. For the first time her death is potentially imminent. Mr. Reyes has wisely staged various services in anticipation of the family's needs. He has understood that participating in too many services at one time might overwhelm the family. However, with increased evidence of HIV disease he has recognized increased tensions in the family and made a referral for counseling. He has recommended that the issues of guardianship of the four HIV-negative Perez children be addressed in the family counseling sessions. His approach has been to gently assert the importance of planning but not to pressure Ms. Perez before she is ready to confront this concern.

Late Phase: Projected Issues and Analysis

The various family issues that have surfaced in the early and middle phases of HIV infection will require ongoing attention. Although the Perez family continues, the concerns of the late phase need to be anticipated. The following plan for coordinating future care has been generated:

1. Ongoing case management will be essential to help this family deal with the HIV-related crises that lie ahead. In particular, the need for a variety of specialized health care services, home health care, and potentially nursing home care need to be anticipated. Mr. Reyes will have to work closely with medical social workers to ensure timely linkages.

2. The issues of temporary and long-term child care and guardianship has not yet been resolved. Efforts to reconnect with Ms. Perez's family should be supported and emphasis given to helping Ms. Perez establish face-to-face contact with them. The feasibility of including the family in the permanency plan can then be addressed.

3. The emotional needs of the Perez family will require ongoing attention. Grief work will be very important as both Rosa's and Ms. Perez's health deteriorates. The family will need assistance in dealing with loss both prior to and following the death of Rosa and Ms. Perez. It will be critical to provide intensive counseling to this family during and following periods of crisis. This should include bereavement services.

4. Contacts with the community need to be facilitated. Ongoing work with family support groups will continue to be essential to counteract increased levels of possible depletion, withdrawal, depression, and isolation. The introduction of a buddy for both Ms. Perez and Rosa will enhance the family's connectedness.

5. As the Perez family moves through this final phase, Mr. Reyes and other service providers must help the family anticipate future events and monitor their own reactions. Recognizing that this work will be very taxing Mr. Reyes and other key services providers will use case consultation and other professional and personal supports to deal with their own depletion.

SUMMARY

As the Perez family case exemplifies, the service needs of HIV-challenged families are extensive and persistent over an extended period. The full gamut of biopsychosocial services are needed in varying combinations with the potential for multiple service providers to overburden and confuse the family. For this reason, case coordination or case management is crucially important and for many families this service is the central component of HIV care. It is the function of the case manager to anticipate the needs of families and stage interventions accordingly. If service providers are inaccessible or respond inappropriately, the case manager should advocate with and on behalf of the family until service needs are appropriately met.

Both the case manager and other HIV professionals should work to empower the family and to connect he family with its surrounding community. Efforts should be made to provide professionals from affected communities and whenever possible use a peer counseling approach. It must be recognized that many families challenged by HIV will also be confronted by other psychosocial problems. Owing to their ethnicity, race, and sexual orientation and to social problems such as poverty and drug use, many families have already been marginalized. Consequently, such families are at risk for depletion and breakdown when confronted with the additional stresses related to HIV. It is essential that HIV services support the capacity of families to provide care to infected members. Using an empowerment proactive model of support and intervention can greatly enhance the family's resilience in dealing with HIV infection.

REFERENCES

Anderson, E. A. (1989). Implications for public policy: Toward a pro-family AIDS social policy. In E. Macklin (Ed.), *AIDS and families* (pp. 187–228). New York: Haworth.

Atkins, R., & Amenta, M. (1991). Family adaptation to AIDS: A comparative study. *Hospice Journal, 7*(1–2), 71–83.

Brown, M., & Powell-Cope, G. (1991). AIDS family caregiving: Transitions through uncertainty. *Nursing Research, 40*, 338–384.

Cates, J., Graham, L., Boeglin, D., & Tielker, S. (1990). The effects of AIDS on the family system. *Families in Society: The Journal of Contemporary Human Services, 71*, 195–201.

Centers for Disease Control. (1995). *Semiannual HIV/AIDS surveillance report.* Atlanta, GA: Author.

Getzel, G. (1991). AIDS. In A. Gitterman (Ed.), *Handbook of social work practice with vulnerable populations.* New York: Columbia University Press.

Groce, N. (1995). Children and AIDS in a multicultural perspective. In S. Geballe, J. Gruendel, & W. Andiman (Eds.), *Forgotten children of the AIDS epidemic.* New Haven, CT: Yale University Press.

Helmquest, M. (1984). *The family guide to AIDS: Responding with your heart.* San Francisco: San Francisco AIDS Foundation.

Hess, H. (1990). *HIV/AIDS health and human services plan for Indiana.* Indianapolis: Indiana State Board of Health.

Hess, H., McGovern, P., & Plasse, B. (1994). *HIV/AIDS, TB, and homelessness in single room occupancy (SRO) hotels: A study of service needs* (Final Report). Washington, DC: American Foundation for AIDS Research (AMFAR).

Hess, H., & O'Rourke, R. (1995). *HIV/AIDS strategic plan for the Tri-County Region (Putnam, Rockland, and Westchester Counties, New York).* New York: Fordham University Graduate School of Social Service and Hudson Valley Health Systems Agency.

Houseman, C., & Pheifer, W. (1988). Potential for unresolved grief in survivors of persons with AIDS. *Archives of Psychiatric Nursing, 2,* 296–301.

Hudes, J. (1995). Adolescents living in families with AIDS. In S. Geballe, J. Gruendel, & W. Andiman (Eds.), *Forgotten children of the AIDS epidemic.* New Haven, CT: Yale University Press.

Indyk, D., Belville, R., Lachapelle, S., Gordon, G., & Dewalt, T. (1993). A community-based approach to HIV case management: Systemizing the unmanageable. *Social Work, 38,* 380–387.

Land, H. (1992). Stress and coping in AIDS caregivers: partners, friends, and family members. In H. Land (Ed.), *AIDS: A complete guide to psychosocial interventions.* Milwaukee, WI: Family Service Association of America.

Landau-Stanton, J., & Clements, C. (1993). *AIDS: Health and mental health: A primary sourcebook.* New York: Brunner-Mazel.

Levine, C. (Ed.). (1993). *A death in the family: Orphans of the HIV epidemic.* New York: United Hospital of New York.

Lockhart, L., & Wodarski. J. (1989). Facing the unknown: Children and adolescents with AIDS. *Social Work, 34,* 215–221.

Macklin, E. (1988). AIDS: Implications for families. *Family Relations, 37,* 141–149.

Medrano, L., & Klopner, M. (1992). AIDS and people of color. In H. Land (Ed.), *AIDS: A complete guide to psychosocial interventions.* Milwaukee, WI: Family Service Association of America.

Nagler, S., Adnopoz, J., & Forsyth, B. (1995). Uncertainty, stigma, and secrecy: Psychological aspects of AIDS for children and adolescents. In S. Geballe, J. Gruendel, & W. Andiman (Eds.), *Forgotten children of the AIDS epidemic.* New Haven, CT: Yale University Press.

Stuntzer-Gibson, D. (1991). Women and HIV disease: An emerging social crisis. *Social Work, 36,* 22–28.

Tiblier, K., Walker, G., & Rolland, J. (1989). Therapeutic issues when working with families of persons with AIDS. In E. Macklin (Ed.), *AIDS and families.* New York: Haworth.

Walker, G. (1987). AIDS and family therapy, pt. 2. *Family Therapy Today, 2,* 1–3, 6–7.

Walker, G., & Small, S. (1991). AIDS, crack, poverty, and race in the African-American community: The need for an ecosystemic approach. *Journal of Independent Social Work, 5,* 69–91.

Winiarski, M. (1991). *AIDS related psychotherapy.* New York: Allyn and Bacon.

Zlotnik, J. (1987). *AIDS: Helping families cope.* Washington, DC: National Association of Social Workers.

Beyond Family Therapy

Family and Group Approaches with Culturally Diverse Families: A Dialogue to Increase Collaboration

Elaine P. Congress
Maxine Lynn

Although family and group therapy approaches are usually studied separately, a dialogue between the two perspectives can help clinicians work more effectively with the complex problems and issues that culturally diverse clients and their families present. This chapter focuses on comparing and contrasting various assessment and intervention skills in family and group work. Each modality contributes to the other, and a dual perspective can enhance clinical practice with culturally diverse clients and their families. In working with families from different cultures the clinician must be very aware of how the family's culture relates to the use of family and/or group therapy methods if interventions are to be successful.

Although there are numerous models for group work and family therapy, a very limited amount of literature focuses on comparing and contrasting the two (Garvin, 1986; Hines, 1988; Ritter, West, & Trotzer, 1987). Family therapists have written about the use of group techniques (Satir, Bitter, & Krestensen, 1988) in working with families. Conversely, group workers have focused on the use of family theory in group work (Trotzer, 1988) and family reenactment as an important theme in working with groups (Yalom, 1985).

A question has been raised about how close or how disparate group and family work are (Garvin, 1985). A focus on the similarities emphasizes the generic nature of practice, and increasing understanding of differences helps family and group workers learn new skills to enhance their work with clients. In addition, workers must be tuned in to their own biases and prejudices and be sensitive to the nuances of cultural differences. A clinician must be aware of the immediate social system and environment, as well as the larger new society to which the immigrant family now belongs (Norton, 1978). A case example is used to illustrate how a group worker and a family therapist would approach a culturally diverse family. Topics in the beginning stages of family and group work are composition, engagement, and assessment. Discussion of contracting, building norms, and workers' roles lead into the middle phase of treatment, where different interventions of both family and group work are compared. Contrasting termination issues for families and groups in the final stage of treatment are discussed. Conclusions and recommendations based on this dialogue between a group worker and family therapist conclude the chapter.

CASE EXAMPLE

Ari, a 10-year-old Lebanese boy was referred to a school-based prevention unit because of his mutism. His family consisted of his 35-year-old mother, Anna; and two sisters: Bada, 13, and Rose, 11. The family had witnessed the murder of his father and two brothers in a recent Lebanese civil war. After this event they left the country and came to the United States via Israel. They had been helped by a maternal aunt who had lived in this country for 10 years. She did not live with the family but continued to provide ongoing support to the family. Despite the fact that the family had lived here for only a year, they spoke and understood English. Although Anna has completed several years of college, she has been forced to take a job as a clerk in a local store because this was the only available position.

SYSTEMS THEORY

Although the unit of attention is different for family and group work, the most obvious similarity between group and family work is that they both rely heavily on systems theory, which suggests that a change in one member affects every other member as well as the system as a whole. A family therapist interprets symptoms in one member as meaning that the family is experiencing stress and is having difficulty maintaining its previous equilibrium. Each family member is seen as both affecting and being affected by external stress. Behavior is seen as circular, rather than lineal. A family therapist believes that not only Ari, who is mute, but each family member has been affected by the traumatic loss of male family members and emigration to a new country.

Both group and family therapists acknowledge the importance of context, both historically and in the here-and-now therapeutic experience, as essential (Hines, 1988). A critical difference, however, is that from the very beginning the family therapist can draw on a vast family history, whereas the group worker must create a history in the group. Everyone has had an initial group experience in the family, and Yalom (1985) speaks of problems in the initial family group experience as the prime motivator for clients seeking group therapy. Both group and family workers see their respective treatment unit as providing the context for change, and both would examine and use process in the therapeutic sessions to help effect change of individual members. Cultural issues form the fabric of the context and need to be examined within the chosen intervention.

INCLUSION

A beginning issue for both family and group workers is inclusion. With families there first appears to be less choice. As a familiar proverb states, "One can choose one's friends, but not one's family." Ideally, family therapists would like to have all family members living in the same household participate in family therapy (Ackerman, 1966). Some family therapists have even included extended family living elsewhere (Boszor-menyi-Nagy & Spark, 1973). Therefore, a family therapist might want to include the maternal aunt in this Lebanese family if the family were to be seen for family therapy. Yet the difficulty of having all family members participate has been acknowledged (Barker, 1986), and most family thera-pists see families in which some members are absent. The motivations of different family members may vary. In the case example presented, Anna and especially Bada and Rose may not want to participate as they might believe that only Ari has the problem. This family experiences further isolation and stigma because there are only a small number of Lebanese in the United States. Furthermore, the different prejudices and biases which many Americans have to people from the Middle East extend to Ari and his family. Thus, the burden of prejudice augments the trauma and pain of the multiple losses and changes they have recently experi-enced.

On the other hand, groups develop because of common needs, and members can choose whether to enter a group. For example, Ari could be considered for a latency-age group for boys who are struggling with issues concerning immigrating. This type of intervention might be viewed as less threatening to other family members. Also, Ari might join a children's activity group that invites participation from a nonverbal child. Early group sessions often focus on membership issues, and questions about whether members belong are frequently raised (Shulman, 1992). Placing Ari in a boys' group is consistent with his culture in which boys are separated from girls.

The issue of heterogeneity versus homogeneity of group composition is often problematic in initial group development. Group therapists know that some heterogeneity encourages growth, but too much leads to scape-goating and early termination (Yalom, 1985). The ''Noah's Ark'' principle of group composition provides a means of introducing heterogeneity with-out encouraging scapegoats (Yalom, 1985). Yet in family therapy there is by definition heterogeneity in terms of age, role, and power, and certainly it is not possible to utilitize this ''Noah's Ark'' principle in a family in which there is one woman, one parent, or one child. The fact that Ari is the only male in this family is particularly significant, given the role of men in the Lebanese society as well as the fact that he is the only remaining male in the family. That status in a family of three women may contribute to him becoming the family scapegoat and the identified patient in this family. On the other hand, Ari's high status in his family could, in effect, make him the patriarch, carrying responsibilities that are not age-appropriate.

A group experience for Ari might help him relate to male peers, and if the group leader is male, help him learn to interact with a male role model. In group, Ari can connect with others in a different way than in his family, as there are no demands on him to assume a specific familial role because of his gender.

Although there is status and gender heterogeneity in families, there is much homogeneity in terms of history and culture. Families share a common history and culture. The therapist is the heterogeneous member, and often it is difficult for the worker to understand a family system that has had a long shared history and culture, including roles, rules, rituals, and communication patterns. With this family there is the family culture as well as a different ethnic culture, which the family therapist must learn to negotiate.

In group work new members have no shared history, and an initial task for the group leader is to facilitate the development of a group culture (Shulman, 1992). Groups are based on the democratic value that each member has equal power, and the therapist continually works toward ensuring that each member has an equal opportunity to participate (Brown, 1991).

In contrast, families have preexisting power differences, and the therapist may choose either to reinforce these differences or to create other power differentials within the family. In the Lebanese family discussed previously, Ari, because of his gender, may have been asked to assume responsibilities beyond his years. A family therapist might strive to restructure the family so that the mother makes more decisions. One might question how culturally sensitive it would be to attempt to change the structure of a Lebanese family and be concerned that this might have unfavorable consequences.

ENGAGEMENT

Engagement of clients is essential in both group work and family therapy. Often it is difficult to engage a family if there is an identified patient, as families often believe that therapists should only treat and cure the family member who is showing symptoms. This belief may be particularly strong among culturally diverse families unfamiliar with the systems perspective in family therapy or the efficacy of therapy in general. It is quite probable that the family therapist who attempts to engage Ari and his family in family therapy may find that the mother is resistant. She may insist that it is Ari who has the problem and may want the therapist to "fix" him. Also, the mother may wonder how a talking cure can help at all.

Another reason that this family may be difficult to engage is that they may not view elective mutism as a problem serious enough to need treatment. Often families rationalize or deny symptoms in children to avoid acknowledging that there are problems with a specific member or in the family in general so that others will not denigrate the family. This may be an important issue for an immigrant family that is trying to survive and "fit" in a new unfamiliar country. This family may be sensitive to the issue that if they have a problem, then the new society will not accept them. Furthermore, in this family, Ari's symptom of elective mutism may symbolize what has become the family's unwritten maxim that it is best to avoid talking about the losses they have experienced or the anxiety they now experience in a new land. The family may be more receptive to Ari's participation in an activity group than in family therapy.

ASSESSMENT

As part of the assessment process a family therapist studies the structure of the family, the hierarchical arrangement, the type and degree of connection between people, communication patterns, decision making, and prevailing values and myths. In Ari's family it soon became apparent that Anna, who had recently become a single parent, was abrogating her parental decision-making role and placing Ari, as the only male child, in charge. Also, this family had become enmeshed in order to survive the stresses produced by war, loss of members, and change of home. The family therapist learned that members rarely communicated with each other, especially on a feeling level. There was a family value that educational achievement was very important. Thus, Ari's symptom of selective mutism is even more upsetting, as this behavior might interfere with his educational achievement. A family myth emerged that if family members did not talk about what had happened in Lebanon, then they could deny the painful losses they had experienced.

A group worker assesses a group in three areas: (1) individual group members; (2) the group as a whole, including dynamics and interaction; and (3) the group's environment. Assuming that Ari was placed in a children's group, the type and amount of his interactions with other children would be noted. The group leader would observe whether Ari assumed a role of deviant group member, gatekeeper, internal leader, quiet member, or group scapegoat (Shulman, 1992). The group becomes a new environment, and Ari does not have to take on an expected role. He can experience an "all in the same boat" phenomenon that allows the other members to share in his experiences and relate to him with different role expectations.

In assessing the group as a whole, the group leader would look at group interactions, cohesion, and the development of group norms and culture. If Ari was in a children's group for new immigrants, one would assess how the different ethnic cultures of group members affected the development of a group culture. Finally, in a group assessment one would look at the environment in which the group takes place. If the group meets in a public school, members might have expectations that it would be conducted like a class, which would affect their participation in group.

CONTRACTING

Contracting takes place in both family treatment and group work. Although engagement may be difficult for this family if they continue to insist that the only problem is Ari, contracting with the family may also be a challenging task if family members do not see the need for family treatment. Also, contracting with this family may be impeded by Ari's lack of communication. In group work a contract must be developed with the therapist or group worker as well as between individual members. Finally, a contract may be difficult to negotiate because children from other cultures may not understand the voluntary nature of contracting implicit in American group work (Congress & Lynn, 1993).

BUILDING NORMS

From the beginning of group treatment and continuing into the middle stage, the group worker must struggle to create group norms. The goal of the latency-age group to which Ari belongs is the development of a mutual aid system. To facilitate achieving this, members must develop appropriate norms, which include listening to each other, respecting differences, and helping others participate. Often this is a challenging prospect in a children's group where members may be exhibiting extreme behaviors not conducive to the development of mutual aid. Ari may, however, benefit a great deal from receiving the support of other group members who have experienced loss and trauma after leaving their homelands.

Families, on the other hand, already have very strong norms. In fact, the existent norms of families may make it difficult for the family therapist, as an outsider, to initially connect with the family. With Ari's family, the family therapist must explore existing norms, especially in terms of relating to strangers, as well as communicating past and present feelings. Also, the family's norms and values in terms of education and work need to be understood, as this information may help them adjust better to life in this country. The family therapist may have to build appropriate norms for becoming involved in therapy. The practitioner can educate clients that family therapy can help them with their problems and can encourage them to develop the norm that makes it appropriate to communicate their feelings openly and honestly in therapy. The family therapist can also reframe their communications to work around cultural differences.

CLINICAL ISSUES IN FAMILY THERAPY AND GROUP WORK

The worker's role, especially in terms of transference and countertransference, is particularly significant in family therapy. Often original family constellations are re-created as the therapist is drawn into the family system. If a male family therapist works with this family, he could very easily become the lost father (husband). This may become apparent when different family members depend on the male family therapist to make important decisions. With this Lebanese family, such a scenario might evoke strong angry feelings in Ari, who has stepped into his father's role within the family, although with ambivalence. If their family therapist is a woman, various members may have negative feelings about her having a position of power and control, especially as this family comes from a culture where women have limited power.

Within the group context, transference issues are often likely to surface. Members often transfer to the leader feelings from relationships in their own families. Latency-age children may place on the leader their desire for a perfect parent. This is especially likely to happen if the group leader is male and is seen by Ari as a replacement for his lost father and/or brothers. The group leader must be astute in recognizing the emergence of transference reactions that can detrimentally affect Ari's progress. For example, Ari may be so intimidated by a male therapist that he may become more mute and withdrawn than previously.

Often scapegoating in a group emerges out of a need to test the leader. Whom will the group leader support? Scapegoating in the family is usually of longer duration and may be very entrenched and difficult to change. In this Lebanese family, Ari may become the family scapegoat. A positive sign is that this role seems to have recently evolved, which bodes well for the therapist's ability to alter the family structure and free Ari from the scapegoat role.

Strong countertransference feelings are often evoked in the family therapist, as all therapists have had their own unique familial experiences. The family therapist guards against perceiving Anna as responsible for Ari's mutism, as single mothers are often blamed for their children's behavior. Another negative countertransference reaction might be to push this family away because of the seriousness of Ari's problems or the feelings of helplessness and hopelessness evoked when one hears about the deaths in Lebanon.

As in family therapy, countertransference feelings often emerge in group work. The group worker must try to avoid overinvolvement with children who have experienced much trauma and are looking for a substitute parent. Although a group leader may be like a good mother or father, he or she is not identical, and it is important for the group leader to always maintain an appropriate professional boundary. The worker needs to be aware of countertransference because there is often a desire to protect and give more attention to a child who has experienced tragic losses.

TREATMENT MODELS AND TECHNIQUES

Both family and group therapists use similar techniques, including support, reframing, confrontation, and interpretation to bring about changes, but social workers must always be cognizant of a significant difference. Group members often do not see each other between sessions. In fact, social contact is usually discouraged in therapy groups (Yalom, 1985), although children involved in group work within the school often see other group members in class.

Families who are seen for family therapy, however, continue to live with each other. This continued close proximity suggests that the family therapist must be careful, especially in the use of confrontation and interpretation or encouraging family members to use these techniques, because of possible negative consequences between sessions.

Different models have been identified for family therapy and group work. Family intervention models include the psychodynamic, structural, humanistic, communication, and strategic. The structural and communication models have been noted for their usefulness in working with immigrant groups (Ho, 1987). Reframing and clear symptom resolution are frequently used effective treatment techniques with culturally diverse families. A psychodynamic family therapist would focus on making more conscious repressed feelings about severe losses. Also, a psychodynamic therapist would look at Ari's mother's earlier life experiences and how they affected Ari's behavior. A structural therapist would try to reorganize the family by making it clear that the mother is in charge and is responsible for all decisions, thus insisting that Ari can no longer be the man in the house. A family therapist from the humanist school, such as Satir, would work on building up the self-esteem of each family member, especially Ari, who has been scapegoated as the family problem. A communication family therapist would encourage family members to speak more openly, especially in terms of their feelings. He or she might identify certain family members who get stuck in certain roles and thus their behavior becomes rigid and solidified. A strategic family therapist would see that Ari is manipulating much power over the family. He or she might circumscribe the symptom with certain limits or reframe the issues in order to change the behavior. Using a paradoxical intervention, the family therapist might tell Ari's family that Ari should continue to remain quiet, as this serves to keep the family together. To this comment Ari may reply (and eliminate his symptom of selective mutism), "What do you mean I don't talk because I want to keep the family together?" No matter which family treatment model the therapist uses, one must remember that the family is continually dealing with its own culture as well as the new American society.

Because the social group work model presumes health, a social group worker would see Ari's behavior not as a symptom, but as an ineffective or nonhelpful adaptation to his environment. Within a social group work framework, Ari might benefit from a reciprocal, mutual aid activity group where he is treated not as having the symptom of mutism but rather as a fully functioning member who chooses to remain quiet. The American culture values verbal communication and interpersonal skills; other cultures may not.

Group work includes a remedial model that reflects a treatment orientation. In this model individual change would be expected, and activities would be directed toward fostering change. With group treatment, the range of interventions can be psychodynamic, supportive, or psychoeducative. Ari's mother could benefit from a supportive group treatment approach if she is motivated to address her recent losses and current life changes. Ari could be placed in a treatment-oriented group that would use activities to help him cope better with the trauma of what he has witnessed and increase his verbalizations. Ari's mother could also benefit from a psychoeducational group in which other immigrants have joined to improve their adjustment to life in this country.

TERMINATION

Termination differs greatly in group work, compared to family therapy. When a group terminates, often members never see each other again. Group workers, however, must not minimize the group experience and must carefully work through individual and group feelings about termination. This may be especially true for a latency-age group in which members have experienced severe losses. When a family terminates, the individual family members will continue to have ongoing contact with each other. If the family therapist believes that the goal of eliminating Ari's mutism has been achieved, therapy can end. Terminating with a family, however, can awaken previous feelings of loss that the family therapist must be prepared to address in the final sessions. Feelings of loss may be especially acute for culturally diverse families who have experienced other severe losses recently. Individual members may be referred for ongoing therapy, or the family may be referred for ongoing treatment. Another perspective to include is that there can be a culture of loss for families who have resided in countries ravaged by war, where loss is an everyday occurrence.

CONCLUSIONS AND RECOMMENDATIONS

This chapter describes the similarities and differences of group and family work in the context of practice with an immigrant family. The knowledge of both group and family therapy theory and techniques should enhance the practice skills of group and family workers. The growing dialogue between the two models should help the profession in making decisions about whether family or group therapy would be more effective in work with specific culturally diverse families. Being attentive to cultural diversity cuts across all modalities. The worker must be sensitive to the cultural nuances and be aware of biases and assumptions about the client's culture. Whatever model is selected, the social worker should be able to maintain a family approach within group therapy as well as a group perspective in working with families. To achieve this goal the following recommendations are made:

1. Students in the helping professions should be prepared for more generic practice by the study of group and family models in work with culturally diverse clients and their families.
2. Practitioners should explore the possibility of their clients being helped by both family and group work.
3. In working with a group a practitioner should always be cognizant of family dynamics that affect group functioning.
4. In working with a family, a family therapist must be mindful that the family is a group and that group processes affect family functioning.
5. The dialogue between family therapy and group work should continue.
6. Research on the interrelationship and effectiveness of a dual perspective can be conducted.
7. Understanding the culture of the client affects the intervention arena and allows for a more integrated approach to helping. Practitioners using both or either modality should address cultural differences in an open and direct manner with their clients.

8. Both family therapists and group workers can benefit from an increased range of interactions by using an integrated model in work with culturally diverse clients.

REFERENCES

Ackerman, N. (1966). *Treating the troubled family.* New York: Basic.

Barker, P. (1986). *Basic family therapy.* New York: Oxford University Press.

Boszormenyi-Nagy, I., & Spark, G. (1973). *Invisible loyalties: Reciprocity in intergenerational family therapy.* Hagerstown, MD: Harper and Row.

Brown, L. (1991). *Groups for growth and change.* New York: Longman.

Congress, E., & Lynn, M. (1994). Developing a group work program in public schools: Ethical dilemmas in social work with culturally diverse students. *Social Work in Education, 16*(2), 107–114.

Garvin, C. (1986). Family therapy and group work: Kissing cousins or distant relatives in social work practice. In M. Parnes (Ed.), *Innovations in social group work: Feedback from practice to theory* (pp. 1–15). New York: Haworth.

Hines, M. (1988). Similarities and differences in group and family therapy. *Journal for Specialists in Group Work, 13*(4), 173–179.

Ho, M. (1987). *Family therapy with ethnic minorities.* Newbury Park, CA: Sage.

Norton, D. (1978). *The dual perspective: Inclusion of ethnic minority content in the social work curriculum.* New York: Council on Social Work Education.

Ritter, K. Y., West J. D., & Trotzer, J. P. (1987). Comparing family counseling and group counseling: An interview with George Gazda, James Hansen, and Alan Hovestadt. *Journal of Counseling and Development, 65,* 295–300.

Satir, V., Bitter, J. R., & Krestensen, K. (1988). Family reconstruction: The family within—group experience. *Journal for Specialists in Group Work, 13*(4), 200–208.

Shulman, L. (1992). *The skills of helping individuals and group* (3rd ed.). Itasca, IL: Peacock.

Trotzner, J. (1988). Family therapy as a group resource. *Journal for Specialists in Group Work, 13*(4), 130–135.

Yalom, I. (1985). *The theory and practice of group psychotherapy* (3rd ed.). New York: Basic.

CHAPTER 17

Substance Abuse and Homeless Mothers: Multiple Oppression and Empowerment

Judith A. B. Lee
Danielle Nisivoccia

To discuss substance abuse and women who are homeless we must tread into the shifting sands of political correctness and defy taboos, stereotypes, and idealized views of women, particularly mothers. Until recently, it has been considered victim blaming to discuss the high prevalence of substance abuse among homeless people although the problem is obvious to the general public in large urban centers (Baum & Burnes, 1993). Sympathetic social workers and researchers have emphasized the structural causes of homelessness and there is no doubt that these are primary (Blau, 1992; Lang, 1989; Liebow, 1993). But it is not the whole picture. It is the tragic interplay of biopsychosocial vulnerabilities (including problems of substance abuse) with structural forces, namely, poverty, oppression, and particularly the lack of affordable housing, that precipitates and maintains homelessness (Bassuk & Salomon, 1993; Buckner, Bassuk, & Zima, 1993). In our outrage at the structural causes and institutionalized lack of concern for people who are homeless, we have minimized the role substance abuse plays in homelessness. In doing so we have rendered ourselves useless to people who are homeless and incredible to the general public. We have failed to design services, programs, and policies that deal effectively with homelessness, especially for mothers with children.

Recent empirical research documents the qualitative data gained from practice experience. This chapter discusses empirical and practice-based data about substance abuse and homeless women with children, most of whom are younger women of color. It concludes with illustrations from practice and implications for practice, policy, and program development.

REVIEW OF EMPIRICAL DATA

Demographic Data on Homeless Women

Homeless women represent a complex heterogeneous population with diverse biopsychosocial needs, multiple problems, and often amazing strengths (Banyard & Graham-Bermann, 1995). Although "the homeless" have been lumped together and consistently undercounted, it is estimated that at least one-third of the homeless population are families headed by a woman (Buckner et al., 1993). Poor women of color are disproportionately represented in both urban and rural homeless populations though in significantly lower numbers in the latter aggregate (First, Rife, & Toomey, 1994; Johnson & Kreuger, 1989). Homeless African American women and families are overrepresented in urban areas; Latinos are consistently underrepresented (Baker, 1994). The average age of homeless women is 31 (Johnson & Krueger, 1989). Extreme poverty, single parenthood, youth, biopsychosocial vulnerabilities, and minority or color status are the highest risk factors for homelessness among women. Affordable housing is an extremely scarce resource for which those who are both poor and hampered by biopsychosocial vulnerabilities, such as substance abuse histories, mental illness, health problems, family dissolution, and the effects of institutional racism (inadequate education and job training and discrimination), cannot successfully compete (Bassuk, 1993). Pregnancy is another risk factor. One 17-city study shows that pregnancy rates among homeless women range from 12% to 24%. Homeless pregnant women are typically younger, have experienced more serious family disruptions as children, and are less likely to have lived independently, compared to other homeless women. Substance abuse rates are higher among pregnant homeless women, compared to both homeless nonpregnant women and domiciled low-income women (Bassuk & Weinreb, 1993).

Homeless women report high rates of childhood and adult physical and sexual abuse (Browne, 1993). It is to be noted, however, that most of these findings have been based on small samples of homeless women. For example, Goodman (1991) studied 50 homeless women who reported high incidents of abuse. Sixteen percent of these women (compared to 4% of those housed) had also spent time in foster care. Browne (1993) cites a notable exception: a 1987 study by Shinn, Knickman, and Weitzman, who surveyed a random sample of 704 homeless families and 524 public assistance–housed families and found that homeless women reported only somewhat higher rates of childhood and adult abuse than their housed counterparts.

Homeless mothers also have more contacts with victimizing and substance-abusing men than do their housed counterparts, and they manifest higher rates of substance abuse, depression, and other medical and psychological symptomatology. Substance abuse often precipitates domestic violence. The long-term effects of victimization may also include higher rates of substance abuse among victims (Browne, 1993).

Women and Substance Abuse

Almost half of all women in their childbearing years, 15 to 44, have used illicit drugs at least once in their lives. AIDS is the fourth leading cause of death in this age group. Of the 40,700 cases of women with AIDS documented by the Centers for Disease Control in 1993, nearly 70% of the women reported injecting drugs or having sex with an injecting drug user (NIDA, 1994). In general, women who are younger drink more heavily and experience episodes of heavy drinking that often place them in precarious situations, including the risk of AIDS, other illnesses, high-risk pregnancy, family breakdown, and homelessness (Robertson, 1991; Van Den Bergh, 1994).

Alcohol and illicit drug use among women present different health challenges, appear to progress differently, and require different treatment approaches than those used with men. Research indicates the following characteristics about women who use alcohol and illicit drugs: about 70% who report using drugs also report that they were sexually abused before the age of 16; more than 80% had at least one parent addicted to alcohol or illicit drugs; and many report that a drug-using male partner introduced them to drugs, another form of victimization.

Women who are substance abusers frequently report feeling powerless and have low self-esteem and little self-confidence. Treatment is not sought because they are afraid of being rejected by their male partner and family, they fear losing their children, and they fear punishment from the legal system. Women become addicted more quickly to some drugs than men do (e.g., crack cocaine). Therefore, experimental or casual use of drugs may led to addiction, and by the time treatment is sought addiction may be severe (Abbott, 1995; Kinney & Leaton, 1991; NIDA, 1994). Traditional male-oriented drug treatment programs often do not provide appropriate services for women. The most beneficial drug treatment programs for women are those that provide comprehensive services or access to such. This includes such services as housing, child care, assertiveness training, and job training. It has also been found that, for women, the importance of a continuous ongoing therapeutic relationship throughout treatment is critical to the recovery process (NIDA, 1994).

Women of Color and Substance Abuse

Research on women of color who are substance abusers can provide knowledge to guide interventions with homeless mothers of color.

African American Women

Alcoholism is considered by some experts to be the number-one health and social problem in the African American community (Wright, Kail, & Creecy, 1990). It is important to note that in the general population African American women tend to be nondrinkers more often than do White women but tend to have a higher rate of heavy drinking when they do drink (Gary & Gary, 1985; Wright et al., 1990). The disease of alcoholism is manifested earlier, beginning in late adolescence and early adulthood, and progresses quickly in African American women. We are dealing with an often fatal disease, as death from alcoholism is more prevalent among Black women than it is among White women (Brisbane & Womble, 1985; Gary & Gary, 1985; Herd, 1989; NCADD, 1990). Some African American feminists (Collins, 1991; Brisbane & Womble, 1985) believe that the role expectations of Family Heroine and Supermom for the African American woman can lead to extreme stress and possible maladaptive behavior, such as alcohol and drug abuse, when the roles cannot be fulfilled. Other factors associated with alcohol abuse include internalized racism, which is also associated with depression and traumatic life events (e.g., assault or homicide of a loved one) (Van Den Bergh, 1994).

According to household surveys, African American women are more likely than African American men or women from other racial and ethnic groups to be using crack cocaine (Straussner, 1993). Of all the polydrug abuse patterns, those involving alcohol are considered the most lethal (Primm & Wesley, 1985).

Gary and Gary (1985) note Carroll's research done in 1981 and 1982 on Black and White women (158 Whites and 67 Blacks in the former, 103 Whites and 97 Blacks in the latter) at the time of admission to a drug treatment facility. The findings on personality variables and substance abuse were that Black female alcoholics were more fearful, guarded, vigilant, and aware of potential danger in their environment than their White counterparts were. These findings have treatment implications for homeless women of color.

Due to social barriers most African Americans do not seek treatment for their drug and/or alcohol problems (Brisbane & Womble, 1985). When they do seek treatment, it is not uncommon for the symptoms to be misdiagnosed as schizophrenia because alcoholism can cause symptoms associated with organic brain syndrome (Bell et al., 1985).

Hispanics

Unfortunately, in most studies the total number of Hispanic women has been small, often making for contradictory findings (Leland, 1984). According to self-report surveys most Hispanic women are infrequent drinkers or are abstainers. Factors associated with substance abuse among Hispanics are the level of acculturation, social class, and rural versus urban environment. Younger, more educated, and acculturated women reported moderate or heavy drinking and marijuana and cocaine use (Alcocer, 1993; USDHHS, 1990; Van Den Bergh, 1994). Stress, family discord, the immigration/acculturation experience, drug use by another family member, and peer influence are seen as major influences on Hispanic drug abuse. When combined with low income and/or poverty and lower levels of education, drug abuse is higher (Mayers & Kail, 1993).

Research suggests universally that alcoholism can often be considered part of a larger substance problem and as a gateway to other drugs (Mayers & Kail, 1993). Mexican American women report heavy drinking and alcohol-related problems more often than do Puerto Rican and Cuban women (Caetano, 1988). According to a national household survey conducted by the National Institute on Drug Abuse, the use of cocaine by Hispanic females between the ages of 12 and 17 exceeds their White and African American counterparts (Mayers & Kail, 1993). Hispanic females are disproportionately represented in the number of AIDS-related cases. Intravenous drug use accounted for 50% to 80.6% of the Hispanic female AIDS cases (Soriano, 1993).

Native Americans

There is extreme cultural heterogeneity among Native American tribes, and studies reveal that tribes vary widely in their use of drugs and alcohol. A sample of a Sioux tribe from California and five tribes of Cherokees and Seminoles in Oklahoma found that women drank less than men, with lifetime abstainers being older middle-class women. Drinking appeared to be somewhat more acceptable for the Plains tribes, with more women being drinkers at all ages. Drinking was rare and unacceptable for women after their mid-20s in the Navajo and Pueblo tribes (Van Den Bergh, 1994). Native Americans on the whole have a very high mortality from alcohol-related causes (May, 1982; Smith, 1989).

Native American women drink less than the men do, but their drinking patterns (either abstinence or heavy drinking) put them at greater risk for alcohol-related health problems. These women account for almost half of all the deaths caused by cirrhosis. Their cirrhosis death rate is six times higher than that of White women (National Institute on Alcohol Abuse and Alcoholism, 1985). In general, women experience the physiological consequences of substance abuse in a shorter time with smaller amounts and accelerated consequences (Abbott, 1995; Corrigan, 1991; Kinney & Leaton, 1991; Nelson-Zlupko, Kauffman, & Dore, 1995). Births of Native American children with fetal alcohol syndrome (FAS) are 33 times that of White children (Chavez, Cordero, & Becerra, 1989).

The 1987 Health Care for the Homeless Study, which provided medical services to 30,000 homeless in 19 cities found that, among women, Native Americans experienced a greater prevalence of alcohol-related problems

(36%), compared to African-American (13%), Latino (4%), and White (12%) women. Homeless women who abuse alcohol or drugs suffer from such ailments as liver disease, seizure disorders, nutritional deficiencies, hypertension, and pulmonary disease (McCarty, Argeriou, Huebner, & Lubran, 1991). Alcoholism merits our best attention in working with young women and mothers of color, who face many levels of oppression within society.

Homeless Women with Children and Substance Abuse

In the past decade, women with children have been one of the fastest-growing subgroups among the homeless population (Thrasher & Mowbray, 1995). Some reports indicate that mothers with children tend to have lower rates of substance abuse than women unaccompanied by their children (Bassuk, 1993; Johnson & Kreuger 1989; Robertson, 1991). However, we must look closer. Early-stage alcoholism and cocaine addiction are more difficult to detect and more likely not be self-reported due to denial, stigma, and fear of having child protective service authorities remove the children and place them in foster care (NCADD, 1990; Robertson, 1991; Weiss & Mirin, 1987).

Research findings in Boston, Los Angeles, and New York City indicate that poor, homeless mothers with children may use less drugs and alcohol than other homeless men and women, but they have higher rates of alcohol and other drug problems than do housed poor women. Alcohol and other substance use adds to the family's vulnerabilities and becomes an important contributing risk factor for homeless mothers as they compete for scarce resources (Robertson, 1991).

There are multiple health risks for infants and children whose homeless mothers use alcohol and other substances, as these women are less likely to obtain prenatal care and other health services, leading to detrimental effects on fetal development, such as prematurity, low birth weight, FAS, crack and other drug withdrawal; higher risk of prenatal HIV exposure and infection; and long-term affects on the child's development. Neglectful and violent behavior, such as extreme mood swings and/or long absences have been associated with homeless mothers' crack and other drug use. Thus, homeless mothers have a higher rate of child abuse and/or neglect or involvement with child protective services agencies than other poor families (Robertson, 1991). Homeless women with children more often report patterns of domestic violence toward themselves and their children than poor housed mothers and often have histories of substance-abusing partners that contributed to the homelessness (Robertson, 1991).

It has also been noted that the care of grandchildren by low-income African American grandmothers has spiked significantly in recent years due to the crack cocaine epidemic (Minkler, Roe, & Robertson-Beckley, 1994). Many homeless women accompanied by one child may have others living with family members who are now unable or unwilling to continue providing care. Many "unaccompanied" women seek reunion with children in the foster care system or with relatives (Johnson & Lee, 1994).

An Example of Institutional Denial and Collusion

A 1994 research study, "The Needs of Young Children Living in Connecticut Shelters and Transitional Housing Programs," surveyed 40 homeless mothers and 26 service providers from 10 agencies in seven Connecticut cities. The mothers' mean age was 27.7 with 2.4 children. Twenty were African-American, 14 were Latinas, and 6 were White. Fifty-three percent were single, 25% divorced or separated, and 9% married. Forty-two percent had lived in shelters before. The sample was small and not random, as people volunteered to participate. Focus groups and questionnaires were used to provide for in-depth information about the needs of homeless women with children. The findings regarding the prevalence of substance abuse among the homeless mothers were predictable. There was

> considerable variation between the perception of shelter staff on the incidence of drug and alcohol use and the self-reporting of parent participants. Of the 40 parents who completed questionnaires, only 17.5% reported any substance abuse problems. On shelter staff questionnaires, respondents thought an average of 56% of parents had alcohol or drug abuse problems, with a range of responses from 10% to 90%. In staff focus groups, some staff thought that up to 95% of parents may have a substance abuse problem. (*Report to the General Assembly*, 1994).

It is remarkable that the recommendations and principles generated from this otherwise comprehensive report and its corollaries included *no* reference to substance abuse. This is, however, an excellent example of how sympathetic professionals including researchers, collude with clients who are in denial about substance abuse, thereby perpetuating it.

SUBSTANCE ABUSE, OPPRESSION,
AND EMPOWERMENT PRACTICE

Substance abuse for women and minorities of color and other stigmatized groups is inevitably related to larger issues of oppression (Lee, 1994). Throughout the years, alcohol has been used to exploit and control women, Native Americans, migrant workers, and tenant farmers. Since slavery alcohol has been used as a tool of oppression with African-Americans to quell rebellion and ensure servitude. Liquor stores are more numerous and laws enforcing the sale of alcohol more loosely enforced in lower-income African-American and Hispanic communities (Leland, 1984; Wright et al., 1990). Drug dealing is proposed to poor minority youth as a glamorous and fast route out of poverty (Anderson, 1990). Drinking and abusing drugs is one way (albeit maladaptive) to deal with the feelings of anger and despair precipitated by bearing stigma and victimization and withstanding discrimination (Gary & Gary, 1985; Wright et al., 1990). Drugs are a potent form of modern day slavery and exploitation. Homeless women must raise consciousness together about this in order to find liberation and power. This is often best done in groups. For example, the following is a narrative of Martha Red Cloud, a Native American member of a women's recovery group that also focused on issues of ethnic pride and critical thinking:

I grew up on a reservation. Almost everyone I knew there was drunk. The families had a lot of problems. I don't know what I felt most ashamed of, my people being drunks or my people being Indians. I was also ashamed to be a women. Since that time I have learned that this was never the way my people set out to be: we have been killed, tortured, and maimed by the white man, for his purposes. I have found out that we have a whole culture, a Native American way of living that is completely different from the way that I grew up. My life on the reservation was living like how the white man wanted us to be, a bunch of drunks too powerless to get up in the morning, let alone to raise our kids with pride in our culture. Then I got involved with men who hurt me; it was as if I let them hurt me the way white people treated Indians. I realized my people must no longer accept that exploitation and treatment and I must no longer accept it either. I realized that if I maintain my recovery, I can help my people, and that is what it really means to be an Indian woman—one who passes on a rich heritage. (Lee, 1994)

Intervention with members of oppressed groups, including homeless women, needs to be ethnic- and class-sensitive and addressed to the sources and realities of oppression as well as to the diseases of drug and alcohol addiction.

The accompanying children must be involved whenever possible. Clinical work with homeless mothers also needs to be family-oriented. Counseling can be offered to the absent father or male partner if he is actively involved in the mother's life and she wants this. Couples counseling may be offered only if there has been no physical abuse. Other counseling referrals may be offered for perpetrators of abuse. The reality is that many apparently single mothers who seek services for themselves and their children will reunite with the male partner once housed. Learning to be independent of male partners who are actively using or otherwise abusive is a major area of work for many homeless women. Empowerment-based practice, including promoting raised consciousness and group pride and action and addressing internalized oppression (including negative self-image and low self-concept when these are present) must go hand in hand with much support and solid confrontation of the addiction and its effects (Gary & Gary, 1985; Lee, 1994). Shelters and other programs for homeless women can enable them in their addictions or they can create opportunities for women to enter and maintain recovery (Scheffler, 1993). Those who work with homeless mothers need training in substance abuse assessment and intervention. Few substance abusers under 35 abuse one drug exclusively. Most are polydrug abusers (Kinney & Leaton, 1991; Lonesome, 1985; Nowinski, 1990). Knowledge about cocaine, alcohol, marijuana, and heroin and their various combinations is critical. There is an increased use in women using heroin. Research reveals that the majority of women are introduced to heroin by a man and that they are twice as likely as men to get dependent after initial use (Ettorre, 1992).

Many shelters have policies that include curfews and attendance at 12-step programs and drug counseling as agreements related to residence. The "faith in a higher power" element of 12-step programs increases their effectiveness with groups for whom religious faith is important: African Americans and others (Knox, 1985; Wright et al., 1990). Maintaining an ecological perspective and facilitating connection to churches, clergy, community groups, and other helping systems that support recovery is important. Drug and alcohol educational programs can be built into life skills meetings and counseling efforts as well. A multisubstance-abuse educational approach is particularly helpful, as many poor and working-class addicts see alcohol and marijuana as "safe and harmless drugs." Combined with a critical education approach that questions oppression and an empowerment philosophy, women who are at various points of living addictive lifestyles can be challenged to live drug-free and be in drug-free relationships as they improve parenting skills and secure housing, education, jobs, and other basic entitlements (Lee, 1994).

EXAMPLES FROM PRACTICE

Pam—A Case of Missed Opportunity

Pam is an attractive 30-year-old African American woman who has just given birth to her second child, a daughter, while in a Connecticut shelter for homeless women and children. Her 6-year-old son resides with her parents in New Jersey. A bright and articulate woman, Pam completed college and held responsible jobs before her addiction to cocaine and alcohol. She completed an inpatient drug treatment program at a well-known treatment center in New Jersey. She moved ostensibly to seek employment. In Connecticut she did not seek counseling or attend 12-step programs. Her baby was low-birthweight and unresponsive initially but without distinct withdrawal symptoms. Pam had abused drugs during the first trimester. By the time the baby was about a month old, Pam found good housing, obtained child care, and started a new job. The worker did not maintain a focus on drug abuse because Pam had convinced her that that was "a closed chapter." Pam was liked at her job and was being considered for a promotion. By the second month of employment, however, she began to miss work and borrow money on the job. The baby's father, a drug dealer, moved into her apartment. By the third month, Pam was terminated from her job for erratic attendance.

By the time the worker focused on drug issues, it was far too late. Pam had returned to a drug-driven lifestyle. Child protective services were involved. Seeing the "first signs," borrowing and uneven attendance at the job, was not enough. The worker needed to maintain a focus on continued drug treatment and 12-step participation from the moment the helping relationship began. Workers cannot afford to buy into the substance abuser's illusions of "handling it." Without a drug focus in the work and referrals to 12-step and drug counseling programs, facilitating recovery is usually impossible (Lee, 1994).

Millie—Alcoholism Undetected

A poignant example of the effects of professionals' minimizing drinking behaviors is the case of Millie, a 38-year-old Irish-American mother of two little girls. Millie is an overweight, slightly disheveled, pleasant, cooperative, and slightly slow (borderline mental retardation) woman. In her third shelter stay, Millie was attending closely to her girls, ages 4 and 5. The 5-year-old was especially bright and resilient.

Millie was so likable that she evoked the caring and giving of all staff members and little of the usual expectation to deal with her problems. Although her friends were all substance abusers, and she said she intended to marry an older alcoholic, her own problem drinking was minimized. She maintained sobriety while in the shelter but clearly slept a great deal after being away for the day on weekends. Millie's 4-year-old began to engage in sexually provocative behavior with male children. Millie confirmed staff suspicions of sexual abuse of the youngest girl by a former male partner. The family was referred for individual and child therapy and family counseling at a reputable agency. Even there, Millie's substance abuse as a major precipitant of the family chaos was overlooked. The shelter social worker attempted active follow-up once Millie found housing. Millie quickly took in another substance-abusing male partner of short acquaintance. The follow-up worker helped to rehouse him, but then there was another. Millie refused agency outreach and discontinued all counseling. The case was referred to the Department of Children and Families. The children were placed in foster care, and within 2 years her parental rights were terminated. Tragically, Millie is now an active middle-stage alcoholic who is barely surviving. The children, who have many emotional problems, remain in the foster care system.

Kaisha—Recovery in Progress

Kaisha, a 32-year-old African American woman, came to the shelter for women and children when she was 7 months pregnant. She said she had been a cocaine addict for 12 years and had just completed a 1-year day treatment recovery program. She got her GED while in this program as well. Her baby's father was in jail on drug-related charges. She could no longer stay with a cousin who was now using drugs and jeopardizing her recovery. She wanted to have a home for her expected child and to resume the care of her two older children, ages 12 and 7, because her mother, who had raised them, had become physically ill. She accepted shelter curfews as positive in her recovery effort but questioned the shelter's encouragement of 12-step meetings. She begrudgingly agreed to attend drug counseling, Narcotics Anonymous (NA), and Cocaine Anonymous (CA) regularly. During her 3-month stay at the shelter, Kaisha gave birth to a baby girl and was also reunited with her 7-year-old son. She resumed her parenting role with her older daughter slowly, through visiting. She began a job training program and sought counseling for herself and her daughter regarding their reunion. She was an active participant in empowerment group meetings and was particularly attuned to issues of oppression and drugs.

Kaisha's ability to discuss her drug addiction was a positive precipitant for other women to examine their own substance abuse histories. But she was also often irritable, angry, and depressed. Staff raised appropriate questions about her recovery process. She was more "dry" than in recovery. "I want what I want when I want it" prevailed in her thinking. On the positive side, her desire for structure, continued job training, and help with parenting spoke to her strengths. The staff decided to go with her strengths and support her request to enter the transitional living facility with her children. She ambivalently contracted to begin work in a recovery program that would include at least three 12-step meetings a week, obtaining a sponsor, and doing step work, as well as continuing with her outside counseling and using the in-house empowerment program. Her strongest motivation was the desire to be a good parent, and she worked hard at this.

Kaisha and her three children recently completed the 2-year transitional living program. They have become a strong family unit. Kaisha became a leader among the residents and excelled in her job training, earning honors at her graduation. She also became interested in the wider issues of homelessness and in acting politically. On occasion she represented the agency and her fellow residents in this arena. Kaisha's recovery is a work in progress with many ups and downs. Overall, she deepened and consolidated her gains in recovery even as she developed the personal, interpersonal, and political power that she needs to live as an empowered woman, mother, and community member. Kaisha was not an "easy client," and there is no glib success story. She has maintained her recovery and her job and apartment for several months, and she continues to be actively involved in parenting her children, including relating to three different schools. She continues working toward empowerment against the odds.

EMPOWERMENT GROUPS AND RECOVERY

Groups are the treatment of choice in work with substance abusers (Nowinski, 1990; Kinney & Leaton, 1991; Straussner, 1993). They enable members to confront denial and learn about addiction as well as provide support, encouragement, and mutual aid in the recovery process. Hudson (1985) and Knox (1985) trace the successful history of AA groups with Blacks of all socioeconomic classes, noting spirituality as one of the strongest connections. Women's groups can be particularly effective as mixed-gender groups tend to be dominated by males (Lee, 1994; Nelson-Zlupko et al., 1995). Whenever possible, consideration should be given by the worker to a women's group being the same gender and ethnicity as group members (Gary & Gary, 1985). Bridges can also be made by culturally sensitive workers from different groups. Delgado and Delgado (1993) note the increasing frequency of groups for Hispanic substance abusers and discuss cultural considerations in using this method of treatment.

The empowerment group blends issues of substance abuse and recovery with mutual support and critical consciousness regarding oppression and the slavery of addiction. This is a particularly effective strategy with people of color (Wright et al., 1990). The focus of the group is on the dynamic connection of the personal and the political, and on assuming responsibility for their lives. Relationships, parenting, preparing to work or pursue education, and issues of daily living as a single parent are also important themes of the work. The worker is a problem poser, asking critical questions to stimulate discussion and reflection. Members are asked to analyze problems on the personal, institutional/systems, and cultural/political levels. The development of a code (picture, chart, song, or poem) is used by the group to further stimulate consciousness raising. The meaning of the code is discussed with the members, using their own perceptions, experiences, and words. This process usually brings new codes and raised consciousness, which is aimed at action on the personal, interpersonal, institutional, and cultural/political levels. The group then reflects on its actions in an ongoing process of praxis, which is action–reflection–action. Empowerment groups also build on strengths and promote ethnic and gender pride and knowledge that bolsters self-esteem (Lee, 1994). The following group examples are excerpted and paraphrased from *The Empowerment Approach to Social Work Practice* (Lee, 1994).

Addiction as Part of the Contract for Empowerment

Present are two social workers for the group, an African American woman who is learning the empowerment approach and a White (Franco-American) woman experienced in this approach. (She is the "I" in the summary below.) Eight women are present: five African Americans, two Puerto Ricans, and one White (Italian American), ages 19 to 36. This is an ongoing open-ended weekly group; therefore, the worker must explain the group's purpose when new members join.

> I began by welcoming the three women who are new to the group today and asked them to tell a little about themselves and why they're here. As each one shared, the others echoed their stories. I said, "Everyone here has had a difficult time before coming here. This group is an opportunity to talk about the things they have experienced and the problems they face that make finding housing difficult. Sometimes they face discrimination and prejudice. Some of the problems are personal, like the ones with relationships you have already described, or trouble with drugs and alcohol abuse for yourself or someone close to you." Daria said, "That's me!" And Maritza said, "Me too. I just got out of a drug program and have nowhere to go." I said, "It was courageous to share that. It is a hard struggle, and one we will work on together here." My coworker said, "Drugs are oppressive." Daria said, "They made me a slave." Maritza said, "And they made me a fool!"
>
> Janine said, "My mother married a guy who drinks. He gets so nasty and makes a play for me. That's why I left. But what I'm upset about is that they lost my application for a Section 8 certificate, and I have to start all over again." Mary said, "No, you don't. You should contact the supervisor. I bet they'll find it."

The worker begins the group by recognizing and welcoming new members and inviting them to tell their story, naming drug abuse as a possible

area of work. Using reflective listening, she empathizes with the struggles
and pain that became their pathway to homelessness and the shelter. She
then moves to develop the contract with the group by telling them what
an empowerment group is and pointing out the common ground. She is
nonjudgmental. She quickly recognizes and praises their courage in sharing
a taboo subject, drugs, and continues to weave this into the group's
contract. The co-worker, who is a woman of color, responds empathically
with a personal-political statement, raising the group's consciousness. The
group members are encouraged and share more of how negatively they
felt about themselves when they used drugs. When Janine shares her
family history of alcohol abuse, then switches gears to Section 8 housing,
the other members jump in to help. They work on problem solving on a
more concrete, easily solvable, less highly charged issue before returning
to drug abuse and oppression later in the meeting.

Recognizing the Effects of Drugs on Homelessness

Present for the meeting at the shelter for women and children are eight
young homeless women who have their children in tow: five are African
American, and three are Puerto Rican. The workers at this meeting are
J, the regular social worker for the shelter, and G, a co-leader experienced
in empowerment group work, who records this meeting. In response to a
critical question about the forces that created their homelessness, Michaela
discusses her cocaine addiction. This is Michaela's second time at the
shelter, although she completed a drug treatment program and had
good housing.

> Michaela said, "I messed up again, and here I am. I'm glad to be here
> and I'm glad for the curfew because sometimes I get the taste again." I
> asked if she was saying that having a curfew helps her to stay away from
> drugs. She said, "Yes, it does, and also encouraging addicts to go to
> Twelve-Step meetings helps." Others nodded.
>   J asked if anyone else had a similar problem with drugs. Ramona said
> that she "felt the pressure" where she was previously living but that since
> she came to the shelter she had not had any alcohol. Michaela talked about
> how she had gone to NA and AA meetings to help her with her craving.
> We spoke about cravings. I then said, "This is what the group is
> about . . . talking about and helping each other with those things that brought

them down . . . to the point that they became homeless.'' The group members indicated that they have had to ''go it alone.'' I said, ''It can be very difficult alone'' and suggested that while they are here they might be able to help one another and possibly continue to help one another after they leave here.

Dora said, ''Finding an apartment is the easy part. The difficult part is keeping it.'' I said, ''That is right, and we have begun to hear from some group members that it was drugs or alcohol that brought them down.'' Dora said she does pot (marijuana), but she has never done alcohol or other drugs like the other members. J said that pot is much more potent now than it was a few years back. Others shared experiences in agreement. I replied that whether it is pot, harder drugs like cocaine and crack, or alcohol, they are all drugs. Ramona and Michaela said that they all get you high, and the group members agreed. Ramona described how addicts often exchange food for drugs and how they will use food money for drugs and then say they do not have any food. If they get food they then sell it for drugs. I nodded and asked if drugs were a problem for those who had been quiet up until now or if they had other things that brought them to the shelter. (Lee, 1994)

Michaela's discussion of the positives in shelter rules are an important piece of work coming from a group member. The worker then clearly invites other members to share their problems with drugs. The worker lends a vision about the group's purpose and contract. Recognizing the difficulty of going it alone, she encourages the group members to be there for one other. Dora makes the transition to some of the difficulties of everyday living without mentioning drugs. The worker, rather than ignoring the latent message, makes the connection to drugs and alcohol being part of the difficulty and asks the members to respond. As Ramona describes the life of an addict, selling food for drugs, for example, she depicts the lives of some of these homeless young mothers. The worker reaches out to draw in the quieter members.

Empowerment group work with substance abuse and recovery as strong themes helps homeless women deal with addiction as a major obstacle to obtaining housing and good parenting. It motivates recovery and prepares women for more meaningful participation in 12-step groups. Parenting issues are also worked on in the empowerment group, and connections are made to substance abuse. There are also life skills groups that focus exclusively on parenting skills and access to resources for parents and children.

SOME PRINCIPLES TO GUIDE PRACTICE,
POLICY, AND PROGRAMS

Substance-abusing homeless women and their children are an extremely high-risk population. Help to enter recovery should be offered to everyone who needs it. Therefore, practice with homeless women who are substance abusers necessitates well-prepared social workers who have the following:

1. In-depth training in the assessment of and intervention/treatment of women with substance abuse problems, including an appreciation of the value of 12-step programs and the skilled use of the group modality.
2. Self-awareness of the way in which collusion with denial and the client's view that she "has it all under control" takes place and is harmful to the professional relationship as well as the client's life chances.
3. A "tough-love" stance. We are dealing with a life-threatening situation.
4. A thorough knowledge of the principles of empowerment practice that appreciates ethnic and class differences, an ecological view, ego-supportive and cognitive-behavioral intervention abilities, and a critical view of oppression and feminist vision.
5. The ability to connect the substance abuse issues of women to gender, class, and racial oppression.
6. Skills in promoting consciousness raising and cultural pride, guiding praxis and facilitating action not only to change substance abuse behaviors but to change the society that contributes structurally to both substance abuse and homelessness among women with and without children. Skills in implementing the empowerment group approach and individual empowerment work.
7. Knowledge and skill in family-oriented work and in developing culturally sensitive parenting skills.
8. A strengths perspective that does not minimize pathology of any sort.
9. A family and community perspective that looks beyond the individual woman to her connection and contribution to her family and her community.

The principles and skills described here are more fully explicated in *The Empowerment Approach to Social Work Practice* (Lee, 1994).

CONCLUSION

We have discussed practice approaches that can empower and liberate homeless mothers who are also substance abusers. There is no empowerment possible unless women begin and maintain a lifelong process of recovery, including evaluating their relationships with substance-abusing partners and learning to "make it" on their own. The use of empowerment groups that include peer support and a focus on the slavery of addiction is an important component of successful services that support people's strengths and challenge addiction.

Most important, services for the homeless are not and should not be treatment centers for the addicted. What is needed are nationwide policies and allocations of resources that mandate and make possible affordable housing for all people (Dattalo, 1991); and ethnic-, class-, and gender-sensitive residential drug treatment programs for women and their children where homeless mothers have priority access. This needs to be followed up by ample availability of halfway houses, outpatient treatment, and permanent housing with comprehensive services, including health care and day care for those who continue to need support. Without such policies and programs, homelessness will be a revolving door for many substance-abusing mothers. Families will be broken and children set adrift in overburdened and costly foster care system (Courtney, 1995). We have already witnessed second-generation homelessness. Optimally, a just society would be preventive of this, and a caring profession would advocate with clients for empowering and life-giving entitlements, opportunities, and services that facilitate recovery and good parenting.

REFERENCES

Abbott, A. (1995). Substance abuse and the feminist perspective. In N. Van Den Bergh (Ed.), *Feminist practice in the 21st century* (pp. 258–277). Washington, DC: National Association of Social Workers.

Alcocer, A. (1993). Patterns of alcohol use among Hispanics. In R. Mayers, B. Kail, T. Watts (Eds.), *Hispanic substance abuse* (pp. 37–50). Springfield, IL: Thomas.

Anderson, E. (1990). *Streetwise: Race, class and change in an urban community.* Chicago: University of Chicago Press.

Baker, S. R. (1994). Gender, ethnicity, and homelessness. *American Behavioral Scientist, 37,* 461–475.

Banyard, V. L., & Graham-Bermann, S. (1995). Building an empowerment policy paradigm: Self-reported strengths of homeless mothers. *American Journal of Orthopsychiatry, 65,* 479–486.

Bassuk, E. (1993). Social and economic hardships of homeless and other poor women. *American Journal of Orthopsychiatry, 63,* 340–347.

Bassuk, E., & Salomon, A. (1993). [*The heart of the social contract* (book review)]. *Readings: A Journal of Reviews and Commentary in Mental Health, 8*(4), 8–12.

Bassuk, E., & Weinreb, L. (1993). Homeless pregnant women: Two generations at risk. *American Journal of Orthopsychiatry, 63,* 348–357.

Baum, A., & Burnes, D. (1993). *A nation in denial: The truth about homelessness.* Boulder, CO: Westview.

Bell, C., Thompson, J., Lewis, D., Redd, J., Shears, M., & Thompson, B. (1985). Misdiagnosis of alcohol-related organic brain syndromes: Implications for treatment. In L. Brisbane & M. Womble (Eds.), *Treatment of Black alcoholics* (pp. 45–65). New York: Haworth.

Blau, J. (1992). *The visible poor: Homelessness in the United States.* New York: Oxford University Press.

Brisbane, F., & Womble, M. (1985). *Treatment of Black alcoholics.* New York: Haworth.

Browne, A. (1993). Family violence in homelessness: The relevance of trauma histories in the lives of homeless women. *American Journal of Orthopsychiatry, 63,* 370–384.

Buckner, J., Bassuk, E., & Zima, B. (1993). Mental health issues affecting homeless women: Implications for intervention. *American Journal of Orthopsychiatry, 63,* 385–399.

Caetano, R. (1988). Alcohol use among Hispanic groups in the United States. *American Journal of Drug and Alcohol Abuse, 14,* 293–308.

Chavez, G., Cordero, J., & Becerra, J. (1989). Leading major congenital malformations among minority groups in the United States, 1981–1986. *Journal of the American Medical Association, 261,* 205–209.

Corrigan, E. (1991). Psychosocial factors in women's alcoholism. In N. Van Den Bergh (Ed.), *Feminist perspectives on addictions* (pp. 67–71). New York: Springer.

Courtney, M. (1995). The foster care crisis and welfare reform. *Journal of Public Welfare*, *53*(3), 27–33.

Dattalo, P. (1991). Moving beyond emergency shelters: Who should fund low-income housing? *Social Work*, *36*, 297–301.

Delgado, M., & Delgado, D. (1993). Chemical dependence, self-help groups, and the Hispanic community. In R. Mayers, B. Kail, & T. Watts (Eds.), *Hispanic substance abuse* (pp. 145–156). Springfield, IL: Thomas.

Ettorre, E. (1992). *Women and substance use*. New Brunswick, NJ: Rutgers University Press.

First, R., Rife, J., & Toomey, B. (1994). Homelessness in rural areas: Causes, patterns and trends. *Social Work*, *39*, 97–108.

Gary, L., & Gary, R. (1985). Treatment needs of Black alcoholic women. In F. Brisbane & M. Womble (Eds.), *Treatment of Black alcoholics* (pp. 97–114). New York: Haworth.

Goodman, L. (1991). The prevalence of abuse in the lives of homeless and housed poor mothers: A comparison study. *American Journal of Orthopsychiatry*, *61*, 489–500.

Herd, D. (1989). The epidemiology of drinking patterns and alcohol related problems among U.S. Blacks. In *Alcohol use among ethnic minorities* (pp. 3–50). (CDHHS Publication No. ADM 89-1435), Rockville, MD: National Institute on Alcohol Abuse and Alcoholism.

Hudson, H. (1985). How and why Alcoholics Anonymous works for Blacks. In F. Brisbane & M. Womble (Eds.), *Treatment of Black alcoholics* (pp. 11–30). New York: Haworth.

Johnson, A., & Kreuger, L. (1989). Toward a better understanding of homelessness. *Social Work*, *34*, 537–540.

Johnson, A., & Lee, J. (1994). Empowerment work with homeless women. In M. Pravder (Ed.), *Women in context: Toward a reconstruction of psychotherapy* (pp. 408–432). New York: Guilford.

Kinney, J., & Leaton, G. (1991). *Loosening the grip: A handbook of alcohol information*. Chicago: Mosby Year Book.

Knox, D. (1985). Spirituality: A tool in the assessment and treatment of Black alcoholics and their families. In F. Brisbane & M. Womble (Eds.), *Treatment of Black alcoholics* (pp. 31–44). New York: Haworth.

Lang, M. (1989). *Homelessness and affluence: Structure and paradox in American economy*. New York: Praeger.

Langelier, R. (1982). *French Canadian families*. In M. McGoldrick, J. Pearce, & J. Giordano (Eds.), *Ethnicity and family therapy*. New York: Guilford.

Leland, J. (1984). Alcohol use and abuse in ethnic minority women. In S. Wilsnack & L. Beckman (Eds.), *Alcohol problems in women*. New York: Guilford.

Lee, J. A. B. (1983). Who's looking out for the homeless? *NASW News*, *28*(8), 4–5.

Lee, J. A. B. (1986). No place to go: Homeless women. In A. Gitterman and L. Shulman (Eds.), *Mutual aid and the life cycle*. New York: Columbia University Press.

Lee, J. A. B. (1994). *The empowerment approach to social work practice*. New York: Columbia University Press.

Leibow, E. (1993). *Tell them who I am: The lives of homeless women*. New York: The Free Press.

Lonesome, R. (1985). In-patient rehabilitation for the Black alcoholic. In F. Brisbane & M. Womble (Eds.), *Treatment of Black alcoholics* (pp. 67–84). New York: Haworth.

May, P. A. (1982). Substance abuse and American Indians: Prevalence and susceptibility. *International Journal of the Addictions*, *17*, 1185–1209.

Mayers, R., & Kail, B. (1993). Hispanic substance abuse: An overview. In R. Mayers, B. Kail, & T. Watts (Eds.), *Hispanic substance abuse* (pp. 5–18). Springfield, IL: Thomas.

McCarty, D., Argeriou, M., Huebner, R., & Lubran, B. (1991). Alcoholism, drug abuse and the homeless. *American Psychologist*, *4*, 1139–1148.

Minkler, M., Roe, K., & Robertson-Beckley, R. (1994). Raising grandchildren from crack-cocaine households: Effects on family and friendship ties of African-American women. *American Journal of Orthopsychiatry*, *64*(1), 20–29.

National Council on Alcoholism and Drug Dependence. (1990). *Fact sheet*. New York: Author.

National Institute on Alcohol Abuse and Alcoholism. (1985). *Alcohol use among U.S. ethnic minorities* (Research Monograph No. 18). Rockville, MD: U.S. Department of Health and Human Services.

National Institute on Drug Abuse. (1994). *Women and drug abuse*. Rockville, MD: Author.

Nelson-Zlupko, L., Kauffman, E., & Dore, M. (1995). Gender differences in drug addiction and treatment: Implications for social work intervention with substance abusing women. *Social Work*, *40*, 45–54.

Nowinski, J. (1990). *Substance abuse in adolescents and young adults: A guide to treatment*. New York: Norton.

Primm, B., & Wesley, J. (1985). Treating the multiply addicted Black alcoholic. In L. Brisbane & M. Womble (Eds.), *Treatment of Black alcoholics* (pp. 155–178). New York: Haworth.

Report to the General Assembly's Select Committee on Children: The needs of young children living in Connecticut shelters and transitional housing programs: Focus group and questionnaire data. (1994a). Unpublished report.

Report to the General Assembly's Select Committee on Children: The needs of young children living in Connecticut shelters and transitional housing programs: Guiding principles and recommendations. (1994b). Unpublished report.

Robertson, M. (1991). Homeless women with children: The role of alcohol and other drug abuse. *American Psychologist, 46,* 1198–1204.

Scheffler, S. (1993). Substance abuse among the homeless. In L. Straussner (Ed.), *Clinical work with substance-abusing clients* (pp. 291–304). New York: Guilford.

Shinn, M., Knickman, J., & Weitzman, B. (1987, August). *Social relationships and vulnerability to becoming homeless among depressed families.* Paper presented at the American Psychological Association meetings, New Orleans.

Smith, E. M. (1989). Services for Native Americans. *Alcohol Health and Research World, 13,* 94.

Soriano, F. (1993). AIDS and intravenous drug use among Hispanic in the U.S.: Considerations for prevention efforts. In R. Mayers, B. Kail, & T. Watts (Eds.), *Hispanic substance abuse.* Springfield, IL: Thomas.

Straussner, S. (1993). *Clinical work with substance-abusing clients.* New York: Guilford.

Thrasher, S., & Mowbray, C. (1995). A strengths perspective: An ethnographic study of homeless women with children. *Health and Social Work, 20*(2), 93–101.

U.S. Department of Health and Human Services. (1990). *Alcohol and women.* Rockville, MD: National Institute on Alcohol Abuse and Alcoholism.

Van Den Bergh, N. (1994, October). *Women's addictions: Multiple problems and multiple needs.* Panel presentation at NASW meeting, Nashville, TN.

Weiss, R., & Mirin, S. (1987). *Cocaine: The human danger, the social costs, the treatment alternatives.* New York: Ballantine.

Wright, R., Kail, B., & Creecy, R. (1990). Culturally sensitive social work practice with Black alcoholics and their families. In S. Logan, E. Freeman, & R. McRoy (Eds.), *Social work practice with Black families* (pp. 102–222). New York: Longman.

CHAPTER 18

The Impact of Culture in Social Work Practice with Groups: The "Grandmothers as Mothers Again" Case Study

Carol Cohen

Social workers must be able to understand and work with cultural differences when practicing with all types of client systems. This chapter focuses on the special challenges posed by the multicultural context of work with women of color in social work groups. It highlights the knowledge and skills social workers need to work with culturally diverse clients in groups and expands workers' options in treating family members who assume new roles.

Many social workers and administrators neglect to consider cultural variables when planning groups. Although simple misinformation may be at the root of some of this neglect, it is more likely that workers' avoidance of cultural issues in planning is a complicated phenomenon. This can have serious consequences, especially when the cultures of clients are different from those of the majority of agency staff. Discussion of culture may raise concerns for the worker and agency, including the "cultural competence" of staff, the agency's vision of "clients' health," and the norms expected in a "good group." In addition, some workers find any groups daunting, and their own fears and fantasies about the group process limit their ability to use their skills and knowledge effectively in a variety of group situations (Kurland, Getzel, & Salmon, 1986). Thus, it appears that culturally diverse groups are at the confluence of two troublesome areas in social work practice.

Groups can be powerful vehicles for family healing and client relief. However, group treatment has not been used as widely as its potential effectiveness warrants. The underutilization of groups for family members is often the result of past failures due to poor preparation. This lack of planning and corresponding failure of group initiatives can be compounded, leading agencies and workers to feel that "groups don't work here" (Cohen, 1993).

For a successful multicultural group, clinicians and administrators must overcome these obstacles, through thoughtful consideration of three layers of analysis. First, workers must understand the culture of the individual family members in relation to ethnic and racial norms, life-stage, gender, and community conditions. Second, they must examine the beliefs and structure of the agency for potential supports and conflicts with the culture of family members and the group. Third, workers must devote their attention to the development of a positive group culture. Success will depend on a high level of group cohesion and mutual aid. Group effectiveness is dependent on the careful analysis of each level, as part of an ongoing planning and evaluation process.

GRANDMOTHERS AS MOTHERS AGAIN

The Grandmothers As Mothers Again (GAMA) support group program serves as a case study to illustrate the impact and implications of multiple cultures in the planning, implementation, and operation of groups serving family members in crisis. The GAMA program is a local response to growing national issue. In the United States the number of households that include grandparents and grandchildren increased by almost 40% from 1980 to 1990 (U.S. Census, 1991). According to the U.S. Census (1994), 3.7 million children under 18 years old live in households with their grandparents. Of these 2.4 million households, 1,487,000 families are identified as Caucasian, 785,000 families as African American, and

356,000 as Latino. Approximately 1.5 million of these grandparent-and-grandchildren households include the children's parents in residence. The remaining 841,000 are households in which parents are not in residence, representing family units in which grandparents take primary caretaking roles. Of those households, 488,000 are identified as Caucasian, 321,000 as African American, and 107,000 as Hispanic.

The American Association of Retired Persons (Chalfie, 1994) documents the existence of 551,025 midlife and older adults, living in 352,945 households with grandparents raising grandchildren without a parent present. More than three fourths (77%) of the grandparents are between 45 and 64 years old, with 39% from 45 to 54 and 38% from 55 to 64 years old. Approximately one quarter of the grandparents (23%) are over 65 years old, with 7% 75 years old or older.

The grandparent heads of households in these families represent the least-educated families of all nontraditional households. Therefore, it is not surprising that they are also the poorest nontraditional households. Whereas only 26% of all households with children have incomes of less than $20,000, 56% of grandparent caregiver households are in this income category. Twenty-seven percent of grandparent caregivers have incomes at or below the poverty level and 14% at the near-poor income level of 100% to 149% of the poverty level (U.S. Bureau of the Census, 1993).

The AARP report confirms that although the overwhelming majority of grandparent caregivers are White, African American grandparents are nearly twice as likely to be grandparent caregivers than are White grandparents. Findings regarding gender indicate that 40% are grandfathers and 60% are grandmothers. However, it is important to consider that 96% of all grandfather caregivers are married, compared to only 63% of the grandmothers. A striking 122,627 grandmothers are raising their grandchildren alone, comprising 93% of all single grandparent caregivers.

Although these reports provide compelling evidence of the need for programs to support grandparents in their struggles, the actual number of grandparents raising grandchildren is probably much higher. The anecdotal evidence of GAMA members indicates that householders often report their grandchildren's parents as being in residence in the household, though they may be substantially or completely absent. Some parents may be physically present in the household but incapacitated and unable to perform parenting roles. As the stories of the GAMA members show, parents leave their children in care of grandparents for a variety of reasons, both voluntarily and involuntarily.

The GAMA program was launched in 1993, to reach out to grandmothers raising their grandchildren in poor neighborhoods of Brooklyn, New York. Two GAMA groups meet biweekly, one operating in English, with African American members and the other in Spanish, with Latina members. Members have assumed their parenting roles through a variety of events, including their children's death from AIDS, incarceration, substance abuse, and abandonment.

The group is an integral program of a large sectarian agency in New York City. GAMA's work is focused on sharing the burdens and blessings of the members' situations, through discussion and activity. Workers facilitate discussions, help members plan group content, bring in outside resources to the group, and provide advocacy and crisis services to individual members as needed. The powerful impact of the group is seen in the words of members, who report: "I'm not isolated anymore," "We all share the same problem," and "When I give help, I feel better."

Given the high level of support currently provided by the group, GAMA's development provides some key lessons in developing groups with culturally diverse clients. The GAMA program eventually flourished through the continual reexamination of the three levels of analysis mentioned earlier: the culture of the members, the culture of the agency, and the culture of the group itself.

CULTURE OF THE MEMBERS

Webster's New World Dictionary (1994) defines culture as: "the ideas, customs, skills, arts, etc. of a people or group, that are transferred, communicated, or passed along, as in or to succeeding generations" (p. 337). Popular usage has expanded this definition to include characteristics (such as race and class) that are shared and form a common identity among a group of people. The members of GAMA appear to belong to a variety of cultures within this broader definition. The primary cultures of the GAMA members include: cultures of gender (women), of life stage (grandmothers), of ethnicity (Latinas and African Americans), and of family crisis (grandparents raising grandchildren through parental incapacity or death). Additional elements, such as social class and level of acculturation with majority culture, also contribute to individual cultural identity (Congress, 1994). Thus, each member can be seen as having a unique cultural reality.

The following sections elaborate on the impact of primary cultural variables on the planning and implementation of the GAMA program. This review of key cultural variables is not intended to provide a "cook book" approach to cultural diversity. Rather, the purpose is to encourage a "kaleidoscopic" view of culture (Middleman & Rhodes, 1985), and its impact in group treatment.

Culture of Gender

As with other cultural variables, gender is a parameter that can both highlight client needs and suggest appropriate service models. Women are disproportionately represented among the poor, and their numbers are rising. Among families in New York receiving Aid to Families with Dependent Children (AFDC), 91% are headed by women. In 1984, 39% of these women were Black, 38.6% were Hispanic, and 13.4% were White. One of every four children in the city was on an AFDC budget (Hatcher, 1984). According to the National Commission on Working Women (1988), only 3% of all males with some college education live in poverty, as compared with more than 20% of women of color with similar educational backgrounds.

Following these patterns, most GAMA members have extremely limited incomes. Some members have had to leave jobs after assuming their unanticipated child-rearing responsibilities. Although some have been able to secure increased benefits through the foster care system, others rely on meager welfare benefits and/or simply stretch other income to accommodate the new family member. GAMA's workers and members understand that although a sense of community with others is critical, it cannot replace adequate food or shelter. GAMA's work focuses on the intimate and compelling concerns of grandmothers raising grandchildren. Program planners must understand the need for workers' advocacy to obtain critical, concrete services, as well as the need for affective support.

The GAMA program is premised on the needs and abilities of women to offer and receive support from others. Feminist theories suggest that women's history of affiliation should be seen as evidence of a "self-in-relation" psychology for women, stressing collective effort, and collaboration (Chodorow, 1978, Gilligan, 1982, Surrey, 1985). According to Berzoff

(1989), "The female self is a relational self. It develops in a web of interconnections (and) it is in the community of relationships (including friendships) that female identity occurs" (p. 49). Whether cooperative strategies are linked with women's unique psychology, or are applicable to all people, group practice approaches that incorporate collective problem solving rather than competitions appear better to serve the needs of the GAMA members for empowerment and support.

Predominant Western ideology places women and members of other oppressed groups in a double bind, in which women risk censure for adopting the action framework of a "generalized competent mature adult" and risk criticism for adopting the more passive roles of a female (Abramovitz & Helly, 1986, p. 84). Consideration of this possible role conflict was critical in the planning of the GAMA support group program. Through the course of the group, workers may be in the position of encouraging clients to take an assertive stance that may be unfamiliar and/or forbidden by cultural and sexual constraint. Staff recognized that strategies such as advocating for increased foster care benefits and the pursuing legal custody might be difficult for the members, given their socialization as women. In this context, the support of group members is essential in taking on new roles and attitudes.

"Mother" is a role familiar to the GAMA members, but it now comes at a time when other roles might have flourished. As Theresa (names have been changed throughout) tells the GAMA group in this excerpt, she experiences competing role demands:

> I'm really thinking of going back to Santo Domingo. When I saw my husband I felt compassion for him. He left me and went back to Santo Domingo, expecting me to follow, but I couldn't leave my grandchildren. . . . I have always been the support of my family since I was 15, 16, 17, they all come to me for help and support.

GAMA members play multiple roles, including those of a grandmother, mother, provider, person of color, worker, lover. To this array, GAMA brings another role, that of a member. Although women are generally seen as adept in balancing roles, competing roles may create role strain, defined as "a problem in existential inauthenticity, arising from conflicting world views in multiple subcultures" (Roberts, 1985, p. 73). Therefore, planners need to consider the role demands of individual members and how members' roles will interface with the group.

Culture of Life Stage

GAMA members are adult women who have taken on new child rearing responsibilities at a time when most of their children are grown and they might otherwise anticipate an "empty" or "emptier" nest. For some, this comes during peak years of employment, and for others, during retirement. Expectations for their own children have been sadly unfulfilled, and conceptions of their own grand motherhood (and great grand motherhood) have been shattered, as they find themselves as mothers again.

The members of GAMA range in age from 40 through 70. Kerson (1989) suggests that role transition, rather than age is the most meaningful marker among women in their middle years (45–65). The GAMA experience confirms this, in that age differences in the group are not an obstacle to the provision of mutual aid and understanding.

The images of grandmothers in our society are varied but generally include stereotypes of the white-haired, cookie-baking granny and the jet-setting, jogging-suited grandmother. Although few meet these images, studies have documented grandmothers' high degree of satisfaction with their role (80%), with 37% finding the role more enjoyable than parenting (Robertson, 1977). Kivnik (1982) found that grandparents who had experienced social losses felt that grandparenthood was more meaningful to them than to other grandparents, suggesting that relationships with grandchildren served compensatory functions. Timberlake and Cipnungu's (1992) study of African American grandmothers found that relationships with grandchildren were influenced by situational factors such as living arrangements, economic class, and role conflicts. Across situational differences, grandmothers were found to place great meaning on their relationships with grandchildren, seeing themselves as linking the generations, "as extended from the past into the present and forward into the future through their grandchildren" (Timberlake & Cipnungu, 1992, p. 220).

Most grandmothers provide some form of caretaking for grandchildren. However, as a full-time parent, the GAMA member cannot "love them, spoil them, and send them home." Grandmothers of color are more likely to live with their grandchildren than are White grandmothers. However, becoming the primary caretaker for their grandchild is quite different from simply living in an extended family household. Members are mourning the loss of their parent and grandmother role, even if they have other "traditional" mother-child and grandparent-child relationships. GAMA acknowledges and incorporates this process of grieving into the group.

A shift to the parenting role has made many changes in the members' lives. The following exchange illustrates how some view these changes:

> *Mildred*: I felt so out of place at the PTA meetings with all those young mothers. But my grands have helped to turn my life around. My grandson saw me at the end of last year and said, "Boy, you sure have changed!" My grand kids keep me dressed all the time. I used to go around the house with robe and curlers unless I had a special place to go. Well, now I'm up and dressed early in the morning and stay that way. And you know, I feel better this way.

> *Joan*: Well, if the truth be told, I'd rather be around children than adults anyway. Most adults are so negative, they depress me.

GAMA has helped negotiate the challenges placed on older women as they take on parenting again. Some members experience greater strains due to aggravated health conditions. These include one member suffering from arthritis aggravated by stress. Other members shared their own remedies with her, including the importance of taking 1 hour alone each day for "quiet time." In another case, when Mary's health attendant was not able to accompany her to the meeting, she expressed concern about falling ill on the way home. Members then volunteered to accompany her.

As Browne (1995) cautions, "the strengths of older women are neglected if a conceptualization of power and empowerment is one of domination and control as opposed to capacity and relatedness" (p. 360). Towle (1952) has pointed out that successful aging requires the reformulation of personal values. She suggests that healthy aging requires replacing the need for acquisition with the need for conservation and replacing the need for self-advancement with the need for self-acceptance. GAMA can help with this complicated transition given their cross-generational roles. GAMA supports the members' development as both an older woman and a new mother, while recognizing that parenting demands control and responsibility for others, as well as caring.

Culture of Ethnicity

The members of the Spanish-speaking GAMA group are Latinas, originally from the Caribbean and Central America. Members of the English-speaking group are African American, from the United States and the

Caribbean. Latino and African American adults are among the fastest-growing groups of adults over 65 years in New York City. From 1980 through 1990 the number of Latinos in this age group increased 60% to become 10% of all older New Yorkers. During the same period the number of African Americans increased by 30%, and they now comprise 30% of the older adult population (Cantor & Brennan, 1993). These ethnic groups have a cultural history of caring for grandchildren through extended family networks. Although consistent with this norm, GAMA members' current child-rearing arrangements represent a dramatic change, due to the devastating events leading the grandmothers to take on parental responsibilities.

Each member of GAMA belongs to the overall culture of "people of color." Therefore, assessment and planning must include an analysis of the impact of oppression on the potential participants. As Pernell (1986) points out, racism and power are inexorably linked, and must be considered in planning a multicultural group.

> The sense of powerlessness to control or alter in any significant way ones life situation or the forces impinging on it leads to a variety of behaviors, from nonlegitimate substitute power and its exercise, to withdrawal. . . . The worker must reach for understanding of the pain and helplessness and the tremendous need for empowerment. This must be true empathy based on real understanding—not a projection of one's own power deficits. (p. 113)

Recognition of the impact of racism and sexism on women of color is critical to this process of developing empathy (Weiler, 1988). Group leaders and planners (of all cultures) must first examine their relative position to clients experiencing oppression. Next, workers must assist participants to see themselves as part of their larger culture, and as a member of the group. In this example, GAMA was designed to help rebuild the often broken links of members to their ethnic reference group and to foster the development of mutual aid among members.

Cross-cultural empathy is difficult to achieve and requires self-awareness and skill. With GAMA, a high level of worker empathy has been achieved although the English-speaking group is led by a White woman from New York, and the Spanish-speaking group is led by an African American woman, originally from Central America. Workers and members built their relationship through understanding the unique position of grandmothers raising grandchildren, and shared sense of group purpose.

Most of the members of GAMA are affiliated with local Catholic and Protestant churches. GAMA may attract an unusually high proportion of religious members due to its sectarian sponsorship, but the members belong to ethnic groups that share strong religious affiliations. GAMA's structure was planned to include this aspect of the members' lives if they wished. Both GAMA groups have decided to have a prayer during the meeting, and they conclude with a ritualized sharing of words of encouragement for each other. Spontaneous demonstrations are also supported as in the following vignette from a worker's recording:

> Martha brought her new baby to the group which added a warm touch to the meeting. Every grandmother commended her for her kindness. The baby was born weighing 3 pounds but is doing well. One grandmother got up and took off a chain which carries a highly religious value, and put it on the baby's neck and said, "I never took this chain off!" It symbolizes the Divine Christ and the Virgin Mary. It means "God will guide you and protect you."

In another example, Lillian shared her feelings about how her 17-year-old granddaughter (and the mother of a 15-month-old child that Lillian was raising) "got herself pregnant again with the same young man." As a highly respected church elder, Lillian felt so embarrassed that she refused to take the baby out of the house, let alone tell other parishioners about the birth. With the group's encouragement, Lillian shared her outrage, and the worker encouraged further discussion of her shame. Members offered stories of how they overcame their own shame so that they could remain in their church, commenting that once they reentered the church, "Other parishioners have sought me out, knowing that I could understand their problems" and "revealing my problems with my daughter has made me stronger." They encouraged Lillian to speak with her pastor. GAMA's workers, and other leaders of groups of women of color, must be open to the free discussion of religion and spirituality in a problem solving context.

Culture of Family Crisis

GAMA members' new caretaking roles have resulted in the realignment of family structures, often accompanied by shattered dreams and economic hardship. As the members quickly note, there are unexpected joys and benefits associated with their new responsibilities, including renewed vigor and interests. All members express love and concern for their grand-children. Yet they are equally clear that the assumption of "second time mothering" has been a difficult transition at best. As corroborated in the study of African American grandmothers in Oakland, California (Min-kler & Roe, 1993), the absence, incapacity, or refusal of their own children to serve as primary caretakers is often a source of anger, guilt, and shame.

Carmen's story poignantly captures the devastation in her family:

> I became a Grandmother as Mother Again when my daughter became involved in drugs. This was a shock to me. She left the house when she became pregnant, and returned when the baby was born. She lived with me for a while, but left again because she didn't want to give up the drugs. I told her to leave the baby because she couldn't take care of her out there. I am also taking care of my niece's son who's mother is in prison for murder. My niece says it was an accident. One night she gave birth in the bathroom. The baby fell in the toilet bowl and was drowned. She was sentenced for four years. I visited my niece in prison to find out she is three months pregnant. She asked me if I would raise her baby when it is born, because she does not want it to be raised by strangers. I agreed. After all, it's my blood.

Her story ended with perhaps surprising words: "Children today need love. I enjoy my grandchildren more than I enjoyed my own children. I wish I knew then what I know now!" Carmen's experiences are not atypical among grandmothers raising their children's children.

Just as GAMA members may be mourning the death of their imagined grand parenthood, they are also mourning the very real loss of children and the perceived failure of their original parenting efforts. Some grand-children's parents have died, others are incarcerated, ill with the AIDS virus, and/or incapacitated from drug use. Many grandmothers stepping into the GAMA role find that their situation can severely isolate them from their natural healing networks. GAMA fills this gap in the member's own neighborhood. The members' experience draws them together in a common culture.

CULTURE OF THE AGENCY

Agency culture is composed of "conditions existing in the agency or host setting that may have an impact on worker action and on the group that is being formed'' (Kurland et al., 1986, p. 61). Prevailing values and institutional norms are conveyed through the client-worker relationship, although these may conflict with client aspirations (Nystrom, 1989). The purpose of GAMA is social support and accessing members' strengths, rather than individual psychological change. Workers must not lose this sense of purpose or they risk psychic damage to clients and/or failure of the group. The worker must use the agency power resources to help clients ''create change,'' not to ''change clients.''

As Reynolds points out, social work practice is imbedded in the societal culture:

> Practice is always shaped by the needs of the times, the problems they present, the fears they generate, the solutions that appeal, and the knowledge and skill available. (Ehrenrich, 1985, p. 13)

Rappaport (1981) shares this view and suggests that as the general society becomes more conservative social workers increasingly turn to intrapsychic rather than environmental explanations for client problems.

Within the agency context, the personal stakes of staff are always present in the launching of a new program. These can become a source of goal displacement without careful monitoring (Perrow, 1986). However, when acknowledged and marshaled effectively, these personal beliefs can fuel a challenging assignment. With GAMA, all of the principal staff members had some kind of personal connection to the project, beyond the necessary commitment to serve clients effectively. The two group leaders were primarily raised by their grandmothers. Their history provided them a legacy of personal experience to draw on and an affinity for each other that bridged their cultural and racial differences with members and each other. Both reported feeling a spiritual reconnection with their grandmothers through their work with the group. Attention to supervision and training ensured that countertransference did not damage the group process. Although such a strong affinity is not necessary for success, the personal connection of the workers to GAMA may help explain the workers' ability to sustain their commitment to the group.

Social workers contemplating support group programs must carefully assess the agency's ideology about groups and then design a complementary structure. Failure to consider the synchronization of group goals and methods with the agency function often places group programs outside the "real" work of the agency (Garland, 1992). When groups are seen as "frills" (Kurland et al., 1986), they are often early failures or the first programs to be abandoned during times of agency constriction.

Agencies often construct barriers to client empowerment and may be hesitant to work with culturally diverse clients of color. Exploring and establishing a "good fit" for empowerment in the agency culture was crucial to the success of the GAMA program. Through integration with the agency mission and goals, the GAMA groups came to represent "the type of program we should be doing" (Cohen, 1995).

CULTURE OF THE GROUP

Successful support groups establish their own culture through the collective efforts of members and workers. Schwartz (1961) suggests that such a group should be viewed as an "organic whole," consisting of "a complex of moving, interdependent human beings, each acting out his changing relationship to society in his present interaction with others engaged in a similar enterprise" (p. 27). The social work group operates as a cultural system with special qualities. Among these qualities is interrelatedness (Hartman & Laird, 1983), in which the interaction of the group's participants leads to an evolving group culture. Changes in one part of the system affect the entire system, through a process of action, reaction, and interaction. Synergy is another term to describe this phenomenon, as in the following definition:

> (1) The interaction of elements that when combined produce a total effect that is greater than the sum of the individual elements, contributions etc.
> (2) The joint action of agents, as drugs, that when taken together increase each other's effectiveness (contrasted with antagonism). (*Random House Dictionary*, 1987, p. 1929)

The primary source of growth in groups is the membership, in the geometric effect of giving and accepting help. Through the phenomenon of mutual aid, members help each other to accomplish individual and collective goals. Although mutual aid often occurs naturally between people, the group worker can foster its development. Conflict is acknowledged as ubiquitous in a positive group culture. The attention of the worker and members is directed toward understanding and resolving conflict through member-to-member relationships. By identifying the group as an ''enterprise in mutual aid'' (Schwartz, 1961), the stage is set for the role of the worker as mediator of the individual-group encounter (Shulman & Gitterman, 1986). The group worker must help the members to weave diverse interests together to operate with ''common goals, by common decision and common action'' (Tropp, 1965, p. 12).

GAMA's purposes encompass major components of self-help groups: (1) eliminating isolation, (2) gaining perspective, and (3) developing a sense of empowerment (Kirkland, 1992). To achieve these goals, careful attention was paid to the multiple cultures of clients and agency. With professional leadership, GAMA's members have created a group culture in the ''open system'' model, giving members ''greater social resources, increased knowledge about the concern that members share, a sense of relief and reassurance, and enhanced skills for coping with their situation'' (Schopler & Galinsky, 1993, p. 201).

GAMA had a very rocky start, and early meetings were sparsely attended, as one worker recalled:

> There was always some excuse for not being able to attend (sick, doctors appointments, grandchild appointments, etc.). Sometimes we had 3, 4, 2 and even one in attendance for the group—however, they were not the same group members from one session to another. Always we had new people showing up and they would talk about their deep inner feelings and would express that they were so glad they had come and had someone to talk to. Then they would leave and promise that they would return for the next session—but never did. By this time we felt overwhelmed with the poor attendance. We tried to understand why the grandmothers would come and then not return. We felt guilty and somewhat confused—that we probably we weren't doing something right.

Using process recordings of the sessions, it appeared that the workers and one regular member encouraged a ''spilling'' pattern for new members. At the time, spotlighting a new member's troubles at her first meeting seemed therapeutic and exciting. With low attendance, focusing the most attention on new participants and their stories seemed reasonable, but this early disclosure pattern was counterproductive to the group's development.

In retrospect, the workers had not effectively considered the impact of cultural variables on group formation and cohesion. It has been noted that women are involved in many reciprocal relationships, yet they are generally more concerned with giving than with receiving assistance. In fact, many older women report fears of asking for help and being unable to reciprocate (Lewittes, 1989). This concern can become a barrier to seeking needed assistance.

In the early GAMA meetings, the small number of other participants had acted as a sponge for the new member's feelings, but they had not conveyed the commonality and potential for support in the group. Potential members who "told everything" at their first meeting felt that they could not face the other women again. The members who encouraged this pattern saw themselves as providing needed assistance because they had the opportunity to serve another woman. The workers were practicing "casework in the group" by focusing on only one member's reality (Kurland & Salmon, 1992) and failed to marshall the power of reciprocity needed to engage new members.

Besides gender, workers failed to consider the impact of ethnicity on the early stages of group development fully. As previously discussed, the two groups represented in the membership, Latinas and African American women, share many similarities but have different views of affiliation. Latinas are more likely to view their family as a source of friends and are less likely to form intimate relationships with women outside the family circle (Sanchez-Ayendez, 1989). When Latinas entered the group and immediately shared "family secrets," they found it extremely difficult to return despite the receptivity of the other women present. The fact that they attended the group at all showed a strong need to go beyond family boundaries for help, but the pattern of the early meetings created barriers to meeting this need. In contrast, African American women form strong relationships with both family and nonfamily members through a process of transforming friends into family (Woehrer, 1982). However, this process also requires mutual sharing and disclosure. The practice of having one member take center stage for an entire meeting was counterproductive to fostering this "family making" process.

Following more extensive group work training, planning, and the replacement of one leader, the groups were revitalized. The reciprocal, focused approach to establishing the commonality of members' experience led to the eventual development of sisterhood in the group. The group members were able to bring their customary ways of behaving into the group. As Hurdle (1991) points out, "Members will interact with each other as they behave toward other people in their social sphere'' (p. 66). GAMA's structure was modified to allow for culturally syntonic, differential participation by the members. As reported in the following excerpt, emphasis shifted to sharing experiences, and away from extended revelations.

> All the members seemed to share a history of family drug abuse. As they realized that all their daughters were addicted to drugs, they began to talk to one another, have eye contact, give support, etc.

The group was then able to progress from the beginning stages of engagement to the middle stages of increased intimacy and maturity.

Within a few months, both groups were meeting biweekly with a steady core of five to ten members. As a special event, the two GAMA groups met together for a bilingual Mother's Day celebration. With both groups in the middle stages of development, the members were secure enough to participate freely and form a quick alliance with the strangers from the other group. Activities included pantomiming scenes from childhood, such as playing games and modeling new clothes. A sense of play and solidarity was evident, with the nonverbal program helping to facilitate communication.

Toward the end of the event the members reflected on the GAMA experience. One member volunteered that she was the first to call and join GAMA and has since learned to appreciate and enjoy her granddaughter more. Another member commented that with GAMA, ''I found a place where I could find support—with mothers like me that can understand my hurt.'' The event ended with a member's song, thanking God and the group for her strength.

New members have been welcomed to become a part of the group in a different way than in the early stages of the group. Now the integration of new members focuses attention back to the purpose of the group. For example, when a new member joined the group she listened as three veteran grandmothers introduced themselves, relating the reasons they cared for their grandchildren and great grandchildren. As the worker documented, the new member then spoke:

> Susan told us, holding back tears, that she did not want to make the same mistakes with her grandchild that she did with her girls. The group

welcomed her and sharing her worries, suggested that we have a speaker talk with us about the development of children.

The members acknowledged her pain, shared their own struggles, and offered positive strategies for collective growth.

In its middle stage of life, GAMA's content has become more diversified, and members have expanded their role in planning. They took active roles in recruitment and created a new flyer that announced: ''We know you need support and we're here for you.'' They decorated and sold T-shirts with a GAMA logo to raise funds, after deciding to begin social outings as part of GAMA. In addition, members and staff are working with the municipal Department for the Aging to create a model child-care respite program. However, the central core of the group remains the support of each other as they raise their grandchildren.

Leadership of treatment groups with multicultural family members requires both general social work knowledge and the specific knowledge of social group work. As demonstrated in the GAMA case study, effective social work encounters require a thorough client assessment and understanding of the agency context. All interventions require thoughtful planning and tuning-in to clients' concerns and needs. Support groups allow members to draw from their individual family experiences, as well as provide opportunities to create new forms of affiliation. This function is particularly important in multicultural work, as noted by Anderson (1991):

> An important function of group work with families in cultural transition is developing their insight both into their own system and its transaction with the world at large. It is this insight which can promote their integrity and choice in determining the present and future strength of their family in preparing members to live fully in an ever-evolving multicultural world. (p. 99)

In particular, social workers who lead groups need to encourage the development of interrelatedness, synergy, and mutual aid. The worker must constantly evaluate and help weave individual strengths into the group culture. The ability to ''scan'' (Middleman & Wood, 1990), taking in information from many sources at once, is critical to the worker's effort in developing a positive group culture. An apt metaphor for the worker's role in this process is that of an orchestra conductor. The maestro's ability to hear individual instruments, sections, and ensemble, all at the same time, is closely allied with the worker' s skill in simultaneously connecting with the individual members, subgroup, and group as a whole.

SUMMARY

The GAMA experience shows that knowledge of clients' cultures is necessary but insufficient for effective group treatment. Three levels of culture, including that of clients, agency, and the group itself, must be analyzed and then drawn together to maximize the potential for member support. Continual evaluation is needed to assess the effective incorporation of cultural norms in the purpose, structure, and content of the group experience. The use of cultural knowledge in the planning and development of a group service leads to client and family growth.

A group's triumphs and troubles are directly related to the level of understanding and use of cultural variables in practice. As illustrated by GAMA, client norms such as those concerning friendship, family boundaries, and religiosity proved to be extremely important in the planning and development of the group. On the level of the agency culture, the ongoing administrative support of the group through a difficult initial stage demonstrated the need for synchronization of agency and group mission. Finally, the development of the unique culture of the GAMA group underscores the need for treatment groups to foster positive norms and healing through the provision of mutual aid.

The members of GAMA serve as partners in this process of analysis and use of cultural variables. The grandmothers clearly identify times of cultural dissonance and times of compatibility through their varying participation and investment in the group. The program's success flows from this agency/client partnership, in which each contributes key cultural elements to create a new, empowering group culture.

REFERENCES

Abramovitz, M., & Helly, D. (1986). *Report on a project to integrate scholarship on women into the introductory courses at Hunter College, 1982–1986* (pp. 83–88). New York: Women's Studies Program of Hunter College.

Anderson, J. D. (1991). Group work with families: A multicultural perspective. In K. Chau (Ed.), *Ethnicity and biculturalism: Perspectives on social group work* (pp. 85–101). New York: Haworth.

Berzoff, J. (1989). From separation to connection: Shifts in understanding women's development. *Affilia, 4*(1), 45–58.

Browne, C. V. (1995). Empowerment in social work practice with older women. *Social Work, 40*, 358–364.

Cantor, M., & Brennan, M. (1993). *Growing older in New York City in the 1990's.* New York: New York Center for Policy on Aging of the New York Community Trust.

Chalfie, D. (1994). *Going it alone: A closer look at grandparents raising grandchildren.* Washington, DC: Women's Initiative, American Association of Retired Persons.

Chodorow, N. (1978). *The reproduction of mothering: Psychoanalysis and the sociology of gender.* Berkeley: University of California Press.

Cohen, C. S. (1993). Enhancing social group work opportunities in field work education. *Dissertation Abstracts International, 54*(01), 317A. (University Microfilms No 9315454).

Cohen, C. S. (1995). Making it happen: From great idea to successful group program. *Social Work with Groups, 19*(1), 67–80.

Congress, E. (1994). The use of culturagrams to assess and empower culturally diverse families. *Families in Society: The Journal of Contemporary Human Services, 75*, 531–539.

Ehrenrich, J. H. (1985). *The altruistic imagination: A history of social work and social policy in the United States.* Ithaca, NY, and London: Cornell University Press.

Garland, J. (1992). Developing and sustaining group work services: A systemic and systematic view. *Social Work with Groups, 15*(4), 89–98.

Gilligan, C. (1982). *In a different voice.* Cambridge, MA: Harvard University Press.

Hartman, A., & Laird, J. (1983). *Family-centered social work practice.* New York: Free Press.

Hatcher, K. J. (1984). *The feminization of poverty: An analysis of poor women in New York City.* New York: Office of Council Member Messinger.

Hurdle, D. E. (1991). The ethnic group experience. In K. Chau (Ed.), *Ethnicity and biculturalism: Perspectives on social group work* (pp. 59–69). New York: Haworth.

Johnson, C. L. (1983). A cultural analysis of the grandmother. *Research on Aging, 5*, 547–567.

Kerson, T. S. (1989). Women and aging: A clinical social work perspective. In J. D. Garner & S. O. Mercer (Eds.), *Challenge, opportunity, and triumph.* New York: Haworth.

Kirkland, B. (1992, February). Definition of a self-help group. *Grandparents United Newsletter*, p. 1.

Kivnick, H. (1982). Grandparenthood: An overview of meaning and mental health. *Gerontologist*, *22*, 59–66.

Kurland, R., Getzel, G., & Salmon, R. (1986). Sowing groups in infertile fields: Curriculum and other strategies to overcome resistance to the formation of new groups. In M. Parnes (Ed.), *Innovations in social group work: Feedback from practice to theory. Proceedings of the Annual Group Work Symposium* (pp. 57–74). New York: Haworth.

Kurland, R., & Salmon, R. (1992). Group work vs. casework in a group: Principles and implications for teaching and practice. *Social Work with Groups*, *15*(4), 3–14.

Ladner, J. A. (1987). Introduction to tomorrow's tomorrow. The Black woman. In S. Harding (Ed.), *Feminism and methodology: Social science issues* (pp. 74–83). Bloomington and Indianapolis: Indiana University Press.

Lewittes, H. (1989). Just being friendly means a lot: Women, friendship, and aging. In L. Grau (Ed.), *Women in the later years: Health, social and cultural perspectives* (pp. 139–159). New York: Haworth.

Middleman, R. R., & Rhodes, G. B. (1985). *Competent supervision: Making imaginative judgments*. Englewood Cliffs, NJ: Prentice-Hall.

Middleman, R. R., & Wood, G. G. (1990). *Skills for direct practice in social work*. New York: Columbia University Press.

Minkler, M., & Roe, K. M. (1993). *Grandmothers as caregivers*. Newbury Park, CA: Sage.

National Commission on Working Women of Wider Opportunities for Women. (1988). *Women, work, and poverty: A fact sheet*. Washington, DC: Author.

Nystrom, J. F. (1989). Empowerment model for delivery of social work services in public schools. *Social Work in Education*, *11*(3), 160–170.

Pernell, R. B. (1986). Empowerment and social group work. In M. Parnes (Ed.), *Innovations in Social Group Work: Feedback from Practice to Theory. Proceedings of the Annual Group Work Symposium*. New York: Haworth.

Perrow, C. (1986). *Complex organizations* (3d ed.). New York: Random House.

Random House Dictionary of the English Language. (1987). New York: Random House.

Rappaport, J. (1981). In praise of paradox: A social policy of empowerment over prevention. *American Journal of Community Psychology*, *9*(1), 1–25.

Roberts, J. I. (1985). A deeper way of looking at multiple roles. *Journal of Thought*, *20*(3), 65–73.

Robertson, J. F. (1977). Grandmotherhood: A study of role conceptions. *Journal of Marriage and the Family*, *39*(1), 165–174.

Sanchez-Ayendez, M. (1989). Puerto Rican elderly women: The cultural dimension of social support networks. In L.Grau (Ed.), *Women in the later years: Health, social and cultural perspectives*. New York: Haworth.

Schopler, J. H., & Galinsky, M. J. (1993). Support groups as open systems: A model for practice and research. *Health and Social Work*, *18*(3), 195–207.

Schwartz, W. (1961). The social worker in the group. *The Social Welfare Forum* (pp. 147–177). New York: Columbia University Press. Reprinted in B. Compton & B. Galaway (Eds.), *Social Work Processes* (pp. 17–37). Homewood, IL: Dorsey.

Shulman, L., & Gitterman, A. (1986). The life model, mutual aid, and the mediating function. In A. Gitterman & L. Shulman (Eds.), *Mutual aid groups and the life cycle* (pp. 3–22). Itasca, IL: F. E. Peacock.

Surrey, J. L. (1985). *Self-in-relation: A theory of women's development*. Wellesley, MA: Wellesley College, Stone Center for Developmental Services and Studies.

Timberlake, E. M., & Cipnungu, S. S. (1992). Grandmotherhood: Contemporary meaning among African American middle-class grandmothers. *Social Work*, *37*, 216–222.

Towle, C. (1952). *Common human needs*. New York: American Association of Social Workers.

Tropp, E. (1965). Group intent and group structure: Essential criteria for group work practice. *Journal of Jewish Communal Service*, *41*, 229–250. Reprinted in Tropp, E. (1971), *A humanistic foundation for group work practice: A collection of writing by Emanuel Tropp* (pp. 7–28). New York: Simon & Schuster.

Webster's New World Dictionary of American English (3rd college ed.). (1994). New York: Prentice-Hall.

Weiler, K. (1988). *Women teaching for change: Gender, class, and power*. Granby, MA: Bergin & Garvey.

Woehrer, C. E. (1982). The influence of ethnic families on intergenerational relationships and later life transitions. *Annals of the American Academy of Political and Social Science*, *464*, 65–78.

U.S. Bureau of the Census. (1991). *Current population reports: Marital status and living arrangements* (Series P20-450). Washington, DC: U.S. Government Printing Office.

U.S. Bureau of the Census. (1993). *Current population reports: Poverty in the United States*. (Series P60-185). Washington, DC: U.S. Government Printing Office.

U.S. Bureau of the Census. (1994). *Current population survey: Marital status and living arrangements*. (Series P20-484). Washington, DC: U.S. Government Printing Office.

Conclusion: Ethical Issues and Future Directions

Elaine P. Congress

Family therapy is always very value-laden, in part because almost all professionals have grown up in families. Although professionals usually do not share a common experience with their clients who are substance abusers or schizophrenics, family therapists, for better or worse, have had a family experience that they may try to re-create or avoid in the families with which they work. Therapists' visions of family may be very connected to their own cultural background. Research has shown that even the most skilled third- or fourth-generation clinicians may still be very influenced by the cultural stereotypes of their own backgrounds (McGoldrick & Rohrbaugh, 1987). Ethical practice with culturally diverse families necessitates that clinicians understand their own cultural background better so as to appreciate the diversity of families they see.

Within the past few decades clinicians have increasingly focused on value and ethical issues in work with individual clients (Levy, 1993; Lowenberg & Dolgoff, 1992; Reamer, 1990, 1994), yet attention to ethics in family work is minimal. A review of literature indicates only two books (Huber, 1994; Walrond-Skinner & Watson, 1987) that focus on the area of ethics in family therapy and nothing on ethical practice with culturally diverse families. The current NASW Code of Ethics barely mentions family therapy (NASW, 1996).

Although most family therapists support self-determination and confidentiality, how are these values translated into ethical practice? How does family therapy affect self-determination? Is the family truly permitted to determine its own behavior or is its behavior prejudged as bad or

dysfunctional? These questions may be particularly relevant for the culturally diverse family whose way of relating may be very different from the
cultural background of the therapist. The clinician often assumes the role
of expert "knower," who evaluates the family in terms of his or her
perception rather than understanding the family as members tell their own
story (Laird, 1995).

Many authors (Boyd-Franklin, 1989; Ho, 1987; McGoldrick, Giordano, & Pearce, 1996) have stressed the importance of family to culturally
diverse families. Yet often the family therapist may assess a culturally
diverse family as being too enmeshed if its members seem very connected
to each other. For example, a mother who must have her adolescent
children accompany her shopping or is reluctant to allow her child to
attend an out-of-state college is described as not encouraging appropriate
boundaries. A family in which older children are asked to care for younger
ones or asked to work in family businesses is seen as exploiting children.
The family therapist must be careful not to label culturally diverse families
as dysfunctional.

An important question is how much family therapy promotes individual
self-determination. Often the family therapist is faced with the fact that
goals of different family members conflict. For example, one spouse may
see family therapy as strengthening the marital relationship, and the other
may see family therapy as a vehicle for making decisions about terminating
the relationship. The family therapist may be in the position of supporting
one member's right to self-determination over the other, especially if there
is conflict. How does a family therapist make decisions of this type? Often
family therapists make these decisions in terms of their own backgrounds.
Family therapists who believe that families should stay together and all
areas of conflict can be resolved are more likely to support the spouse
who wants to continue the relationship. Family therapists who see separation and divorce as valid options for seriously conflictual relationships
may tend to support the spouse who wants to terminate the relationship.

Often ethical problems arise in helping families reconcile conflicts.
How should the family therapist intervene when there are conflicts over
acculturation? It is well known that children and adolescents, probably
because of their greater association with the American educational system
and peer culture, often become acculturated faster than their parents. This
may lead to family conflict, especially when there are adolescents. How
does the family therapist recognize individual self-determination when

adolescent clients seek more association with peers and activities outside the home, while their parents maintain that adolescents should primarily be involved with family responsibilities? This conflict is particularly challenging for family therapists raised and trained within American culture, which usually views making peer contacts outside the home as appropriate for normal adolescent development. Family therapists must be careful to maintain a focus on the total family system. They must avoid allying themselves with adolescents in the family they serve, lest they lose the adults within the family.

Confidentiality is often a challenging issue for the family therapist. Practitioners often have differing opinions as to what information should be kept confidential and from whom. Although some therapists believe that whatever is divulged in individual sessions should be kept confidential, others maintain that whatever is shared individually must be discussed by the family as a whole (Corey, Corey, & Callahan, 1993). The handling of confidentiality is especially challenging for those who work with culturally diverse families, who may have a very different understanding of confidentiality. In a previous article on culturally diverse children this author reported that often culturally diverse clients have a very different concept of confidentiality, compared with the prevailing social work value of confidentiality (Congress, 1994).

Although rights to privacy and confidentiality are stressed in American culture in general and social work practice in particular, these values may not have the same meaning in work with culturally diverse clients. For example, culturally diverse families may be reluctant to share information with family therapists if they are undocumented. They may fear that the clinician, whom they view as an unknown authority figure, may share this information with immigration officials, which will lead to their deportation. Even if the family has legal status, past oppression and discrimination experienced by family members may make them reluctant to share information (Boyd-Franklin, 1990). Furthermore, some culturally diverse families believe that it is inappropriate to share family matters with outsiders.

All families have different ways of communicating and sharing personal information. In some families there is very open communication (perhaps too open) between family members; other families have many secrets which are kept confidential, especially from children. Not only do family therapists often have different ways of handling confidentiality but so do different families. Some of these ways may be characteristic of many families from similar cultural backgrounds; others may be unique to a specific family. The ethical family therapist working with culturally diverse clients must explore their beliefs about confidentiality and maintaining secrets. Otherwise, the therapy may be doomed to failure. For example, a family therapist who insists that there be no secrets and forces a Hispanic father to share in a session his feelings of inadequacy over his unemployment may find that this culturally diverse family will not continue in therapy.

Different family members may have different understandings about confidentiality. Culturally diverse families may feel that their adolescents should share openly and not maintain secrets, but adolescents influenced by American adolescent culture, which stresses emotional independence from parents, may want to hide personal information from other family members. Recent court decisions that have upheld adolescents' right to confidentiality also affect family therapy with culturally diverse clients.

Informed consent is considered an important principle in the delivery of ethical clinical services (Corey et al., 1993). Informed consent can occur, however, only if clients and families understand the nature of the treatment they will receive. How can the family therapist practice informed consent with culturally diverse families if there are significant language and cultural differences? Family therapists with culturally diverse families must be able to communicate with families in a language they can understand. This points to the need for family therapists who can speak the language of the families they see. Using children as interpreters is problematic in family therapy, as this affects the family functioning and structure. Even if the therapist is able to communicate in the language of the family, ensuring informed consent may still be problematic. Whereas informed consent may occur in terms of parents, how much informed consent occurs with children? This may be an issue in all family therapy but may be more acute in culturally diverse families in which children are not seen as having rights. Family therapists can be influenced by culturally diverse parents who have not explained to children why they are coming for therapy, and furthermore do not see the need for therapy. The ethical family therapist must strive to enable all members of a family to experience informed consent. It may be necessary to explain what family therapy means in a way that children and those not familiar with family therapy can understand.

What is family therapy, and what will family therapy be like in the 21st century? Mental health treatment has already been greatly affected by a managed care model, and one can predict that family therapy services will continue to be provided in a managed care environment. The impact of managed care on family therapy will be to move toward more short-term, solution-focused models of treatment. This may be very effective with culturally diverse families who previously have often sought treatment that is time-limited and focused on specific treatment objectives.

The trend toward managed care also necessitates a specific focus on clear goals and objectives that will make family therapy more appealing to culturally diverse families who are reluctant to become involved in less structured treatment. An initial responsibility for the family therapist will be to identify to the client the focus of treatment and appropriate treatment objectives.

With the current focus on managed care, there is concern that family therapy is not always considered reimbursable. There is no accepted diagnostic system comparable to *DSM-IV*, which is used to measure individual dysfunction and symptomatology. Yet family therapy seems an effective way to treat a number of people simultaneously, and many people will continue to seek treatment for family problems.

Family therapy seems particularly appropriate for treating culturally diverse families, as often these families seek treatment as a group—in contrast to many Americans, who often pursue treatment as individuals.

Because of increased poverty and violence, many culturally diverse communities are currently under siege and can provide only limited support for their residents. One can predict that this situation will not improve with cutbacks in financial and social services resources for poor people. Culturally competent family treatment that focuses on strengthening families provides much support for families who function within a challenging social environment.

REFERENCES

Boyd-Franklin, N. (1989). *Black families in therapy*. New York: Guilford.

Congress, E. (1994). Group work programs in public schools: Ethical dilemmas and cultural diversity. *Social Work in Education, 16*(2), 107–114.

Corey, G., Corey, M., & Callahan, P. (1993). *Issues and ethics in the helping professions* (4th ed.). Pacific Grove, CA: Brooks Cole.

Ho, M. (1987). *Family therapy with ethnic minorities.* Newbury Park, CA: Sage.

Huber, C. (1994). *Ethical, legal, and professional issues in practice of marriage and family therapy.* New York: Merrill.

Laird, J. (1995). Family centered practice in post modern era. *Families in Society, 76*(3), 150–160.

Levy, C. (1993). *Social work ethics on the line.* New York: Haworth.

Lowenberg, F., & Dolgoff, R. (1992). *Ethical decisions for social work practice* (4th ed.). Itasca, IL: Peacock.

McGoldrick, M., Pearce, J., & Giordano, J. (1996). *Ethnicity and family therapy* (2nd ed.). New York: Guilford.

McGoldrick, M., & Rohrbaugh, M. (1987). Researching ethnic stereotypes. *Family Process, 26*(1), 89–99.

National Association of Social Workers. (1996). *Code of ethics of National Association of Social Workers.* Washington, DC: Author.

Reamer, F. (1990). *Ethical dilemmas in social service* (2nd ed.). New York: Columbia University Press.

Reamer. F. (1994). *Social work values and ethics.* New York: Columbia University Press.

Waldron-Skinner, S., & Watson, D. (1987). *Ethical issues in family therapy.* London: Routledge and Kegan Paul.

Index

⑤ *Springer Publishing Company*

Helping Families Through Divorce
An Eclectic Approach
Ellen Bogolub, MSW, PhD

Using an eclectic, goal-oriented approach, Dr. Bogolub guides mental health professionals helping today's clients cope with a broad range of divorce-related problems. Her book is unique in its attention to people of varied ethnicity, age, and socioeconomic class.

HELPING
FAMILIES
THROUGH
DIVORCE

An Eclectic Approach

Ellen B. Bogolub

After an overview of current trends, controversies and demographics about divorce, the volume presents a three-stage divorce model (predivorce phase, divorce transition, postdivorce phase). A final section presents implications for legal reform, social policy, and research. Featuring lively illustrative vignettes, this book is useful for psychiatrists, psychologists, social workers, and students in these fields.

Contents:

1995   264pp   0-8261-9060-X   hardcover

536 Broadway, New York, NY 10012-3955 • (212) 431-4370 • Fax (212) 941-7842

Springer Publishing Company

Beyond the Traditional Family
Voices of Diversity
Betty Polisar Reigot and **Rita K. Spina,** PhD

In this innovative text, the authors present original qualitative research based on personal interviews with selected modern families. These interviews reveal the new variety of domestic relationships that are emerging today, including single mothers by choice, adolescent mothers,

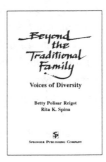

fathers as caretakers, homosexual parents, grandparents as parents, and parents by technology. The stories carry important implications for social policy and provide an insightful qualitative resource for professionals including sociologists, family therapists and academics in social work and psychology.

Contents:

Preface • Introduction • The Interviews

1995   224pp   0-8261-9030-8   hardcover

536 Broadway, New York, NY 10012-3955 • (212) 431-4370 • Fax (212) 941-7842

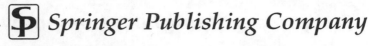
Springer Publishing Company

Battered Women and Their Families, 2nd Edition
Intervention Strategies and Treatment Programs
Albert R. Roberts, PhD, Editor

"...a landmark achievement. Every clinical social worker, nurse specialist, and physician should read this book. This is the first comprehensive book to examine domestic violence from a multi-cultural perspective. This brilliantly written and all-inclusive resource provides new clinical knowledge and practice wisdom to alleviate the emotional pain and trauma of battered women and their children. I have been searching for a book like this for years, especially when I was Consultant to the Army Surgeon General."
—Jesse J. Harris, PhD, BCD, ACSW
Professor and Dean, School of Social Work, University of Maryland
Colonel Retired

Partial Contents:
I. Crisis Intervention and Short-Term Treatment. Crisis Intervention and Cognitive Problem-Solving Therapy with Battered Women: A National Survey and Practice Model, *A.R. Roberts and S. Burman* •The Stress-Crisis Continuum: Its Application to Domestic Violence, *P.V. Valentine, A.R. Roberts and A.W. Burgess* • The Organizational Structure and Function of Shelters for Battered Women and Their Children: A National Survey, *A.R. Roberts* • Conjoint Therapy for the Treatment of Partner Abuse: Indications and ContraIndications, *J.A. Geller* **II. Children and Adolescents from Violent Homes.** Crisis Intervention with Traumatized Child Witnesses in Shelters for Battered Women, *P. Lehmann and B.E. Carlson* **III. Health Care and Welfare Policies and Practices with Battered Women.** Battered Women in the Emergency Room: Emerging Roles for the ER Social Worker and Clinical Nurse Specialist, *M.E. Boes* **IV. High Risk Group and Vulnerable Populations.** Elder Abuse, *P. Brownell and I. Abelman* **V. Cross-Cultural Issues, Policies and Practices with Battered Women.** Application of the Culturagram to Assess and Empower Culturally and Ethnically Diverse Battered Women, *P. Brownell and E.P. Congress* • Domestic Violence in Japan: Research, Program Developments and Emerging Movement, *M. Yoskihama* • Chinese Battered Women in the United States , *M.Y. Lee and P. Au* • Validating Coping Strategies and Empowering Latino Battered Women in Puerto Rico, *D. Valle Ferrer*
1998   544pp (est)   0-8261-4591-4   hardcover

536 Broadway, New York, NY 10012-3955 • (212) 431-4370 • Fax (212) 941-7842